THE BETTER HALF

By the same author

Fiction

THE RAKER

THE PARADISE BUM

MY FRIEND JUDAS

THE PROJECT

THE BREAKING OF BUMBO

Nonfiction

THE AVAILABLE MAN: THE LIFE BEHIND
THE MASKS OF WARREN GAMALIEL HARDING

PROHIBITION: THE ERA OF EXCESS

THE
BETTER HALF

The Emancipation
of the American Woman

by

ANDREW SINCLAIR

HARPER & ROW, PUBLISHERS
NEW YORK

FIRST EDITION

LIBRARY OF CONGRESS CATALOG CARD NUMBER: 65–14659

E-P

CONTENTS

[v]

PART FOUR

The American Lady

PART FIVE

Working Women

PART SIX

Allies and Enemies

PART SEVEN

The Birth of the Modern Woman

PART EIGHT
The English Example

PART NINE
Nothing but the Vote

PART TEN
The New Victorians

Regarding her as I *do,* as the *better half* of *humanity*—with a more *delicate* and *sensitive* nature than man—with a more *refined* and *spiritual organization*—*WOMAN* should be the conservator of *public morals!*

We may call this a part of her divine mission.

Public morality will be very much what *she* makes it.

MARY LIVERMORE
on the Sphere and Influence of Woman

INTRODUCTION

IN THE EARLY American colonies, the struggle for survival took priority over the struggle for rights. The Founding Fathers and Mothers held by the old customs which they had brought with them; there was no other way of surviving on the edge of the wilderness. There were a few spiritual rebellions and one political one by audacious women; but the scattering of settlements along the Atlantic coast and the difficulty of communications meant that the early rebels could find few followers among their own sex. Moreover, the first great American rebellion was against the control of England, not of men. The attack on foreign tyranny rightly preceded the attack on internal injustice.

The growth of the cities along the Atlantic seaboard provided the first societies which felt secure and settled enough to question the established ways. The accumulation of money and the use of servants allowed the growth of a new class of leisured women—the American ladies. These ladies were to be both the supporters and the sworn enemies of the early American feminists. In the first American cities and in their surrounding small towns, these women had the time and the education—if they had the wish—to stir up the early agitation for women's rights. Only by understanding the urban situation in the early nineteenth century can one understand the roots of feminism in the United States.

Women, however, did not merely look for the freedom of their own sex. What I hope to make very clear is that reforms do not come singly; one leads to another, and the reformers are linked by time and place. There is both a society and a geography of reform. If a particular class or sex or group is brought nearer to equality with those who are dominant, a third depressed section of the community will demand advance, for advance will have been proved to be *possible*. Agitation for one reform sparks off agitation for others, the atmosphere of change and ferment spreads. When, in addition, it is a time of great immigration and social change as in the United States in the early nineteenth century, the possibility of the infinite improvement of society seems imminent. "In the history of the world," Emerson declared in 1841, "the doctrine of Reform had never such scope as at the present hour."[1]

The reform wave surged in certain areas of America in the 1830's and 1840's, receded before and during the Civil War, surged again in the hope of the reconstruction of society after the war, receded for twenty years while large industry dominated the government, and surged again in the two decades before the First World War. At these times, there was an interaction among reforms, and a geography of reform. Those reforms which successfully changed the position of great numbers were the movements for the rights of Negroes, of women, and of labour, the three major groups deprived of the American promise of liberty and equality of opportunity.

The movement to free the slave was split up geographically into four sections. From the quiet and ladylike Philadelphia section, pressure on the South was discreet. Despite the burning of a reform hall in 1838, there were few riots in the Quaker City. Although many early reform leaders, such as Lucretia Mott, came from Philadelphia, urban society kept a discreet and aristocratic flavour. Pennsylvania itself was full of conservative German and Dutch farmers, who did not like reform. There was no ring of radical small towns and manufacturing towns around Philadelphia to stimulate its politics through immigration. As the anti-slavery Quaker, Elizabeth Neall, wrote in 1842,

New England Abolitionism differs so from ours here in Pennsylvania that I often wish for a little of the fiery spirit that lives and thrives among the rocky fastnesses and rough bleak hills of our Yankee Caledonia. . . . Whether from our quiet temperament or from our near vicinity to the South and its influence which always paralyze whatever comes within their reach that is good or true, that we are so far wanting in action, I cannot tell, but certainly we are far in the rear.[2]

There was, indeed, a fiery spirit in New England. For fifty years after the American Revolution, New England had been in a state of change. Regular religious revivals kept the Yankees in a spirit of flux. The "Western fever" removed the populations of whole farming communities and small towns, settlers in the Connecticut Valley moved up to Vermont, while emigration from the farms to the seaboard continued.

It was not Boston alone that was in a ferment of the mind. In Portland, Maine, in the 1830's, the writer Elizabeth Oakes Smith found a "pet City to the divine eye." It had its Peace Societies, its Anti-Slavery Societies, its Temperance Societies, its Missionary Societies, and its continual controversy over Unitarianism and Universalism. "Everybody was out to hear, and everybody talked and studied and took sides." Once the ladies of Portland even went to a political meeting in a group, during the heady Jacksonian days. The men there welcomed them with clapping and cheering. "Politics ran high at this time, and every man . . . and every woman was partisan. All the issues of every shade were heartily endorsed or rejected by both sexes," including clairvoyance, magnetism, phrenology, and gymnastics. Yet, Elizabeth Oakes Smith admitted, "Not a man there read the handwriting of woman suffrage on the wall!"[3]

These seething seaboard cities, with their small groups of excited educated people, threw the current ideas of America or Europe into some of the small towns that surrounded them. As Frederick Jackson Turner pointed out in a neglected part of his famous essay on the frontier, the frontier was settled by the Eastern cities in the way that the Greek city-states planted their colony cities around the Mediterranean. The American cities founded the small towns near them. These, in their turn, founded towns on the frontier, which, as it receded West, became more and more distant from its original mother cities and from Europe. The frontier virtues that Turner celebrated were the virtues of the towns *behind* the frontier, where the first farmers in their sod huts found their supplies and their schools and their contacts with civilization.

The rise of the new Western towns and cities was one of the dominant factors in frontier life. There were many of these settlements as far West as Ohio, before the agitation for abolition or women's rights grew powerful. Their quick growth explained the rapid spread of ideas from seaboard city to neighbouring small town to Western settlement, despite the horrific difficulties of communication. In a real sense, the Burned-Over District of New York and the Western Reserve of Ohio, Rochester and Cleveland and Cincinnati, were the cultural sons of the Atlantic ports. Boston and New York sought influence over them, and, in their turn, the Westerners sought to influence Boston and New York with the radical ideas of the new frontier town.

Boston was, with Philadelphia, the leading reform city of the 1830's. It was the chosen home of Garrison and the extreme abolitionists. Garrison adopted a great many other reforms by the end of the decade, including perfectionism, women's rights, non-resistance, and withdrawal from politics. Radical Boston women stuck by him and the *Liberator,* but the majority of the Boston lady reformers preferred more conservative and single-minded leaders. The struggles in the anti-slavery movement between Garrison and his opponents after 1837 split the Female Anti-Slavery Societies as well. But the split had always been present in Boston social life, between the merchant or intellectual aristocracy and the small-town radical immigrants like Garrison, between the Brahmin ladies and other reforming women. Moreover, both groups were split from the greater part of the people of Boston—the immigrants from Yankee or Southern or Irish farms who clung to their traditional ideas.

The prominence of a few radical Boston women, such as Maria Weston Chapman, Abby Kelley, and Lydia Maria Child, obscured the fact that most Bostonian ladies were interested only in conservative and respectable reform work. These were the learned spinsters, whom Theodore Parker called "the glorious phalanx of old maids." Margaret Fuller, with her dislike of the radical activities of the early feminists, was more characteristic of the learned and fastidious Bostonian reformer. After its ferment of the 1830's, polite Boston was to become the home of the apostles of gradual change. Moderate reformers converted such urban ladies as Julia Ward Howe, who found in their company a relief "from a sense of isolation and eccentricity."[4] The fine fury of a decade passed, to leave Boston no more than a Northern Philadelphia.

The third home of the anti-slavery movement, New York, was not led by a cohesive and learned clique, as were its two Atlantic rival cities. It was an incoherent and booming place, especially after the Erie Canal gave it the waterway to the West, and condemned Boston and Philadelphia to slower growth. Pro-slavery riots and mob rule were common in New York; they were rare elsewhere. One drunken election there was so savage that even Lydia Maria Child hoped that the city would blow up with the rest of the world, and begin again.[5]

New York was also the home of Arthur and Lewis Tappan, who were the chief financiers behind the abolition movement. There was a readiness in the city to invest in the potential of the West, allied with a lack of pride in cultural superiority, which made it seem less condescending to the Westerners than its competitors for influence beyond the Alleghenies. As Theodore Weld, the leader of the early anti-slavery agitation in Ohio and western New York State, wrote to some anti-slavery ladies in Massachusetts, "I am a *Backwoodsman untamed*. My bearish proportions have never been licked into *city shape*, and are quite too uncombed and shaggy for 'Boston notions.' "[6] This opinion of himself did not stop Weld from coming to New York City to work for the Tappans.

The success of the New York abolitionists with the Ohio group of reformers gave them the support of much of the Burned-Over District and the Western Reserve. Garrison, whose radicalism made him a notorious figure in his adopted city of Boston, also appealed with his many-sided doctrines to these same Western areas a decade later, through the equally incongruous Irish Quaker from Boston, Abby Kelley. Her radicalism was so extreme that even the Garrisonian, Lydia Child, could lament that "the devil helped her to drive away all the tender-spirited and judicious from our ranks."[7]

Yet the radical Western towns, in a sense, were always independent of the East. They cooperated with that reform group which would give them money and would appeal to their sense of independence. They wanted speakers and funds from the East, not direction. In time, Western anti-slavery feeling deserted both the Tappans and Garrison, to support the political solution of the Republican Party. The history of every American national reform organization is a history of quarrels within that organization between West and East—and South, if Southerners join the movement.

The geographical splits in the movement for women's rights were to parallel the splits in the anti-slavery ranks between Philadelphia and Boston and New York and the Western areas. The first anti-slavery agitation had risen in the Eastern cities. But, within a few years, some of the small towns of Massachusetts were already more radical over abolition than Boston, as the Western Reserve was more radical than New York or Philadelphia. As early as 1838, Lydia Child declared on the matter of anti-slavery feeling, "Boston, like other cities, is very far behind the country towns on this subject; so much so that it is getting to be Boston *versus* Massachusetts."[8]

In the same way, the early feminist leaders worked in Boston and Philadelphia—Lucretia Mott, Abby Kelley, Maria Chapman, Lydia Child, and the sisters Grimké. Except for Frances Gage of Ohio, nearly all of the early feminists came from Quaker or seaport backgrounds. But they burned up their enthusiasm in anti-slavery work in the 1830's and 1840's. If some of them did turn to women's rights, they remained fearful of injuring "that blessed cause" of the slave. "When slavery is abolished," Lydia Child confessed, "I think I shall get so as not to dislike anything. I may safely say so; for when that *is* abolished throughout the world, the millennium must be near at hand."⁹

The next generation of feminist leaders, however, came from the radical small towns of New England or further West. Elizabeth Cady Stanton, Paulina Wright, Antoinette Brown, Matilda Gage, Sally Holley, and Elizabeth Smith Miller, all came from upper New York State. Lucy Stone, although she was brought up in Massachusetts, was educated at Oberlin in Ohio. Susan Anthony, reared in small-town Massachusetts, chose to live in Rochester. These new leaders were usually brought up in reform homes, where anti-slavery agitation was taken for granted. Although they began as anti-slavery or temperance speakers, they were only followers in that movement. When they switched to women's rights as the *first* reform in their calendar, they became leaders. All the opening conventions on women's rights were held in Western towns, two in upper New York State, two in upstate Massachusetts, and four in Ohio. Radicalism grew the further towns were settled from their founding Eastern cities.

Not all the Western towns were radical, and those that were radical were so in limited ways. The towns settled mainly by conservative Southerners remained conservative and pro-slavery, those settled almost entirely by religious sects kept a preoccupation with the millennium in heaven rather than on earth. When founded by a wealthy entrepreneur, the town could remain stifled by his semi-feudal rule for decades; or if set up merely to make money through mines or stockyards, it often made little else. It was the other Western towns, which grew up on rivers or railways or as market-places for farmers, which sometimes contained radicalism because of widespread immigration from North and South and even from Europe. People with conflicting traditions found themselves mingling to found a new community. And in this situation of friction, the immigrant social reformer, full of the latest ideas from the Eastern city, could use his or her influence to attract a wide following—particularly for any reform which could be called holy. If he or she could never quell local conservative opposition, reforming ideas could be spread in the new settlements. The town, on its advance through the West, was quick to champion or oppose the new. It was not an indifferent place, as many cities were.

The reason for the success of some reforms in many Western towns, and for the failure of others, lay in their religious appeal. The drive to prohibit the liquor trade was particularly popular, because it was an evangelical crusade, led by the Protestant churches. It was a dry crusade for purity and womanhood without the taint of politics, a crusade against the infidel power of Rum and Rome in the big cities without the taint of sectionalism. Southerners could join with Northerners, and men with women, in the fight against the saloon. The centre of temperance agitation, as of abolition and woman suffrage, advanced from the Atlantic Coast through the small towns of New England towards the West.

Anti-slavery, too, was popular here and there in the Middle West, because it was chiefly an evangelical crusade—the failure of most of the abolitionists to concern themselves with the future of the freed slaves after the Civil War showed how little they were concerned with the *social* consequences of emancipation (of course, anti-slavery agitation failed in the South exactly because the Southerners could see little more than the social upheaval involved in freeing the slaves). The demand for women's rights, which also began chiefly as an evangelical reform, again appealed in some Western towns as part of the crusade to better the earth; but when, in the later stages of the crusade, it became more of a movement of social criticism to help the working women in the cities, it lost some of its appeal to the Western settlements. And as for labour reform, that had little appeal in the Western towns, for it seemed only a movement of social reform and possibly contrary to the will of the Almighty. The large cities had, anyway, brought the problem upon themselves, for the wealthy industrialists there had encouraged the influx of alien "new immigrants" from Latin and Balkan Europe.

There were general causes, too, which led to a climate of opinion favourable to radicalism in many of the new settlements at the back of the frontier. The pioneers were often those people who were discontented with the established way of life on the Eastern seaboard. The new towns abounded with speculators of all sorts, both in dollars and ideas. They depended for survival on a boom psychology. They had to encourage more immigration to develop themselves; and, through this new immigration, local ideas were kept in a state of flux. They were fertile ground for religious revivals and evangelical drives. And they were proud of their distinction and difference from the old cities and the old ways. "Let the great cities *alone,*" Theodore Weld wrote to Lewis Tappan in New York, "They must be burned down by *back fires.* The springs to touch in order to move them lie in the *country."* The way to conquer the Eastern city was to agitate in the Western village and town "and smaller cities in the interior."[10]

In building up these Western towns, women enjoyed an equality with men. But once the nucleus of the town was established, with its bank and its churches and its store and its main street, a small group of women with Eastern and urban ideas found themselves with leisure time, bought for them by Irish servants and the wealth of husbands or fathers. Most of the feminist leaders came from homes where the father was a professional man, interested in Eastern reforms. They lived continually in the ferment of speculation, which characterized the speedy development of the West. And yet they could not occupy themselves in the business of money-making, which kept their men-folk busy from morning to night.

For the small town, then as now, was boring for educated women. Nothing contributed more to the calling of the first women's convention at Seneca Falls in 1848 than the ennui of Elizabeth Stanton, who found herself suddenly, after four years in Boston, in a dreary factory town, with five children and nothing to occupy her mind. She remembered Emerson's remark, "A healthy discontent is the first step to progress." When a chance for reform or political action came up, educated women in small towns leapt at the opportunity to forget themselves in work. Reform activity was the theatre of the small town in its early days. It was difficult for women there to take refuge in the time-consuming devices of the ladies in the cities or in the old towns of the East; there were too few people to visit, and too few opportunities to dress up and dance and play cards. These diversions were, in any case, intolerable to the leaders of community life—the evangelical ministers, whose social leadership continued until the end of the century, when, as a commentator noticed, a small town contained as many social groups as it contained religious bodies.[11] These ministers, often allied with immigrant Eastern ladies, pushed many Western towns into holy crusades for a purer and better civilization.

Moreover, the wish to be different from the Eastern lady with her airs of superiority, to reform *her* rather than be corrupted by her effete ways, led some aggressive Western women to adopt bloomers and water cures and spiritualism and Mental Science. Novelty was in the air in many of the new Western towns. Any reformer could find an audience there, only too pleased to be amused by new fashions. The feminist movement, in particular, was recruited through personal contact. In the small town, the reform speaker could meet his or her audience face to face. Sponsors would board out speakers; sympathizers would speak to them before and after the lecture. Such immediate contact was not to be found in the vast assembly rooms of the city, or through the badly distributed press. The forced neighbourliness of the new small town led to the rapid spread of new ideas, once one social leader had been converted to the faith.

Yet the period of radicalism in a new small town was often as brief as the period of revolutionary fervour in America before the writing of the Constitution. The years were short between the founding of a town and its government by a clique of conservative and wealthy bankers and merchants and farmers, whose wives considered themselves to be settled ladies. In a matter of a decade, social power could become invested in hands almost as safe as those which ran the polite suburbs of the Eastern cities. The fringe of radical new towns moved ever westward, while the conditions of small town life in the land east of the Mississippi River became as secure and conservative as in any New England rural settlement. "Ohio," Lucretia Mott commented as early as 1850, "indeed is beginning to seem an *old* country, when compared with the Wisconsins and Iowas and Minnesotas."[12]

When the new National Woman Suffrage Association parted with the American Woman Suffrage Association in 1869, exactly as the anti-slavery movement had split in 1840, Elizabeth Stanton and Susan Anthony used New York as their base to attach the West to them, as the Tappans had once done to attract Weld and the Ohio reformers. Their rival, Lucy Stone in Boston, soon found herself with the mere support of the East Coast ladies in her American Association, and little else. In fact, when Stanton and Anthony used their own agent in Massachusetts to set up a rival organization, it grew up outside Boston in the envious small towns, in the same way as Garrison had once found his supporters in western Massachusetts and not in the state capital.

Of course, Stanton was brought up, and Anthony chose to live, further West than Lucy Stone. Anthony had started as a temperance speaker, and she understood the importance of that reform in the new small towns. Stanton had been enthusiastic about the Middle West ever since the suffrage campaign of 1867 in Kansas, when she wrote that she could not "endure the thoughts of living again that contracted eastern existence."[13] Under the leadership of Stanton and Anthony, the National Woman Suffrage Association did not allow the differences between East and West to become serious. For they themselves had been born in the small town and had emigrated to work in the large cities. Moreover, decades of travelling all over the nation on lecture tours after the Civil War kept them in contact with the feelings of the distant settlements.

Yet this very understanding of small-town life prevented both of them from understanding the ways in which suffrage reform could be linked with labour reform in the large cities. They understood evangelical reform, not social reform. Although their newspaper, *The Revolution,* supported the cause of workingmen, it did not convince workers to support votes for women any more than they were convinced that their interests were the same as those of the radical farm movements of the West. In fact, Anthony's only attempt at forming a women's union brought down on her head the wrath of the labour movement. For, in her anxiety to find jobs for her women printers, she had used them as scabs and strike-breakers. She was too eager to

advance the opportunities of her sex to understand the need of all
working people to stick together.

Lucy Stone, on the other hand, hated the West. Her own hard
childhood on a poor farm made her dislike rural life. In 1850, she
had had to go to Illinois to nurse a dying brother. She had found the
prairie communities very uncongenial. "Profanity, Intemperance, and
Licentiousness *abound,*" she had written. "They are not yet prepared
for Anti-Slavery, and will have to grow fifty years, before they can
see a moral principle, much more, recognize its claims. Of course, *all*
are not so, but the *majority* of influence is."[14] She herself had nearly
died of typhoid fever on her way back to the East.

Her poor opinion of the morality of the West persisted. Despite
her husband Henry Blackwell's enthusiasm, she persuaded him not to
live in the West, and to diminish his business interests there. Her bias
in favour of city life made her think it was there that women's rights
should be won. Her strategy was the opposite of Theodore Weld's. "It
is very important for the *cause,*" she wrote to Susan Anthony in
1854, "that we should get a favourable hearing in the large cities,
and places of most influence. The *little* places will always approve of
what the *large* ones do."[15] She did campaign for woman suffrage in
Kansas in 1867, but briefly. After that the only influence that the
American Woman Suffrage Association had on the West during its
twenty years of life was through the efforts of Henry Blackwell, who
had been brought up in Ohio and who knew to a nicety the blend of
materialism and evangelism in the small-town mind.

The anti-slavery crusade sank into apathy after the Civil War,
despite the wrongs done the freed slaves. For God had won his
victory; the ex-slaves should look after themselves. And labour reform was not to become an issue in the West until the spreading cities
of America had become broadcast across the land. In the thirty years
after the Civil War, it was temperance that chiefly engaged the attention of progressive women in the small towns. The Woman's Christian Temperance Union trained a generation of agitators, who later
entered the suffrage movement, exactly as the anti-slavery crusade had
trained the first feminists. Gradually, the priority of educated West-

ern women changed from abolishing the saloon to getting the vote for themselves. Often, their interests went hand in hand, for a woman's vote was presumed to be a dry vote. And, as with the early abolitionists and feminists, they brought their success in the West to the help of the presumably backward East.

Owing to the longevity of the second generation of feminists, there were few new leaders in the movement during the three decades after the Civil War. The aged chiefs of the suffrage cause made it almost respectable, for old ladies outlive the accusation of sin. They drove ambitious younger women into the ranks of the Woman's Christian Temperance Union, where these could play a leader's part. In the 1890's, however, the retirement and death of the Old Guard began. At every convention, the obituaries of two or three of the pioneer feminists were lamented. Most of them, kept young by political activity, reached the age of eighty before they were buried. Lucy Stone was the first to die; Elizabeth Stanton and Susan Anthony followed her into retirement and the grave. But, before they left the scene, they joined together the two wings of the suffrage movement which they had split apart.

The third generation of the leaders of the National American Woman Suffrage Association came from further West. Anna Shaw was brought up in a log cabin in Michigan, Carrie Chapman Catt on an Iowa farm. Both were educated and worked in large Western communities. The new cities had reached the Middle West and the Mountain States, and had begun to mingle the causes of evangelical and social reform. It was from Portland, Oregon, not Portland, Maine, that the farmer's wife, Abigail Scott Duniway, fought an isolated and successful battle for women's suffrage in the Northwest. The cleansing of the politics of the cities did not begin on the East Coast, but in Cleveland, Ohio—that early centre of abolitionism— and in the cities of Wisconsin, where Robert La Follette welded the vote of the educated middle classes of Madison and Milwaukee into an alliance with the vote of discontented German farmers and immigrant factory workers.

The problem of labour reform came to the West, previously interested only in evangelical crusades, with the growth of cities there. The Mountain States were the home of the most militant of the union organizations, the Industrial Workers of the World. But the Populists, and later the Progressives, were equally strong in the West, with their demands for the regulation of railroads and trusts, and for decent farm and factory legislation. Yet even there, the rural Progressives often quarrelled with the urban Progressives, and the alliance of farmer and factory worker was usually uneasy, with recurring differences over material and religious matters.

Anna Shaw, when she became the president of the national women's movement, remained too much the rural Westerner to understand the need of combining with urban Progressive and labour forces to win over the Eastern cities. She could only understand the need of working with the evangelical churches and temperance women of the small Western towns, and here woman suffrage was successful. By her tacit acceptance of Southern vice-presidents in the woman's organization, who were not prepared to let Negro women have the vote or to accept the principle of a federal suffrage amendment, she further alienated those brought up in the anti-slavery tradition of the East. When she gave up the leadership in 1915, the West had already been won for woman suffrage, state by state; but neither the South nor the East had been touched.

The final leader of the suffragists was a new breed of Westerner. Where Anna Shaw had been the essential Victorian in piety and intensity and primness, Carrie Chapman Catt was the new professional woman, diplomatic and politic and shrewd. Although she was born on a farm, she had worked in towns and cities most of her life. She had been a superintendent of schools in a Midwestern city and a journalist in San Francisco. A prototype of a new managerial class of women, she would run smoothly what the pioneer mothers had built. She could manipulate the politics necessary for legal change and the details necessary for social change without committing herself to the enmities bred by aggressive principles.

Anna Shaw, with her evangelical ideas and vocabulary, had been unable to communicate with the educated professional women and the union organizers of the cities. This failure had led to the revolt of the Eastern cities from the control of the Western and small-town mind, as once Lucy Stone and the Bostonian women had broken away from Stanton and Anthony. The new and militant Woman's Party, however, was not modelled on the discreet American Woman Suffrage Association. It was modelled, as the first Female Anti-Slavery Societies had been, on the example of England, where the militants were organized and powerful. Its spirit was so like the spirit of the early abolitionists and feminists that the eighty-year-old Reverend Olympia Brown felt that she was born to her youth again. Its use of aggressive strike tactics brought support from union organizers in the East and the West.[16]

The new vitality of Eastern suffrage leadership was another sign that the savagery of slum conditions had moved the frontier of civilization back from the settled towns of the West to the line between tenement and middle-class suburb in the cities. The problem now was to tame not the Indian but the hoodlum. The evangelical circuit riders and priests were now more necessary in the urban immigrant enclaves than in the backwoods; barbarism was more frequent in the streets than the forests. Progressive reform had to deal with the city jungle as well as the subsistence farm.

The shifting of the focus of reform activity back to the Eastern city came just at the time that the suffrage movement needed to conquer the Eastern States. By this time, nearly all of the small towns of the West had been settled long enough to become conservative. The difference between the rural crusade of Populism in the 1890's and of the Ku Klux Klan in the 1920's showed how the fine frenzy of radicalism could change in a few decades from reforming zeal to conservative suspicion and hate. It was the difference between the psychology of possible boom and the knowledge of probable bust. In Victorian times, most villages still hoped to become cities. By the 1920's, most villages feared to become ghost towns. Their zeal was now to conserve, not to change; to exclude, not to welcome.

Even as far West as Nebraska, the small towns that had been founded by a community of equals had split into castes and classes by the end of the nineteenth century. The old-stock Americans, who controlled the banks and the stores of the small town, resented the new European peasant farmers, or the poor whites leasing their eroded lands. In Willa Cather's town of Black Hawk, the merchants' lazy daughters "had a confident, uninquiring belief that they were 'refined,' and that the country girls, who 'worked out,' were not."[17] Unless the old-stock American girls could teach, they were made to sit at home like any Eastern lady. Radicalism died in many of the small towns as the new immigration of Eastern European and poor white farmers made change something to be resisted rather than incorporated. The pride of the settled Western town came to lie more in its past blood than in its future size. The frontier of radicalism continued mainly within the expanding Western city.

The last victory of the small town over the city was prohibition. It was an attempt to impose rural evangelical morality on urban fact, and it did not succeed. In the same way, the urban attempt to convince the small towns of the virtue of labour unions was a conspicuous failure in an atmosphere that distrusted mass organizations and social upheaval. On woman suffrage, however, the Western townswoman could sometimes agree with the Eastern working or professional woman that a vote would help their dignity and their chances of getting a better society.

Only in the South was the suffrage movement a failure, although enough state legislatures ratified the Nineteenth Amendment to make it the law of the land. The use of the vote by Southern women was to remain well below the average set by the rest of the nation. For after the Civil War and the forced emancipation of the Negro, the South turned in on itself and isolated its ways from the geography of reform. If it accepted the prohibition of the liquor trade, this was because prohibition was a church crusade, as well as a useful legal method of keeping liquor from Negroes without banning the possession of strong drink by Caucasians. When federal laws made new reforms legal, Southern men and women ignored them as far as possible, so that they could concentrate on the worship of the power and glory of their mythical plantation past. Legal reform is ineffective without social observance.

In a curious way, the geography of evangelical reform followed the geography of the frontier town. Crusades for change followed the westward march of the small town and of the Yankees who settled in them—"the *eastern-intelligent*" men and women credited by Susan Anthony with bringing the gospel of woman suffrage to the Far West.[18] The Eastern city itself, which many a radical deserted because of its Victorian conservatism, remained facing towards Europe; the Western town remained facing towards a new America. English example began the anti-slavery crusade for Eastern women. The English book of Mary Wollstonecraft was the revolutionary text for the early American feminists. But once woman suffrage had been taken up by the radical townswomen of the West from the lips of Eastern immigrants, they obtained the vote in presidential elections some thirty years before English women were allowed to vote in more than municipal elections.

The Eastern cities, however, grew as the new immigrants from Europe poured in during the decades before the First World War. And the interests of the educated reformers shifted back to those cities where immigrants from the westward towns had already begun to return. Not only did Europe send its millions into the sprawling American cities, but the sons and daughters of those pioneers who had rejected the cities returned there in flight from the bare opportunities of the land. For women, especially, who could not perform the back-breaking labour of the fields, the city was the frontier of work and independence. It was there that Western women found a pride in their new professions, and Western college girls came to talk with factory women in the new settlement houses, built after the example of Hull-House and its founder from rural Illinois, Jane Addams. And English example helped to complete what English example had helped to begin, the winning of the suffrage for women in the East. The geography of reform had crossed a continent, and had returned to its birthplace.

After winning the vote, American women began to work out the consequences of their political victory in the growing cities and suburbs. With the coming of mass communications, Lucy Stone was proved right and the small towns came increasingly under direct urban influence through radio, newspaper, movies, and, eventually, television. The geography of reform remained located in the expanding megalopolis. The new sexual freedom of women, permitted by the invention and diffusion of efficient contraceptives before the First World War, became the normalcy of many young women by the 1930's. Their sexual revolution, which put an end to the double standard and the red-light districts, succeeded where evangelical reform had not. Nothing showed the failure of rural morality more, indeed, than the repeal of prohibition in 1933—the only part of the Constitution ever to be repealed.

After sexual advance came political and economic advance. Increasingly, women took an independent line in politics, until, by the 1960's, the majority of them claimed to be voting their own choice. The world wars and the great depression increased the proportion of women in the labour force to one person in three. The principle of equal pay for equal work was endorsed in law, although not always in practice. And yet, although women seemed to have achieved nearly all the freedoms possible to men, social taboos still restricted their opportunities in some fields as much as it had their Victorian grandmothers. Custom can lag a century behind a changed way of life.

The cities and their attached suburbs continued to absorb the attentions of reforming women, whose priorities returned to matters of schooling and local affairs. The militant reformers came to back the cause of the Negro a second time, for the economic and political opportunities of coloured people had failed to advance as fast as those of white women. The 1960's resembled the 1840's as a decade when the Negro's position filled the minds of reformers. The cause of feminism, with women apparently equal with men in all except social usage and business opportunity, lagged.

Yet when the Negroes gain their desired liberties and many women realize that they are still excluded from some of the social and economic privileges of men, the preoccupation of reformers may swing back to the status of women. Certainly, the problems of the new cities will remain dominant in our thought. For, along with problems of population and armaments, urbanization is the third major obsession of our time. More than one in five of mankind now lives in a great city; by the end of the century, at the present rate of urban growth, it will be one human being in two. And the cities and the suburbs particularly cater to the needs and opportunities of women. Rural society usually makes drudges of them, while the city allows them to become equal human beings. The geography of reform will remain centred on the city and on the position of the underprivileged there, including Negroes and women.

In the history of woman's search for the freedoms of the body and of the mind and of the spirit in America, nothing has aided her more than the advance of technology and urbanization. Her quest for liberty has been interacting with the spread of an industrial civilization across a continent. The revolving wheels of progress have brought leisure to American women and time for them to seek the subtle liberties of feeling free. It is too soon to say that the emancipation of women in America has failed, just because they received the vote less than fifty years ago and have done no better with it than men. The long quest for the freedoms of women is still in its infancy; only the more obvious discriminations have been removed. The geography of liberty still has many frontiers to cross.

PART ONE

American Heritage

Men like to see women pick up the drunken and fallen!—repair the *damages* of society!—that *patching business* is in "woman's proper sphere"— But to be *master* of *circumstances*—that is man's sphere!

SUSAN B. ANTHONY

I

❦

EARLY CONDITIONS

TWENTY-FOUR WOMEN landed at Plymouth with the Pilgrims. Nine
were dead at the end of the first winter. Their successors fared better.
If they survived the crossing, they could expect to find a settlement of
some kind already in existence either along the coasts or in the
wilderness, and a choice of possible husbands. The frontier was
always short of women, but they usually preferred the settled small
towns and later the cities; any existence other than that of the pioneer
assured them of a certain freedom from incessant, bodily toil.

The sod hut was the first home of the Pilgrim woman, and later
the first home of the prairie settler. Half a pit and half a tent of earth
supported on branches, it was nasty, dirty, dank, and cold. Later,
when the woman had helped clear the land for the first harvest, her
man built her a log cabin, windy and wet, but at least above the
ground. Eventually, clay or mud or plaster could be used to fill
the cracks between the logs; bricks might be made or bought to
build a hearth; wooden floors might be set in to raise feet above the
trodden earth. Then the woman could think about making a home.

In the primitive rural society of colonial days, and in the later West
and poor white South, women lived either in mud or dust. These were
the two seasons. Refuse heaps and middens and cess-pits bred epi-

demics about the house, closets were unspeakable (when the first efficient one was invented, it was given a testimonial by the great reformer, William Lloyd Garrison), nightfall put an end to all outdoor work. Travel was slow and dangerous; in winter, people risked drowning in pools on the main roads. Isolation was normal on farms, and visitors rare.

Where people were so few, every hand was needed. There was a rough division of labour between men and women on the farms—the men produced the raw materials, the women manufactured them for use. Few women outside the Indian and slave and German immigrant groups worked in the fields, except in time of harvest. Although the women looked after the livestock in the farmyard, their province was the house, which was a little factory that employed old men, women, and children. The younger men brought in the timber, the grain, the wool, and the meat; the women and children prepared and preserved the food, spun, sewed, washed and ironed the clothes, and made candles for light. Every colonial woman was a perpetual housekeeper, even when she had servants—and these were rare.

Early American women were almost treated like Negro slaves, inside and outside the home. Both were expected to behave with deference and obedience towards owner or husband; both did not exist officially under the law; both had few rights and little education; both found it difficult to run away; both worked for their masters without pay; both had to breed on command, and to nurse the results. As George Fitzhugh wrote in his *Sociology for the South* as late as 1854, "The kind of slavery is adapted to the men enslaved. Wives and apprentices are slaves; not in theory only, but often in fact. Children are slaves to their parents, guardians and teachers."[1] The only slavemaster was the free sane white male. Outside his jurisdiction lived the despised of society, free Negroes, spinsters, widows, and the inhabitants of the wilderness.

Of course, a colonial wife was treated better than a slave, as a household Negro or concubine was treated better than a field hand. She could even be promoted to a position of responsibility, as an overseer in her master's absence. She could discipline her own servants, as a Negro steward could discipline his minions. Although she could not be sold—except in Smithfield Market, London—she lost control over her possessions during the lifetime of the master who chose her. The authority of a husband was as absolute and unquestionable as that of a plantation owner.

If colonial husbands and fathers treated their women with respect and some equality, it was by their own free choice. The law, literally interpreted and untempered by equity, gave them almost unlimited power over the persons of their wives and daughters, although public opinion did not allow wife-beating in New England (public opinion did allow the beating of slaves in the South, short of maiming or murder, and whereas the churches chose to protect the dignity of white women, they rarely chose to protect the morality of Negroes). The white woman was considered as another human being, even if an inferior one; the slave was hardly considered as much better than a beast with a soul.

In the early colonies, marriage was the duty of every woman. She married young, as soon as she could bear children. Men married again on the death of their wives, and widows were courted immediately their husbands were buried. These early and repeated marriages produced many children. By 1675, the average family in New England consisted of nine people—some women bore up to twenty children. Wives had a commandment to multiply and replenish the earth of a continent. Their fertility was extraordinary. If occasionally a pious and poor father prayed for "churchyard luck" and, like John Donne, for God to ease him with burials, most of the children who lived were useful in an expanding community of farmers. Continual pregnancies gave wives no respite from the ills of the flesh. They aged early and suffered much pain, but their simple diet and dress gave them good health for the time.

In the strict founding settlements of America, women had no need to settle for less than the security of marriage. Throughout the eighteenth century, there were three men to every two women. Even the female criminals shipped to Virginia as bond servants found husbands quickly. But freedom to enjoy the pleasures of the body demanded the servitude of marriage. As John Milton had written, marriage was "a prescribed satisfaction for irrational heat." Under the famous Blue Laws, fornication and adultery in New England were punished by whipping, branding, banishment, the stocks, the scarlet letter, and, in one case, by hanging. But the effect of these laws on the American character then and now has been exaggerated. They were, in some ways, necessary in their own age, and disused afterwards.

The fact of living on the edge of savagery, in contact with the primitive morality of the Indian and the Negro, made the authorities in the colonies necessarily strict. They had led their people to settle in the unknown, and they insisted on trying to defend the souls of these followers through their bodies. The terrible liberty of isolation and the wilderness made some of the first settlers discard their European moral restraints. Cases of bestiality, according to Cotton Mather, were not unknown. The possession of slave and bondwomen made their masters and mistresses free to do what they wished. Indian squaws could easily be found by frontiersmen, and easily abandoned.

As the first missionaries to the West were told, barbarism was the chief danger to the pioneers. "They will think it no degradation to do before the woods and wild animals, what, in the presence of a cultivated social state, they would blush to perpetrate."[2] Until a stern public opinion could govern the ethics of a scattered and immigrant society, small governments tried to do what they could to keep up the standards of civilization. Their success was impressive. If repression led to the occasional excesses of witch-hunts and women appearing naked at sermons, yet the growing societies were preserved from savagery.

The strictness of behaviour forced upon the women of New England in their small communities gave them little freedom in the years after marriage, but much in the months before. Every inducement was placed in front of a girl to find a husband. The custom of bundling, when courting couples were allowed to spend the night fully dressed in the same bed, was not only due to the shortage of heat and beds. As petting is now, it was an incentive to early marriage. The punishments of the courts were lax in respect to offences committed before wedlock. In fact, the French traveller Chastellux found that in the moderately liberal society of Connecticut a seduced girl was not ruined; her misfortune could be and was easily remedied by finding a husband. An immigrant society did not dwell on the failures of its past too much.

After marriage, American women sometimes appeared more godly than they were. Any journey by their husbands meant a long time absent in those days of slow travel. The court records are full of cases of erring wives. The Journal of Nicholas Cresswell, an Englishman on a visit to New York just before the Revolution, told of an episode which cast a curious light on the difference between public observance and private practice. He met a major's wife, who asked him to supper in the absence of her husband. During the meal, she ran over the Scriptures from Genesis to Revelations, for sentences to prove the heinous crime of fornication. But after supper, this wife with the apparent neatness of a Quaker and modesty of a vestal, showed, "in private, the air and behaviour of a professed courtesan, and in bed the lechery of a guinea pig." The episode proved her hypocrisy to Cresswell, but it also proves more—both the care colonial woman had to take of moral opinion, even in American cities, and the care historians have to take in showing that early American moral laws were honoured more in the observance than the breach.

As manners moved South, they became even more relaxed. From Maryland to South Carolina, morals were less strict than in the North. This was mainly due to the system of agriculture, with its large land-holdings and quantities of servants and slaves. Society there was patriarchal and aristocratic enough to take pride in the number of its bastards, especially when these added to the number of its slaves. Where Negroes were bred as openly as animals, the owner's children were often fitted by the sights they saw to become no more than the masters of slaves. The lives of such pioneer planters as William Byrd II of Westover show that the elevation of planters' wives to the estate of goddesses was not a colonial phenomenon. Byrd kissed his fellow citizens' womenfolk with familiarity and impunity, although he was a little scared of his own wife. Women drank too much and quarrelled openly with their husbands. There was a great degree of equality between the sexes in all the deadly sins, except lechery. In fact, Byrd's diaries have more the flavour of *Tom Jones* than *Ivanhoe*.

The colonies could not be settled without women. They could not remain civilized unless these women came from Europe. No man could, indeed, run his farm well without the labour of women and children. "A bachelor," declared a traveller in 1822, "has no business in the backwoods; for in a wild country where it is almost impossible to hire assistance of any kind, either male or female, a man is thrown entirely upon his own resources."[3] No merchant or fisherman could easily leave for long periods without trusting his business to his wife. In Nantucket, the Quaker women were rewarded on their husbands' return with his approval and the remark, "Wife, thee hast done well." As Crèvecoeur asked, what would the men have done "without the agency of these faithful mates?" The necessity for women made their sexual characteristics less important; up until the end of the nineteenth century, ugly women could always find Western farmers to marry them. Wives were needed to work rather than to please. But woman's freedom to work and to rear children lay only within marriage or in the ultimate independence of widowhood.

Elizabeth Oakes Smith, a pioneer feminist in the early days of the movement, was one of those New England girls who was pushed young into marriage with a middle-aged man. Although she later tended to idealize her maidenhood, she gave an accurate picture of the pressures put on a Puritan girl to make her marry.

Puritan Maidens with their unselfish, unworldly, and supreme conscientiousness were easily managed by careful mothers who took the settlement of their daughters mostly into their own hands, and these found themselves on the road to matrimony they hardly knew how. . . . To be a wife to mother children was esteemed the proper thing—the right thing, and the beautiful thing. . . . The passion of a Puritan maiden existed, but it was buried Pelion upon Ossa, under a vast substratum of Duty, never volcano-like to break forth, and carry destruction in its path.

Elizabeth Oakes Smith wrote in the days of romanticism, when love was held to be more important than duty; but the failure of her own youthful marriage gives some truth to her dictum, "To be rushed from the cradle to the altar is to make the great life-long mistake."[4]

An early manual, *The Whole Duty of a Woman: Or, an Infallible Guide to the Fair Sex,* defined the colonial opportunities of women. "There are but three States of Life, through which they can regularly pass, *viz.* Virginity, Marriage, and Widowhood, two of them are States of Subjection, the First to the Parent, the Second to the Husband, and the Third, as it is casual, whether ever they arrive to it or no . . . a Condition the most desolate and deplorable."[5] The number of young women with old husbands—a fact which shocked many travellers in New England—may have been a tribute to the wisdom of the girls, who knew that in the hope of widowhood lay their greatest liberty. The difficulty which Samuel Sewall had in finding a rich widow to marry was due to the widows' wish to keep their freedom and fortune as much as to his own avarice in negotiating a marriage settlement. The most desolate and deplorable condition was, in truth, that of an old maid. As a sea captain complained about his dependent sisters in a letter to his brother, "Old Maids are useless trouble to all the human flesh and if you live as I have done you will find it out, and I hope you never will."[6]

A single woman had no hope of freeing her body from the control of her father or brothers until she could find work and a place to live in outside her home. Privacy was too expensive a thing to exist in most early American houses. Space was lacking and dear. But work for a woman which paid her enough to house and feed and clothe herself was equally lacking. As late as the 1830's, Harriet Martineau found England superior to America in that respect. Only the nun, and the occasional lucky school-teacher, could support herself well in the eyes of God and the world.

Single women had to stay inside the home of any relative who would endure them. In this state of grateful subservience, the strictest marriage could look like relative freedom, and provide some form of sexual release. That was, provided a man offered marriage. As Polly Baker once complained after she had been whipped, fined, and imprisoned for bearing a bastard, "I readily consented to the only offer of marriage that ever was made me. . . . What must poor young women do? Custom forbids their making overtures to men; they cannot, however heartily they wish it, marry when they please."[7]

Those women who could or did not please made up some sort of rationale to preserve their self-respect. Rebecca Gratz, a spinster in a wealthy Jewish family in Philadelphia and possibly the original for Walter Scott's Rebecca, tried to justify her position in a private letter:

The man who has no one to influence and console him, when vehement passions, painful diseases and disappointed pride cross his vexed spirits—is a sad spectacle of suffering and helplessness—I should be frightened for our own single brothers when such a picture is presented to my mind—if it were not for the hope that I may be able to repay all their goodness to me—by keeping up a domestic home with those charities alive, which may rescue them from the worst effects of bachelorship—a care-for-nobody independence.

Yet even this intelligent and conservative and generous woman could not repress her doubts at her position as an unpaid nurse and housekeeper in her brothers' household. "This is giving a new turn to self-importance is it not?" she asked herself, only to answer, "But indeed, we who have neither fortune to support, nor other right to an establishment must endeavour to set up a claim to usefulness in some subordinate way to reconcile us to the idea of not being a burden to our relations."[8] The Devil's gift to the early Americans was to make single women feel uneasy about enjoying the bodily comforts of family dependence, and yet to restrict their opportunities for respectable work outside the house. It surprised travellers at the time of de Tocqueville to find out that many American mechanics kept their women in idleness and did not allow them to work.

The Puritan pressure on women to marry did not spare the men. "The Bachelor," declared the *Ladies' Miscellany* in 1830, "God pity him. Man nor woman nor child will not. He is as one marked out and fitted for the abuse and cavillings of his neighbours."[9] Bachelors were thought to be odd, as they still are. This was so much the case that a book appeared in 1852 called *Single Blessedness; Or, Single Ladies and Gentlemen, Against the Slanders of The Pulpit, The*

Press, and The Lecture-room, addressed to Those Who Are Really Wise, and To Those Who Fancy Themselves So. It claimed to be the first defence of the bachelor state for men and women after eighteen centuries of assault. The anonymous author maintained that bachelors checked extravagance, worked harder for the state, helped charity, and supported parents and the aged. As for their reasons for choosing to be single, "Why men remain unmarried is nobody's concern but their own." The author was unsuccessful in his plea for singleness. The bachelor and the bachelor girl are still rarer in America than in any other civilized country. Although there were many spinsters on the East Coast in early Victorian times, the Puritan emphasis on early and frequent marriage still operates in a continent where more than nine in ten modern girls marry at least once before their early thirties. America remains the land Nicholas Cresswell called "a paradise on earth" for women because there were so few old maids.

The early feminists of Victorian times resented this concentration on marriage by young girls and their mothers. They said that women were warped permanently by failing to get an education in the hope of getting a husband instead. Fathers thought that it was stupid to waste money on schooling a girl beyond adolescence; many girls had to fight like Lucy Stone to reach college. So the usual daughter was condemned to stay at home for years in hope of a suitor, or to fill up the innumerable boarding-houses in the cities and the spas with the same expectation. She had to endure "that purgatory between school and marriage, that death in life," to which social arrangements doomed middle-class girls. These young creatures passed their days, in the words of Oliver Wendell Holmes, "sittin' like shopkeepers behind their goods, waitin' and waitin' and waitin'."

It was small wonder that some girls decided to make men pay for this period of degradation. A woman dictated before marriage, George Eliot declared, that she might have an appetite for submission afterwards. Lillie Devereux Blake, a Southern belle and heiress, recorded her female fury at the age of sixteen, and her intention to torment Southern men for their faithlessness to women. "For this men's hearts must be attacked and then trifled with; therefore I give myself heart and soul to making men miserable; if they love me I will refuse them, no matter how much I may be interested. I will live but to redress these terrible wrongs."[10] If she married four years later a man who squandered her fortune, and married yet again a man whom she had sometimes to support, yet she became a leading suffragist in New York and helped to avenge in her late life some of the wrongs of her sex that her violent youth had failed to right.

Early marriage in early America was a religious, family, and economic duty. It also meant freedom from a parents' home and freedom to run a husband's. Above all, it meant freedom to escape from the daily worry of being left an old maid in a marrying society. A good wife and mother could feel that she earned her keep, and even earned a kind of equality with her husband. A maiden aunt found it nearly impossible to feel her own worth. Moreover, the widow then, as the widow now, could be one of the most independent and rich members of her society. By the law of most states, she received at least a third of her husband's estate during her life. By marriage contract, she could well have preserved her own fortune. Usually, she inherited more than the law allowed. She owned enough, if she was lucky, to force respect. If she had children, she had the power of a mother in a fatherless home. The moral and economic supremacy of many American widows and mothers set an example in colonial times.

Except for the brief period of courtship, when each year meant diminishing choices, marriage was the liberty and opportunity of the American girl. Her freedom inside marriage, however small, was greater than her freedom inside a relative's house. But the lot of both the wife and the female relative was slavery to the home.

The women who were most exploited in early America were the slaves and the bond servants on the farms and in the towns. These women were often treated little better than animals. They were kept apart from their master's family, although space was sometimes so short that they were included. The bond servants could be treated even worse than the slaves, since a Negro belonged all his life to his

owner, while a servant was bound for seven years or less. The Sot-
Weed Factor's maid was not fortunate.

> . . . now at the Hoe,
> I daily work, and Bare-foot go,
> In weeding Corn or feeding Swine,
> I spend my melancholy Time.

Although the myth was that the servants often rose in the social scale
after their period of service and sometimes employed servants of their
own, this was rarely true, except for those few who rose into the
aristocracy of Virginia. The women tended to marry labourers or
small farmers, and to become the ancestors of the present poor
whites.

Increasingly, servants worked freely for wages. As colonial America was chiefly a domestic economy, women had to find employment
within the homes of others. But no American free servant would give
up her right to equality. She was merely accepting a job until she had
an opportunity to become as good as her mistress, or better. As de
Tocqueville noticed, "The condition of domestic service does not
degrade the character of those who enter upon it, because it is freely
chosen and adopted for a time only, because it is not stigmatized by
public opinion and creates no permanent inequality between the servant and the master."[11] Indeed, Mrs. Trollope found it more than
petty treason to the Republic to call a free citizen a *servant*. They had
to be called *helps* or *domestics*.

Before Irish immigration introduced a division of background and
religion between servant and mistress, the American household without slaves or bond servants was an integrated community. Everybody
worked in it, for there was work for everybody. The Devil found
work for nobody to do, because there could be no idle hands. If there
was leisure time for some women in a large household, they devoted
it to earning money for the household through handicrafts. Before
the factory system was imported from England, women could make
low wages by piece-work in spinning, weaving, knitting, and sewing.
Upper New York State, for instance, was a centre of the home indus-

try of glove-making. The fact that they could not legally keep their wages from their husbands sent some women in 1848 to the first feminist convention at Seneca Falls.

In the colonial and revolutionary period, the family and the household were the economic basis of society. Only a few exceptional women in the towns made their living outside the home. At the head of the family stood the husband. It was his duty to feed, clothe, and house all his dependents. These could be a large number. When Samuel Blackwell sailed for America in 1832, he took with him fifteen people: a wife, eight children, four sisters, a governess, and a nurse; only on his death did they have to begin earning a living. It was a man's duty to look after all his female relatives and to keep his self-supporting society in working order. Therefore, it was only reasonable that he should control the income of all its members.

When the home was the workshop of America and a barter economy flourished as much as a money economy, both men and women could feel that their tasks were necessary and useful. The services provided by the colonial woman were essential for the colonial man—some of them he could hardly buy elsewhere. The economic value of women and children was shown by the fact that Western widowers preferred, for a second wife, a healthy widow with several children who knew how to work a farm. When a farmer in pioneer Illinois was asked whether he had married his wife because of her great size, he replied, "I reckon women are some like horses and oxen, the biggest can do the most work, and that's what I want one for."[12]

Until the coming of the American factory and city, American women could hardly complain about the slavery of their lives. There were no alternatives. A woman might be a drudge from birth, but so was a man. The taming of the soil meant an equality in bondage to the earth. What the man found or grew, the woman cooked or made. In primitive America, only the wives of those frontiersmen who preferred to hunt rather than till the soil lived a life of dirty leisure. Crèvecoeur found that many of the wives and children of hunters lived in sloth and inactivity, and that hunting quickly reduced poor whites to the level of Indians. The freedom of the woods was no freedom to the women who had to set up a home there without any of the contrivances of civilization. Small wonder if, under the dread of isolation and under the toil of existence, they relapsed into torpor or sluttishness or even madness. In the early lunatic asylums, a large proportion of the inmates were the wives of countrymen.

In the colonies, a woman had to work in some home or another. Given this choice, she preferred to work in her husband's—that home was more especially her own. The worship of the American home began when the household was the focus of all daily life and the workshop for it. The church, if available, was the only other meeting-place. Naturally, the one supported the other against the terror of the wilderness, as they were to support each other long after the home had lost its function as a maker of goods.

Many women were content with their subordinate roles within their churches. But for the rebels who were not strong enough to be heretics or to found their own churches, religious freedom lay in increasing their role within their own churches, or in joining another church of more liberal views. Despite the blaze of Jonathan Edwards and the Great Awakening, America after the Revolution was probably in the most heathen period of its history. Rationalism was at its brief zenith. Crèvecoeur forecast that religious indifference, already one of the strongest characteristics of the Americans in his opinion, would increase and conquer the whole continent. "Persecution, religious pride, the love of contradiction, are the food of what the world commonly calls religion. These motives have ceased here; zeal in Europe is confined; here it evaporates in the great distance it has to travel; there it is a grain of powder inclosed; here it burns away in the open air and consumes without effect."[18]

New England still kept the grain of Calvin's powder inclosed, in spite of the Western fever that drained off its population. The diaries of women in the eighteenth and early nineteenth century still suffered from a heavy burden of sin. At the age of nine, one New England girl baked something for her amusement on Sunday; she fell into the fire and burned her hand, which she presently thought came justly upon her for playing on the Sabbath day.[14] Another Connecticut girl died at the age of eleven, saying, "There is none that doeth good, no, not one," and confessing, "I *have* been a *very* great sinner. I have sinned ever since I got out of my cradle."[15]

Calvinist preachers used the ever-present facts of death and pain and disease to keep their flocks mindful of God. In every family, young girls were used to nursing their sick or dying brothers and sisters, mothers and fathers. Every family provided its own nurses. The suffering of loved relations was never far away.

A sixteen-year-old Puritan child recognized herself as "carnal and sitting loose from God," and held that she was rightly punished with smallpox as a "proper rebuke to her pride and vanity."[16] Another girl spent two months nursing her mad mother before her death, and then reproached herself with her own inadequacy in failing to imitate her mother's virtues. A Massachusetts wife reflected at the death-bed of her grandmother, "I must leave my own body also, no longer to rejoice the eyes of my friends, but to moulder in the dust powerless to defend its narrow house from the intruding reptile to whom my wasting flesh must be a prey."[17] Women at this time had to dwell on death, for it was all around them from childhood, even if they did not share in the strange joy of Samuel Sewall, who passed Christmas Day in his family tomb, where he was "entertained with a view of, and converse with, the Coffins. . . . 'Twas an awful yet pleasing Treat."[18]

This fear of pain and death was the greatest lever of the old Calvinist and the new evangelical religion. The hope of a heaven and of a future meeting with the loved dead gave sorrowing women consolation and freed them from some agony in resignation to the will of God. "It is indeed a heavy stroke to lose my little Brother," another sixteen-year-old girl wrote, "but it is wrong to repine. He is doubtless gone, to happier scenes and it now remains for me to be prepared to follow him whenever it shall please my Heavenly Father to call me home."[19] Although death could not be escaped, hope could be kept alive of a future encounter in heaven.

Even the great Unitarian preacher, William Ellery Channing, who

EARLY CONDITIONS   [17]

later taught God's love and man's perfection for the inspiration of the Transcendentalists, began with more traditional methods of bringing sinners to their Maker. An account of a sermon of his by a young Boston spinster shows the effect that sermons could have. Channing's text for New Year's Eve, 1815, was, "Now my days are swifter than a frost; they flee away, they see no good." He spoke "in his own peculiarly impressive and *unequalled manner.*" He said that, although he was a young man, he had seen all the other pulpits in Boston suddenly left vacant. He talked of the next New Year's Eve, then repeated twice, *"If I live, if I live."* Before ending with rules of conduct, he declared, "I then speak to you as a dying man, one standing on the borders of eternity. I beseech of you to reform." The spinster's comment on the sermon was the pious hope, "May it be the means in some measure of making me more prepared for that hour which must come. I know not *how soon.*"[20]

The churches, which were to convert the South and West of America, learnt the emphasis on death and sin of the Calvinist and other Massachusetts churches. Although church membership had declined to only one person in eight in New England and only one in twenty in the South by 1760, the techniques of English revivalism allied to the Puritan emphasis on sin were to spot the continent with evangelical churches. The Baptists and the Methodists sent their circuit riders round the backwoods, which took to the drama and the immediate redemption of the camp-meetings.[21] The fear of God of the old New England towns was broadcast across the land in the wake of emigrant and missionary preachers, although the villages of America could rarely afford to pay for a permanent clergyman. As Frances Trollope noticed, the frontiersmen contrived to marry, christen, and bury by themselves. Their wives worked on Sundays, and one of them, when taxed with this, replied, "I beant a Christian, Ma'am; we have got no opportunity."[22]

Meanwhile, some of the larger sea towns grew into cities through further emigration from Europe—one in three Americans was foreign-born by the middle of the eighteenth century. These new cities at Philadelphia, New York, Boston, Charles Town, and Newport looked towards Europe. They were big enough, with populations running to the tens of thousands, to allow religious toleration. For the uniformity of old-time Boston had depended on its village size. If religious indifference, as Crèvecoeur had thought, was not to be the result of the American spaces, religious diversity was.

The first American cities felt the impact of the Enlightenment from Europe, and the following romanticism. The Enlightenment in turn led to a questioning about man's freedom and equality which was to provide the ideology for the American Revolution and the women's revolution. The Eastern American city always remained open to the influence of Europe, and this, in time, led to a reaction against such "alien" growths on the part of the Western small town and farm. For the country was inland, jealous, poorer, and soon to consider itself more religious and patriotic than the city. The American who wished to think himself as virtuous as Thoreau was to follow his example of "ever . . . leaving the city more and more and withdrawing into the wilderness," for he "must walk toward Oregon and not toward Europe."[23]

In these new cities and in the older small towns about them, religious freedom flourished. A schoolgirl, after hearing her first Unitarian sermon near Boston, wrote of "the beautiful ideas constantly instilled—that they are entirely an original class—original in their conceptions and feelings—the only enlightened, liberal thinkers in the world."[24] The Brahmin class with its Unitarian leaders dominated wealthy Boston and Cambridge and Concord—the Calvinist Lyman Beecher found that all the literary men of Massachusetts were Unitarian; all the trustees and professors of Harvard College were Unitarian; all the elite of wealth and fashion crowded Unitarian churches; and the judges on the bench were Unitarian.

This group produced many fearless anti-slavery women, and the first philosopher of feminism in America, Margaret Fuller. The freedom from sin preached by the Unitarians, and the concept of love of all, was a driving force behind the Massachusetts reformers of the early nineteenth century. One woman convert to Unitarianism confessed that it gave her "a responsibility of self-culture which was self-torture." The doctrine was to prove as powerful as the Quakerism of

Philadelphia in training the first American feminists. For the crusade for women's rights began in the Eastern American city, before its leadership passed to those brought up in the Western small town.

Universalism was the poor woman's version of Unitarianism. Its simple doctrines preached the oneness of love and religion. God was too good to damn the men and women that He had made. Mary Livermore, who became an important feminist, was brought up in the North End of Boston in the 1820's with such Calvinistic sternness that she often expressed to her father "a bitter regret that she had ever been born." But later she was to marry a Universalist minister and feel an extraordinary freedom in doing so. She freed herself further by going out to Chicago with her husband, escaping her childhood in everything except her own character, which bound her to serve others all her life.[25] In the same way, the Boston author and reformer, Lydia Maria Child, was to hope that "some time or other, there will be a Universal Church," and was already to see signs of its imminent arrival.[26]

Unitarianism and Universalism loosened the rigours of New England religion. They gave a liberty of the spirit to women who did not dare to give up religion altogether for fear of public opinion, and yet who could not live with the burden of sin always upon their hearts. The conformity of American life, noticed by every European visitor, never freed a woman from the habits of her neighbours; but she could find a congenial faith to free her from the duties exacted by a stern male God. The liberal religions brought emancipation to their believers, whom Harriet Martineau had pitied under the yoke of Calvinism:

women [who] go wearily to church, Sunday after Sunday, to hear what they do not believe; lie down at night full of self-reproach for a want of piety which they do not know how to attain; and rise up in the morning hopelessly, seeing nothing in the day before them but the misery of carrying their secret concealed from parents, husband, sisters, friends.[27]

At the same time, revivalism, led in the Burned-Over District after 1825 by the extraordinary Charles Grandison Finney, converted upper New York State and the Western Reserve of Ohio. A missionary was already lamenting that, although the settlers had come from a land of Bibles and Sabbaths, they found themselves in a country where they could "fight against God without fearing man," a land "of sinful liberty."[28] Finney's "New Measures" proved wildly successful in converting the frontier. He encouraged the participation of women at prayer-meetings and "promiscuous" assemblies. Both at Rochester and later at Oberlin, he trained preachers—including one woman—to follow his path.

The spiritual ferment which Finney brought to some women and his encouragement of their testimony were potent forces behind the later prominence of the Burned-Over District and Ohio in the struggle for the rights of Negroes and women. The very scarcity of religious people in the West gave women their chance. Often, there was only a woman who could testify at a meeting. Women clutched onto religion in the West as the first coming of civilization, and their first freedom from the savage terrors of the unknown and the brute male.

In the South, the Methodist and the Baptist churches had their great successes among the poor white farmers and among the Negro slaves. In the first fifty years of the nineteenth century, the Protestant churches increased their membership nearly ten times over. Where one in fifteen Americans had been a member of a Protestant church in 1800, one in seven was by 1850. The wealthy New York abolitionist, Lewis Tappan, had more grounds than optimism when he wrote at the time of the Finney revivals:

A great spirit of improvement prevails in our country, and in foreign countries. Never, I suppose, was so much mind at work, and never was matter in such agitation. We are certainly more active than our fathers, if not wiser, and I verily believe we excel them in energy and wisdom. Poor mother earth was never so beat and exercised as now, and she must think a new race dwells on her surface.[29]

Yet it was to be decades before that spirit of improvement affected politics and changed the law.

II

⧅

THE FIRST REBELS

BEFORE THE RISE of the pioneering feminists of the early nineteenth century, the general condition of American women was accepted by all but the most exceptional. The records of the beginnings of American feminism are conspicuous by their barrenness. There was only one important political rebel, perhaps because there were so few aristocrats in the American colonies strong enough to rebel. Religious rebels were more numerous. The New World had attracted the outcasts from established religions and allowed room for rebellion. Even so, the heretic seekers after God were few.

It was for religious freedom that the first colonists from England had crossed the Atlantic. The women who came to be with the men worshipped alongside them. As the weary and despondent Quaker Eliza Hard, without food in the wilderness, reproached herself on her knees, "Didst thou not come for liberty of conscience, and hast thou not got it,—also being provided far beyond thy expectations?" When she looked up, she found her cat with a rabbit in its mouth.[1] God, through the abundance of the New World, seemed to have answered her prayers.

Yet, if the early colonists fled from religious persecution, they did not flee to religious anarchy. The churches which they planted in America were organized after the model of old churches; the society they established had to be well ordered under God to survive and repel the savage continent. Thus women who came to Massachusetts to worship in freedom were still bound by the tenets of their churches in Europe, and the strict Presbyterians of the Massachusetts colony did nothing to soften the teaching of John Knox upon women.

Woman in her greatest perfection, was made to serve and obey man, not to rule and command him: As Saint Paul doth reason in these words. Man is not of the woman but the woman of the man. . . . After her fall and rebellion committed against God, there was put upon her a new necessity, and she was made subject to man by the irrevocable sentence of God.

In the church especially, she should listen and obey. "Let woman keep silence in the congregation, for it is not permitted to them to speak, but to be subject as the law sayeth."[2]

It was just, therefore, that the first protest of a woman against her position as the social and intellectual inferior of man should be a religious protest. Anne Hutchinson had fled to Boston from Lincolnshire in 1634 to seek freedom of worship. She was dominant over her well-to-do husband and family, and once her chosen preacher, John Cotton, had left for Massachusetts, she had to follow. She was particularly attracted to the doctrine of the Covenant of Grace. Her restless, quick temper and mind needed a faith that allowed her to claim utter and direct dependence on God, and thus utter and direct dependence on her own words as the revelation of God.

When she arrived in Boston, she quickly endeared herself to a large circle of people through her knowledge of herbal healing; at that time, pain and slow dying were part of normal family life. She began a weekly meeting for women, at which she expounded the sermons of John Cotton; she later added a weekly meeting for men and women. Soon her doctrines spoke more of the freedom of God's grace and of her own visions than of the words of Cotton himself.

Her support grew among the tolerant, the individualistic, the entrepreneurs, the unsuccessful, and women. As one of her extreme supporters promised a newcomer, "I'll bring you to a woman that preaches better Gospel than any of your black-coats that have been at the Ninniversity, a Woman of another kind of spirit, who hath many revelations of things to come. . . . I had rather hear such a one that speaks from the mere motion of the spirit, without any study at all, than any of your learned Scholars, although they may be fuller of Scripture."

This charismatic healer, with the gift of fluent and inspired speech, attracted the hatred of the powers in Massachusetts, especially John Winthrop, who had become Governor of the colony after fleeing there to escape the dictatorship of Archbishop Laud in England. He himself became more dictatorial than the Archbishop. He rightly saw the danger of prophetesses and their "immediate revelation" to the theocracy of Massachusetts, where church and state were fused. If one woman defied the established powers over religion, how many men would do so over business and the laws?

John Cotton was eventually weaned towards a Covenant of Works and turned on Anne Hutchinson when she was brought to trial. He told her that her doctrine of individualism was so dangerous that, although he did not think "you have been unfaithful to your Husband in his Marriage Covenant, yet that will follow upon it." To question the state church was to question all morality. Anne Hutchinson was sentenced "as a Leper to withdraw," and went to Rhode Island, where another religious rebel from Boston, Roger Williams, had founded a colony. Many families followed her example. But she provoked more strife with her mystical doctrines in Rhode Island, and, on her husband's death, she moved with her six younger children to a lonely farm on Long Island Sound. There she and five of her children were killed by Indians.

The struggle for religious freedom, which in Stuart England had led to a political struggle and emigration to America, in Anne Hutchinson's case made her a political danger to the Massachusetts government. Her enemy, Governor Winthrop, wrote: "She walked by such a rule as cannot stand with the peace of any State; for such bottomless revelations . . . if they be allowed in one thing, must be admitted a rule in all things; for they being above reason and Scripture, they are not subject to control." The individual, man or woman, coming to America in search of a particular freedom was bound to adjust himself to the small churches and governments already there, or to flee from them to the wilderness and set up his own society or God.

Anne Hutchinson sought religious freedom because it seemed to her the most important freedom in her time. Political liberty was necessarily involved. Her friend, Mary Dyer, a convert to Quakerism, was to die later on the Boston gallows for coming a second time to the town to "publish Truth" and "look the Law in the face." Both strong women, seeking the primary freedom of their time, were victims of political societies. And both were criminals twice over. To be a religious rebel was wicked, but to be a woman rebel was devilish. The first of Anne Hutchinson's crimes, according to her male accusers, was to inspire other women to be "rather . . . a Husband than a Wife." It was worse than inspiring them to be rather "a preacher than a Hearer; and a Magistrate than a Subject."[3]

Yet the ostracism of one woman and the hanging of another for preaching were mild compared to the execution of certain women for the sake of religion in the small towns of Massachusetts. Witches were thought to have emigrated from Europe with the godly. Satan had been a fellow passenger. Half a dozen witches had already been hanged—mainly for opposition to the local minister—before the famous Salem trials of 1692. In the hysteria of that year, nineteen people were put to death on the evidence of frenzied children and popular superstition. As Cotton Mather said, "A witch is not to be endured in heaven or on earth."

Most of the victims were aged and friendless old women. If an occasional one of them, driven half-mad by loneliness and the repression of sexuality and degradation, confessed to being the Devil's own, her lie was a fearful stretching after the dangerous liberty of feeling important, at least in evil. For the churches claimed the right of judging those who were important in doing good, and these could hardly be female. To hang a witch was a symbolic choking of sin in all women. And the freedom of women to do wrong, according to their natures, could never be allowed by any society under the rule of God.

The Puritans were sure that they knew the right place of men and women on earth. They felt that survival on the rim of the wilderness depended upon the approval of God, and that His approval depended upon the obedience of men and women. To question was to commit a form of treason. And, despite their excesses, the Puritans did "as much for freedom of conscience as could have been expected, and were in that respect in advance of the age in which they lived." For, as their apologist in the time of de Tocqueville continued, "if they were intolerant, so were others."[4] The religious excesses of Massachusetts were mild compared with the religious wars of Europe.

Religious intolerance in the colonies outside Massachusetts and the rest of New England was less violent. It excluded certain people from power, particularly those who were not members of the founding sect, or who were thought inferior within the sect. In the Southern colonies, the Church of England was established, and worked with the powers that were. When New York was still New Amsterdam, the Dutch Reformed churches were dominant, and, although women were given some schooling and legal protection, they were held back by a stern religion. The German Pietists and Moravians in Pennsylvania also educated their women; but it was the ruling Quakers in that state who first gave women the chance of religious equality and liberty.

The founder of the Society of Friends, George Fox, had begun by converting a Baptist woman—the Baptists alone in their time recognized "she-preachers." Fox's wife, Margaret Fell, proved as important in founding the faith as he. Twelve of the original sixty-six Quaker apostles in England were women, for, as Fox wrote in his *Epistles,* "Women are to take up the Cross daily and follow Christ daily as well as the men . . . they have an office as well as the men, for they have a stewardship to the Lord as well as man."[5]

Although the followers of Fox in England and America tried to diminish the role of women in the Quaker churches, they could not prevent women from preaching when they received the call. Many English Quakeresses crossed the Atlantic to testify, although, like Anna Braithwaite, who left her seven children to make the crossing three times, they did not "look for great things" in their "steppings along." Many Quaker churches, particularly in aristocratic Rhode Island, did manage to separate the meetings of men and women. Male domination made Quakeresses adopt their sober and distinctive dress, despite Margaret Fell's love of bright colours and hatred of such a "silly, poor gospel."

Yet the Quakers did give boys and girls an equal education, did make both feel that their souls and their rights were equal before God, and did make women feel as strong as men through pacifism. The early feminists in America were to come from among the Quakers. And, before their coming, a Quaker sect was to produce the first woman to carry Anne Hutchinson's revolt to its logical end, and to set herself up as God in the New World.

Ann Lee was born in 1736 in Manchester, England. Her father was a blacksmith. She worked as a cotton-spinner, a fur-cutter, and a cook. Although she was early conscious of sin, she married a blacksmith and had four children, all of whom died in infancy. At the age of twenty-three, she joined a heretic Quaker sect, the Shakers, who lived in chastity and openly confessed their sins. After agonies of the spirit, in which bloody sweat pressed through the pores of her skin and made her as helpless as an infant, she felt reborn and pure. She began to testify publicly against "fleshly lusts, which war against the soul." She was put in jail, in a cell too small to lie in, called "Bedlam." There, after many days, Jesus Christ appeared to her. She came out to lead the sect of Shakers, saying "I am Ann the Word."

From that time, Mother Ann Lee preached continence. Her followers remained continent through the outlet of shaking and dancing and testifying. She had more visions. Once, when one of her brothers beat her unconscious, she ascribed her release from pain and the stars before her eyes to "the bright rays of the glory of God." She took her flock with her to America. Although persecution continued there, the Shakers survived and prospered.

For Mother Lee was fantastically devoted to cleanliness and hard work and eternity. Even if she died at the age of only forty-eight years and was succeeded by a man, she had served as God to a sect that was to endure. Her justification for being a female God was shrewd, and even conservative. She admitted that God and Jesus Christ were masculine, and that a father was the natural head of the divine and the human family. But, she said, "when the man is gone, the right of government does not belong to the children, but to the *woman:* so *is the family of Christ."*[6] Thus she was the Mother of the family of the absent Christ.

Another woman, Jemima Wilkinson, who called herself the Universal Friend, tried to set herself up as God in the late eighteenth century. The headstrong and handsome daughter of a wealthy Rhode Island farmer, she believed, as the Shaker leader had, that her body was possessed by the soul of Christ. She gave herself the title of the Universal Friend, and began to hold revival meetings. She claimed that she could heal the sick and reveal the future. In a compelling and persuasive manner, she preached world-wide love and peace, at a time when Unitarianism and Universalism were yet to come with their messages of hope and release from sin. She supported celibacy and communal living, and thought that the spirit within her would live for a thousand years before returning to heaven in glory.

She found followers among the rich and the poor, in Pennsylvania and New England. But the churches there turned against her, when her flock declared that she was Christ come again, and when wives began refusing to sleep with their husbands. The Universal Friend decided to follow the course of Anne Hutchinson and to remove herself to the wilderness. She settled with her followers in western New York near Seneca Lake, in that part of the country which was to be known as the Burned-Over District, because of the revivals that were to sweep over it like fire and leave behind a spiritual ferment that goaded women into protest for their rights. Unfortunately, she died at the age of sixty-seven years, and her disillusioned people split apart.

The great religious oppression and excitement in the early colonial period encouraged the revolt of some women against the established churches. These women were intelligent, and excessive by nature. They were not content to feel their souls to be free within them. They had to express their freedom of the spirit through an outward revolt. The fact of the American forest allowed them to withdraw to the wilderness to worship or to be worshipped. The fact of American distance allowed them to be moderately free from local persecution. The very space of the expanding colonies made religious liberty a real thing. Aristotle had said that anybody could live in the city-state except a god or a wild beast. These could live on the American frontier.

The American Revolution guaranteed religious freedom and put an end to the spectre of an established church. The religious rebels, who happened to be women, helped in a general victory for the freedom of the individual to found his or her own church, if so desired, but they had not done anything to help the freedom of women in any other way, let alone inside the conventional churches.

Two of the early religious rebels had been educated women from wealthy backgrounds. Ann Lee was the exceptional case of an uneducated woman who managed to hold together an organized following. Yet before education became normal for the daughters of the middle classes, sustained rebellion for a woman was only possible for those few aristocrats who had the leisure and special training to make themselves necessary in a primitive society.

In colonial days, education was a spotty affair. In the villages, boys and girls were lucky to get a grounding in the Bible, grammar, and arithmetic before they were absorbed in the labours of the farm. Occasionally, a minister would teach some unusual girl Latin, Greek, or Hebrew; but outside Philadelphia and Boston few young women had the chance of a thorough education, unless their rich father could pay for a succession of good tutors. It was no coincidence that these two cities were to lead in the pioneer movement for women's rights.

Women especially received little teaching before the nineteenth century because of the backward educational theories of the time. From Lord Halifax and Abbé Fénélon to Dr. Gregory and Jean-

Jacques Rousseau—with the honorable exceptions of Mary Astell and Daniel Defoe—it was held that girls were unfit in brain and character for serious study; even Jefferson agreed with this. Girls should be taught how to run a household, and, if suitable, how to display the graces of a lady. Music, dancing, French, embroidery, these should be the mathematics, astronomy, philosophy, and classics of the female mind. Some history and geography could be studied, but not enough to disturb the prospective wife's deference to her husband's opinions. If, by any chance, intelligent young ladies acquired a great deal of knowledge from their brothers' tutors, they should keep silent. "Their stockings may be as blue as they please," Lord Jeffreys conceded, "if their petticoats are but long enough."

The only effective political rebel of colonial America had been fortunate to acquire just such a rare aristocratic education. In the founding days of Maryland, the aggressive and wealthy Margaret Brent could behave rather as Queen Elizabeth the First had behaved, tempting and cowing men through hope of marriage. She was a legal expert, and a competent manager of lands and servants. As a Roman Catholic, she did much to bring about the passage of a toleration act in the colony. On the death of her suitor, Governor Calvert of Maryland, in 1647, she was appointed sole executrix of his estate through his order, "Take all and pay all." In this position, she became the unauthorized attorney for Lord Baltimore in his absence, with full control over all the rents of that proprietory landlord.

Margaret Brent, however, overreached herself when she applied for two votes in the General Assembly of Maryland—one as Calvert's executrix and one as Baltimore's attorney. She was refused by the new Governor, despite her claim that all meetings of the General Assembly would be illegal without her presence. Nonetheless, for the next fifteen years, she remained the power behind the scenes in the colony. Without her, the Assembly declared to Lord Baltimore, "All would have gone to ruin."

The demand of this self-confident aristocrat for a vote in early colonial days was echoed by the demand of the wife of a leader of the American Revolution, although Abigail Adams was married, where

Margaret Brent had been a wealthy spinster. Thus she had to use the power of her influence over her husband, not her direct contact with the makers of the laws. In a famous and mocking letter in 1777, she asked John Adams to remember the ladies under the new code of laws which would be necessary with American Independence. "Remember," she wrote, "all men would be tyrants if they could. If particular care and attention is not paid to the ladies, we are determined to foment a rebellion, and will not hold ourselves bound by any laws in which we have no voice or representation."[7] Although Abigail Adams probably hoped for no more than protection for married women's property under the law, her use of the revolutionary jargon of the day took the same basis as the feminist Elizabeth Stanton's use of the Declaration of Independence in 1848 to draft her pioneer demand for women's rights. The fact that the United States originated in rebellion meant that future rebellions by members of minority groups or the weaker sex would be justified in the very terms of the original revolt.

As it happened, the haste of Revolution did give the vote effectively to the women of New Jersey. There was no time for debate or fine political considerations when the new constitutions of the states were being written. Women had legally had the vote in many of the early colonies, although there is hardly a recorded instance of their use of the ballot. But colonial legislatures had taken away the right, until revolutionary New Jersey restored it in 1776, by permitting "all inhabitants" to vote who were over twenty-one, had been resident in the state for one year, and possessed an estate worth fifty pounds. The revised constitution of the state of 1790 specifically referred to "he or she" in the clause about voting qualifications.

Six years later, a group of conservative "widows and maids" in Elizabethtown, organized by the Federalist candidate, nearly defeated his opponent in a state election. The Newark *Centinel* noticed proudly that "the *Rights of Man* have been warmly insisted on by Tom Paine and other democrats, but we outstrip them in the science of government, and not only preach the *Rights of Women,* but boldly push it into practice."

Yet this election of 1796 was unusual, for the Elizabethtown women had been manipulated for political expediency. Political parties, in their earliest days, used the woman's vote as a tool of partisan politics. One contemporary observer confessed that "women are admitted or rejected, just as it may suit the views of the persons in direction."[8] Politics were so corrupt in New Jersey in the decades after the Revolution that the woman's vote was no better than any venal element in the situation. When, in 1806, Newark battled with Elizabethtown for the site of the new courthouse, women and Negroes and servants and boys were marshalled into the polling booths. The resulting scandal led the politician who had nearly been defeated by the women ten years before to sponsor a bill restricting the suffrage to "free, white, male citizens," as in most of the other states. The preamble to the bill talked of the great diversities of practice owing to the voting of aliens, females, and Negroes, and excluded them from the polls. In fact, the voting of the women of New Jersey was a mere accident of time and place; it had no consequences, except the setting of a precedent, since these women produced no political leader of importance and no future feminist.

By the early nineteenth century, women and many free Negroes had lost the few political rights which they had once had. These rights had only existed fleetingly because of the haste and egalitarian fervour of revolutionary times. The considered laws of the nation and the states effectively restricted the vote to free, white, male, property-owning citizens—about one in eight of the total population. Free Negro men seem to have been allowed to vote in New England and New York until 1860; but elsewhere they were gradually excluded from the franchise along with women. The lawmaking of the independent Americans proved even more exclusive than the lawmaking of the colonists, for there were no longer loopholes for aristocratic females.

Yet, with the promise of equality after the Revolution, the division of society that preoccupied reformers was no longer between aristocrats and others, but between white men and black men, between good men and sinners, and, to a lesser degree, between white men and all women. There, inequality remained a social fact. After aristocracy had officially foundered in revolution, the other distinctions of race and morality and sex were bound to "foment a rebellion," once American society had thrown up a group of educated women, nourished in the promise of equality for all, trained in the techniques of reform, and willing to do battle for their whole sex.

The first female rebels were merely rebels who happened to be women. They were not champions of their sex; they were champions of themselves. They demanded the right to be treated as individuals, without distinction of sex; but they did not consider themselves as other than exceptions. They never questioned that the general rule was the rule of women by men. Thus they were not feminists so much as female rebels, made so by the accidents of birth and place and inspiration. These accidents had to become widespread in order that a group of female rebels might meet and discover that their sense of wrong was not a solitary one, but part of a sense shared by others, united by their sex. In fact, the American Revolution, by allowing the diffusion of wealth, was to permit many women to share in the education and leisure given to a Margaret Brent. From these women came the first feminists.

PART TWO

The Pioneer Feminists

It looks as if the first reformer of a thing has to meet such a hard opposition and gets so bothered and bespattered that afterwards, when people find they have to accept this reform, they will accept it more easily from any other man.

ABRAHAM LINCOLN, of William Lloyd Garrison

The empty *name* is everywhere,—*free* government, *free* men, *free* speech, *free* people, *free* schools, and *free* churches . . . FREE! The word and sound are omnipresent masks, and mockers! An impious lie! unless they stand for free *Lynch Law,* and free *murder!* for they *are* free.

THEODORE WELD

III

❧❧❧

WOMAN OR SLAVE

THE FIRST FAMOUS speaker for women's rights in America nearly put an end to the subject in polite society. She happened to support most of the theories that the later feminists felt bound to repudiate. Frances Wright was born in Scotland. The early death of her parents made her an heiress. She was brought up by strict relatives in England, where she developed an enthusiasm for America; she believed that liberty was possible for women there. As soon as she was able, she and her sister crossed the Atlantic. A bad play of hers about the struggle for republicanism in Switzerland was performed in New York and Philadelphia in 1819. She followed up its failure by writing a good travel-book of her journeys in the United States, and later, she brought over Mrs. Trollope to emulate her example.

Frances Wright became the friend of Mary Shelley, the daughter of Mary Wollstonecraft; she also became the reputed mistress of Lafayette and Robert Dale Owen. She believed in her freedom to speak and live by her own rules; her money gave her power to do so. She bought land at Nashoba, Tennessee, and tried to run a plantation where slaves could free themselves through the earnings from their labour. Racial, legal, and economic customs were relaxed inside the community, for its owner thought that the free mulatto was the answer to the Negro problem in the South. In her notes on Nashoba, she wrote:

The marriage law existing without the pale of the institution is of no force within that pale. No woman can forfeit her individual rights or independent existence, and no man assert over her any rights or power whatsoever beyond what he may exercise over her free and voluntary affection. . . . Let us not attach ideas of purity to monastic chastity, impossible to man or woman without consequences fraught with evil, nor ideas of vice to connections formed under the auspices of kind feeling.

The experiment at Nashoba failed. And the bold assertion of the freedom of a woman to give her body outside marriage raised nearly every voice against Frances Wright. Her courageous speeches for public education in the election of 1828 and her support of the Workingman's Party of New York meant that the democratic theories of "the great she-Loco-Foco" could be denounced as the ravings of a loose woman. Like Victoria Woodhull after her, Frances Wright claimed too much too soon. Even a century later, only small bohemias in cities and suburbs would approve of her theories of sexual freedom outside marriage. As a reformer, she was too far ahead of the weight of public opinion. No novelty, particularly a sexual one, can be tolerated before the mass of opinion has come to recognize the truth of its existence. The voice of the reformer may cry in the wilderness, but the people must be prepared to follow.

Yet, despite the fury she aroused, Frances Wright set a precedent for a woman's right to speak on morality and politics in public. The later feminists were grateful for her example. As a contemporary ballad conceded:

> . . . If you want to raise the wind
> Or breed a moral storm,
> You must have one bold lady-man
> To prate about reform.[1]

Women reformers with diffuse theories on free love were to plague the organized movement for women's rights throughout its history. As Henry Blackwell later wrote to his wife, Lucy Stone, "It would be an infinite shame and pity to allow the just claims of women to liberty of person, to rights of property, to industrial, social and political equality, to be associated with a conspiracy against purity and virtue and all the holiest relations of life."[2] Nothing played into the hands of those who opposed women's rights more than a woman who advocated both free love and the emancipation of women.

Yet for every Frances Wright who claimed the liberty of choosing her bed-fellow, there were to be a thousand Harriet Martineaus who would term that liberty "the dastardly tyranny of licentiousness." Freedom of the sexual appetite was thought to be slavery to lust by most Victorian women. Freedom of the body meant to them freedom only to enjoy the body in its prescribed place and at its due time within marriage and social life.

The concern that turned certain women into pioneer reformers was less an attack on sexual bondage than an assault on the actual slavery of the Negro people. "We have good cause to be grateful to the slave," wrote the feminist and abolitionist Abby Kelley, "for the benefit we have received to *ourselves*, in working for *him*. In striving to strike his irons off, we found most surely, that *we* were manacled *ourselves*."[3] In seeking to free the slaves, radical women became conscious of their own lack of freedom. Through helping others, they learned to help themselves. The destiny of American women and American Negroes has been interacting, and still is.

Women learnt the techniques of reform within the churches. The churches of Britain had made charity and some reforms such as anti-slavery respectable for religious women. From 1810 onwards, a network of female religious societies spread over New England. Their function was to raise money for home and foreign missionary societies, Bible societies, improved prisons, homes for fallen women, and the urban poor. Particularly important was the huge spread of "moral reform" societies in the 1830's. Their emphasis changed from saving the prostitute to preventing men from ruining her. For the first time, church women were brought into contact with the facts of prostitution, and with the connection of the men in their own families with the social evil. They began to understand the workings of the "double standard." And the early feminists found the questioning of that standard and the doubt now cast on the good character of respectable men to be one of their most powerful weapons.

The money raised by women for the "cent" missionary societies —a donation of one cent would help save a soul—was through work done in their own homes. But inevitably women were drawn outside their homes to sell their goods in the great fund-raising fairs. They learnt to organize clubs and finance speakers. It was only a question of time before they turned their talents to helping their own sex in their own place rather than a male missionary abroad. As Elizabeth Cady Stanton was to declare to a Woman's Temperance Convention in 1852, "Inasmuch as charity begins at home, let us withdraw our mite from all associations for sending the gospel to the heathen across the ocean, for the education of young men for the ministry, for the building up of a theological aristocracy and gorgeous temples to the unknown God, and devote ourselves to the poor and suffering about us."[4]

The churches taught their women members to combine and to operate outside their houses. They taught that it was *good* to do so. A woman's place might still be in the home, but it was also at the charity club. A lady's place could even be in the slum, visiting the poor. The very fact that the Protestant evangelical churches were reform-minded gave the women in them a taste for reforming others. Bronson Alcott was to scoff at the humanitarian ministers of his time as "The Lord's chore boys," but they raised to their support hosts of the Lord's chore girls.

These trained women were not to stop short at the limits which their ministers set on their reforms. As Edmund Burke had once observed, all Protestantism, even the most cold and passive, was a sort of dissent; but the American colonists represented the dissidence of dissent. This contagion was to be a fever to some Protestant women. The churches had sowed the dragon's teeth by making reform respectable for women in the first place. When religious women spoke up in public, as the Grimké sisters did in 1837, it was too late to denounce such immodest behaviour. For the women of New England had been organized by the churches themselves.

The famous Pastoral Letter of the Congregational churches of Massachusetts against the Grimkés was remarkable in its failure. It stirred up ten feminists, such as Lucy Stone, for each one that it deterred. The Quaker Grimkés were too pious to be denounced in the same way as the atheistic Frances Wright, who had been condemned eight years before after speaking out for "free love" and the working-man. The Letter may have deplored "the mistaken conduct of those who encourage females to bear an obtrusive and ostentatious part in measures of reform"; but that conduct had been the conduct of many Congregational ministers, who were grateful enough for funds and free work from the women in their churches. It was true that few Congregationalist ministers had countenanced any women "who so far forgot themselves as to itinerate in the character of public lecturers and speakers"; but it was the revivalist preachers who had borrowed many of the shock tactics of the old Puritans, and had taught women how to use them.

Protestantism, by its very nature, cannot set limits to the protests of its believers. The United States was both Protestant and republican, and, as Michel Chevalier noticed, "Protestantism, republicanism, and individuality are all one." The ideal, if not the fact, of all three faiths was human equality. This ideal was bound to inspire women to protest, once they had learned how to organize against the fact of their inequality. The churches helped to free women by teaching them how to protest. And once their protest had begun, a Pastoral Letter would not stop them any more than a Papal Bull had stopped Luther.

When Northern American women in the 1830's began to organize to free the slave, they learned the politics of agitation for human rights. Letters to the press opened the debate. As early as 1829, the conservative *Ladies' Magazine* printed a letter from a Southern woman, asking her sex to form societies to free the slaves. She appealed to the instinct for moral reform in women, on behalf of their helpless Negro sisters. She claimed that women were already powerful enough to end slavery. "American women! Your power is sufficient for its extinction! and, oh! by every sympathy most holy to the breast of woman, are ye called upon for the exercise of that potency!" The opinion of the editors, however, expressed the caution of most American women of the time.

Women certainly have, in our country, a great influence over public opinion but . . . the slave question is not one of humanity merely. It is political in its bearings. Let us beware of exerting our power *politically*. We should do no good to the *slave*, and much evil might result to the *free*. The influence of woman, to be beneficial, must depend mainly on the respect inspired by her *moral* excellence, not on the political address or energy she may display.

The question of indirect influence or direct action continued to haunt respectable women throughout the century. Anti-slavery work inevitably led to political action; Angelina Grimké began by speaking to small groups of women in private homes, progressed to addressing mass meetings of both sexes, and finished by pleading in front of the Massachusetts legislature. Any work outside the home inexorably led to politics. Tradition demanded that women should work through their influence within the home. The secret behind a statesman was always his mother and his wife. "Woman's true greatness consists in rendering others useful, rather than in being directly useful herself." By tumbling into the dirt of partisan politics, women would lose their precious influence for good and become the shoddy equals of political men. It was only a few radical women who dared to applaud Harriet Martineau's witty summary of the argument:

In regard to this old controversy—of Influence *vs.* Office—it appears to me that, if Influence is good and Office is bad for human morals and character, Man's present position is one of such hardship as it is almost profane to contemplate; and if, on the contrary, Office is good and a life of Influence is bad, Woman has an instant right to claim that her position be amended.[5]

However fearful the ladies of New England might be, the mechanics of anti-slavery agitation drew them into politics. Letters to editors were followed by petitions to Congress, on behalf of persecuted Indians as well as Negroes. The collection of signatures on the petition meant a trudge from door to door and political argument with diffident women. When the women's petitions were sent up to Congress, they became the cause of a constitutional debate. John Quincy Adams, no friend of the abolitionists although a devotee of the Constitution, supported the right of men and women to petition against an angry majority of the House of Representatives. When Congress, after 1836, put a gag on petitions, Adams found himself fighting for the right of women to present them. The son of Abigail Adams, who had asked her husband to remember the ladies under the new code of laws after the Revolution, became himself the unwitting defender of the one political right of women under the federal Constitution.

The organization of petitions parallelled the organization of Female Anti-Slavery Societies; the first one in Boston was formed in 1832. Although these groups of women believed in gradual emancipation, they did not all support the leader in the field, the American Colonization Society. That society wanted to deport the Negro back to Africa rather than accept him as an equal in America. It thought that the North was as guilty in shipping the Negro to America as the South was in exploiting his labour. The guilt of both could be expiated by shipping the Negro back to Africa or to Haiti. The Colonization Society agreed that Negroes were degraded beings, unfit for the American way of life. Most of the free Negroes in America—one in eight of the Negro population by the time of the Civil War—bitterly opposed the society. They wished to be free to become good Americans. As one of them said, the Society "wants us to go to Liberia if we will; if we won't go there, we may go to hell."[6]

Some radical Quakers had always worked for a different solution to the problem of slavery. They held that a man was a man, whether his skin were black or white. Education was the answer to the Negro problem, not deportation. When one of these early anti-slavery Quakers, Benjamin Lundy, converted a young Boston editor, William Lloyd Garrison, to the need for emancipating the Negroes, he was unknowingly helping all American women, white and black, to demand their equality with white men.

Garrison, a creature of a hundred causes, was no early supporter of women's rights. His famous newspaper, the *Liberator,* founded in 1831, did not approve of women leaving their appointed sphere until Garrison himself needed their votes to take over the organization of the official anti-slavery movement. He taught a generation of women the subtleties of fighting within organizations, a lesson that the Boston wing of the women's movement never forgot. By supporting women's rights after 1838, he made his followers make propaganda for both slaves and women. Garrison linked the ideas of female and Negro degradation in many minds. The language of the feminists, through Garrison, became founded on the language of the abolitionists.

Radical women had only to substitute the word "husband" for the word "slave-owner" to see themselves as slaves. They had been promised by the Declaration of Independence their liberty and equality, as the slaves had been. If the promise had been ignored by the Constitution, yet the Declaration of Independence remained a written and revolutionary creed. Reform is based on the gap between generally accepted ideal and actual fact. Jefferson had said that all men were created equal, and by that phrase he had meant mankind. It was useless for Calhoun to sneer, "Taking the proposition literally, there is not a word of truth in it." The proposition still remained in its original and accepted form. Reformers still intended to establish the legal and political truth of it. When the first proclamation of women's rights was sent from Seneca Falls in 1848, it was naturally a paraphrase of the Declaration of Independence, with the words "all men" substituted for "King George." Independence for white American men had been won; now their own Declaration could be used to win independence from them.

The debate over the ideal or the fact remained the debate between feminists and champions of the Negro on one side and conservative ladies and Southerners on the other. Arguments about Ought To Be cannot be answered by arguments about Is. The possibility of change cannot be denied by the virtue of the *status quo.* But such considerations never stopped the great debate, once it had begun. Abby Folsom whom Emerson called "the Flea of Conventions," could say, "Let man but acknowledge the equality of woman, and there is but little doubt of the right behaviour of my sex."[7] But man had not recognized woman's equality, and many women thought their sex behaved rightly by remaining where it was. *"Perfect* freedom is," a planter's wife could reply, "incompatible with society. *Equal* freedom, a freedom setting all men upon the same footing, has been dreamed of, has been talked of, but never seriously aimed at by any government. . . . Mr. Jefferson's great humbug flourish of 'Free and equal,' has made trouble enough, and it is full time that its mischievous influence should end."[8] Yet that great humbug flourish *did* make abolition a political force in the North and West, because many people believed that it *should* be the truth. The debate between North and South over the rights of women and Negroes was a sequel to the differences between the Declaration of Independence, which sought to overturn a settled government, and the Constitution of the United States, which sought to found one.

In one particular way, the anti-slavery crusade was a woman's crusade, even for the Southern woman. No one accused the planters' wives of using Negro men to satisfy their lust, for, by definition, they had no lust. But every Northern abolitionist—and some Southern ladies—accused the planter himself of assaulting his female slaves. "The negro woman is unprotected either by law or public opinion," wrote Lydia Maria Child in *An Appeal in Favour of that class of Americans called Africans*. "She is the property of her master, and her daughters are his property. They are allowed to have no conscientious scruples, no sense of shame, no regard for the feelings of husband, or parent; they must be entirely subservient to the will of their owner, on pain of being whipped as near unto death as will comport with his interest, or quite to death, if it suit his pleasure."[9] Any woman who feared rape herself could identify with the female slave, and transfer her hatred from the plantation owner to the whole male sex. In that way, the wrongs inflicted on Negro women were the wrongs of womankind. What was the difference between a lustful slave-owner and a lustful husband? To show the similar position of all wives with that of Negro slave women, the feminists coined the term "the slavery of sex."

The public debate over the rights of women and Negroes was brought to a head by the brief careers of Sarah and Angelina Grimké. They were the daughters of an intelligent and conservative planter and judge in South Carolina. They were brought up at the beginning of the nineteenth century to be secluded ladies, content with their influence upon their family, and perhaps upon their slaves. Sarah Grimké broke away from Charleston society and joined an Orthodox Quaker sect in Philadelphia. In the duty of prayer and plain living, she found some satisfaction for her ascetic nature. Her strong influence over her younger sister, Angelina, brought her also as a novice into the Quaker faith.

The Philadelphia Friends were, however, too discreet on the issue of slavery for the sisters. Sarah might have endured in silence, while she waited to be called to the Quaker ministry, but Angelina chafed at the restraints of cautious religion. The chains of Quaker belief galled her as badly as the chains of plantation idleness. She commented in Sarah's religious diary: "It is hard for me to *be* and to *do* nothing. My restless, ambitious temper, so different from dear sister's, craves high duties and high attainments. . . . The hope of attaining to great eminence in the divine life has often prompted me to give up in little things. . . . These are my temptations."

The rise of anti-slavery sentiment in the North gave the Grimké sisters their chance. They found freedom of the spirit in anti-slavery circles in New York and in Boston, and they began their first local attempts at speaking to small groups of ladies. "O sister," Angelina wrote to Sarah, "I feel as if I could give up not only friends, but life itself, for the slave, if it is called for. I feel as if I could go anywhere to save him, even down to the South if I am called there." She wrote a pamphlet, *An Appeal to the Christian Women of the South,* which was promptly burned in her home city.

The Grimké sisters were invaluable to the anti-slavery cause. They were the daughters of a planter and slave-owner; they knew the peculiar institution at first hand, and loathed it. They could not be accused of Yankee bias and ignorance. Their small meetings of 1836 spread to mass meetings of both sexes the following year. They followed where Frances Wright had led; but, in their Quaker dress, they seemed as respectable as nuns. Sarah Grimké felt freedom even from her own sex. "How little, how very little I supposed, when I used so often to say 'I wish I were a man,' that I could go forth and lecture, that *I* ever would do such a thing. The idea never crossed my mind that as a *woman* such work could possibly be assigned to me." The possibility of public speaking for respectable women immediately became a right to be defended, once it was proved successful. "The denial of our duty to act in this cause," Angelina Grimké declared, "is the denial of our right to act; and if we have no right to act, then may *we* well be termed 'the white slaves of the North,' for, like our brethren in bonds, we must seal our lips in silence and despair."[10]

Unfortunately for the cause of anti-slavery, the Grimkés were too intelligent not to stress the connection between the wrongs of women and Negroes. Sarah Grimké led the way, and the speeches of both began to swing towards women's rights. These called down thundering denunciations from the pulpits, many of which had been open to them before. The conservative elements of the anti-slavery cause itself were angry. But Angelina Grimké was proud of the huge crowds of women who came to hear them speak, walking up to eight miles to get there. It was obvious to her that the women of New England had long been waiting for someone to voice their dissatisfactions. If that voice was a Southern one, it was still a true voice, when it asserted in Sarah Grimké's words, that *"Whatsoever it is morally right for a man to do, it is morally right for a woman to do."*[11]

Outside the group led by Garrison, the leaders of the anti-slavery movement tried to stop the intrusive Grimké sisters from speaking on women's rights. Angelina Grimké herself confessed to "some regret" that the question of women had come up before the question of slavery was settled, so fearful was she of injuring "that blessed cause." Yet her faith told her that the time was ripe for women's rights, because it "must be the Lord's time and therefore the *best* time."

Her correspondent and future husband, Theodore Weld, did not agree with her. She and her sister were best employed speaking on slavery alone. They were unique, in that they knew about slavery. Any Northern woman could speak up for women's rights. They must continue as they had begun, with their emphasis on the wrongs of the slave.

Angelina Grimké was not convinced. She had to establish the right of women to engage in political action, or else it would be impossible for her and her sister to go on with their anti-slavery work. "And can you not see that women *could* do, and *would* do a hundred times more for the slave if she were not fettered?" The immediate emancipation of women would help all reforms, not hinder them. She prophetically added, "The slave may be freed and woman be where she is, but woman cannot be freed and the slave remain where he is."

Weld urged her that reform must come at its due, human time. The reform drive must concentrate on one object at once. No moral enterprise ever failed so long as its conductors "pushed the *main* principle and did not strike off until they got to the summit level. On the other hand every reform that ever foundered in mid sea was capsized by one of these gusty side winds." The Grimké sisters were doing positive harm to the cause of the slaves, by diverting attention from their wrongs. "Your woman's rights! You put the cart before the horse; you drag the tree by the top in attempting to push your *woman's* rights, until human rights have gone ahead and broken the *path.*" Freedom of the slave, both male and female, must come before the freedom of all women. Weld did not point out that, in numerical terms, American women outnumbered American Negroes in a proportion of five to one, and thus, given the number of individual rights involved, women could be said to have the priority. And Weld could not, being a religious and absolute man, take refuge in the correct political argument, that the emancipation of the Negro had already taken place in England and in Canada and in the Northern states of America. It would be likely, therefore, to take place in the near future throughout America. The same could not be said for the emancipation of women.[12]

Theodore Weld married Angelina Grimké after their disagreement. At the ceremony, without benefit of clergy, they transferred their ideals to their relationship. Weld gave up his legal rights over his wife's person and property; Angelina Grimké said that she would love Weld "with a pure heart fervently." The marriage put an end to the careers of both Grimkés, and of Weld. The three of them retired to a farm, where Weld practiced his ideas of manual labour. Occasionally, they appeared at anti-slavery and suffrage meetings, and they personally helped some coloured people, including the illegitimate half-brothers of the Grimkés.

The reason of the retirement of the Welds into marriage was the reason that many reformers gave throughout the century. They told the feminist Henry Blackwell that, although there was a "fighting era in every one's life," there was also "another and a higher view" to be found in a perfect and equal marriage and in the rearing of children. Public protest should be followed by private example. Blackwell used their example to press his suit of Lucy Stone. "If ever there was a true marriage it is theirs—Both preserve their separate individuality *per-fectly* and on many points differ heartily with the utmost good will."[13]

Angelina Grimké Weld achieved the equality between man and woman in her marriage which she had preached before it. Others were to follow her example and apply the faith behind abolitionism to their private lives. "I believe nineteen women out of twenty," Henry Blackwell wrote again during his courtship, "would be unhappy with a husband who, like myself, would repudiate supremacy —The proof of my opinion is that the great majority of people, in endeavouring to imagine a contrary state of things, conceive of the woman as the *leader* and the man as the *subservient*."[14] But the twentieth Victorian wife did achieve the equality of relationship with her husband that the abolitionists hoped would be possible between master and slave.

For every free Negro who educated himself into becoming a leader of his people, such as Frederick Douglass, there was a feminist who made her ideas triumph over the slavery of marriage. For the possibility of equality with the white male had now been proved. It was not just a public outcry but a personal commitment. This is again shown clearly in the correspondence of Elizabeth Smith, the daughter of the anti-slavery crusader Gerrit Smith, before her marriage with Charles Miller in 1843. She praised him for taking neither wine nor tobacco, and said that she would follow him wherever he went. But she said she could not go to a pro-slavery church. Wherever they lived, she had to go to "the Free Church," even if it were a "comparatively despised Church." And the reform creed that people could be *persuaded* into doing right should be applied in marriage.

"We must both be open to conviction," Elizabeth Smith continued.

If I become convinced that I am wrong and you right, I must go with you. If, on the other hand, you become convinced that you are wrong, and I right, you must go with me. Where a thing is neither right nor wrong, I trust I may have sufficient love for you, to make your desires mine, but we know very well, my dear Charlie, that our *highest object* in this life, whether married, or unmarried, should be to serve the Lord, and in matters of right and wrong, we must take the right, whatever may be the hazard—don't you agree with me? You are at liberty, Charlie, to change my views in regard to Churches but you must not ask me to attend a proslavery Church *against my conscience*.[15]

In an extreme or a moderate form, the arguments over the equality of the slave were applied by some educated women in their marriages. They set an example for their sex, which was to become a normal part of life in middle-class marriage in the twentieth century. The white man could be matched by his wife or his slave; the mother was the equal of the father; no human being should be the master of another. Those women who wanted to become equal with white men found themselves in the struggle for the slave's equality with white men. The support of him became the support of themselves. And if many anti-slavery men thought that the cause of the Negro came before the cause of women, it was because they were not women.

IV

THE FEMINIST BIBLES

"Rousseau exerts himself to prove that all *was* right originally," wrote Mary Wollstonecraft, "a crowd of authors that all *is* now right: and I, that all will *be* right." In this faith, she wrote the first feminist bible, *A Vindication of the Rights of Woman,* published in England in 1792. No one had more influence over the early American feminists than she had.

For Mary Wollstonecraft, liberty and equality and reason were more important than sexual characteristics. "The first object of laudable ambition is to obtain a character as a human being, regardless of the distinction of sex . . . secondary views should be brought to this simple touchstone." In her Lockian view, biology counted for nothing and education for all. She refused to believe Rousseau when he declared that woman was *naturally* subject to man; it was her false training that made her consider herself so. "Trifling employments have rendered woman a trifler." The sexes were equal by nature and should be developed equally by schooling. "I here throw down my gauntlet, and deny the existence of sexual virtues, not excepting modesty. For man and woman, truth, if I understand the meaning of the word, must be the same." Of course, this did not mean that the sexes should do identical jobs. "Women, I allow, may have different duties to fulfil; but they are *human* duties, and the principles that should regulate the discharge of them, I sturdily maintain, must be the same."

Mary Wollstonecraft based all the faith of her own emotional nature on the faculty of reason. She was a good disciple of the *philosophes*. Women must come to rely on their own judgement as the rule of their lives—"They must only bow to the authority of reason, instead of being the *modest* slaves of opinion." Reason was the jury of all things; it would condemn the customs and usages that had kept mankind from being free and equal. "If laws exist, made by the strong to oppress the weak," said Wollstonecraft's heroine Maria, "I appeal to my own sense of justice."[1] The supreme court was the individual mind if right reason had been learned. And right reason would be learned by all the earth. At that time, "the distinction of sex" would be "confounded in society, unless where love animates the behaviour."[2]

Such a passionate belief in human reason and in the concepts of freedom and equality put Mary Wollstonecraft in the mainstream of the ideas that were used to justify the American and the French Revolutions. Briefly, those with discontented temperaments were all rebels and Jacobins, and, like rebels or Jacobins, they were denied in the constitutions of their countries. The *Vindication*, however, along with the Declaration of Independence, was to inspire such feminists as Frances Wright, Lucretia Mott, Elizabeth Stanton, and Susan Anthony. It was to become a respectable book when the equality of the sexes became a social fact in all but the important training of the sexes.

In her personal life, Mary Wollstonecraft was herself influenced by the American experience. While she was in Paris, she took a lover from New Jersey, Gilbert Imlay, a speculator and explorer and author. On the basis of his accounts of the Kentucky wilderness, where he had spent two years trying to make a fortune, she thought him a true child of nature. She found out soon enough that he was a natural businessman, as were most American men who went to the West. For him as for them, nature might be described in the terms of

Eden, but it was to be exploited in the terms of Eldorado. The only
child of nature in the relationship was her bastard daughter, which
Imlay left with her when he deserted her. She later lived with the
English anarchist, William Godwin, married him before the birth of
another daughter, and died at the age of thirty-eight in child-bed,
giving birth to a girl child who was to create *Frankenstein*. Her life
showed the passion and freedom and boldness of her work.

The United States did not produce its own philosopher of feminism until the publication of Margaret Fuller's *Woman in the Nineteenth Century* in 1845. Written in as graceless a style as the *Vindication,* the book is inferior in power and content to its predecessor. It
was more popular merely because it was safer and less offensive, the
work of a Boston lady rather than an Anglo-Irish anarchist. Wollstonecraft dismissed religious feeling, Fuller glorified it. Reason was
replaced by a transcendental "divine energy." The goal of woman's
emancipation was not so much her freedom as the need to bring
harmony to the universe. Clouds of mysticism obscure Fuller's tortu-
ous arguments. Like the *Vindication,* the book does not think the vote
important for women; but, unlike the *Vindication,* it does not preach
the actual equality of the sexes. "What Woman needs is not as a
woman to act or rule, but as a nature to grow, as an intellect to
discern, as a soul to live freely and unimpeded." Swedenborgian
concepts are substituted for the companionship of the sexes. "Man
and Woman share an angelic ministry; the union is of one with one,
permanent and pure. . . . I wish Woman to live, *first* for God's
sake. Then she will not make an imperfect man her god, and thus
sink to idolatry."[3]

Yet, in Italy, Margaret Fuller did make an imperfect man her god.
Like Wollstonecraft during the Terror in Paris, she took a foreign
lover at the time of the Siege of Rome. This man, the handsome but
stupid Ossoli, made her pregnant, as Imlay had done with her forerunner. But she immediately showed how much more of a Bostonian
and a lady she was than the title-hating and unconventional Wollstonecraft; she married Ossoli and claimed that he was a count. Death
came to her almost immediately, at the age of forty, only two years

older than her predecessor. Shipwreck killed her and her husband and her child off Fire Island. Her end made her seem a pioneer in the cause of feminism, a position which she had scarcely earned by her life or writings. It is not necessary to die for a cause to become a martyr; it is only necessary to seem to support a cause and to die at the appropriate time.

Despite her intellectual gifts and her friends in Transcendental circles in Boston, Margaret Fuller was arrogant and disliked. "There is no modesty or moderation in me," she confessed; nor was there much sympathy or enthusiasm in her for the pioneer feminists whom she knew. She sneered at all their early attempts. If she had come to be their leader on her return from Italy, as some of the lady feminists hoped, she would have made the woman's movement even more exclusive, Bostonian, and cliquish than it was—a sort of privileged extension of her famous Conversations. Death ensured her reputation as the philosopher of the American feminists, although Elizabeth Stanton was to deserve that position. Unfortunately, Stanton's life and nature were too spasmodic to allow her to write anything philosophical much longer than a speech.

The third and greatest of the feminist bibles was written by a man, John Stuart Mill, although many of his ideas came from his wife, Harriet Taylor. In an important article in the *Westminster Review* in 1851, which was widely circulated in feminist circles in America, Harriet Taylor put forward the reasonable case for votes for women. The whole manner of the article was politic and restrained. While Mary Wollstonecraft was the first militant feminist, Harriet Taylor was the first political feminist. Gone was the language of the *philosophes* and of the Transcendentalists, that women needed opportunities to use their reason and develop their souls. Harriet Taylor wanted equality of the sexes through the utilitarian world—equal chances in jobs, government, schools, and the courts of law.

Although her language is cool and subtle, her solution is both more practical and radical than that of her predecessors. She avoids emotional arguments about reason in order to persuade through the rational process. Above all, she stresses the need for the economic and educational opportunity of women to compete with men, and rejects the idea of her sex as housewives and mothers. "Numbers of women are wives and mothers only because there is no other career open to them. . . . To say that women must be excluded from active life because maternity disqualifies them for it, is in fact to say that every other career should be forbidden them, in order that maternity may be their only resource."[4]

After her death John Stuart Mill published his masterpiece, *On the Subjection of Women,* in 1869; it was the most important feminist text in late Victorian times on both sides of the Atlantic. He claimed, without an excess of chivalry, that all his ideas were those of his wife and his step-daughter. Certainly, it was they who had persuaded him into becoming a feminist. What he added to their ideas was the logic of a professional philosopher, a cutting wit, and a style that was lucid and persuasive. "Women are declared to be better than men," he pointed out, "an empty compliment which must provoke a bitter smile from every woman of spirit, since there is no other situation in life in which it is the established order, and quite natural and suitable, that the better should obey the worse."[5] In the manner of his dead wife, he pleaded for specific rights for women. Through his prestige and words, he did much to convince educated people on both sides of the Atlantic that rights for women should not be long denied. Curiously enough, it was he who wrote on the rights of women, while Mary Wollstonecraft wrote on their subjection.

What the two Mills advocated has been gained. In legal and economic terms, women are more or less the equals of men. But what Mary Wollstonecraft wanted, and Margaret Fuller imitated, is still absent. Women have not been educated to feel responsible only to their own reason or soul. The "accident of birth" of sex is still considered important by many educators, for they listen to the psychologists. They do not heed Margaret Fuller's caution, "As you would not educate a soul to be an aristocrat, so do not to be a woman."[6] The concepts of the sexual equality of human reason and of the human soul have been discarded, particularly in America, for the concept of the biological and psychological differences of the sexes. If the first feminists used their ideals to protest against the worship of the mother in the home, modern feminists tend to use their lack of ideals and reliance on sociology to renew that worship. They have forgotten what all crusaders have always known, that the ideal believed can become the social fact, and that the progress of society demands the denial of present society. The problem is not to adjust people to their way of life, but to improve it.

V

THE FIRST SUFFRAGISTS

IF PRINT LEADS to a voicing of wrongs, organization leads to their redress. The feminists needed both their prophets crying in the wilderness and their bureaucrats working in the cities. The first of the organization women was Lucretia Coffin Mott. In her own life she united the colonial woman with the Victorian feminist. She was brought up at the close of the eighteenth century in the Quaker settlement of Nantucket, where, as she wrote, "the women have long been regarded as the stronger part."[1] There, she learnt the thrifty and thorough organization of a house. Her father, Thomas Coffin, was a whaler, but he soon turned to the business of the land. Lucretia was educated in Boston and New York. After a brief period as a school-teacher, she married a young Quaker businessman, James Mott, who set up business with her father in Philadelphia.

The marriage proved successful and equal. If Lucretia Coffin took her husband's name, she later observed, "People would sooner call my husband Mr. Lucretia Mott than me Mrs. James Mott." She became a minister of the Quaker faith and a public speaker. When the Hicksite controversy arose, however, she took the liberal and heretic side. For the Hicksites were to the Orthodox Quakers what the Unitarians and Universalists were to the old Calvinists. These religious controversies first loosed women from religious prohibitions, and set them spiritually free to crusade for the slave and their own rights.

During the 1830's, Lucretia Mott became a worker in the anti-slavery movement; her home was a stop on the underground railroad for fugitive slaves. She was a supporter of Garrison and the sisters Grimké, and she even expressed approval of Frances Wright. Her feelings about her own sex grew radical. She was an early disciple of Mary Wollstonecraft's *Vindication*. It remained her "pet book or one of them" for most of her married life. "Lucretia, I admire thy independence," Sarah Grimké said, when she saw the revolutionary text on Mrs. Mott's centre table.

Yet Lucretia Mott had more than independence of judgement. She had a taste for power and organization, which she applied outwards from her family life to the anti-slavery movement. She was no Sarah Grimké, to retire after a few years as a public speaker with the words, "I do not know, but my business is simply to open doors, or do the first rough work." Lucretia Mott both opened doors and worked to keep them open. The first national women's anti-slavery convention was held in New York in 1837, and a resolution was passed upholding women's right to engage in political work. In the following three years, Garrison used the anti-slavery women to take over the organization of the American Anti-Slavery Society. In 1840, he succeeded, and put Lucretia Mott, along with Abby Kelley and Maria Chapman, to serve on the committee of the Society. Lydia Child was engaged as the editor of a Garrisonian newspaper in the enemy stronghold of New York. The Tappans and the conservative abolitionists from Massachusetts and elsewhere walked out of the Society and founded a rival group of abolitionists. Lewis Tappan himself was disgusted with their sectional quarrels, saying, "I loathe the spirit that comes from the east."

The organizational battle which Garrison and the early feminists won in America was lost at a world anti-slavery convention in England that same year. There, the Orthodox Quakers and abolitionists were in full strength. Many female delegates from Garrison's group of women made the voyage to London, but they were refused seats as delegates from America in the convention. Lucretia Mott's diary of the trip spells out the humiliation of her rejection. Also rejected were Abby Kimber and Sarah Pugh and Elizabeth Neall—three more Quaker women from Philadelphia—and Elizabeth Smith and Ann Greene Phillips, who was to convert her fluent husband, Wendell Phillips, to the cause of woman suffrage. Garrison himself took his seat with the rejected women in the gallery of the convention hall.

The opponents of the female delegates claimed that by excluding women they were sticking to the one subject of anti-slavery. Garrison's retort was that by excluding women "they *did* undertake to settle another great question."[2] There was no answer to his objection, nor to another one which pointed out the inconsistency of calling a world convention to abolish slavery, "and at its threshold depriving half the world their liberty." In Elizabeth Stanton's indignant words, the abolitionists "would have been horrified at the idea of burning the flesh of the distinguished women present with red-hot irons, but the crucifixion of their pride and self-respect, the humiliation of the spirit, seemed to them a most trifling matter."[3]

The rejection of the women delegates was, however, vital for the organization of a political woman's movement *separate* from the anti-slavery movement. Nothing succeeds in raising a rival like exclusion. English patriarchalism had triumphed where American paternalism had failed. Most galling and prophetic of all, a Negro delegate had spoken against the seating of the women, in case the convention seemed ridiculous to the outside world. Lucretia Mott became friendly with the young Elizabeth Stanton, who had come to the convention with her husband on her wedding trip. For the first time, the young small-town Western woman met a group of women from the large Eastern cities who believed in the equality of the sexes and disbelieved in popular orthodox religion. Between themselves, Mrs. Mott and Mrs. Stanton planned an organization for women's rights. The world convention was to prove more important in the history of those it kept out than of those it included.

In the middle years of the 1840's, Lucretia Mott and Elizabeth Stanton continued to plan. But nothing was done. Elizabeth Stanton was kept busy having five children, and in educating herself within the "enthusiastically literary and reform latitude" of Boston. Lucretia Mott gave up much of her time to her own husband and children, and to the causes of abolition and peace and temperance; but, in 1845, she delivered to Quaker women in Ohio at a Yearly Meeting what one of her listeners called "the first public Suffrage speech by a woman, for a woman in that region of the country."[4] It was not until chance, however, led to her meeting with the bored Elizabeth Stanton in western New York that anything was done about calling the first convention on women's rights.

Political organizations begin in casual ways, through the meetings of friends. At the tea parties in the farmhouses near Seneca Falls in the July of 1848—the Year of Revolutions in Europe—Elizabeth Stanton met with Lucretia Mott and her circle of local Quaker women. Stanton was the driving force behind the decision to call a women's convention. She poured out the torrent of her "long-accumulating discontent" until she stirred herself and the rest "to do and dare anything." The next day, July the Fourteenth—the anniversary of the fall of the Bastille—an advertisement appeared in the *Seneca County Courier,* announcing that a convention on women's rights would be held within the week. The women who had called the convention did not know what to do, but some of them prepared speeches, and Stanton had the idea of paraphrasing the Declaration of Independence to serve as a document for revolution. As it was harvest time, they expected a small audience and little publicity.

In spite of the notoriety of the convention at Seneca Falls, recent observers have minimized its significance, as merely the first and most local of many conventions on women's rights. But it was the first in the world, outside the fiction of *Lysistrata;* it did set a precedent and show that such a convention was possible; and it did attract a large audience and much publicity. By its very calling in a small manufacturing town in western New York, it gave an illuminating insight into the forces behind early feminism.

A long-time resident of Seneca Falls, Mary Bull, gave her picture of conditions in the town in the 1840's before the arrival of the bored

Elizabeth Stanton, too spoiled by the excitement of Boston to discern the ferment on a lower intellectual level in the neighbourhood. Mary Bull, however, found that "a spirit of reform, of dissatisfaction with existing things, a reaching out for perfection, characterized many of the inhabitants of this village." A newspaper devoted to legal reform was published there, and was one of the forces behind the calling of the state constitutional convention of 1846. The Second Adventists or Millerites had a large following there, and the end of the world was, at one time, expected hourly. There were two temperance societies, one for women; reformed drunkards were local heroes. There was a Unitarian society formed by disciples of William Ellery Channing, and there was an anti-slavery group. Abby Kelley had lectured in the town as early as 1843, but she was so obnoxious that she had had to speak from the stoop of a house. The anti-slavery heroes, Douglass and Redmond and Garrison and George Thompson, had also spoken there. Homeopathy flourished and fought with conventional ideas of medicine. The "community fever" afflicted whole families, who moved off to exist in hopeless utopias. There were also groups of vegetarian Grahamites and a Non-Resistance Society.

When Elizabeth Stanton arrived, with all the latest Boston ideas and fads fresh in her mind, she immediately "exerted a widespread influence over the younger and more advanced portion of society," although she herself missed the "isms" of the city. Her disregard of Sunday shocked older people, as did her public appearances with Negro orators, but she was respected for her admirable care of her home, husband, and children. As an undisputed social leader, she could even win over her enemies, as when she cajoled the quiet lawyer's wife, Amelia Bloomer, into changing her temperance sheet, *The Lily*, to a women's rights paper, and into doffing her long skirts for the trousers that were to bear her name.[5]

Thus Elizabeth Stanton could count on an audience of curious and even enthusiastic townspeople for any crusade that she was prepared to lead. There was also another audience, which the ladylike Mary Bull did not mention. For Seneca Falls was a factory town that made gloves. A cluster of Irish immigrants was firmly in the motherly and

reforming grasp of Mrs. Stanton, although few of them were occupied with the woman question. Many of the processes of glove-
making were distributed to the daughters and wives of neighbouring
farmers, who thought themselves too respectable to allow their
womenfolk to work outside the house. One of these women, the
nineteen-year-old Charlotte Woodward, signed the famous Declaration of Sentiments at the convention. She was the only one of the
hundred signatories who lived to see women get the vote in the
United States.

Charlotte Woodward's reason for going to the convention was
more serious than curiosity or boredom. She and other female glove-
makers, already being pinched by the factory system, were bitter
about their legal and economic position.

We women did more than keep house, cook, sew, wash, spin and weave,
and garden. Many of us were under the necessity of earning money
besides. . . . We worked secretly, in the seclusion of our bedchambers,
because all society was built on the theory that men, not women, earned
money, and that men alone supported the family. . . . Most women
accepted this condition of society as normal and God-ordained and therefore changeless. But I do not believe that there was any community anywhere in which the souls of some women were not beating their wings
in rebellion. For my own obscure self I can say that every fibre of my
being rebelled, although silently, all the hours that I sat and sewed gloves
for a miserable pittance which, after it was earned, could never be mine.
I wanted to work, but I wanted to choose my task and I wanted to collect
my wages. That was my form of rebellion against the life into which I
was born.

When the notice of the convention appeared in the local newspaper, the women of Charlotte Woodward's family decided to attend
it. "I do clearly remember," she continued in her reminiscences of
1920,

the wonderful beauty of the early morning when we dropped all our
alloted tasks and climbed in the family waggon to drive over the rough
roads to Seneca Falls. At first we travelled quite alone under the over-
hanging tree branches and wild vines, but before we had gone many miles

we came on other waggon-loads of women, bound in the same direction. As we reached different cross-roads we saw waggons coming from every part of the county, and long before we reached Seneca Falls we were a procession.

The crowds arrived to find a locked door on the Wesleyan chapel, where the meeting was due to be held. A man was pushed through a window so that he could open the door from the inside. "Mr. Lucretia Mott" presided over the convention, as no woman knew how to do so. Mrs. Lucretia Mott and Mrs. Stanton and other men and women spoke or read speeches. But the greatest feeling was generated when Elizabeth Stanton's "young voice, trembling with emotion, yet clear and strong," read out the paraphrase of the Declaration of Independence. "Remember," Charlotte Woodward said, "we were all American born then, and not very far removed in our thoughts from the events of the Revolution." As propaganda it was a stroke of genius for Elizabeth Stanton to choose to rewrite the document of American liberties, even if it had been drawn up by men.

Only over the matter of women and the vote was the meeting cautious. It welcomed all the other resolutions demanding for women opportunities in education, trade, commerce, and the professions, and rights in property, free speech, and the guardianship of children. But when the vote was demanded for women, "the thing was too nearly unthinkable to be real."[6] A small majority, however, carried the resolution, after fiery speeches in its favour by Elizabeth Stanton and Frederick Douglass, who had come over from nearby Rochester. Henry Stanton had been so angry at his wife's decision to demand the vote that he had left town rather than witness the farce. Even Lucretia Mott, a year later, said that she asked for the ballot with reluctance, "because this claim is so distasteful to the age."[7]

The convention at Seneca Falls showed how much one bold woman in a small town could achieve. If she had "city" ideas and was a social leader, she could gather a large audience, especially if there were a religious group such as the Quakers interested in her principles. She could, through personal contacts, bring in well-known speakers, such as Lucretia Mott and Frederick Douglass. She could appeal to dissatisfied women within a radius of fifty miles, who had little enough excitement to break up the long drudgery of their lives. She could continue her influence by writing weekly in the small-town newspaper, and by persuading travelling lecturers to stop in the town.

Moreover, Seneca Falls itself was in an interesting stage of growth. It was a new town, hardly a generation old. Yet the factory system had already reached there. Women, even in their homes, had been unsettled by the possibility of earning wages and leaving those homes. Under the added disturbance of millennial ideas and various reform notions, any change in society seemed possible in a place that had been a forest and was now a settlement. Women especially felt drawn towards the salvation of their sex. The crusade for the freedom of the slave gave only a vicarious satisfaction, while the crusade for women's rights promised immediate deliverance. As a spinster in Cambridgeport declared in the local newspaper in the flurry after the convention of 1848, women should "declare themselves *absolutely* independent of the men," for then the "millennium of woman's glory" would come upon man "like a flash of lightning."

The reaction of the New York press to the convention was mixed. It ranged from the Oneida *Whig's* comment, "This bolt is the most shocking and unnatural incident ever recorded in the history of womanity," to the Auburn *Daily Advertiser's* praise, "This is emphatically the age of 'democratic progression,'—of *equality* and *fraternization*—the age when all colours and sexes—the bond and free, black and white, male and female—are, as they by right ought to be, all tending downward and upward towards the common level of equality." But the most interesting criticism came from the *Mechanics Advocate* of Albany:

> The women who demand for their sex so many supposed *Rights,* and who aim to be placed upon an equal footing with the sterner sex, in all the relations of life, belong to a class that is, for the most part, unaffected by the serious evils that weigh so crushingly upon all classes of female operatives. . . . Work out a reform in *them;* bring about a diminution of the hours of toil, and an increase in wages, and *then* it will be time enough for you to preach up the strange doctrines contained in your Declaration of Rights.[8]

There were already labour leaders in 1848 who quarrelled with the first suffragists over the priorities of reform. The quarrel was to continue until women were given the vote, and afterwards, when the vote was not used to help workers in the factories.

The appetite created at Seneca Falls led to the immediate call for another women's convention in nearby Rochester. There, a Quaker woman presided, Abigail Bush. "On my taking the chair," she wrote fifty years later to Susan Anthony, "Lucretia Mott and Elizabeth Cady Stanton left the platform and took their seats in the audience, but it did not move me from performing all my duties, and at the close of the meeting Lucretia Mott came forward and folded me tenderly in her arms, and thanked me for presiding. That settled the question of men presiding at a woman's convention."9 Women quickly learned to manage all the techniques of protest meetings, once they faced the necessity of doing so.

Interested feminists soon followed the example of the two conventions in New York State. The first of four conventions held in small towns in Ohio took place at Salem in 1850, an area that was strong for Garrison and abolition. All men were barred from speaking at this convention. The idea of woman, separate and alone, reached an apogee as the towns approached the frontier. But at the first truly national women's convention, held at Worcester, Massachusetts, in the same year, the leading orators of the anti-slavery movement spoke, including Wendell Phillips and Theodore Parker. "It was fitting," wrote Harriet Taylor in the *Westminster Review* of July, 1851, "that the men whose names will remain associated with the extirpation from the democratic soil of America of the aristocracy of colour, should be among the originators, for America and for the rest of the world, of the first collective protest against the aristocracy of sex; a distinction as accidental as that of colour, and fully as irrelevant to all questions of government."

At a second convention at Worcester in 1851, Abby Kelley paid just tribute to herself, as the only woman who had kept up a continual agitation in public since the meteoric career of the Grimkés. Her bloody feet, she said, had worn smooth the path that the feminists now climbed with such ease. And she called them to work. "You will not need to speak when you speak by your every-day life. Oh, how truly does Webster say, Action, action, is eloquence!"[10] The other steady but quiet labourer in the same field, Lucretia Mott, further pointed out that Jesus was an agitator.

The truth was, however, that the feminists had no means of political action. They had no national organization. As so many of the leading Garrisonians supported them, they did not feel it necessary to hold more than sporadic conventions. In the decade before the Civil War, there was a women's convention nearly every year in Massachusetts, occasionally in New York and Pennsylvania and Ohio, and once in Indiana. Speakers continued to point out the need to do something. "Poverty is essentially slavery if not legal yet actual," cried Paulina Wright Davis in 1851. "The women of the time, the women worthy of the time must understand this and they must *go to work!* They must *press* into every avenue, every open door that custom and law leaves unguarded. . . . They *must* purchase themselves out of bondage."[11] Yet she herself did not go to work as a professional woman, nor as a permanent organizer for the feminists.

The advocates of women's rights before the Civil War were mainly married ladies, who spent most of their time looking after husbands and children. They were content to leave steady organizational work to the paid agents of the anti-slavery societies. Until a section of these radical women felt betrayed by the anti-slavery movement, they would not work to set up an organization of their own. "I shall be glad," Lucy Stone declared to Lucretia Mott, "when the Woman Question is allowed to rest *on its own merits.*"[12] But it could not rest on its own merits while its supporters remained a restive auxiliary of groups formed to free the slave.

Even if the early feminists had formed an organization, they would have faced the same barrier which met the early abolitionists. Could they *persuade* men to give them the vote any more than Yankees could *persuade* Southern slave-owners to free their slaves? They could agitate and make public speeches and collect signatures to petitions, but they could not take direct political action—the course which was open to the anti-slavery movement. When Henry Stanton wanted to support the Liberty Party and the later Republican Party, he could vote for the party of his choice and even be elected to Congress. His wife could not, although once she ran in an election in New York and secured twenty-four votes.

The techniques of agitation were effective in raising the wind for a cause; they were not effective in securing laws to make a cause part of the social landscape. The early suffragists had to win over a large body of educated, male opinion to their side. Even the abolitionists, who did not have to surmount the barrier of sex, had no effect on Congress until they began to infiltrate it. The supporters of women's rights fared even worse. They might address polite or impolite legislative committees year after year, but they could not make legislators see that some women did not feel adequately represented by men alone. "Here, gentlemen, is our difficulty," Elizabeth Stanton told the legislature of New York in 1854.

When we plead our cause before the law makers and *savants* of the republic, they cannot take in the idea that men and women are alike; and so long as the mass rest in this delusion, the public mind will not be so much startled by the revelations made of the injustice and degradation of woman's position as by the fact that she should at length wake up to a sense of it.

If you, too, are thus deluded, what avails it that we show by your statute books that your laws are unjust—that woman is the victim of avarice and power? What avails it that we point out the wrongs of woman in social life; the victim of passion and lust? You scorn the thought that she has any natural love of freedom burning in her breast, any clear perception of justice urging her on to demand her rights.[13]

It was clear that the slave was not represented by his owner, but the majority agreed that men did represent women. While the difference of the sexes was thought natural, no legislature would dream of giving women power through the vote over their ordained male representatives.

With general agreement on the inequality of the sexes in nature as well as in society, the early leaders of the feminists were judicious in keeping their cause attached to the cause of the Negro. For the Negro

man was likely to get the vote—he already had it if he was a freed-
man and state law permitted. If the suffragists could identify the
cause of the Negro male slave with that of all women, they might
hope that gratitude for their help in the cause of abolition would
persuade the anti-slavery forces to help them towards the vote for
women. The mission of anti-slavery, Elizabeth Stanton urged, was
not "to the African slave alone, but to the slaves of custom, creed,
and sex as well." The Civil War was both to teach American feminists to organize alone and to split some of them from their past
friends and helpers. Their priority was to become women first, even
at the expense of the Negro.

The vote remained improbable to radical women before the Civil
War, low in the list of their expected freedoms. Even Elizabeth Stanton, as late as 1852, thought that woman should only vote and not
hold office, because of the disgusting state of politics.

I disclaim all desire or intention to meddle with *vulgar* politics . . .
to sit in council with vulgar, rum drinking, wine bibbing, tobacco chewing
men, with thick lipped voluptuaries, gourmands and licentiates, who disgrace our national councils with their grossness and profanity, their
savage rudeness, and uncurbed ferocity; who, instead of sound reason
and strong argument, resort to fist-cuffing, dirking and duelling, to settle
nice questions of honour and statesmanship. No, until a new type of man be
placed at the helm of the ship of state, rest assured we women shall
decline all nominations for office.[14]

With politics violent, the press hostile, pulpits barred, and public
opinion apathetic to the idea of ballots for women, there was nothing
that the few suffragists could do but agitate locally, recruit future
leaders, and attach their cause to a more successful one.

Two of the most important leaders of the woman's movement,
Lucy Stone and Elizabeth Stanton, were drawn into their lifelong
crusades by anger at woman's wrongs within marriage. They both
insisted that a wife should have the right to her own body, although
the law made her subject to her husband's will. The fact that Elizabeth Stanton had a husband only made her voice rise louder, although

marriage was eventually to stop Lucy Stone's mouth with the gag of respectability.

Lucy Stone was brought up in a situation of man's dominance and woman's resignation. Her autocratic father wore out her mother with toil on his stony Massachusetts farm. She herself grew up strong, dogged, plain, assertive, shrewd, and excessively clean. The example of Abby Kelley and the Grimké sisters made her an early supporter of abolition and women's rights. At the age of twenty, she wrote to one brother that the Grimkés were "first rate," and had helped her resolutions "to call no man master."[15] After nine years of toil as a local school-teacher, she scraped and borrowed enough money to go to Oberlin. Unlike her loved friend, Antoinette Brown, she did not become more religious there. She found Oberlin the place "to *harden* sinners," because of the excessive preaching there.

After graduation, Lucy Stone determined to make her living as a public lecturer. Her family objected, particularly her mother. But the daughter replied, "If in this hour of the world's need I should refuse to lend my aid, however small it may be, I should have no right to think myself a Christian, and I should forever despise Lucy Stone. . . . Especially do I mean to labour for the elevation of my sex."[16]

Lucy Stone was early preoccupied with marriage and procreation. She had seen her mother aged by overwork and the rearing of nine children. While she was still at Oberlin in 1846 and 1847, she advised her married brothers about the need for moral reform inside marriage. She quoted the example of Angelina Grimké, who believed in spacing out her children through self-restraint in her marriage with Theodore Weld. The three preserved replies to her letters show the frankness possible between farm people of the time despite the conventions of prudery, and the acceptance or rejection of current sexual folkways and reforms.

The wife of the Reverend William Stone rejected the idea that wedded people could commit adultery within marriage. Her mother had told her on the subject, "To avoid fornication let every man have his own wife," for nobody ever committed fornication for the sake of offspring. Her husband agreed with her that married people should sleep together and that nothing was wrong which was "the necessary result of so doing"; but he also agreed with his sister that whatever was injurious to health was wrong.[17]

Lucy Stone's other two brothers were less tolerant. One supported her, and one opposed her. Frank Stone had just become a father again.

> Some think as you do that it is having them rather too fast. . . . This waiting three years Sis, as you intimate is all nonsense. Have them as fast as you can if you can, take care of them, and if you can't, trust Providence and obey the command given to our first parents to multiply and replenish the Earth and subdue it. Were all to follow the example of Mrs Weld and the advice of yourself, when think you would the wilderness and the solitary place in the natural world, bud and blossom as the rose? Your own good sense will answer never. . . . Then think of the multitudes that have lived and that will live who would never have had an existence, had the generations past, and the generations yet to come acted as you advise. You spoke of cohabiting only for the sake of children . . . for what do you take your regular meals each day? Do you eat that you may live, or do you eat because you are hungry? So then I suppose individuals do not cohabit for the sake of children only, but because they want to.[18]

Only with Luther Stone did his sister's ideas on marriage reform find some sort of acceptance:

> In answer to your inquiry about sexual intercourse I shall say in brief, that God made the whole of man for his own glory—All the organs he has given to man are to be used with reference to His glory. Our Generative organs should never be used except for propagation and we should always be able to ask God's blessing to follow their use. Nine-tenths of all the half grown men and of all the invalids, and men of half minds have become what they are by their own or their fathers' indulgence in the Beastlike use of their generative organs—But I am not yet through. *Lucy, I think It As Great A Sin To not Suffer These Organs to Be Used At All As To Use Them Too Much.*[19]

The three letters demonstrate the great importance the Bible played in the sexual lives of a reasonably devout rural family from New

England. One brother took the Bible to guide his life of self-restraint in marriage; another took it to mean a reasonable tolerance of sex within wedlock; a third believed in replenishing the earth according to Biblical injunction, and in the demands of human nature. Each adopted or rejected the folkways of sex according to his own character, whether stern or liberal or lusty. If the brothers resented the reforming impulse of their sister, yet they replied to her with honesty and in certainty of their righteousness. The letters are unique in the correspondence of the time and provide the only commentary on the effect of the moral reforms preached by the feminists. Lucy Stone was to forget her own preaching when she married. She wrote then to Susan Anthony that she did not "intend to lose *any* opportunity of securing the blessing of motherhood." She would not leave home and husband unless she knew motherhood was "not possible" or unless she was ready to *"wait* for *results."*[20]

Her fear of marriage made Lucy Stone a difficult woman to court. Henry Blackwell was determined to win her, and he did. He had been strongly attached to his elder sister Elizabeth, the pioneer doctor. Lucy Stone, as his brother Samuel pointed out, was very like Elizabeth "by her quiet decision, steady purpose, and lofty principle . . . and by a certain precision and distinctness of utterance, and personal neatness and good judgement."[21] The Blackwells all loved and worked for each other. Henry had gone into business at the age of fourteen years to help his mother and sisters, although like his brother Samuel, he had been bitten by reform and the fame of his doctor sisters Elizabeth and Emily. The closeness of the family tie certainly helped the businessmen brothers in the choice of their wives. As they could not marry their sisters, they did the next best thing and married two eminent feminists who loved one another, Lucy Stone and Antoinette Brown.

The courtship of Lucy Stone by Henry Blackwell showed up the great pride which the pioneer feminists put on their independence. Blackwell was a shrewd salesman and a tough land speculator; once he was nearly lynched in the West for forcing up the price of local real estate, although he quietened the mob of angry farmers by telling them that he was only doing what they would all do gladly if they were able. In his campaign of courtship over many years, he showed an incredible persistence. Lucy Stone refused him often. She said that she had dedicated her life to reform. She would not give up her "absolute freedom." She was already in her middle thirties, while her suitor was seven years younger than herself. "Excessive toil, and excessive grief," she wrote, "gave me a *premature* womanhood, and so, by a natural law, premature physical decay will come all the sooner— Do not forget either that a man is *younger* than a woman of the *same* age."[22]

Yet Henry Blackwell wore down her resistance. He promised her *"perfect equality"* in marriage. He said that he would free her to do more work for women by giving her a home. The law of marriage could not affect a woman who was determined to keep free. "Surely you enormously exaggerate the scope and force of *external* laws," he wrote to her, "at the expense of *internal* power."[23] By a marriage settlement and a public protest, he gave up all moral and economic power over Lucy Stone's possessions and person. As far as possible, he allowed her to stick to her youthful resolution to call no man master.

But marriage changed Lucy Stone. She began to defend the institution. She became a devoted wife and mother to her husband and her only daughter, Alice Stone Blackwell. Nothing showed her conversion more than her attitude to her husband's business dealings. At the beginning of his courtship, she had tried to wean him from business and put him to work at moral reform. *"No* consideration should ever make us sacrifice our spiritual growth, for any *material* good—that which is to be part of us *forever* must have the *higher* place—It is much less important that we be rich in *money."*[24] But soon Henry Blackwell was investing her savings in Wisconsin farmland; he promised her a profit of several hundred percent and made her represent part of that absentee Eastern capital that was to anger the West. After his marriage, Henry Blackwell remained a good businessman. He did not change to being a mediocre reformer. As he had once boasted when he thought he would become a millionaire, "Better to reign in Hell than serve in Heaven!"[25] He speculated in land for many of the reformers and kept his wife's newspaper, the *Woman's Journal,* afloat for twenty years.

In Lucy Stone's old age, Henry Blackwell began to reign in heaven. As he retired from his business dealings, he increasingly took over his wife's share of the leadership of the woman's movement, until his daughter was old enough to take over from him. He found, through his reforming wife, the salvation of himself through works. By sharp business practices, he had helped to keep his family and his wife virtuous in moral reform. His price, which was the price of many American businessmen, was to feel and admit the superior nature of his womenfolk, who were freed to push forward their reforms. In the same way, Carrie Catt's husband was to make the money for both of them, while she performed the service. When Lucy Stone gave up the liberty of her body to marry Henry Blackwell, she provided herself with money, a husband, and a daughter to carry on the cause of women beyond her death. The five Blackwell sisters, however, were more consistent. Each kept their freedom and remained single. Moreover, each adopted a daughter to carry on her ideas without impediment of husband.

Elizabeth Cady Stanton had a different kind of marriage. Like Lucy Stone, she had rebelled against her father, Daniel Cady, a wealthy judge with a brood of daughters in upper New York State. Although she was educated at the conservative Troy Female Seminary, she was infected early with abolition and women's rights in the reform circle around her cousin Gerrit Smith and his daughter Elizabeth, the pioneer of the bloomer dress. She heard discussions there about Ernestine Rose's early work for a married woman's property act in New York. Secretly, she fell in love with her brother-in-law, which made her chafe against the difficulty of divorce. Luckily, before she decided to elope with her sister's husband, she met Henry Stanton. He was ten years her senior, a fiery abolitionist, and a vigorous and assertive man. He made her his wife, although she refused to use the word "obey" in her marriage ceremony.

Elizabeth Stanton was always outspoken against women's wrongs in marriage. She had difficulties in her own. Both she and her husband had strong, autocratic, passionate natures. They quarrelled immediately and publicly. After three years of wedlock, Henry Stanton wrote to his wife asking her to forgive his coldness and unkindness.[26] A close friend of Elizabeth Stanton's wrote to another friend that she could not understand what Elizabeth saw in her husband; she personally would pick his eyes out if she were treated so badly.[27]

The salvation of the marriage lay in Elizabeth Stanton's mothering of seven children, including five boys. If she may not have wished for so many, she was proud of her efforts once she was successful. She enjoyed being a mother and her husband enjoyed being a father, and thus they learned to live with each other and disagree. It was an equal relationship, but not a compatible one. Although Elizabeth Stanton declared that she and her husband had lived for fifty years together without more than the usual matrimonial friction, she might have been declaring only her lack of knowledge about other marriages.

Yet whatever the cause—her early infatuation with her brother-in-law, her differences with her husband, or her sympathy with her own sex—Elizabeth Stanton was fired throughout her life with indignation against women's wrongs. It was her obsession; one of her cousins found out that all conversations returned to that subject. In her anger, she became one of the best propagandists of her age. And she put marriage reform before everything else. "The right idea of marriage," she wrote to her new friend Susan Anthony in 1853,

is at the foundation of all reforms. . . . A child conceived in the midst of hate, sin, and discord, nurtured on abuse and injustice, cannot do much to bless the world or himself. . . . Man in his lust has regulated this whole question of sexual intercourse. Long Enough! Let the Mother of Mankind, whose prerogative it is to set bounds to his indulgence, rouse up and give this whole matter a thorough fearless examination.[28]

Susan Anthony counselled caution on attacking the sexual habits of husbands. Even Lucy Stone, still a spinster at that time and still preoccupied with marriage, was enough of a politician to see that marriage reform had to be treated separately from the subject of

THE FIRST SUFFRAGISTS [73]

women's rights. Yet she added to the case-histories of Elizabeth Stanton by telling her of a woman who had fled from her husband to the chaste Shakers "because he gave her no peace either during menstruation, pregnancy, or nursing." And still the law gave a husband rights over his wife's body. "Shall we keep silence when such curses are inflicted through woman, upon the race?" Indeed, morality demanded that people should speak up for the rights of women within marriage. "The Free Love theories grow out of their wrongs." Lucy Stone ended with high praise for her later opponent, Elizabeth Stanton. "There is not another woman in our ranks, who thinks, or who dares speak, what she thinks on the topic, as far as I know."[29]

For the rest of her life, Elizabeth Stanton spoke out on marriage and divorce. And once she had wept at the first insults hurled at her for attacking the holy of holies, she was prepared to attack anything and anyone in the name of woman. "I would rather make a few slanders from a superabundance of life," she declared, "than to have all the proprieties of a well embalmed mummy."[30] She definitely had what Lucy Stone lacked, a strong sense of the war between the sexes. Marriage was to her "man-marriage." Man made all the laws, gained his wife's estate and submission, wreaked his lust on her, and kept the children, if he wished, after a divorce. This made no sense if the American mother were really dominant in the home and in the rearing of children. Because this made no sense, educated opinion began to back Elizabeth Stanton and liberalize the marriage and divorce laws.

Until the end of her public life, the aged crusader remained married herself and tried to help those who did not wish to do so. Her arguments were unanswerable:

Limiting the causes of divorce to physical defects or delinquencies; making the proceedings public; prying into all the personal affairs of unhappy men and women; regarding the step as quasi criminal; punishing the guilty party in the suit; all this will not strengthen frail human nature, will not insure happy homes, will not banish scandals and purge society of prostitution.

No, no; the enemy of marriage, of the State, of society is not liberal divorce laws, but the unhealthy atmosphere that exists in the home itself. A legislative act cannot make a unit of a divided family.[31]

Despite her own genius for propaganda, perhaps Elizabeth Stanton's greatest service to the cause of woman was to make a suffragist out of Susan Brownell Anthony, who was made to be an organization woman. Anthony had been born in a small town in Massachusetts, of Quaker parents. Her father had rebelled, as Lucretia Mott and the Grimkés had rebelled, from the orthodox discipline of the Society of Friends. He had eventually joined the Universalists, and had crusaded against strong drink and slavery. He had been wealthy when his daughter was young, and had sent her to a good school in Philadelphia. He had lost his fortune, however, and had retired to a farm near Rochester. Susan Anthony had gone out to teach; she had sent home some of her small salary. She had had suitors, but none of them had matched up to the perfection of her father. So she had not married. She was to end her life justifying the freedom of spinsterhood, preaching a "new epoch of single women" who might dominate affairs from homes of their own.

Susan Anthony's first reform work had been temperance. It was the most respectable of the reforms to enter, although the dry organizations imitated the abolitionists in making it difficult for women to speak out at conventions. During the disillusion of trying to raise funds from women who had no money to give because it was kept in their husbands' pockets, Susan Anthony met Elizabeth Stanton. They took an instant liking to each other. Gradually, Anthony began to accept her friend's priorities. Woman suffrage came to play a greater part in her speeches, especially when she dared to speak out at a male-dominated teachers' convention in 1853. There, she complained bitterly that the degraded status of women teachers made even the male teachers seem inferior by sharing in the same profession. Yet she was no *"speaking* Medium"; her style was awkward and diffident.[32] Antoinette Brown, who went on a speaking tour with her at this time, wrote that Anthony would never get along smoothly in this world. It was as much her manner as the matter of what she said.

The ebullient Elizabeth Stanton gradually freed Susan Anthony from her sense of isolation and her inhibitions. While the worried and dedicated Anthony wrote endless letters and made continual arrangements and scratched up meagre funds, the lazy and corpulent Stanton was goaded into writing speeches. "It is too cruel," Anthony once wrote of her friend, "that such mental powers must be hampered with such a *clumsy body*—oh—if we could only give her elasticity of limbs—and locomotive powers."[33] Anthony was included in the Stanton family life, which freed her from loneliness and her friend for work. Although Anthony spent her life in the shadow of the forceful Stanton, she outlived her and became the saint of the woman's movement. Her very perseverance and doggedness made her known in every hamlet in America; girls who were tomboys were called "Susan Bs." The reason for her fame had a lot to do with her appearance, that of the "schoolmarm," a withered, tall, raw-boned, single-minded old maid. But her reputation changed from being a byword into being a holy invocation. Even her speaking style became reasonably emotional and inspiring, as practice gave her confidence. She was a living example of how much good a public life does for a single woman.

The driving force behind Anthony was partly her meticulous and conscientious temperament, partly her discovery of the right cause at the right time, partly a fierce desire for power and dominance, and partly a sense of deprivation of the family that she never had. In the woman's movement, Susan Anthony found the daughters that she was not free to have without a husband. There was no one that she loved so much as the young "Joan of Arc" of the feminists, Anna Dickinson, when the girl was at the height of her fame as a speaker after the Civil War, and Susan Anthony was in her late forties. In a long correspondence with Anna Dickinson, in which she tried to make the girl put the cause of women before that of the Negro, she declared her love.

Anthony's letters abound in addresses to "Dicky darling Anna" and "Dear Chick a dee dee." She is always wanting to give the girl "one awful long squeeze." She tries to make her promise "not to *marry* a *man."* She preaches the virtues of her spinster flat in New York. "I have *plain quarters*—at 44 Bond St.—*double bed*—and big enough and good enough to take you *in*—So come and see me." Although busy night and day as the editor of *The Revolution,* she would travel anywhere to see Anna. "I do so long for the scolding and pinched ears and every thing I know awaits me. . . . What worlds of experience since I last snuggled the wee child in my long arms."

Yet, throughout her letters, Anthony never asserted that her desperate love was more than a maternal feeling. She could not think in other terms, nor give her passion a modern name. "Anna," she wrote in a scrawled hand in 1869, with tears blotting the ink, "my soul goes out to you in real mother yearnings—I don't believe you have believed the depths thereof." When time abated her passion, and Anna Dickinson aged and grew a little mad, Anthony did not forget her. In 1895, she wrote a letter of fond reminiscence. "I have had several lovely *Anna* girls—'nieces'—they call themselves now-a-day —since my *first Anna*—but none of them—ever has or ever can fill the niche in my heart that you did."[34]

This dogged, yearning, spinster resented the housework and marriage which took most of the time of the other leading suffragists. Practically all of the feminists were married, many of them more than once, and practically all of them had children, sometimes many of them. Anthony's letters are full of resentment at their periodic retirements into child-bearing. At one period in the early days, Antoinette Brown and Lucy Stone and Elizabeth Stanton were all pregnant, and Anthony complained bitterly, "Those of you who have the *talent* to do honour to poor—and how poor—Womanhood, have all given yourselves over to *baby* making, and left poor brainless *me* to battle alone—It is a shame,—such a Lady as *I might* be *spared* to *such cradles,* but it is a *crime* for *you*."[35] Interestingly and wrongly enough, Anthony presumed that the educated and married feminists had enough knowledge of contraception, or enough power of self-restraint, to choose when they wanted to have their children.

On the other hand, Anthony was Victorian enough over motherhood. She never questioned that reproduction was "the highest and holiest function of the physical organism . . . to be a *Mother*, to be a *Father*, is the best and highest wish of any human being."[36] If she learned to justify the fact that she was single, it was a defence against the low opinion of old maids held by society, allied with the satisfaction of a life well spent in the education of many feminists. For Susan Anthony, her suffrage organization and her "nieces" were her family, once she could head that organization.

The personal bitterness between Anthony and Lucy Stone that was to split the woman's movement in 1869 was dormant in their early attitudes to one another. Lucy Stone never hated Elizabeth Stanton, whom she treated as an equal, both as a pioneer suffragist and as a mother. But Anthony came late to the woman's movement. In the early days, Lucy Stone patronized her as a follower, and basked in Anthony's admiration. Marriage made Lucy Stone still more patronizing. "It is very absurd of you, you little naughty thing," she wrote to Anthony in 1856, "to feel that you are left *alone*—are all the married ones dead and gone? Have we neither life, character nor use? You are a little wretch, to even *intimate* that we are nothing *now* . . . just quit thinking that you are left in possession of the whole world alone—for we shall claim our share, and what is better still, we shall get it too."[37]

Lucy Stone's added adoption of Boston as her home city made her still more intolerable to Anthony, who remained very much the ambitious small-town woman. She sometimes referred to the capital of Massachusetts as "Boss-town." The basic desire of both women to lead and organize and dominate was bound to bring about a personal conflict between the respectable urban wife and the aggressive rural spinster, once a national woman's organization had been set up.

In a real sense, this personal quarrel was a reflection of the geographical conflict between condescending Boston and the West led from New York. At least, when the split came, Anthony thought in those terms. When Lucy Stone tried to call a women's convention in New York in 1870 because Westerners would not travel to Boston, Anthony called it an attempt "to *steal New York's thunder*." She added contemptuously, however, "Bostonianism don't flourish with *the people—Let 'em come."* A few weeks later, she claimed that Lucy Stone was trying to overthrow her personally. "And am I to be compelled to *concede* my position *to her—to Boston!* . . . No—No."[38]

Susan Anthony chose to make her home in Rochester, not in New York or Washington, the centre of her life of organization. She remained very much the farmer's daughter—at least in the belief of returning to one's roots. Nothing is more revealing of the attitudes that lay behind her dislike of the educated intellectuals of the Eastern cities than a speech which she delivered at a country fair in upper New York State in 1858 to an audience of farmers. She claimed that she herself was a farmer, although her attempt to grow raspberries scientifically had failed. What farmers needed to do was to become more progressive and to make their jobs more stimulating. "If the farmers of New-York would save their children from the sickly employments, and debasing vices of our cities, they must conduct their pursuits on scientific principles, that shall command the respect and attention of young men and women of intelligence, taste and refinement."

She spoke to magnify the calling of the farmer. For the American race could only be redeemed through outdoor work, face to face with nature.

When, in the progress of civilization, the tide shall flow backward,— when, with higher and better views of life, we shall turn from the crowded marts of commerce, to cultivate the land once more,—then may we confidently look for a new race of men and women—sound in body and mind—with renovated moral forces and power. . . . Farming is the only natural and enduring employment, which has been, and will be through the ages, the true condition of the race. All the trades and professions grow out of the artificial necessities and diseases of civilized life; —and, to a greater or less extent, compel false habits. . . . Crimes spring not from the soil, but from the whirl and strife of competition and excess.

In language that was a paraphrase of Jefferson's eulogy of the small farmer, and that was to echo again in the revolt of the Greenbackers and the Populists, Anthony continued: "To the farmers, then, of this republic, belong the care and keeping of our sacred rights to life, liberty and happiness.—The battles of the revolution were not fought by perfumed dandies, carpet knights, and half crazed scholars, —but by stout men, with sound heads and hearts." Every farmer should be a statesman. The science of government was simple enough when it was based on the broad principles of justice. And everybody had the same principles of right and wrong. "Alone with his plough and his God," the farmer should settle "what is right among families, States and Nations:—For one law governs all. The land owners,—the *producers,* should be at the *helm* of *government.* Those who spend their time in mere management and talk, are but leeches on social and governmental life.—The farmer being independent is the man above all others to give true politics."[39]

Although Anthony may have exaggerated her sentiments in view of her audience of farmers, she displayed a fundamental belief in American rural values that was extraordinary in an educated and emancipated woman. Her hatred of the city and its ways, her belief that only the land was good, her simple ideas on the running of a government, her bias against intellectual life, and her contempt for the expanding commerce that was to develop the continent betray her underlying conservatism and her sentiment for a lost heritage. These views, of course, made her a great success in the small towns of the West. She knew the chords to strike to make a countrywoman feel proud of herself. But such beliefs made her useless in her attempts to secure the backing of slum or factory women.

Susan Anthony lived all her life within the values of the small town. An aggressive spirit, taught the language of radicalism by Elizabeth Stanton, made her seem a pioneer in her age, but she looked back steadily to the past. In fact, her novelty was, as was that of Elizabeth Stanton, to believe in the literal words of the Declaration of Independence.

PART THREE

First Successes

I'd rather be a free spinster and paddle my own canoe.

LOUISA M. ALCOTT

VI

❧❧❧

THE REVOLT AGAINST
CIVIL DEATH

WHEN COMMON LAW had crossed the Atlantic, it had lost much of its
severity. Few American lawyers had been trained enough to understand the complexities of English case law, or even to know of many
of the cases. Thus a wide field had been left open for the exercise of
equity and the common sense of judges. The rigours of English law
had been softened by the ignorance and practical verdicts of American
courts. Equity had already begun to change the law in Stuart and
Georgian England, but this process of change had accelerated in the
New World. In trying to imitate the rule of common law, the colonies
had proved uncommonly kind to American women. The freedom of
colonial wives had been relatively great, because the laws to restrain
them had not been applied.

The famous *Commentaries* of Sir William Blackstone were the law
to most American lawyers. They presented a readable digest of an
outdated and labyrinthine legal system. Blackstone's assertion of the
"civil death" of women in marriage was a formidable support for
those who wished to exploit their wives. It was also marvellous
propaganda for the early feminists. No wife who valued her identity

would submit to Blackstone's definition of her status: "By marriage, the husband and the wife are one person in law; that is, the very being or legal existence of the woman is suspended during her marriage, or at least, is consolidated into that of her husband under whose wing, protection and *cover,* she performs everything."[1] Even if a wife were assaulted or raped, she could not prosecute her attackers unless her husband would bring the suit.

Yet those American lawyers who used Blackstone and those feminists who rebelled against him were using a text that had little practical application in American case law. Different conditions in the colonies had bred different precedents, which varied from state to state. Even when a federal system had come to the United States with the Constitution, federal law had merely been imposed on the various laws of the states. The changing of the laws relating to women had to be done piecemeal. Even today, a woman is legally a different person in the states of the North and West and South.

The colonial courts had recognized some of the rights of the wife. She had the right to live with her husband in house and bed. She had the right to be supported by him, even if he abandoned her. She had the right to be protected from violence at his hands. All of these rights for wives showed that the colonial courts had recognized a certain equality in marriage between husband and wife, since both were economically necessary to one another. None of these rights had been recognized under contemporary English law.

Because of the shortage of skills and of women, and because of the long absences of seafaring husbands, married American women also received more independence than their English counterparts. Some were allowed to run estates and businesses on their own, even when they had husbands. According to Blackstone, wives were classed with minors and idiots; they had no responsibility under the law. But in America, where every hand was needed to develop the virgin land, married women with dependents were given acres of their own to till. Need brought justice to the law in particular cases.

Although a woman gave up control over her property to her husband, she did not lose the property outright, except in Connecticut.

Even under English law, a husband was only allowed to administer and use his wife's property during his lifetime; he could not dispose of it. Moreover, nearly all wealthy families, who gave a dowry with their daughter, protected her inheritance by means of a marriage contract or a trust. As a Victorian commentator pointed out, only the wives of the poor, who were ignorant of the law, lost everything to their husbands. The aristocracy and the middle class knew how to evade the law, and did evade it. "Every marriage settlement was a protest against the law; but every marriage settlement was a guarantee for the continuance of the law. The wealthy classes insisted upon a settlement at the marriage of every daughter."² When a married woman's property bill was finally passed in New York State, it was less due to popular agitation than to the pressure of wealthy New Yorkers who wanted to safeguard their daughters' inheritances. If the interests of the rich were threatened, they had the law changed. It so happened that in American democracy the law applied to everyone. Thus even the wives of the poor benefited, if they possessed something in the first place.

Marriage contracts were a normal part of life, when marriage was an economic business and a lifelong partnership. In the rare cases where a marriage ended in separation or divorce, the property of husband and wife could be clearly divided. Without a contract, a husband had the rights on even his wife's personal possessions, down to the dress on her back. But, in fact, the clothing of a wife was not seized by her husband or his creditors. Unjust laws are rarely applied in civil suits.

Although American colonial courts had not treated a woman equally with a man, because of the fiction that husband and wife were one person, the laws had given back a little of what they had taken away. If a wife lost control of all her possessions to her husband, she was heir upon his death to the use of one-third of his estate during her life, and to certain household goods. If she was childless, she received one-half. When the estate was small, she received it all. Equity was frequently applied by the courts to make special provisions for a widow and her children from an estate. And if the wife died, her husband only had the use of her estate during his lifetime. On his death, it went to their children. Moreover, if a husband owned all his wife's possessions, he was also responsible for her debts before and during marriage. Even in cases of slander, husbands had to pay the fines of their wives.

Yet the paternalism of the law merely emphasized the dependence of the married woman. Obviously, she was not the same person as her husband, and frequently she did not want to be thought his subordinate. The law, anyway, was not invoked in a marriage of respect and equality between husband and wife. It was when the marriage was out of joint that the law was summoned. If, then, the law favoured the husband heavily at the expense of his wife, her small freedom from the laws through the fiction of her "civil death" was turned into a monstrous burden of injustice. Freedom from the law is all very well until the law is applied. Then it is equality under the law that is important.

With the ideology of the American Revolution, and with the democratic ferment during the age of Jackson, the concept of equality under the law was bound to affect the position of women. American laws patently needed reform, now that the American legal system was independent of English precedent. With the frequent calling of state constitutional conventions, reformers could convince delegates to convert the decisions of American equity into fundamental law. The position of women was, indeed, idiotic, in terms of equality and liberty. If the function of the law was to protect the weak, women needed its protection. Thus legal reform became one of the first successful campaigns of American feminists. For it allowed American lawyers to boast of the superiority of their legal system to those of European countries, most of which now possessed a version of the Code Napoléon that was based on his dictum, "Woman is given to man to bear children; she is therefore his property, as the tree is the gardener's."

If many of the more idiotic laws against wives were not applied, some were. Where a bad law exists, injustice will occasionally be done. The instances of injustice, where a married woman's clothes were seized by her husband's creditors or a farmer's wife's egg money went to her drunken husband, gave the early feminists the excuse to drum up support for women's rights. In New York State, it was the twelve years' campaign for the Married Women's Property Act of 1848 that led to the calling of the first women's rights convention in the same year. The bill was first introduced into the state legislature by a conservative judge, who had married a woman of property, and who wanted to secure that property from his creditors in case of financial disaster. He disliked the vagueness of the state law on the subject of the property of wives. He was backed by other legislators, who wanted to protect their daughters' marriage portions.

The bill was talked over in committee for twelve years. During that time, support for the measure grew among wealthy and powerful families in the state. Although the bill appeared to be a radical one which would alter the place of married women in society, it was in fact an aristocratic measure, designed to protect the daughters and wives of the rich. Its peculiar by-product was the rise of the woman's movement in New York State. The Polish reformer, Ernestine Rose, fresh from contact with Robert Owen in England, stumped from door to door in New York City collecting signatures to petition for the bill. She even spoke in public, in the manner of Frances Wright. Through her agitation she met and combined forces with the feminists in upper New York State, Paulina Wright Davis and Elizabeth Cady Stanton. The immigrant woman, and the two women from small towns, spoke to legislative committees and organized agitation through petition, speeches, and lobbying. Although Ernestine Rose had only got five signatures to her first petition, thousands of women signed the later petitions.

The bitterness of the small-town ladies was particularly evident, for in a small town the injustice of a husband to his wife could not be hidden. One petition from western New York read: "Our numerous and yearly petitions for this most desirable object having been disregarded, we now ask your *august* body to abolish all laws which hold married women more accountable for their acts than *infants, idiots and lunatics.*" It was this female frustration which reached its peak in the convention at Seneca Falls.

The act was passed, giving a wife full control over her real and personal property at the time of her marriage, and excepting it from her husband's debts. The wages earned by a wife were still, however, the property of her husband. The act was not worth much, Ernestine Rose conceded, "for at best it was only for the favoured few and not for the suffering many."[3] But it was a legal advance for women, in which the self-interest of the rich happened to coincide with the wishes of the early feminists.

Legal reform had a special appeal to the middle-class feminists in the early days of the woman's movement. It was possible in the way that dress reform or physical reform was not. Rich and powerful men could be made to see that their daughters and grandchildren could benefit from the protection of their family possessions. "The law which alienates the wife's right to the control of her own property, her own earnings," Clarina Nichols declared in 1851, "lies at the foundation of all her social and legal wrongs."[4] In a way, she was right. Once a wife was separated from her husband in the most important matter in Victorian married life—property—the fiction that she was one person with her husband disappeared. With this protection, she could campaign for other reforms in the law, which would give her control of her children after a divorce, which would protect her wages, and which would raise the age of consent in marriage.

Where New York led, the other states followed. In the North and in the West, liberal property laws came into being to protect the married woman. The South, already retiring upon itself, resisted Yankee innovation. And, during the passage of these laws, the feminists had all the ammunition they desired. Blackstone's "civil death" became their favourite whipping-boy. The being of a wife, Ernestine Rose mocked, "is said to be merged in her husband. Has nature there merged it? Has she ceased to exist or feel pleasure and pain? When she violates the laws of her being, does he pay the penalty?" Of course he did not. For the law is never more than a fiction until it is applied in fact.

It was, indeed, not so much the *fact* of the law that the feminists resented, for that could be evaded or used for propaganda. It was the concept behind the law which humiliated them. "The husband provides for his wife," Ernestine Rose continued. "Oh! the degradation of that idea! Yes, he keeps her, so he does his horse."[5] Even the reasonable legal provision giving a minimum of one-third of large estates to a widow for her lifetime became shocking, when it was applied by Clarina Nichols to the case of the widow of a small householder. This woman would have to exist in a third of a house, in "a corner in the kitchen, a corner in the garret, and a *'privilege'* in the cellar . . . as if she were a *rat!"*

Of course, equity gave more of her husband's estate to the widow when that estate was small. But, to the feminists, the charity of equity was merely another proof of the galling condescension of male judges. Women should be equal with men under the law. For the law offered them written and incontrovertible proof of their inferiority. When Lydia Child made a will and her husband had to sign it to make it legal, she was "toweringly indignant." It was not against him, for he believed in the freedom of all women on principle, but against the insult done to women by law, literature, and custom. "The very phrases used with regard to us are abominable. 'Dead in the law,' 'Femme couverte.' How I detest such language! I must come out with a broadside on that subject before I die. If I don't, I shall walk and rap afterward."[6]

Thus the law was the first to be attacked and the first to be changed. Among the many inchoate strivings of Victorian women after equality with men in all fields, equality under the law was the most coherent idea to grasp and apply. The law was defined. Political pressure on legislators could change it. While spiritual and social equality was hard to define and harder to attain, the law was a palpable and a malleable thing, the positive evidence of degradation.

Yet the slowly improving position of Victorian women under the law told against the feminists. As factory laws were passed, and property laws, and laws to give the innocent party custody of the children in case of divorce, as even the Southern states raised the age of consent to sixteen years old, so the anti-suffragists used legal reform as proof that women did not need the vote. By indirect influence, women had caused men to give them their legal rights. Mark Twain commented that "men could not have done as much for themselves in that time, without bloodshed—at least they never have; and that is argument that they didn't know how."[7] At the end of the nineteenth century, Lord Bryce found that women were equal to men "as respects all private rights." Even where the divorce law was unsatisfactory, it was equally unjust to husband and wife. By their legal fairness to women, the anti-feminists concluded, men had proved that they always kept the interests of the other sex at heart.

The suffragists found this argument hard to answer. They could only enumerate those states—and there were always bad laws in some states—where women's rights lagged behind those of men. What they were really protesting about was the lack of legal power of the federal government to intervene in matters of state law. Even where state law helped women, its application was limited to the area of the state. Thus the hard campaigns for changes in the laws of individual states taught the national women's organizations to press for federal amendments to the Constitution, whenever possible. For it was better to make woman's right to vote a national rather than a local right.

Even after the vote was won, concern over the unfair discrimination between men and women under the law—particularly in the South—persisted in the women's organizations. In some states, the law favoured the authority of the father, yet freed the father from responsibility for his child if the child was a bastard. The double standard in marriage was still recognized in some states; a man could divorce his wife for being unchaste before marriage, while she could not. Arrests for prostitution still resulted only in the punishment of the girls, not of their customers. The labour of a woman in her husband's business could still be judged valueless in the case of divorce. And because of the factory laws designed to protect women workers, many of these women found that they were jobless because they could not work overtime or at night.[8]

Those feminists who have retained the militant belief in the total equality of men and women have lobbied Congress until this day for an Equal Rights Amendment to the Constitution. This would provide for no discrimination between the sexes in legislation. Those suffragists who once believed in the need to protect women from exploitation in the factories still oppose this measure. The quarrel in the feminist ranks continues. It is the echo of the same debate that has never been resolved in law or out of it. Should women be treated as the equals of men in all ways, or should the sexes recognize their biological differences?

VII

THE ALPHABET OF REFORM

"IF AMERICAN MEN intend always to keep women slaves, political and civil," Mary Clay asserted to a Congressional committee, "they make a great mistake when they let the girls, with the boys, learn the alphabet, for no educated class will long remain in subjection."[1]

The scarcity of cities had told against education in colonial America. Public education has always fared better in the city than the countryside, because of the unwillingness of farmers to pay taxes. When marriage was early and farm work continual, a village girl could not be expected to learn much from the local school—if there was one. What schools there were had operated only in the winter, and the teachers had been underpaid and ill-taught themselves. In some of the larger towns, schools of some efficiency had existed; but girls had rarely been allowed to progress beyond the rudimentary stages of education. Fewer than two women in five who signed surviving deeds in colonial Massachusetts could write their names, and Massachusetts had led the rest of the country in schools.

Only in the major cities had female academies been set up in the eighteenth century for the daughters of the well-to-do. Female education had only been for ladies, to make them more ladylike. "If you complain of education in sons," Abigail Adams had written to her husband during the great debate over the Constitution of the new Republic,

what shall I say of daughters who every day experience the want of it? With regard to the education of my own children I feel myself soon out of my depth, destitute in every part of education. I most sincerely wish that some more liberal plan might be laid and executed for the benefit of the rising generation and that our new Constitution may be distinguished for encouraging learning and virtue. If we mean to have heroes, statesmen, and philosophers, we should have learned women.[2]

The new Constitution had not provided for the encouragement of learning and virtue. In fact, although educational opportunity had been poor during the colonial period, it grew poorer in the years between the American Revolution and the Civil War. Opportunities for technological training through apprenticeship diminished, owing to the factory system in the North and slavery in the South and tenuous settlement in the West. The common schools of the country became badly neglected, as the wish to impose a uniform religious education on children grew less. By 1840, only one child in two in Massachusetts, one in four in the Middle Atlantic States, one in six in the West, and one in twelve in the South received a free education.

Yet the growing populations of the American cities and manufacturing towns demanded training in skills. If the American dream of opportunity for all had any meaning, it meant education for all. "Inequality is often of the mind as well as of property," Robert Dale Owen wrote in 1829. "The only security for the enjoyment of equal rights is, not agrarian laws or any laws whatever, but equal, national, republican education."[3] If the mechanic was to rise, he had to know more, even if the farmer could grow materially rich through dull toil. By 1840, more than half of the population of Massachusetts lived in towns or cities; the population of Boston had more than doubled in twenty years. The demand for learning in the cities surged.

The democratic ferment of the age of Jackson pushed middle-class reformers into action to protect themselves. Horace Mann supported a new system of public schools and equal education for boys and girls.

"The rulers of our country need knowledge (God only knows how much they need it!); but mothers need it more."[4] The evangelical circuit riders took travelling schools with them into the barbarous West. The popular lyceum enabled every village and city quarter to have its fortnight of higher education through visiting lecturers. The areas where the lyceum flourished, in Massachusetts, in New York City and the Burned-Over District, and in Ohio, were to be the centres of support for abolition and women's rights. For often the lyceum audience was chiefly an audience of women. It was the high school which they had never been able to attend. The thirst for education went hand in hand with the thirst for reform, and no places were more thirsty than the new small towns of the West.

This popular demand for education of both the sexes had to be staffed by teachers. And these teachers were to come from the improvised female seminaries, the first state normal schools, and the pioneer women's colleges. In 1818, Hannah Mather Crocker had published the first plea for women's education written by an American woman. She repudiated Mary Wollstonecraft's demands for the equality of the sexes, for God had rightly deprived woman of equality with man in Eden; but the Gospel was removing God's curse, and women should now be educated. Since the Christian era, man was no longer commanded to rule over woman. Therefore, women should be taught to rule over themselves, as men did. The sexes were equal in their capacities, short of women governing the state or speaking in public. "Mind," Hannah Crocker declared, "has no sex."[5]

Three women from New England made education the priority of lady reformers there. All were brought up on farms or in small towns, all were religious and conservative, and all opposed the giving of the vote to the mass of their sex. In a way, their conservatism was forced upon them, since they had to attract girls from well-to-do families to their schools in order to earn a living. Any woman who tried to educate young ladies could only support respectable reforms. Discretion was the price of success.

Emma Hart had an unusual education for a girl, as she was taught by her Universalist and free-thinking father. She picked up more learning from a Yale graduate, and went into school-teaching. She made a shrewd marriage at the age of twenty-two to a fifty-year-old banker in a small town. When his bank failed, the new Mrs. Willard set up a school for young ladies in her house. But she had greater ambitions, and presented a Plan for Improving Female Education to the Governor and legislature of New York. The plan asked the state to endow the teaching of religion and domestic science to young girls. Such training would fit them to become good women and good wives. It would be absurd to suppose that just because a few educated women with masculine minds chose to compete with men the mass of educated girls would dare to do so. Their proper training would rescue them from any trace of "unwonted officiousness."

The booming town of Troy on the Hudson River near its junction with the Erie Canal was impressed enough to set up Emma Willard in 1821 at the head of a female seminary there. In this conservative institution, the daughters of the middle classes were educated; Elizabeth Cady went there as a girl. The emphasis of the syllabus lay on religious and moral instruction, which Emma Willard thought "the true end of all education." An adequate amount of history and arithmetic and geography was taught along with the graces of a lady. Also included were lectures on physiology, for Emma Willard had studied a little medicine and had her own theory on the circulation of the blood. In the textbooks, however, heavy paper was pasted over all drawings of the human body. Poor girls were sometimes trained as teachers at Troy, on a system of repayable grants. Emma Willard, while accumulating a small fortune, also helped her sex.

Mary Lyon was brought up, like Lucy Stone, on a rocky farm in Massachusetts. She lived on the verge of starvation, for her father died when she was young. She had a passionate religious faith and a dogged, persevering mind. Lucky contacts with a kind minister and a rich man's daughter led to her education and a career in teaching. She remained a spinster, and was converted to the creed of faith through works, when a clergyman preached that "education was to fit one to do good." She followed Emma Willard's example and founded a ladies' school, Mount Holyoke, which was to become the oldest women's college in the United States. More selfless and dedicated than her predecessor, Mary Lyon achieved more. She selected most pupils by their brains rather than their parents' incomes, she gave them a three years' course that included moral philosophy and botany and chemistry, and she made them take formal examinations. Annual religious revivals also kept the girls in a ferment of the spirit. Mount Holyoke was the testing ground for all the later women's colleges. It also produced hundreds of teachers for American schools. Mary Lyon fitted her pupils to do good as mothers and teachers of children.

The third of the pioneers in female education was Catherine Beecher. Daughter of the widely-known Congregationalist preacher, Lyman Beecher, she was proud of being "the daughter or sister of nine ministers." Like most of the eleven Beecher children, she was to free herself from the Calvinistic dogma of sin by a belief in salvation through good works. The early death of her intended husband set her off on a long career as an educational propagandist. The schools and the organizations which she founded were failures; she did not have the attention to detail of Emma Willard or Mary Lyon. But she did stump the Eastern seaboard to raise money for Western education, and for the training of women to serve as teachers in the West. More than any other person, she made conservative reformers and church people see the importance of bringing religion and education to the West, before its barbaric people rebelled against the wealthy East. Jackson's election to the White House had already showed the power of the Western vote. It was both right and expedient for the East to educate its masters.

Catherine Beecher quoted pictures of Western life that were worthy of an abolitionist's description of the horrors of slavery. The Negro slave and the wage-slave lived in luxury compared to the slaves of the backwoods. These places were full of thin, illiterate, ragged children, brought up among "irreligion, ignorance, abject poverty, filth, and wretched vice." Even in civilized New York State in 1844, many of the self-styled teachers were "low, vulgar, obscene, intemperate, and utterly incompetent to teach anything good." Ten thousand teachers were needed in Ohio and Kentucky alone to teach two hundred thousand children, "who otherwise must grow up in utter ignorance."[6]

The conservatism of Catherine Beecher, who openly opposed the abolitionist as well as the feminist, was illustrative of the reforming lady in Massachusetts rather than the reforming woman. Education of girls to become good wives, or of Negroes to become devout, was a proper interest for any New England lady. Reform should be a gradual affair. First things must come first. After women and Negroes were educated and holy, then was the time to talk about the rights of women and the wrongs of slavery. Those who stirred up hatred between North and South, or between women and men, were wicked and irreligious. For the conservative lady in the city or small town of New England, Catherine Beecher was in the vanguard of right reform. Her priorities were correct: freedom from stern religion through a growing emphasis on the love of God, freedom for ladies to learn to become better wives and mothers, freedom for the Negro when his Southern owner could be persuaded to release him, and freedom for the West to learn the secure wisdom of the East.

But the radical Westerner was not content to be educated by the conservative Easterner. He decided to educate himself and to convert the East to radicalism. Lyman Beecher had left his safe Boston pulpit to head the Lane Theological Seminary in Cincinnati, and to lead the advance of Eastern education into the heathen wilderness. "If we gain the West, all is safe," he wrote to his daughter Catherine; "if we lose it, all is lost."[7] But Theodore Weld made the safe seminary a hot-bed of anti-slavery agitation. Beecher told him that if he wished to educate coloured people, his pockets could be filled with money; but if he walked with them in the streets, he would be overwhelmed.

Weld and forty fellow students withdrew in 1834 to a communal enterprise at Oberlin, a small place in Ohio. They persuaded the wealthy Tappans, who had brought Beecher to Lane Seminary, to transfer their support to the new college at Oberlin. The West had shaken itself free from the leadership of New England, even if it held to many of the early Puritan values. The first college that admitted students without regard to their colour or sex was founded several hundred miles inland from the Atlantic Coast. In the same year, a young woman who tried to run a school for coloured children in a small town in Connecticut was threatened and persecuted until she closed its doors.

Oberlin was vital for the feminist movement. Although there had been some co-education in a few female seminaries, Oberlin publicized the fact of men and women working together with equality and decency. A report in 1836 commented on the strict control over contacts between the two sexes and quoted one of the founders of the college, that "the female appendage has done more to recommend the Institution, than any other cause."[8] Even if the college professors intended to fit women students "for intelligent motherhood and a properly subservient wifehood," the student body itself was rabid with abolitionists and feminists. Radical women there learned to identify their wrongs with the wrongs of slaves. All the major reformers of the time visited the college to give speeches. Oberlin became an important point on the underground railroad for smuggling slaves to Canada. Many Negroes began to live there, and many radicals. Some families, like that of Olympia Brown, even emigrated back to Oberlin from the Middle West to educate their daughters. Above all, by its emphasis on faith through works and continual revivalism, Oberlin fulfilled Harriet Martineau's hopes for women's learning. "Women, like men, must be educated with a view to action, or their studies cannot be called Education."[9]

Where Oberlin led, others followed. Although opportunities for women to find a higher education remained few until the Civil War, a determined girl could go to college. Women graduates from Oberlin, such as Lucy Stone and Antoinette Brown, were becoming famous in reform circles. Their example set off a revolution in many women's hearts. Even the basic tenets of women's education as practiced at Oberlin came under question.

Of the four wings of the early feminist movement, those in Philadelphia and Massachusetts were the more conservative, although Boston was the base of William Lloyd Garrison. The New York group was fairly vocal, under the leadership of the fiery Elizabeth

Cady Stanton. But it was the Ohio group, where Garrisonians were locally as thick on the ground as Southern conservatives, that questioned the very assumptions of most Eastern reformers. The women's rights convention at Salem, Ohio, in 1852, wanted a clean sweep of the despicable theory behind the education of the female sex, in and out of college.

From the cradle upward through all the instructions of the nursery, the school, the pulpit, the forum, and the chamber of the muse—there has sounded one tedious monotonous refrain, reiterating,

> Obedience, patience, meekness;
> Meekness, patience, obedience;
> And *"soft, attractive grace,"*

as the long catalogue of womanly virtues; the one appointed preparation for the duties, the one security for the happiness of the married state—the Alpha and Omega of her duty and destiny![10]

It was time for women to demand equality with men everywhere, and in the West first of all.

That equality was easy to find in the pioneer conditions of the West, where both skills and women were few and educated people of both sexes were highly prized. In the Middle West alone, the cause of women's college education advanced before the Civil War. Antioch, Iowa State, and Wisconsin universities opened their doors to women, to be followed after the war by Syracuse, Northwestern, Michigan, Illinois, and Ohio State. In the Far West, California University also admitted women in 1869. In the East, while Swarthmore was founded for the purposes of co-education, the conservative example of segregated Mount Holyoke set the pattern for the new women's colleges of Vassar and Wellesley and Smith and Bryn Mawr. The "Harvard Annex" became Radcliffe, and women were admitted to the male institutions of Boston University, the Massachusetts Institute of Technology, Wesleyan, and Cornell. The East was half-hearted in following the Western idea of co-education, but it did gradually follow. Only in the South were Victorian women kept free from the possible taint of higher education, outside a few backward female colleges.

Although education in Victorian women's colleges was inferior in quality, so was education at Harvard and elsewhere. Good professors of either sex were spread thinly round; scholarship was at a premium. And yet a little learning was possible to the daughters of the middle class, and if that little learning was a dangerous thing, it was a help to feminism. A conservative Frenchwoman who visited Wellesley in 1895 already found it far too large with its seven hundred students, and commented on another danger that threatened the United States —"too much culture in all ranks of society, since culture thus spread broadcast cannot be very profound."[11] But this danger was to the good of progressivism, which was largely backed by educated middle-class opinion.

The spread of opportunities for women in higher education was also matched by the spread of public schools and high schools after the Civil War. Generations of dedicated spinsters went out to teach the children of the land. Teaching also became the way to fill in time before marriage for the intelligent but undedicated girl. Women were cheaper to hire than men—in New York in 1853, they were given one-tenth of the pay of male teachers. Education was everywhere considered the proper function of their sex; the schoolmistress was the temporary mother of the children of others.

Gradually women took over three in four of the teaching jobs available. Their status was recognized by the National Teachers' Association after the Civil War as equal to that of men. And with the spread of the public schools, the illiterate girls from the farms and villages of the West and South were taught to read and write. By the end of the century, any intelligent girl of native-born white parents had an opportunity of free education, at least to the level of literacy. Indian and Negro and Mexican and immigrant women had little opportunity in education, as they had little in everything.

Although the teaching profession had been encouraged by anti-feminists such as Catherine Beecher as a proper and decent occupation for single women, it became a training ground for feminists. Many of the early leaders of the women's rights movement had been teachers, for it was the only common profession outside literature open to an intelligent woman before the middle of the nineteenth century. These women became accustomed to earning their own bread by their own work. They knew the injustice of receiving one dollar for every ten that a man received; they became aware of discrimination against their sex. They knew at first hand how badly society needed reforming, when children had so little opportunity to learn. They were surrounded daily by case histories of the evils resulting to children from the drunkenness and ignorance and squalor of their parents. No teacher in a village school could afford the graces of a lady in the city. If she was a reformer by temperament, she was tempted to come out and do battle for her sex.

The right of a woman to get an education equal to that of a man made progress early, as did the right of a woman to be treated by the law as the equal of her husband. For both educational and legal reforms were popular in the Eastern as well as in the Western States in Victorian times. Ladies could safely help to educate the heathen at home as well as abroad, and even their own sex must benefit from institutions which made religion the centre of the curriculum. Most of the early Western colleges were founded by evangelical sects, and the figure of God loomed large in the syllabus.

In education and under the law, Victorian women were free to advance through steady pressure. For a large body of conservative, educated opinion supported them. Through education—the theory of the conservative reformers ran—women would receive their freedom. There was no need for any other agitation for female rights. As the small-town heiress from Massachusetts, Sophia Smith, wrote when she gave her fortune to found the women's college that bears her name, "It is my belief that by the higher and more thorough Christian education of women, what are called their 'wrongs' will be redressed, their wages adjusted, their weight of influence in reforming the evils of society will be greatly increased."[12] For the lady, education was the panacea for her sex, but the radical woman could only be satisfied by the vote.

VIII

꧁꧂

A SWEET ORDER
IN THE DRESS

If ERNESTINE ROSE thought that legal reform should come first of all, and if Catherine Beecher gave the priority to female education, Harriot Hunt, the pioneer psychotherapist, opted for physical reform, as "the ultimate of all reforms. . . . Without a healthy form in which to manifest itself, the soul *may* struggle for *use,* and find all its desires crushed."[1] To bring about this physical reform, Harriot Hunt lectured on physiology to groups of women. Her emphasis was on their need for exercise. She also believed, as Elizabeth Stanton did, in reform of dress. The corset of the Victorian woman was the symbol of her bodily bondage.

Corsets had hardly ever been worn in American country districts. Although in the colonies certain fashionable ladies had worn hoops and paniers and stays and stomachers, the normal dress for women had been an apron over a woollen gown that did not touch the ground, petticoats, stockings, a hood on the head and low shoes on the feet. In the poor sectors of the West and South, women went barefoot and wore only a cotton or calico gown. Even rich women were not content to be constricted round the waist all of the time; in the house, they wore sacques, polonezes, levites, trollopees, and slammerkins—all versions of the modern dressing-gown.

The French Revolution had an effect on the clothes of men and women. Both gave up stockings and began to wear trousers. Two women, Dorothy Sampson Gannet and Mad Ann Bailey, had worn men's clothes and fought like men in the American Revolution. But they had changed their sex temporarily. When women first took to trousers in any number, it was no parade of French fashion and equality. They made their trousers of cambric and hid them under their skirts, except for a brief period when pantaloons became the fashion in a few cities. These female trousers became the drawers of the Victorian age, which "Lady Chesterfield" called "those comfortable garments which we have borrowed from the other sex, and which all of us wear and none of us talk about."[2] Victorian women may have wanted to feel equal to men, but they hid it. Once the drawers were made in broad-cloth and exposed under a short skirt, all hell broke loose on those who dared to ape men openly.

The fashions that followed the French Revolution also seemed about to liberate women from their stays. Its ideas of nature and freedom loosed the female body. The Empire dress briefly stripped fashionable women nearly naked. Muslin and cambric were the fabrics—the style was borrowed from Greek and Roman dress. New England ladies ran even more risk of the local disease, consumption, when they wore the flimsy outfits. "Americans could hardly run into absurdities of these kinds," a contemporary complained, "were they to consult their own taste or interest. It is the authority of foreign manners which keeps us in subjection, and gives a kind of sanction to follies which are pardonable in Europe, but inexcusable in America."[3]

But the authority of France over the American lady-to-be was superseded by the authority of Queen Victoria. She became the model for most respectable American mothers. And fashion swung backwards to the incredible constriction of the old stays, now called corsets. Steel ribs and whalebone were pressed into service to make the cage of tight laces into a more rigid prison. Trailing skirts and petticoats up to the weight of fifteen pounds hung from the hips and dragged in the dirt. A woman could and did reduce her waist up to fifteen inches. In some finishing schools, young girls were made to sleep in their corsets. The corset itself pressed so intolerably into the lower ribs, pelvis, stomach, and back that some doctors accused it of causing nine-tenths of female diseases. In fact, many of women's complaints were the result of their follies. One woman doctor said that medical students called the livers of women in the dissecting-room the "corset-liver." These livers were so deeply indented where the ribs had been crowded against them that a wrist could easily be laid inside the groove.[4]

The strange fact about the Victorian corset was its long life. Perhaps it was no stranger than the long life of Victoria. It remained in fashion for nearly a century. While women progressed towards economic and legal and even some sexual freedom, they did not discard the corset. "Is it because," one dress reformer asked, "woman has a fancy for voluntary tortures, and believes that the more secret pain she inflicts upon herself, in the way of distorted ribs, squeezed liver, pinched feet, and fettered arms, the better it will be for her in the world to come?"[5] Or was the corset a private pleasure to some? Women, once used to tight lacing, felt ill without their stays, and one of them even confessed that a tight corset produced "delicious sensations, half pleasure, half pain."[6]

The pleasure of the corset, however, was outweighed tenfold by its discomfort. The real reason for its success was the American woman's search for equality. Like the American man, she did not want to be equal with her poor neighbour, but with a lady or even a queen. She wanted freedom to wear a tight corset and prove herself superior to the working woman who could not afford to wear one. The tighter the corset, the more ladylike the sufferer. She could not even exert herself without fainting. She had to be kept by her menfolk in relative idleness. She had given up the heretic liberty of French dress for the constraint of polite English society. The return of the American woman to the traditional corset parallelled the return of the American nation to its traditional values and stability after the dangerous period

of revolutionary ideas. It was curious that the dominance of romanticism over the female mind should have made ladies seek liberation
inside a whalebone frame. But how else could a healthy woman feel
suitably fragile?

The early feminists rightly thought dress important in women's
search for physical freedom. Until she could wear her clothes in
comfort, she could not work properly or even exercise her body. Her
long skirts and hoops prevented a woman from competing with men
for jobs, and the high cost of clothes made her more reliant on the
income of a man. "So long as she remains in her clothes-prison,"
Gerrit Smith declared, "she will be dependent and poor."[7] Current
fashion also prevented her from exercising her muscles and increased
the gap between male and female strength. This caused the delicate
nature of urban women—and the Victorian age was preoccupied with
the delicacy of women. Above all, female fashion, which emphasized
the breasts and the waist and the buttocks, made women conscious of
their sex and men conscious of their lust. Every part of a woman's
dress, Elizabeth Stanton complained, had been faithfully developed
"by some French courtesan to produce this effect." In fact, woman's
dress perfectly described woman's ambition. Tight waists, long trailing skirts, and paper sleeves deprived her of all freedom of breathing
and moving and taught her "the *poetry* of dependence."[8]

Elizabeth Smith Miller, the daughter of the wealthy landowner
and reformer Gerrit Smith, first put on the bloomer dress. It was
based on a mountain-climbing costume of the British actress, Fanny
Kemble, although patriotic Westerners claimed that "it originated in
the necessities of a new country, where women must hunt cows hid in
tall weeds and coarse grass on dewy or frosty mornings."[9] In fact,
Fanny Kemble had copied the Empire pantaloons, which had become
the standard costume of little girls. Also the example of Middle
Eastern and Chinese women, who wore trousers regularly, had become
well-known through the writings of such popular authors as Lydia
Maria Child. Baggy Turkish trousers under a short knee-length skirt,
topped by a blouse and a belted jacket, gave Elizabeth Miller freedom
to walk about and work in house and garden. She found the costume

clean, convenient, and modest. It was soon adopted by the braver feminists, including Elizabeth Stanton, Susan Anthony, Lucy Stone, the Grimké sisters, and the publisher of a temperance newspaper in Seneca Falls, Amelia Bloomer. Elizabeth Stanton even tried to discard the trousers and wear just a short skirt, but she was seventy years too far ahead of fashion. "She *cannot* do so," Susan Anthony wrote to Lucy Stone, "it will only be said the Bloomers have doffed their Pants the better to display their legs."[10]

The campaign for dress reform in the 1850's was a failure, as it was to be throughout the century. Although some thousands of women put on the bloomer costume, they soon took it off. Elizabeth Miller and Amelia Bloomer wore it for nearly a decade, but only because they both looked exquisite in it. The truth was that few women could get away with such a dress. Elizabeth Stanton looked fat in bloomers, Lucy Stone looked dumpy, and Susan Anthony impossibly angular. A friend of Mrs. Stanton's in Seneca Falls wrote:

Imagine her then in a full black satin frock cut off at the knee, with Turkish trowsers of the same material, her wrap a double broche shawl, and on her head the hideous great bonnet then in fashion. I have seen scarecrows that did credit to farmers' boys' ingenuity, but never one better calculated to scare all birds, beasts and human beings.[11]

All who wore the reform dress were greeted with derision in public. Susan Anthony, sensitive enough about her plainness and awkwardness, became the "scape-goat" of the movement, and the others quailed. Elizabeth Stanton broke first and laid aside the short dress. "We put it on for greater freedom," she wrote to Lucy Stone, "but what is physical freedom compared with mental bondage? By all means, have the new dress made long."[12]

The continual failure of dress reform showed that it was premature. As a would-be reformer said sadly in 1873, "The second nature of conventionality has always appeared stronger to women's minds than nature at first hand."[13] Education and opportunity to exercise were to give more freedom to women's dress. Vassar College refused to allow its pupils to wear corsets. Girls were admitted to gymnasiums. The fashion of hiking shortened the skirt, and the craze of bicycling divided it. If women clung to the long skirt until they had the vote, it was because they could not believe in their coming liberty. The success of feminism and the ferment of the progressive era and the First World War produced another excitable situation as in the era after the French Revolution. It was only then that women accepted freedom of their bodies within their dress and returned to near-nudity. Unfortunately, Charlotte Gilman's hope that more nakedness would make for more morality was not realized.

Harriot Hunt's other crusade for physical reform through exercise was successful earlier. With the spread of higher education for women, the gymnasium became a popular place for girl students. The best gymnasts at the Boston Normal School for Physical Education regularly proved to be women. At another physical training school in Massachusetts, girl pupils gained two and a half inches round the chest and five round the waist in a course of eight months. They all thought that they could not live without a corset when they began their training; by the end, they could not live within one.

The bicycle was the second great giver of freedom to women's bodies. It took them out of the cities and small towns and beyond the eyes of their parents; it gave equality to both sexes in travelling far and together; and it forced the skirt to divide and resemble a pair of flapping trousers. "Whin is a woman not a woman?" Mr. Dooley asked in disgust. "Whin she's on a bicycle, by dad."[14]

By shedding their clothing, women made themselves healthier. They no longer dragged around yards of street-spattered cloth in their trailing skirts and petticoats. The drudgery of keeping their clothes in order diminished and less time was spent at the wash-tub and the needle. When women put aside their long skirts and petticoats and whalebone corsets and took to hardening their bodies, they put on an equality with men in physical freedom. It had been so, as Amelia Bloomer pointed out, back in the Garden of Eden. When Adam and Eve sewed fig-leaves together, there was no evidence of any difference in the style of their aprons.[15]

The experience of the pioneer feminists with the reform of law and education and dress showed one thing, that American society in city and town was dominated by the lady—or the woman who thought herself a lady. Law reform was first successful, because it protected the dowry and inheritance of ladies. The first good colleges for women were set up to provide education for ladies; Elizabeth Stanton was trained to be a lady at Troy, while, even at Oberlin, Lucy Stone protested against the obedience and humility demanded from the female students. However passionately Stanton and Stone embraced the cause of all women later in their lives, they never forgot that they themselves were ladies; Lucy Stone, indeed, became too much of a lady from contact with polite Boston society.

The failure of dress reform in the 1850's further showed how dominant was the concept of what a lady could or could not do, even in feminist circles. The reform had only been sparked off because a leader of fashion, Fanny Kemble, had begun wearing trousers under a short skirt; it was pushed onwards by an heiress in Upper New York State, Elizabeth Smith Miller; its brief success in the Western towns depended on the fact that local ladies thought they were being smart. But the moment that women's trousers became derided as "bloomers" and made no progress with urban society, skirts dropped to the ground —and sometimes trailed in the dust—in every small town. A few committed feminists toiled on in their trousers; but they too yielded to fashion. What broke them down was that majority opinion thought their costumes ungenteel, if not obscene. When Elizabeth Stanton declared that wearing bloomers put her in "mental bondage," she was saying that she only felt free when she felt herself accepted as a lady.

The feminist insistence on being treated by men in a gentlemanly way was a good tactic for the time. The nineteenth century was a century in which society was dominated by successful men, who demanded that the women who influenced them must play the part of ladies. Perhaps male opinion and oppression forced the role of gentility on American women; but there is no question that, once most American women were given the chance of playing the lady, they enjoyed the part. To insist on being treated as a lady was, after all, the one way by which a woman might protect herself from barbarism and male violence.

The early feminists rightly saw how the role of the lady had enslaved American women. Yet they themselves only felt free when they were playing the part of ladies. They never came to terms with this anomaly, and thus feminism in the nineteenth century remained largely a middle-class and ladylike business. When shocking feminist leaders appeared, such as Frances Wright and Victoria Woodhull, they were soon excluded from the official ranks of feminism. In fact, most American ladies—by their very social position—opposed anything other than safe and mild reforms of a religious or educational nature. Elizabeth Stanton's more revolutionary ideas were bound to fail. Most ladies remained indifferent or hostile to any social change which might upset their hard-won status in society. Against every lady for reform in principle—whether extreme or mild—there was one bitterly opposed to reform, and ten who were generally opposed out of indifference and absorption in their established households.

The education and social position of the American lady has to be understood, in order to make sense of feminism in the increasingly class-conscious towns and cities of Victorian America. More important, too, than the education of the lady were the subconscious drives which made her act as she did, her fears and her sexual beliefs. The lady was the only woman who had the leisure and the position to be a reformer; those rare reformers who began as women usually ended as ladies. For the lady did not have to earn her living; her husband bought her the time for reform work; nearly all the leading feminists were married. Yet, at the same time, the lady was the biggest obstacle to reform, except when her secret fears were aroused.

The feminists sometimes played on the fears of the rich part of society and sometimes on the fears of the middle-class lady. Thus they won their early reforms, because a majority within the ruling group accepted certain remedies for their worries, even if these meant a change in convention. Behind the ladies stood the great mass of American women, the working women and wives of the farms and the slums, and the small group of professional women in the United States. Yet, in the society of early Victorian times, the lady was the dominant factor in reform and in the search for the freedoms of women.

PART FOUR

The American Lady

When the female descends the scale of moral excellence, instead of rising in it, as nature intended, it cannot with certainty be foretold where she will stop. Depravity in the sex is of a deeper and a darker cast, as the strongest acids are obtained from the sweetest base.

The Ladies' Magazine, 1828

IX

THE OSTRICH GAME

THE EUROPEAN LADY had not found a place in the colonies during the first hard years of the clearing of the soil. She had not flourished until the European city had crossed the Atlantic and the cotton plantation had grown up on the backs of slave labour. Then the concept of the lady had spread out from the cities into the settled small towns, until even the well-to-do farmer began to send his daughters East to learn to be ladies and to grow ashamed of life on the farm. Only a rich society where men work hard can afford ladies, and America afforded many.

The first ladies in America had been those that came from England with their husbands, working in government or the army. They had brought with them some ideas of Court fashion and behaviour in polite London society. Each American small city in the eighteenth century had boasted its little aristocracy, dominated by a clique of the wealthy and well-born. A group of rich merchants and land-owners had held power in most American seaports, although the small towns inland had been governed by the more democratic town meeting.

A small class of leisured ladies had led the social life in these cities. They had dressed up and called on each other and consumed the luxuries of Europe. They had developed special habits and accents to distinguish themselves from other Americans. Although Poor Richard had advised people to write with the learned and pronounce with the vulgar, the ladies had been proud of the refinement of their voices. Even if urban ladies were rare before the American Revolution, they were present and already set standards for the rest.

Although the ranks of the urban rich had been depleted when the Tories had fled, some ladies had remained. If Elizabeth Perkins Cabot had protested that there was no exclusiveness in Boston society after independence, she had gone on to say that she "should as soon have expected to see a *cow* in a drawing-room as a *Jacobin*."[1] In Boston and New York and Philadelphia, lines of caste and class were strongly marked by the 1830's. As a contemporary ladies' magazine said, "The lower class of women in the cities are profane, impudent, masculine, and even filthy in their persons."[2] Twenty years later, the idleness of the American lady was the concern of every traveller who came to the New World expecting to see nothing but thrifty and industrious republican women. The English feminist, Barbara Bodichon, found the lady class of America more utterly idle than anywhere outside the harems of the East. A huge population of young ladies cluttered up the boarding-houses, waiting to get married. These women reminded her of those she had seen in seraglios, "with this difference, the ladies of the East spend their days in adorning themselves to please one lord and master—the ladies of the West to please all the lords of creation. Which is the noblest ambition?" The answer was, for all ladies to work, "to save their souls from the devil, and to save their husbands, too, from that terrible treadmill, that 'everlasting grind' in which American men live."[3]

Yet the American lady in Victorian times was not as idle as she seemed. She usually had to run a large and complicated household, in a land of few good servants. Although her home in a city or a town meant that she could buy the necessaries of life without having to make them, she still had to organize the cooking and washing and cleaning. Irish maids became the stand-by and curse of every would-be lady. Even the feminists displayed signs of racial prejudice against their sex when confronted with raw Irish girls to train. Eliza-

beth Stanton found that she had no time for the woman's cause with
two babies and two "daughters of Erin" to teach.

In the intervals between maids—and these were frequent because
of the temptations of factories or marriage—the lady had to do her
own work. The amount of food served daily in the American home
was immense; as Chastellux had once noted, the whole day passed in
heaping indigestions on one another. The pretended idleness of the
Victorian lady was a sop to fashion. She often had to toil desperately behind the scenes in order to seem to be doing nothing in front
of them. Mrs. Trollope noticed how almost all the wives and daughters of the opulent performed in their families "the sordid offices of
household drudgery." Even in the slave states, the highest of the
planters' wives occupied herself in her household concerns.

The Southern lady had to cope with a world of public opinion and
daily fact even more separate than the Northern lady. The fact of
slavery gave a small planter class of men and women some leisure,
which they devoted to denying the fact of slavery. Once the cotton
gin had made the cotton crop and the plantation system the most
profitable part of the Southern economy, the South had to justify
its peculiar institution. To the Virginian version of the English
squire was added the myth of *Ivanhoe*. Mark Twain held Walter
Scott to be one of the chief causes of the Civil War; in fact, his main
effect was to give emotional release to isolated people on plantations.
The shortest way to a day-dream was through the Waverley novels.
Scott also fostered the cult of the lady. By definition, Southern ladies
had to become more pure and virtuous, as the slaves that made them
possible bred and multiplied. The one guaranteed the other. The lady
has to find someone to do her work.

Of course, the price of being a Southern lady was high. She had to
be the organizer of a household of hundreds of people. If she was
merciful by nature, her nursing of the sick and the wounded never
ceased. Although Fanny Kemble went to her husband's plantation in
Georgia with anti-slavery principles clearly in her mind, her Journal
also showed the continual worry and horror and difficulties that faced
the mistress of slaves. If no lady endured any pain to compare with

the child-bearing and field work and whipping forced on Negro women, her prized delicacy gave her pain enough. "I used to pity the slaves," Fanny Kemble wrote, "and I do pity them with all my soul; but oh dear! oh dear! their case is a bed of roses to that of their owners."[4] Mary Chesnut, also a planter's wife, was more outspoken: "Any lady is ready to tell you who is the father of all the mulatto children in everybody's household but her own. Those, she seems to think, drop from the clouds."

Yet in the same way as the poor whites accepted the leadership of the plantation owners in the vague dream of owning a plantation themselves one fine day, so the ladies on the plantations accepted their men's definition of themselves. It was gratifying for them to be flattered, coddled, and assured of their superiority. Constant repetition seemed like the truth. In a society where black women were held inferior, white women were naturally held superior; white men, who knew both well, held a middle position as human beings. If Southern men deprived wealthy Southern women of any pretence of legal or economic equality, yet there was no pretence of equality between the Southern men. The lady was obviously less bound than the male slave.

With all the attention and gallantry, the shadow of female superiority often seemed more real than the fact of male dominance. The hierarchy of status had to be preserved, or the whole society of unequals might collapse in a riot of levelling. Good manners towards women were more than a convention; they were proof of the actual delicacy and purity of the Southern lady. Even the bitter Mary Chesnut did not dare to have an affair of her own to revenge herself on her husband, nor did she complain in public. She merely wrote in her diary: "Bad books are not allowed house room . . . but bad women, if they are not white and serve in a menial capacity, may swarm the house unmolested. The ostrich game is thought a Christian act."[5]

The curious fact about the Victorian lady was that her husband was prepared to work himself almost to death to support her. It was a point of pride to him that his womenfolk should not have to work outside the home, even if they wanted to work. Status in society depended on idle women. In the immigrant and fluid society of North and West, this proof of social position was important for the rising man. His wish to keep his women in his home was partly a relic of rural morality, where a man expected his wife never to leave his farm; but it was also an imitation of European society, where the rich man was judged by the uselessness of his dependent women.

Prosperity, as Veblen pointed out, required respectable women to be freed from any taint of utility. They had to make more of a show of leisure than men of the same social class. A lady's sphere was in the household, which she should "beautify," and of which she should be the "chief ornament." The male head of the household was not spoken of as its ornament.

Increasing American riches meant an increase in the class of American ladies. The Victorian lady stands halfway between the farm wife, with her appalling drudgery, and the modern housewife, with her working day of a few hours. The Victorian lady was still close enough to the farm to insist on doing a great deal of her own cooking, even when she had servants. "Our women are cooking themselves to death," a mid-Victorian complained, "and cooking the nation into a materialism worse than death."[6] Packaged food, brand goods, laundries, and washing-machines have lifted the load of both cooking and housework from the modern housewife. In its place, she still has the dissatisfaction of a queen whose subjects give her no trouble. The home is too easy to rule now. It takes up too little time. Its running gives cheap satisfaction when all its services can be easily bought outside. The wife remains on her throne there, dominant in her petty kingdom, and aware that she is no longer necessary except as the mother of children.

X

THE MAKING OF THE LADY

"EVERY AMERICAN WOMAN," a lady's lecturer declared in 1841, "has reason to thank God every day of her life, that she was born in this happy country. She cannot read of any portion or period of the world, without becoming more and more convinced, that America is the Paradise of women." This fortunate state of affairs had been brought about by the combination of "physical comfort and abundance with the subjection of society to the restraints of morality and religion." Yet, in this heaven for women, who were treated as ladies in the settled East, the lecturer struck one warning note. "The consideration with which women are treated in this country is carried to excess." A woman "suffers for it in the end, by the feebleness, effeminacy, helplessness and bad health which it induces."[1]

The courtesy of the American man to all white women in North and South and West amazed early travellers. It seemed that American democracy made every woman expect the rights of the lady. "No *cavaliere servente* of a lady of fashion," Frances Wright declared, "no sighing lover, who has just penned a sonnet to his 'mistress's eyebrow,' ever rendered more delicate attentions to the idol of his fancy than . . . an American farmer or mechanic, not to say gentleman, to the companion of his life."[2] Everywhere they went, curious European ladies met with exquisite manners on the part of American men. Only Harriet Martineau took this amiss. The fact that women had the best place in stage-coaches and were always seated while men stood only gave them indulgence as a substitute for justice. The greater the chivalry of men, the less possible it was for a woman to get her true rights. As Havelock Ellis was to say later, chivalry was an ideal by which a woman was treated as a cross between an angel and an idiot.

Yet it was the women who exacted this deference from the men. A lady is, after all, merely a woman who thinks herself a lady, and expects recognition as such. The American lady, fresh off the farm, did not feel easy in her new position. She had to assert her right to it. A British traveller in 1833 noted that the American woman was "always conscious of the full extent of her claims to preference and admiration," and was never satisfied until she felt them to be acknowledged. There were no female republicans, for no lady would admit her equality with men. Six years later, Francis Grund found that in high society in the cities the women talked not only much more, but also much louder, than the men, who always approached women with "the most indubitable consciousness of their own inferiority."[3]

The supremacy of the urban lady in social life was a curious phenomenon to those who were used to the leadership of men in Europe. It was partly because the American lady had the leisure to cultivate her mind while her man worked; partly because the drawing-room was held to be her province; partly because she was a new and rare being in the civilization that had just been hacked out from the wilderness; and partly because of the early obedience to his mother instilled in the American child.

Yet the real reason for the lady's supremacy was that men and women hardly ever mixed in American social life. The lady was excluded from the saloon and the club and the sporting match, even in the countryside. Men and women usually took their pleasures apart. A gay English captain in the 1840's found only nine women in a crowd of thousands at a Massachusetts fair; when he heard music, he found four men solemnly dancing a reel. Charles Dickens found no social amusements when he reached New York. At night there were only the evening service or lecture for ladies, and the counting-house, the store, and the bar-room for gentlemen. When a group of men did meet with their ladies, they were unused to polite conversation. To cover this gap in communication, they were excessively polite and allowed the women to talk. Those who learn to play apart find it difficult to talk together.

The fact that a lady was kept in the home so much and was excluded from male pleasures gave her a determination to exact the homage that was her due. If she was made to stay in the house, at least she could make her men worship her there. Although ladies' guides told her that she should show "the consciousness of dependence," she made her husband pay for taking away her freedom. The price for giving up the liberty of girlhood was to insist upon the respect due to the wife. The fact that she was thought "inferior to man, but near to angels," made her a Lucifer when a man tried to treat her as anything but a lady.

The early feminists, naturally, abhorred the Lady, although nearly all of them thought themselves ladies. Although they agreed that it was "not the tyranny, but the chivalry of men that we American women have to fear," they did not forego the courtesies of social life. When women acquired legal and political equality with men, they did not leave the men free to treat them as equal beings. The cult of acting the lady never liberated the American man from the cult of acting the gentleman. In the same way as the lessening functions of the home hardly diminished the adoration of the woman inside it, so the increasing equality of men and women hardly affected the deference paid to the lady. American women in the nineteenth century were often reproached for their bad manners to men; but these, at least, could be excused as the small revenges of the weaker vessels, who were preserving their self-respect by acting the lady. With equality, however, their manners did not improve. Respect for the woman as lady continued to be a manly duty; respect for the man as gentleman, a female concession. Customs lag for generations behind the changing culture which evolves them.

The American lady was not born, but bred. Because the finished product was meant to be so pure and delicate, especial care was taken in the training of girl children. Usually, the permissiveness of American parents amazed visitors, used to the stern disciplines of Europe. Only in the New World could the most popular woman's magazine, *Godey's Lady's Book,* carry on a continual campaign for "The Rights of Children." The freedom of American children and their equality with their parents seemed a living proof of the land of liberty for all. "The instincts of children," Elizabeth Stanton asserted, "are quite as often right as the perverted reason of Parents and Teachers."⁴ Families seemed determined that the children should be blessed by the promise of America, even if the adults had not been so. If one generation had been slaves to the clearing of the soil, the next should be free to enjoy the fruits of the earth. Only in the making of the urban lady were American mothers as strict as any dowager in the Old World. For the Eastern city was particularly planted by Europe.

The biological theory behind the training of the lady was that girls were more emotional than boys, and therefore more in need of control. The seat of a woman's reason lay in her womb, even though, by nature, she was more pure than the male. In the female, "the uterus was an animal inside an animal." While sinful man was controlled by his brain, delicate woman was controlled by her reproductive organs. Thus she had always to restrain herself, from cradle to grave. For her very innocence made her easily corrupted. "Women often show a strange facility of debasement and moral abandonment, when they have once given way consentingly to wrong. Men go down by a descent—*facilis descensus*—women, by a precipitation."⁵

The young lady was segregated early from boys. To keep back the foul fiend, she was not allowed to drink tea or coffee or other stimulating drinks. The theatre, music, and dancing—except with other young ladies—were forbidden for fear of exciting the tender passions. With puberty, the restrictions grew. Habits contracted at this age were thought to be very powerful and intimately connected with future health or disgrace. Young girls should not be allowed to lie on soft beds or to sit on soft chairs or to lean against anything to rest their muscles. Exercise was even necessary for young women, "to prevent attachment to fanciful objects, as well as the tendency to dwell on those subjects which it is desirable to avoid."

Chilly clothes and cold baths diminished "the sensibility which must otherwise do mischief." No girl should be allowed to sit with her legs crossed or to ride upon a stick or a see-saw. The reading of novels was sure "to falsify the judgement of the young by the most absurd exaggerations, to render their duties distasteful, and even to predispose to disease." A young lady should always sleep alone and be kept from the intimacy of boarding schools, which were "a hot-bed of vice to all who have reached puberty." Too much education at that age would weaken an already weakened constitution.[6]

The young lady should be taught early how to avoid seduction, although not about the workings of her own body. By self-control and corsets, she must keep her nature back. If she showed any signs of solitary vice, she had to be supervised night and day. For, if her depravity were not arrested, she would reach "the grave, the mad-house, or, worse yet, the brothel."[7] Equally well, too much chastity might make her morbid. "If marriage be not permitted to terminate this state, injury fatal to life may be its consequence."[8] Early marriage was necessary to the health of both sexes. Then, in their turn, young ladies could rear young ladies—"Parents are not only the agents but also the models for their children."[9]

Such was the prescribed pattern for the early Victorian lady. Of course, as with the pattern for the Puritan girl, it was an ideal. But even so, the ideal was enforced in many strict homes, in order that the daughters might reflect the virtue of their parents. This long training produced a being of some price, and it cost any buyer a great deal of money. The expense of producing the Victorian lady is the only cause besides prolonged economic depression that has ever stopped most American women from marrying early. The Victorian age was full of complaints about late marriages and bachelors too selfish to support wives. The Eastern urban spinster was the by-product of the lady, who had to be kept as luxuriously as she had been brought up. An acute modern observer has plotted the connection between Victorian marriage and the "paraphernalia of gentility" in England, and has concluded that late marriage and fewer children were forced on the times by the expenses of an acceptable standard of living in the cities.[10]

The feminists campaigned with increasing success against the education of the lady. The American desire for self-improvement was, basically, a stronger force than the desire to imitate European fashion. Elizabeth Stanton's most popular lyceum lecture was one in which she praised an equal education and training for both sexes. The young girl should never try to become the ideal lady.

With iron shoes, steel ribbed corsets, hoops, trails, high heels, chignons, paniers, limping gait, feeble muscles, with her cultivated fears of everything seen and unseen, of snakes and spiders, mice and millers, curs and caterpillars, dogs and drunken men, fire crackers and cannon, thunder and lightning, ghosts and gentlemen, women die ten thousand deaths, when if educated to be brave and self-dependent they would die but one. This sheer affectation of fear and feebleness men too have become so depraved in their tastes as to admire.[11]

The answer was equal education and a life for women outside the home.

The success of girl students at the new colleges open to women, at Oberlin and Mount Holyoke and Michigan and Antioch and Vassar, and their obvious equality with men in health and intellect, strained the theory of the lady to its breaking point. For if women could be as healthy and clever as men, where was the emotional and delicate lady? In 1874 Dr. Edward Clarke fired the last popular blast against the equal education of the sexes. He blamed the thousand ills of the American middle-class woman on her college education. By forcing their brains in puberty, they had used up blood which was needed for menstruation. The young lady rested and remained healthy, while the girl student developed anemia and nervous diseases from overstrain. In fact, Dr. Clarke had once been fortunate enough to make a medical examination of a harem. He praised the inmates for "their well-developed forms, their brown skins, rich with the blood and sun of the East, and their unintelligent, sensuous faces." All they needed was a smattering of Western liberty and intellect to make them perfect ladies.[12]

The feminists quoted statistics in vain against Dr. Clarke's "dreadful little book." The idea of the lady died hard. Six years later, *Popular Science Monthly* still carried an article saying that the cranium of a woman was smaller than that of a man, and that the weight of the average female brain was six ounces less than that of the male. Education for women in other than the graces of the lady resulted in "symptoms of nervousness, hysteria, hypochondriasis, and insanity . . . emaciation and other diseases, the offspring of an exhausted constitution." Women should only be educated to become mothers, and not to work outside the home.[13]

The similarity of many Victorian beliefs about the lady to the thesis of some influential Neo-Freudians, that all the true happiness of women lies in motherhood and home-making, needs no comment. More emphasis on permissive child-rearing and sexual satisfaction within marriage has not attacked the Victorian idols of woman as the goddess of her hearth and her children. The fact that most American women choose to be influenced by Freud rather than Havelock Ellis merely shows how deeply involved they are with the Victorian past. Ellis could have provided them with a justification for the single, childless woman, living as she wished. Neo-Freudianism blesses what the dominant folkway wishes to believe, that a woman is happiest as a mother within her own house. Only the rising influence of feminism and higher education disturbs the peace around the family barbecue as it once disturbed the Victorian lady from her idle fireside.

For the concept of the lady changed with the success of the early feminists in education. Exercise and diet became fashionable. The very shape of the ideal lady altered, from a woman fat in hip and breast to a woman lean in both. Fresh air came to the rescue of those who had had to stay indoors to keep up their pallor. Fresh food stripped the fat from those who lived "in the zone of perpetual pie and doughnuts." Willy-nilly, the lady followed where the emancipated woman led.

The last sad trickles of the education of the Victorian lady reached the small towns of America. When the middle-class girl in the city had been constricted, the small-town girl had been freed. Country and farm life were too near the new Western towns to allow for the education of ladies. They could not be kept from seeing the facts of human and animal nature all around them. It was not until a second and third generation of girls had been brought up in the same small town that ladies became the curse of Western upbringing. For when, by 1900, the education of the city girl was becoming more healthy and relaxed, the morbid Victorian emphasis on purity came to roost in the settled small town of the Bible Belt. It was in Purity Congresses and books on "Perfect Girlhood" published in Marietta, Ohio, that the strict rules on female education were now repeated. Girls should be made to sleep with their hands outside the bedclothes, should never sit on their feet, and should not even sleep at another girl's house, for fear of sin and the mental collapse that was sure to follow.

The small town is heir to the morality of the city; but usually a generation too late. If emigration back to the city takes place, urban people can suddenly be confronted with a caricature of their own grandmothers' beliefs. The very distance of city from country makes the imitation, practiced in the small town, a distortion. The country lady had perhaps the greatest load to bear, for her daily life bore no relation to her pretensions.

Yet children are wise in the ways of their world, especially when there is a gap between profession and practice. The huge difference between the excessive emphasis on purity and the facts of life in a country town were described in many reminiscences. Yet few children seemed to suffer from this discrepancy. Occasionally, some Western children met with the rigorous supervision needed to train a lady. But these cases were rare, and usually found in large Western cities. A Chicago girl, born in a wealthy family in 1871, recorded that sex had not been part of her education, and that she wished that it had been. "Just a hint of such a thing would have been vastly more useful to me than trips with Caesar into Gaul." But she was a rarity, and already part of the new aristocracy of the West.[14]

In the slums and on the farms, ladies were hardly ever found. Space was too short, dirt was too near, the example of the beast in man and woman and animal too close. The lady is the product of the refined society of the city or of the settled town or of the plantation. The fact that there were and are so many self-styled ladies in America is a tribute to the phenomenal growth of the American city and suburb rather than to the natural delicacy of the American woman.

XI

࿐

THE UNMENTIONABLE
FEARS

"FEAR PERHAPS, has injured the health of the ladies," a marriage guide warned in 1808, "more frequently than any of the passions." Ladies should be taught courage, for "terrible apprehensions" have brought about more deaths "than parturition itself." To cowardly women, "the very possibility of sickness and death, is a continual source of the most destructive terror, so that through fear of death, they are all their life-time subject to bondage."[1]

The irrational fears of women in the nineteenth century were based on the rational knowledge of the uselessness of contemporary medicine. The fanaticism with which women clutched at each new medical or quack remedy showed the extent of their fears. Homeopathy, hydropathy, spiritualism, mesmerism, galvanism, vegetable and mineral cures, all had their devotees. If the Bible, the novel, and women's magazines were the first reading of this religious and sentimental age, marriage and medical manuals were nearly as popular. It is ridiculous to suppose that any American woman who could read and get hold of books was ignorant of her physiology in the nineteenth century. If public prudery was the fashion, private self-education was the rule.

There were volumes to satisfy the curiosity of the American woman, who knew that the proper study of mankind began with herself. De Tocqueville was correct when he noticed the precocious knowledge on all subjects of the young American girl, who was "remarkable rather for purity of manners than for chastity of mind."

The marriage manuals fed on feminine modesty as well as the desire for self-improvement. As *The Young Married Lady's Private Medical Guide* stressed, a woman had to know

the physiology of her own private organs . . . to judge of her *own* diseases, without offending the most delicate and sensitive feelings of woman's nature, by obliging her to consult another regarding complaints of so delicate a nature, at first trifling and insidious, but which, when neglected, result in blasted hopes, ruined health, infinite suffering, and a premature grave.[2]

It was unthinkable for an American woman to consult a male doctor about certain diseases in Victorian times, and many women would not trust a female doctor, where available. The ill woman had to doctor herself. Some American medical men were even proud of this state of affairs and praised women who preferred to suffer danger and pain rather than waive their scruples of delicacy. It was "evidence of a fine morality" in American society.[3]

The early medical guides were horrific in their remedies. To bleed, to blister, and to purge was the cure for all female ills, including fear of death. Given these alternatives, many women shunned doctors altogether. There were only two effective medicines at the time, Peruvian bark or quinine and soporifics such as opium or morphia, which could free women from pain. The other twenty normal remedies only increased discomfort, from calomel and aloes taken internally to lancets and leeches applied externally.

The malevolence of early American medicine, which seemed to be designed to purify the soul through torture of the body, explained the enthusiasm which greeted the early water and diet cures. Particularly in child-birth, which had meant a period of long confinement and morbidity, the use of fresh air and water and food brought an incredible release. Harriet Robinson, a one-time mill-girl, turned feminist, had her third child with the plentiful use of cold water. "I was never so well," she wrote in her diary, "nor so free from sick days and nights as at this time, no long wearisome confinement, no fever, no medicine, not even *castor oil,* all to be attributed to the free and faithful use of *Cold Water.*"[4]

Although there were no antibiotics to help in serious diseases such as puerperal fever, these modern ideas on child-bearing did give many women great relief in early Victorian times. When even the stoical Queen of England received ether during the birth of one of her many children, ease during woman's greatest labour became respectable over the objections of those clergymen who quoted the Bible to prove that women were fated to bring forth in sorrow. Indeed, after the huge interest in physiological lectures during the reform wave of the 1830's, women could no longer be kept in ignorance of the workings of their own bodies.

The folk beliefs of pregnancy needed to be swept away. They had caused much fear and pain. It was thought that the imagination of the mother could influence the child in her womb, although anatomy had already proved that the embryo had its own distinct nerves and circulation. General myth also ran that the mother should eat for two during pregnancy; she should not take exercise; she should not sleep with her husband; she should be bled and purged frequently to ease her plethoric condition; she should wear tight corsets to support the child; and she should lie in for months after the birth of her baby. If a woman came out of child-birth in a healthy condition, her own constitution deserved praise, not the folkways. Even then, she had every chance of conceiving another child at once, since popular myth held that a woman was sterile during the nursing period, and since her husband could not be denied after the long chastity of pregnancy. Some women insisted on remaining chaste through lactation as well, and were surprised that their husbands went to prostitutes during these years. It was no wonder that city women suffered more with the problems of child-birth than countrywomen, who could not leave their farm work long enough to indulge in the errors of the folk mind.

The most popular medical book of its time was written by a physiological lecturer and doctor, Frederick Hollick. More than any other work, it freed the Victorian woman of her darkest fears. Hollick's *The Matron's Manual of Midwifery, and The Diseases of Women during Pregnancy and in Child Bed* went into forty-seven editions in the seven years before 1850. It was a serious, competent, and factual book. It was devoted to dispelling "the wondering ignorance" and "morbid imagination" of women who believed in the silly folkways of child-bearing. It advised against bleeding, blistering, and purging—"*Try almost anything and everything first.*" It recommended regular baths, exercise, and a light diet, including salads. It chose as antiseptics, warm soap-suds, Peruvian bark in water, and weak chloride of lime. Hollick even came out against the most popular fallacy of the time, that intercourse during pregnancy led to the premature birth of monsters. "In some persons miscarriage is caused by *too eager* gratification of certain desires, but in others it may arise *from the opposite cause.*"

Hollick's manual spoke up for everything then known which could release a woman from fear and pain in child-birth. He supported the use of ether during operations; to him, no suffering was ordained by God if men could prevent it. He even went so far as to recommend premature delivery, "when needed to preserve life, and to escape great suffering and danger." He recommended every young woman to be medically examined before marriage, so that, if she was incapable of bearing children, means of avoiding conception could be provided. "When I know that the *life,* or *life-long health,* of a female, depends on her not becoming pregnant, I consider it my duty to put such means at her disposal, if she desires it."[5]

Then, as now, the popularity of marriage manuals was partly because they provided some knowledge of contraception. The high birthrate in America before the Civil War has misled many people into thinking that American women *wanted* many children. Every marriage manual, and the evidence of nearly every doctor, denied this. Every woman's physician repeated endless cases of women begging him for methods to stop having children. Most of the methods peddled by the doctors were worse than useless; but the logic of humanitarianism and eugenics and the need to prevent abortion was soon brought to bear in favour of birth-control.

Birth-control became more and more necessary as the hygienic practices of the nineteenth century lowered the rate of infant mortality in the small towns and cities. "Churchyard luck" came less and less to help poor fathers, who felt morally bound to provide their wives and children with an urban and middle-class standard of living. Richer Americans wanted fewer and better children. In the first half of the nineteenth century, four in five children were calculated to die before the age of five years. What if four in five now survived?

Robert Dale Owen's *Moral Physiology* was the first guide to birth-control to be published in America. It appeared in 1831. Its frontispiece showed a young woman abandoning her baby at the Foundling Hospital in Paris; the caption read: "Alas! that it should ever have been born." Owen denied the idea that a woman who had been taught to avoid the fruits of sin would immediately become a sinner. If fear of conception was the only safeguard of chastity, the virtue of women was worth nothing. "Vice is never the offspring of just knowledge." Letters reached Owen which testified to the release from fear that his ineffective methods seemed to have brought to some husbands. One young father called the book the most useful one since Tom Paine's *Common Sense;* after reading it, he had become "a free agent, and, in a degree, the arbiter" of his own destiny.[6]

Moral Physiology was shortly followed by Charles Knowlton's *Fruits of Philosophy*. It advocated the first moderately effective female contraceptive, a sponge dipped in vinegar or alum, and douching. Both of these books were based on the pioneer attempts of Francis Place in England to provide a check on population and to find a way out from the starvation predicted by Malthus for most of the world. The books were essentially *moral* efforts to give men and women freedom of choice over the number of children which they desired. Chastity was not a method of contraception for Owen—he defined the word as his father had done, "sexual intercourse *with* affection." As the feminist John Stuart Mill declared, "Little advance can be expected in *morality* until the producing of large families is regarded in the same way as drunkenness or any other physical excess."[7] It was time to end what the first Lord Birkenhead defined as the male view of a mother—a mere "conduit pipe" whose misfortunes were comic or negligible.

Unfortunately, early contraceptive practices were all inadequate, unless husbands and wives showed great care and restraint. This restraint was not found outside small educated groups in some towns and cities. Many editions of *Moral Physiology* and the *Fruits of Philosophy* were produced by various inventors of contraceptives, who added advertisements for their own devices at the back of the book. The most effective method advocated by Owen was *coitus interruptus,* which he claimed had reduced the French population due to the chivalry of Frenchmen. But this method left the choice to the man, not to the woman, who could only use Knowlton's sponge. Electric shocks, powders, pills, and other devices were claimed to cause temporary sterility in women; but these were quack remedies. None of the contraceptive devices for American women in the nineteenth century could remove her fear of having another child, although a nascent industry in devices made from vulcanized rubber grew up after the Civil War.

Yet, as the death-rate fell in America, so the birth-rate fell. Outside the slums and the farms of the nation, American women had fewer children. Various causes have been given to this, declining fertility, ill-health caused by corsets, industrialism, loss of function, moral pressure on husbands, growing wealth, every reason under the skin except the proper one. A woman in marriage had one natural method of contraception in her power, the rhythm method. Even the Roman Catholic Church was to endorse this method. Provided that the woman could control her own and her husband's desires, she had a good chance of escaping conception.

It has been assumed that, from colonial times, women knew when they were most fertile. Therefore, they *chose* to have many children. In fact, they did not. Until the 1840's, most doctors worked on the analogy of animals and thought that women were most fertile near their menstruation. "Conception," as a widely read London doctor declared in 1842, "generally takes place a day or two after the last menstrual period."[8] It was not until the publication of an article in 1849 by a London professor that this theory was exploded.

Professor Oldham, the author of the article, had examined the wives of seamen, whose going to sea could reasonably date the conception of their children. He found out, after careful research, that women had conceived eight, ten, twelve, fourteen, sixteen, and even twenty-one days after their menstruation, but not immediately afterwards. He finally made clear that the believed "safe period" for women was, in fact, the time when they were most fertile.[9] Once his conclusions had been widely printed in medical textbooks of the 1850's, middle-class women with control over themselves and their husbands could begin to limit the number of their children. Sexual freedom of the body had begun for American women.

The restraint on sexuality in the nineteenth century, which was necessary to limit the number of children, imposed severe strains on the woman of leisure. The Puritan emphasis that all flesh was sinful, and female flesh more so (except in marriage), changed to the Victorian emphasis that a woman's body was pure, though weak, and only a man's body wicked. The excessive sentimentality and longing for purity of many Victorian ladies was often a reaction from making the sexual act a rare and abnormal thing in their married life. In fact, the morbid fear of the consequences of loving men led to the passionate, if discreet, relationships among many Victorian women. To give a heart to a man meant children and pain and sin. To give a heart to a woman meant purity and freedom and understanding.

Although most women were hardly the passive and enduring sex partners that Victorian myth made them out to be, men were told that they should not have intercourse more than once a month, or at the most twice. Each male orgasm was said to cause the loss of the equivalent of eight ounces of the "best human blood." Intercourse was strictly for the purpose of creating children. Indulgence meant warped babies and premature graves. For the sake of himself and the woman and the race, a man must control himself.[10]

The infrequency of intercourse allowed inside a respectable marriage did much to push men to seek satisfaction outside. Women were to turn bitterly on men for the hypocrisy of the double standard, which asked them to be chaste while their husbands visited prostitutes. But that standard had been erected by the whole of Victorian society, which insisted that a man could not marry until he could support a wife in middle-class comfort, and could not sleep often with his wife even when he was married. A censorious society puts up its own double standard, which is the distance between public opinion and human weakness. The young Victorian male had to be chaste or visit prostitutes. The middle-aged Victorian husband was often forced by moral pressure to be chaste, and return to the habits of his youth. It was not until the American wife could feel free to be as available as the American whore that the double standard was to topple.

Prostitution in America had been common in all the colonies except New England. Young Indian and Negro girls had had little legal protection. Later, immigrant girls found themselves in a similar position in the slums of the new cities. Jobs were hard to find for unskilled labour; wages were too low to live on. A servant girl who lost her place in the cities had few alternatives to the streets. Until there were enough jobs at a decent wage, whores were plentiful in America, even though the life was short because of rampant venereal diseases and inadequate mercury remedies. "The higher sense of mankind," Emily Blackwell commented bitterly, "says that the family is the essential unit of the state. Our practice says that the family plus prostitution is the essential unit."[11]

It was the general belief of reformers of "the social evil" that "no woman leads a life of shame through choice."[12] She could not, for woman, by definition, was pure. Hard times made the prostitute. This was obviously untrue of the women who followed the gold miners in the West; but in the East the Victorian mind preferred to think that men were to blame for "the social evil." They first ruined a girl, and then they paid her. If there were no patrons of prostitutes, there would be no prostitutes.

Men had, indeed, created the vicious economic situation which created most of the whores in the slums. And they were to blame for a worse crime in the eyes of the feminists. Not only did they sin outside the home, but they brought the diseases of sin inside the home, to infect their wives and unborn children. Fear of syphilis was a driving force at the back of feminism all through the nineteenth century, once the first statistics of prostitution had been published in the 1830's. Although irresponsible estimates claimed that one in two Americans was tainted by the disease through sin or heredity, one in ten was a fair estimate by the end of the century. The somewhat morbid concentration of the Victorian churches and women on purity was as reasonable as the Puritan emphasis on moral law. Neither campaign meant to chase the taint of sex from the American home and marriage; each meant to protect that home and marriage. The emphasis of both was excessive only because the horror of venereal disease or the wilderness provoked an extreme reaction.

In the same way, the Southern woman's fear of rape at the hands of the Negro and the Western woman's at the hands of the Indian produced a horrible vengeance on these peoples by Southern and Western men, worse than the Puritan vengeance on witches. Lynching and Indian massacre were produced by the irrational frenzy of men who feared the worst for their women. No Western wife captured by Indians could admit to being outraged. Therefore, the presumption was that she had been. Equally, no Southern women could admit to contact with a Negro man. Thus, once a Negro man was seen talking familiarly with a Southern woman, he had practically admitted his lust. With the Victorian prudery of women, and in the silence demanded by polite society, the fears of the men ran riot. Thousands of Indians and Negroes were brutally murdered as a sacrifice to the mere suspicions bred by the modesty of the American woman, and to the fear that "savage" men might prove more potent than "civilized" lovers.

The advance of medical science, psychology, and technology was to free women from many of their unmentionable fears. Salvarsan and antibiotics and cheap contraceptives were to diminish their horror of venereal disease and child-bearing. And the seamy confessional of the

psychologist's couch—even more satisfactory than the hysterical testimony of the revival meeting—was to compensate for the silence of
the Victorian lady. Social pressure was to change from approval of
those who told nothing to approval of those who told all. And with
this change in public opinion, the American woman would change
the outlets which she would choose to take in her search for the
freedom of her body.

When the feminists wanted to put an end to the double standard,
they did not seek equality with men in lechery. They wanted men to
imitate the restraint of Victorian wives. The relaxed sexuality of
modern women inside marriage would have seemed to them adultery
within wedlock. On the basis of the fears of the lady and of the
mother, the feminists attacked prostitution in the large cities and had
laws passed against the evil. And they could always apply moral
pressure on men, who felt that their wives were superior and more
ethical because they did not go to brothels.

If the lady patronized movements for moral reform, because she
had the time to brood over the injustice of her sexual position and
to seek for equality between the sexes in marriage, the working or
professional woman had another priority. She was concerned with
feeding herself, because she did not have a husband or relative who
could support her, or because she was desperate for independence.
Moral reform was the luxury of the lady of leisure; economic progress was the necessity of the woman who had to earn her bread.

PART FIVE

Working Women

We can never expect to prove anything upon such a point. It is a difference of opinion which does not admit of proof. We each begin, probably, with a little bias towards our own sex, and upon that bias build every circumstance in favour of it which has occurred within our own circle.
JANE AUSTEN, in *Persuasion*

XII

❦

THE FREEDOM OF
THE FACTORY

WHEN THE HOME had been the scene of all woman's work, the opportunity of working in a factory had seemed like freedom. Hard work for twelve hours a day, or more, had been normal for most American women in the eighteenth century. Their tasks had been heavy and endless and unpaid. The early factory system meant a semi-skilled and repetitive job, which demanded little physical exertion. Although the working day could be thirteen hours long, no girl had to operate many machines, and she could rest at intervals. It was the shorter working day and the system of piece-work that drove later working girls to unremitting labour. The refinements of grinding greater output out of the system took time to develop.

At the beginning of the American industrial revolution, factories were thought to be a blessing to women and children. Men were needed at the more arduous task of tilling the soil; it was wrong to waste their labour in factories. But once the machine had taken the place of muscle, women and children could operate the power looms and spinning jenneys. Weaving and spinning had traditionally been household tasks. All that the machine did was to move the women and children from the home into a large shed. And now they were paid wages, which could help them and their husbands. Sloth, moreover, was held to be the chief evil of the poor. Factories would rescue village women "doomed to idleness and its inseparable attendants, vice and guilt."[1]

The first American factories were set up near the source of waterpower in small rural towns in Massachusetts. They hardly changed the customs around their sites, which remained patriarchal and Puritan. They were staffed by farm girls and seamen's daughters, and they were surrounded by countryside. Although the memoirs of the Lowell mill-girls have spread gilt over early factory conditions, the girls there did feel freed from the home. Outside the power of the overseer, they became their own mistresses for the first time in their lives. Although they worked thirteen hours a day, they did have their few evening hours and Sundays free from the commands of a father or mother or brother. And if some of them worked "to secure the means of education for some *male* member of the family," many single women kept their low wages. A Lowell mill-girl once described the feeling that earnings gave to the unmarried women of the time. "They could earn money and spend it as they pleased. They could gratify their tastes and desires without restraint and without rendering an account to anybody. At last they had found a place in the universe, and were no longer obliged to finish out their faded lives a burden to their male relatives."[2]

Until the coming of the factories, women had merely saved money for their men. They could make little as servants, sewing-women, keepers of boarding-houses, or teachers. But the first New England mills offered tolerable wages and conditions for the time, because labour was still short. Not until the Irish immigration of the 1840's did the necessary condition for the late Victorian sweatshops come about, the presence of a large surplus of unemployed women on the Eastern seaboard. From the first days of Western migration, women had outnumbered men in Massachusetts. And this state of affairs only worsened when immigration brought the European slum into the American city and factory town.

Even during the brief golden age of the New England mill town, when conditions seemed like paradise in comparison with the dark Satanic mills of England, there were strikes because of wage-cutting. These strikes were broken by lock-outs and black-listing. However paternal the employers, they believed in keeping their factory girls in their proper position of gratitude. The hope of earning enough money in the mills to go back home with a nest-egg or dowry was a mirage, like so much of the early American dream of equal opportunity. The two famous Lowell girls who emancipated themselves, Lucy Larcom and Harriet Robinson, did not do so on money earned from the looms; one became a teacher and author, and the other married. By 1840, a commentator noted that the great mass of the Lowell girls "wear out their health, spirits and morals without becoming one whit better off than when they commenced labour. The bills of mortality in these factory towns are not striking, we admit, for the poor girls when they can toil no longer go home to die."[3]

Economic freedom under any conditions seemed important to women who had none. The drudgery of the Lowell girls was less than the drudgery within their farm homes. Women in the first mills could feel free by comparison with the small opportunities offered to their mothers outside the home. But their daughters would demand more freedom from the factory, to do what they wished in their spare time. The first factories meant freedom from the incessant workshop of the home; but the later factories meant a time of bondage needed to buy hours of leisure within the city block. As early as 1884 in Midwestern Cincinnati, a pioneer suffragist noticed one great change in the city. "We can see at all times, in the evening and the morning, throngs of girls passing to and from their day's work, lunch-basket in hand, as unconcerned as though it had been done in all the years of the past."[4] These unconcerned girls would demand new freedoms in the future.

Freedom is, above all, a sense of the spirit. To feel more free, each generation has to fight for and win better conditions of life than were once possible. The psychology of liberty demands continual advance, higher wages, shorter hours, less discrimination, more leisure. But the particular freedom for which each generation is prepared to fight depends on the temper of current society. No new freedom can be achieved without agitation and mass support. If one of the first practical advances of women towards emancipation took place in the economic sphere, it was because technology and public opinion had given them the chance of earning a wage outside the house. They took this opportunity, meagre as it was, in their search for emancipation. If the work day of thirteen hours seems an intolerable slavery to the modern factory girl, it was, to the early girls at Lowell, a fantastic liberty.

The new textile factories hardly affected women in their chief employment, sewing. As sewing could be done in the home, the trade was always overcrowded and underpaid. Even when the invention of the sewing-machine came to free women from the worst of their labours with a needle, the device was still small enough to be used in the house. The rates for piece-work in sewing went down. Immigration from Europe and the influx of Southern widows into the Eastern cities after the Civil War further lowered wages in the profession. By 1870, women were making shirts at six cents apiece. In New York, seven thousand women lived in cellars and twenty thousand on the edge of starvation. With a maximum wage of three dollars a week, what woman could hope to stay or become a lady? Her only escape was through marriage or prostitution. Her low wages allowed her to save nothing. In a slump, the only remedy was the streets. Of two thousand prostitutes interviewed in New York in 1858, nearly half had been servants and one-third sewing-women, while the remainder had depended on male relatives. At this time, there was one prostitute for every fifty men in the American city. "If women are compelled to undergo merely the slavery of life," the interviewer concluded, "no moral advancement can ever be expected from them."[5]

Yet, although factory wages and sweatshops brought some urban women into worse toil and degradation than in the harshest of homes, they did free the servant from her mistress and the mistress from her servant. Even if two million of the five million women employed in 1900 were still in domestic service, their numbers steadily decreased as factory conditions improved. The machines which were made within the factories, in their turn, allowed the household to manage without servants. The toil of the factory bench allowed the home-maker to sit at her ease. If machines took women from housework, they and their servants made more machines to take housework from women.

Once Elizabeth Stanton begged men to use their imaginations to lighten women's burden in the home, "for the mass of my sex hate iron facts, rules and machinery."[6] Yet these same iron facts, rules, and machinery were eventually to take away a wife's servants and give her a gas-stove for her kitchen range, an electric light for her candle, a washing-machine for her tub, and a vacuum-cleaner for her broom. The factory destroyed the workshop home and the household with servants. It gave single women and domestics freedom to leave the humiliation of other people's houses. But it gave back to the mistress of the home the servants of gas and electricity and technology. Woman's economic freedom from the home began in the factory, and her domestic work in the home was lightened by the factory. If the factories became the slave-drivers of poor women, the fault lay in their operators, not in their existence. Their coming was an answer to the cry of women such as the anonymous wife who wrote to *The Revolution:* "My life has been aimless, objectless, and now I am poor and dependent, and dependence is far worse and harder to bear than pure poverty. I would be willing to take the position of door-keeper to earn my own living, that my hands might be freed from padlocks and my feet from chains, that I could live as well as last."[7]

XIII

☙❧

THE PROFESSIONAL WOMAN

IF THE WORKING WOMAN was ill-equipped to fight her way into
skilled trades and higher earnings, the educated woman had more
advantages. Although it was difficult for her to break into the male
professions, it was possible. She could depend on a certain reforming
impulse in middle-class society and a chivalry even in her opponents.
Some of the professions fell ripe into her lap. Others demanded a
struggle.

In *A Woman of the Century,* Frances Willard and Mary Livermore collected 1,470 biographies of the most distinguished Victorian
women. Despite a bias in favour of temperance workers and con-
temporaries, an analysis of these biographies reveals where the main
success of the professional woman lay. One in four of the famous
American women of their century was a writer, a poet, or a novelist—
Hawthorne's "damned mob of scribbling women." The second
distinguished field for women was education, where one in eight of
the successful women was employed. After that, professional acclaim
was found in the entertainment world, journalism, temperance reform, medicine, suffrage work, and philanthropy. Few women were
known for their work in business, law, or the church.

Certain factors were at the back of the success of these women. A

high proportion of them were the daughters of ministers or of reformers, and many married ministers. More than one in four remained single. Those who married did so early or late; one in three
of them was soon widowed and did not remarry. Therefore, nearly
one in two of these successful Victorian women spent most of her
adult life as a single woman. Of these, many had dependents, although their children frequently died young. A large number moved
from the East to the West and became professionals owing to the
shortage of skills in the new territories—particularly in journalism,
medicine, and temperance work. Nearly all of the women came from
Protestant, old American stock. Few came from a farm or from an
urban background. The majority came from the Puritan small towns
of the Eastern states.

Victorian professional women, therefore, came mainly from old
families. Their backgrounds were connected with reform, and their
parents were interested in the particular reform of the East—education. They learned their skills in Eastern colleges. The high proportion of spinsters and widows shows how the stimulus of need drove
many women to break down the established patterns of their age.
Equally, although the usual lot of Victorian women was marriage,
only one in two of the outstanding women of the century was married
for most of her adult life. The masculine temper of the age is further
shown by the few professions in which women did succeed.

Literature could be written by any lady in her home; books could
and did appear under pseudonyms. Teaching, at a level below university, had long been the province of women; three in four teachers
by the end of the century were women, because they were cheaper to
hire and easily available. Temperance work and philanthropy were
female businesses blessed by the evangelical churches, and suffrage
work was particularly a woman's concern. A male society had always
approved of women as entertainers, although a lady found it difficult
to go on the stage until the success of Fanny Kemble. Only in journalism and medicine did women achieve a break-through. Even then,
journalism was allied to writing, and women were traditionally useful as news-gatherers. Women doctors also flourished, more because

of the modesty of their sex than because of their exceptional qualities. As *Godey's Lady's Book* said, "The education of women for the treatment of women is the only remedy for concealment and irremediable disease."[1] Only in the new profession of nursing did women become dominant, and that was an occupation which they had performed within the family throughout the ages.

Although some women broke through into most professions during Victorian times, they were few and extraordinary. If they set an example, women have not rushed forward to imitate them in the United States. The professional woman in Russia is usual, in America abnormal. Many trades have not accepted the equality of the sexes. The Victorian pattern of male dominance in many of the traditional areas of working life was not altered significantly by the feminist pioneers, and their weaker heirs in kinder times have not shown more courage.

The drives and frustrations of the Victorian woman who tried to break into a closed profession are clear in the lives of Elizabeth and Emily Blackwell, who both qualified as doctors. Elizabeth Blackwell was the first to do so in America. She came from an immigrant English family. Her father had been in the sugar trade in Bristol and was an anti-slavery reformer; he failed in business in New York, and moved West to Cincinnati, Ohio, with his wife and eight children. There he and his family came under the influence of the Boston Unitarians. When he died in his middle age, Elizabeth Blackwell was forced to become a school-teacher to support her mother and sisters, while her brothers went into business as youths.

Her limited opportunities for earning money galled Elizabeth Blackwell. In 1837, at the age of sixteen, she wrote in her diary: "I wish I could devise some good way of maintaining myself but the restrictions which confine my dear sex render all my aspirations useless."[2] She chose to become a doctor because a woman friend died of a painful disease, hating her treatment at the hands of male doctors. Her choice was made in spite of a strong aversion to physiology, particularly to the classroom memory of "a bullock's eye resting on its cushion of rather bloody fat." She felt a strong distaste for the idea of marriage, although her intimacy with her brothers prevented her from ever hating men. Above all, she was of the nature that enjoys conquering aversion and attempting the difficult. For her, reform began within herself and spread over the world. Personal indignation at the fact that the infamous abortioner, Madame Restell, was known as a "female physician" also drove on this champion of motherhood. She was refused admission repeatedly by medical schools. "You cannot expect us to furnish you with a stick to break our heads with," one male dean replied. Finally, the vote of the student body had her admitted to a small medical college in Geneva, New York.

There she persevered in her isolation, hating small-town life. "Geneva is a very immoral place," she recorded, "the lower classes of women being often worthless, the higher ones fastidious and exclusive, so that there is no healthy blending of the sexes." Geneva had been settled long enough to boast of its caste system and clique of ladies, who stopped to stare at Elizabeth Blackwell "as at a curious animal." Their theory was that she was either "a bad woman, whose designs would gradually become evident, or that, being insane, an outbreak of insanity would soon be apparent." The male medical students, however, never molested her, and she qualified for her medical degree with ease.[3]

She finished her studies in Paris and London. Unfortunately, she contracted an eye disease, nearly went blind, and lost one eye. This made her morbidly sensitive. She returned to New York and set up a female hospital there, helped by her younger sister Emily and another woman doctor. She found great satisfaction in her work, although never the excitement of overcoming her first obstacles. Her letters to the sculptress Barbara Bodichon in 1860 are some of the most revealing documents written by the pioneer feminists. They show how the delight of these women lay in the search for freedom in a new field, not in the enjoyment of that freedom gained. Qualification was worth more than practice; liberty meant more as an idea than as a job.

"I am happy," Elizabeth Blackwell wrote,

in my steady work as medical practitioner, because in the present age, it has its universal bearings, as a new and noble field for woman's work— but also, it has its monotonous routine of poor and insignificant relations, which drives me constantly within, for refreshment, and recreating strength. It is thus I imagine, with every work in the present age, no matter how divine in itself, nor how glorious in its enthusiastic initiation—the practical application of grand ideas is necessarily a disappointment, and a degradation of the ideal. . . .[4]

Yet, even so, work was everything for a single woman.

How good work is—work that has a soul in it! I cannot conceive that anything can supply its wants to a woman. In all human relations the woman has to yield, to modify her individuality—the strong personality of even the best husband and children compels some daily sacrifice of self—some loving condescension to the less spiritual and more imperious natures—but true work is perfect freedom, and full satisfaction.[5]

The fact that Elizabeth Blackwell went back to England after the Civil War, to live out her life among her aristocratic friends, showed how much of the lady there was in her. Yet her conscience had made her quell every shudder of delicacy and had even driven her through foul work in a syphilitics' ward. It was no wonder that the moral reform of others became one of her preoccupations.

Her determination and practical efficiency were somewhat fearsome to her sister Emily, who struggled after her in the bondage of self-doubt. When, as a girl, Emily Blackwell had nursed her mother, ill with a discharging tumour, she confessed in her diary that she did not love her parent, but that her idea of duty and love prevented her from showing this. She also had to teach, and also found it difficult to be accepted in a medical school. Yet she struggled on, determined to be a Washington or Kossuth of women, for her sex had never equalled men only because it had never been free. She was finally accepted as a medical student in Chicago, and got her degree in Cleveland, Ohio.

Yet the moment that she qualified as a doctor, Emily Blackwell decided that she had made a mistake. What had been for her sister a passing fear was for her a life-long doubt. "Oh my God," she wrote in 1856, "is the end of all my aspiration, of my prayers and dreams, to be that this long earnest struggle has been a mistake, that this life of a Physician is so utterly not my life that I can not express myself through it—and worse—worse—that I might have done more in other ways? . . . I could bear anything but the feeling of failure, show me the way, be with me!"[6] She was never particularly happy as a women's doctor, and tried to give it up to become an artist. But she never made enough money to do so. She became the dean of a women's medical college, and passed her life in teaching other women to become what she did not enjoy being herself.

Now that it is possible for women to enter most professions, they feel little of the achievement that the pioneer feminists felt. Even those women knew more the pleasure of the struggle than of the duty of service. Once they found themselves single and qualified, they found themselves bound by daily work. They had cleared the way for their sex, but their followers were few and often untalented. To strive is more inspiring than to teach. And they had given up the ideal of their time, that of a happy marriage and love.

The practical Elizabeth Blackwell did what she could to fill this need. She adopted a daughter and set up a household. "I have recognized the truth of this part of my nature," she wrote, "and the necessity of satisfying its wants that I may be calm and free for the wider work."[7] Emily followed her example, as did the other three spinster Blackwell sisters. They each chose to adopt a daughter outside marriage and to remain free of the influence of all men except their brothers.

Other spinster doctors found an outlet for their emotions in strong attachments to their women patients, within the Victorian pattern of propriety. The letters of Dr. Helen Morton of Boston to Mrs. Mary Hopkinson, whose two children she had delivered, give an insight into the desperate loneliness of these medical pioneers. Helen Morton found only drudgery and a bare living in her profession; her liberty was in the love of her friends.

"You are one of the people," she wrote,

who gave me freedom. I, the inside I, am at home, at ease, and clear with you, as if heart and soul had found blue sky and sunshine.

Can friends do more?

I wish you would try to bore me with your affection, and I wish I might be sure of never losing it.[8]

As with the first girls who escaped from the home into the factory, the liberty of finding a job soon evaporated in the slavery of doing the job. Only the dedicated such as Elizabeth Blackwell could still feel free in doing their duty. The women who followed her into the professions were to find a hard choice between the difficult dedication of singleness and the satisfactory diversion of love and marriage. The freedom of the spirit seemed to demand a home as well as a job, and their interests were often in conflict. There was no choice for the professional woman who wanted children, except that of periods of retirement from her chosen work. And even on return to her career, thoughts of home played continually on her nerves.

When Fanny Kemble returned to the stage in 1849 after her wrecked marriage with her Georgian planter, she earned a fortune. She had more professional fame and individual freedom than any woman of her time. She had had the satisfactions of having a rich husband and children. Yet her return to liberty was hard for her. "This is too childish I know," she wrote to a friend, "but the fact is that I was intended by nature for quite another sort of an existence than this strolling Independence which I relish infinitely little—a home where I could have been excessively spoilt and petted would have suited me vastly better than this vagabonding freedom and the general affections of a whole population."[9]

XIV

❧❧❧

THE REVEREND
SUFFRAGISTS

EXCEPT AMONG THE QUAKERS, where women were free to become ministers, and among other small and esoteric sects, the holiest thing a Protestant woman could do in the nineteenth century was to become a minister's wife. Fear of being unworthy, and a greater fear of being forced to be worthy through the hardship of such a station, caused much hesitation before marriage. One girl, asked to become the wife of a minister, decided to consult a woman who had already married a minister. Her diary reads: "She is decidedly in favour of ministers marrying; thinks it is 'not good for man to be alone.' She thinks my *happiness will*, and my *usefulness ought* to be greatly augmented by the union."[1] In fact, the great toil of clergymen in the nineteenth century often meant even greater toil for their wives—too often, the happiness of these women was lessened and only their usefulness augmented.

Although marriage to a minister meant freedom to leave home and to do good, it had its restrictions, even in the cities. One Boston clergyman's wife defined her position well:

The wife of a clergyman is more narrowly watched than almost anyone else. Her deviations from duty are very seldom overlooked; her opinions are minutely examined and often repeated. She is thought to take her notions of things, to a considerable extent, from her husband; and, of course, he suffers if she is imprudent. When I reflect on the responsibility of this situation, I tremble.[2]

As missionary and evangelical influence was the most important civilizing force on the frontier and the most important reform force in the small town and city, the missionary's wife played a key role in her community. Yet she passes almost unnoticed. Even the selfless lives of the nuns inside their convent walls in Louisiana and Baltimore and New York were more noticed than hers. Her reward was thought to be her husband's sacrifice; her own was forgotten.

In one series of letters, the courtship and disillusion of a missionary's wife is preserved. The Reverend William Thompson wanted to marry Miss Harriot Boynton Sawyer. In the summer of 1842, he proposed to her.

DEAR FRIEND,

I desire, to a greater extent than I have yet enjoyed, the refining and elevating influence of the female sex; and I have been the more desirous to enjoy the benefit of your influence, because the visions and principles which you have adopted so much accord, in my view, with the *true spirit* of our holy religion. . . .

Permit me to say that I think you qualified to fill a station of more than ordinary influence. I think, moreover, that you would be happy in *doing* good, though you should be called to endure self-denial, and that you are *just the one,* to sympathize with one who would devote himself to toil in the vineyard of the Lord.

Miss Sawyer refused the offer of marriage. She said that she felt at home in Boston. Whenever she returned there, there was "a feeling of gladness at heart which makes my step bound freely, and my spirit rise rejoicing." She thought herself to have "so little true piety," and to be "so destitute of holy zeal," that it seemed mockery for her to talk of duty calling.

But the Reverend Thompson pressed his suit, and claimed a *"particular providence"* in their meeting. Miss Sawyer weakened, and said that she did not want to make up her mind. "I would not be, or have

you think me to be, a coquette or a prude. . . . I respect, and esteem
you, but do not know you well enough to feel at present a warmer
sentiment." But, by the following summer, she had decided to marry
him and follow him wherever he went. He was to be her master. "I
suppose that in determining where to go you will feel it to be necessary that the location should be a healthy one, farther than this I
think *I* should have no choice. . . ."

Even though she gave up her freedom of choice, the new Mrs.
Thompson hardly expected to find herself where she did a year later,
in a log cabin in the farthest West in Iowa Territory. She wrote back
to a woman friend in Boston in despair that they were the only
missionaries in the Territory southwest of Des Moines. They had had
ten weeks of constant rain, with hogsheads of water coming through
the roof.

We have been obliged to "endure hardness" of many kinds, which I
hope will work for our spiritual good, though I have doubted sometimes
whether it was duty for a missionary with a family to remain in a place
where their health was necessarily so much exposed. During the wet
weather, we were at one time without money, flour, meal, and wood, and
owing to the state of the roads and mill streams were unable to get any.

They lived fifteen miles from the nearest small town, and their
neighbours were too poor to help them.

Mrs. Thompson continued:

I am willing to deny myself in all things when it is necessary but I
have thought we were exposing ourselves more than is consistent with
prudence. We have comparatively few comforts, and almost no conven-
iences, and I think I have done harder and dirtier work than much of the
hired help in Boston. Certainly I have felt it to be harder and yet it is
bodily exercise which profiteth but little. I have often thought it would
do all repining and complaining Christians good to live a few months in
our cabin and to be situated in all respects as we are. Still we hope it will
not be in vain.

They had only converted two young girls, but they had started four
Sunday schools, and were making progress with the women and chil-

dren. The letter and the correspondence ended: "This is cause for gratitude but I never felt that my heart was so cold. Pray for us, you know not how much we need your prayers."[3] In such despair, a woman could regret the exchange of her spinster freedom for a life of service, and find it difficult to see that her self-denial might open for her a way to God.

Those women who chose to become preachers themselves rather than the wives of ministers are better known. One of the first of these, outside the Quaker faith, was Salome Lincoln. Her career was curious, the career of a woman born a century before her time. Salome Lincoln was a mill-girl in various small towns in Massachusetts. Like Ann Lee, she had an obsession about cleanliness, and was converted at a revival of the Freewill Baptists. She began to preach in public, and, when her funds ran out, she returned to the mills. In 1829 she became a strike leader, when the wages of the girls at the Hopewell factory were reduced. The strike was broken; but Salome Lincoln refused to return to work. She continued to preach without being ordained, married a church elder, and died in childbirth at the age of thirty-four years. Her life as a factory worker, strike leader, and preacher foretold the lives of a group of important women who were to bring the factory girls and women's trade unions into contact with the middle-class suffrage movement, through the social gospel of the early twentieth century.[4]

The reason that some women broke down the walls against female ministers in Protestant churches was the same reason that had led Anne Hutchinson to try to set herself up as an unofficial preacher in Boston. These few women were highly religious and felt that their freedom in religion demanded their ability to preach. They also wished to earn their living like male ministers. Once one woman had become an ordained minister in a Protestant church, a few hundred women were encouraged to follow her example. The churches, however, were never welcoming. And the objection proved illusory which met Olympia Brown at her ordination, that "women will flock to the ministry" and "bring down the price of preaching." The churches have remained dominated by men and attended by women, even though many of them have provided for a token integration.

The first woman to become an ordained Protestant minister was a quiet emotional girl, who was to fail as a public lecturer from want of self-confidence. Antoinette Brown was the daughter of a comfortable and progressive farmer in the Burned-Over District, near Rochester, which was also the home town of Susan Anthony. She was brought up with kindness among religious and anti-slavery influences. Her father and her brothers and sisters were converted by Finney himself. She believed from the age of nine years in a liberal type of orthodox Congregationalism. She remained religious ever afterwards. While she was still young, the Mormons and the Fox sisters with their rappings disturbed the peace of the neighbourhood. Antoinette Brown's dry comment was that "the region has been rather noted for originating peculiar doctrines and practices."

She was secretly in favour of women's rights before she went to Oberlin College, where Finney himself had gone to be a professor of theology, and to keep the students fired by revivals—"His pictures of the condition of sinners in the next world were fearfully vivid, artistic and realistic to an intense degree." Once there, Antoinette Brown found herself among her like. "The class which graduated in 1847," she wrote, "was probably one of the most eccentric that Oberlin has ever seen. Several of the young men and women believed in the equal rights of women. One or two were not members of churches but most at least of the older students were. Someone said of the class of 1847 that we were made up of the odds and ends of creation."[5]

The history of women's rights in the United States is a history of *personal* contacts. The movement grew by the laying on of hands. At Oberlin, Antoinette Brown fell in love with Lucy Stone, with all the passion and sentimental licence possible between women of the time, before they learned to question their subconscious motives. Lucy Stone was older, determined, tidy, forceful, aggressive, unorthodox, anti-clerical, the stuff of martyrs—"the epitome of system." Antoinette Brown was gushing, imitative, lonely, dependent, compromising in all except her religion—"the personification of vagabondism." For a decade, she adored Lucy Stone. She wrote endless letters to her friend, who left Oberlin to earn her living as a public lecturer in favour of temperance, abolition, and women's rights. Even the fact that Antoinette Brown returned to Oberlin to study theology did not break their relationship. On religion alone, the two women agreed to disagree.

Antoinette Brown's letters to Lucy Stone reveal the intensity of the emotion which the younger woman felt for religion and for her friend. Freedom, for her, lay in pursuing both. After studying theology for a few months, she wrote: "I have never been happier in the world for the last few months but it is a new kind of happiness and I have kept it all buried up in my heart. If you had been here it would not have been so and it shall not be so now." Yet it was a strange and lonely experience to be the first female divinity student in America, among suspicious people. "Sometimes they own me not to be a Fanny Wright man, sometimes believe I am joking, sometimes stare at me with amazement and sometimes seem to start back with a kind of horror. Men and women are about equal and seem to have their mouths opened and their tongues loosed to about the same extent."[6]

But her belief in her God and Lucy Stone buoyed her up, although she complained, "I am forever wanting to lean over on to somebody, but no body will support me, and I think seriously of swallowing the yard stick or putting on a buckram corset, so as to get a little assistance somehow, for I am determined to maintain the perpendicular position."[7] She was ordained by a liberal-minded minister, and became the pastor of a small town in New York. Before her coming, the small town had been served by a Negro clergyman, so, "of course, after that, they were quite ready to invite the woman." But she found the life of a minister there as restrictive as that of a minister's wife. She begged her "dearest little cow boy" to come and visit her. "I love you Lucy any way, and if you would only come and take a nap with me here on my bed my head would get rested a great deal faster for it is aching now."[8]

She contributed to Horace Greeley's New York *Tribune* and insisted that he knew her worth. "Preaching with me has been deliberately chosen as a life profession and will not be lightly abandoned; but I am beginning to feel the need of freer surroundings." Even so, she was proud of her status.

Since I am really *legally* ordained and fully entitled to the technical prefix, Rev., will it not be well for the *cause* of *woman* that you should use it in connection with a woman's name? . . . . If it was an absurd title in the beginning, and is now no better than a worn out caricature, it still has a few specific uses remaining, since it is still too hard a mouthful for conservative orthodoxy to swallow with any great relish.[9]

In a year, she had given up her pastorate after spiritual doubts. "I can never again be the *pastor of a Church*," she wrote to Greeley, "but must be *a preacher for the people*." She left the Congregationalists. "My present religion is a free one—all its truths are revelations from Nature's God to the soul; and one must be outside of all sectarian pressure to speak it freely." Ambition also made her choose. Her preaching could "be better done in the city than the country—in New York than in any smaller place."[10] Like many a small-town woman, Antoinette Brown wanted to storm the big city.

She had had her first taste of success before her pastorate. She had become famous for trying to speak for an hour and a half at a world temperance convention in New York, where she was shouted down. She had gone on a lecture tour with Amelia Bloomer and Susan Anthony, although she alone had worn long skirts while the others wore short skirts and trousers. Her hard efforts for the freedom of becoming an ordained minister seemed wasted in the prison of being an ordained minister.

She failed in New York. She was a dull lecturer, a nothing compared to the fiery Lucy Stone and Elizabeth Cady Stanton. She married Samuel Blackwell, another businessman from the famous Blackwell family. She had six children and found refuge in domesticity, much to the annoyance of Susan Anthony, who wrote to her sharply at the birth of her second child: "*Not another baby, is my peremptory command, two* will solve the *problem* whether a *woman can* be anything *more* than a *wife* and *mother* better than half a dozen or *ten even*."[11]

Antoinette Brown Blackwell was perfectly contented in marriage and child-rearing. Although she always thought of herself as a preacher and joined the Universalist Church for greater freedom, she preached rarely. Her value in her later years was to act as a moderator between Lucy Stone in Boston and Susan Anthony and Elizabeth Stanton in New York, when the suffrage movement had split into two parts. Her career seemed to show what every anti-feminist said, that marriage was the proper and most fulfilling career for a woman.

She did inspire a girl from a Michigan log cabin to follow her into the ministry. Once Olympia Brown had heard her first woman minister preach, "the sense of victory" lifted her up, and she felt "as though the Kingdom of Heaven were at hand." Although she came from a poorer background than Antoinette Brown, her parents were equally religious and concerned with anti-slavery and education. She went to college at Antioch, the scene of Horace Mann's "great experiment," and later attended the Universalist Divinity School. She was the first woman preacher to be ordained by a proper church body, and she passed much of her life as a minister.

She moved West to Wisconsin and became involved in the woman suffrage movement. She played a great part in the losing Kansas campaign of 1867, when the feminists began their split with the abolitionists. She married late in life, but she kept her maiden name after the example of Lucy Stone, to show that she was still a free woman, not "as in slavery times when the negro changed his name on gaining a new owner." She lived long, through what she called the "dark ages" of the woman suffrage movement, when the old leaders were very old and the new ones were too politic for her crusading taste. In her eighties, she came out of retirement to join the militant Woman's Party and to picket the White House. "I belonged to this party," she declared, "before it was born."[12]

Olympia Brown was enduring and active. She did much to spread the word of women's rights throughout the West. It was part of the aggressive spirit of the frontier to think that all things were possible for woman as well as for man. She does not seem to have suffered from the fears of Antoinette Brown that she would not succeed in her chosen career, or that she had chosen wrongly. Another woman minister, Augusta Chapin, who was ordained in Michigan in the same year as Olympia Brown, expressed this curious freedom from doubt and forgetfulness of sex in work that seemed to be the gift of the West to its stronger women.

I have no recollection of ever considering the question of whether I would preach or not. I never deliberately chose the profession of the ministry; from the moment I believed in Universalism it was a matter of course that I was to preach it. I never questioned as to how I came by this purpose, nor did it ever seem in the least strange that I should preach, nor had I any real conception of how my course must appear to my friends and the world until I had been more than ten years in the active work. So when people have asked me how I came to enter the ministry I have answered truly that they knew as much about it as I; and I think it was this wondering question so often asked that finally made me aware that my position and work were unusual for a woman. Yet I have never been able to realize this fact except by strong effort, and have almost forgotten it utterly at other times; and when engaged in my work I have never felt it necessary, as so many do, to assert myself, or to maintain my position, or to explain myself, or to apologize for it.[13]

By the twentieth century, a few hundred women had been admitted to some of the Protestant churches as ministers. Preaching had become a possible, if not a normal, career for their sex. The Free Methodist and the Methodist Episcopal churches admitted deaconesses, who fulfilled something of the role of nuns in the Roman Catholic Church. But the Lutheran, the Presbyterian, the Protestant Episcopal, and the Reformed churches refused to admit women to a much higher place than kneeling in their pews. Religion was to remain for women a solace rather than a profession; their spiritual need for release could be more profitably employed through the pen than the pulpit.

XV

⁓⁓⁓

BOOK-MAKING
PROPENSITIES

"I THINK SOME GOOD," wrote one mid-Victorian father to his daughter about *Uncle Tom's Cabin,* "will come out of these book-making propensities of the age."[1] In terms of the freedom of women, that good was economic and psychological rather than creative. Authorship offered the first opportunity for some women to make a fortune off the stage. It provided a reasonable living for others. And the critical and popular success of occasional women as authors gave a feeling of pride to many of their sex. "A *grand* poem, isn't it?" Lucy Larcom wrote after reading "Aurora Leigh." "I think woman is *some body* in these days, if all the talk and writing amount to anything."[2]

Women had distinguished themselves in literature in American colonial days, but they had been few and their influence limited. Classical and English male authors had still dominated the American mind. The pleas for recognition by women had been muted. As Anne Bradstreet had declared:

> Men can do best, and women know it well,
> Pre-eminence in all and each is yours,
> Yet grant some small acknowledgment of ours.[3]

When Mercy Warren had died, with her plays and other writings at last published under her own name, she had died satisfied. In her will, she had left the copyright on her work to her favourite son, saying that it was "the only thing she could properly call her own."[4] Yet even that little claim had been too great, for the copyright had legally belonged to her husband.

Not until the early nineteenth century did literature begin to reflect and encourage the growing importance of feminism. Although literary circles in the young cities offered the true frontier of opportunity for the ambitious woman, it was not strange that Fenimore Cooper gave the qualities prized by the feminists to the pioneer women. The heroines of *The Last of the Mohicans* may have been conventional and ladylike creatures—in Lowell's words, as flat as the prairies and sappy as the maples. Yet Esther in *The Prairie* is tough, ruthless, domineering, sometimes braver than the frontiersmen, the true equal and partner of her husband Ishmael. She can shoulder a rifle, shoot Indians, survive raids, overcome hardships, and keep her whole family under her thumb. Her sex is secondary to her qualities and vices. She is respected solely for her endurance and courage. Cooper goes so far as to say that her character is a "singular mixture of good and evil," which would have made her remarkable in a wider sphere of action. Even he recognized that the life of a squatter's wife may have developed her formidable qualities, and at the same time restricted her opportunities.[5]

Yet Eastern writers could hardly know of the fact of Western life. As an early Westerner complained, "The mass of the Atlantic people have less exact knowledge about us, than they have about the Chinese. . . . Most of the people imagine a western backwoods man to be a kind of humanized Ourang Outang, like my lord Monboddo's man, recently divested of the unsightly appendage of a tail."[6] It was apt that the first refutation of Cooper's version of Western woman should come from the pen of a Western woman. Caroline Kirkland, in her description of life in a Michigan village, *A New Home— Who'll Follow*, gave the lie to Cooper. For every Esther to be found on the prairies, there were ten sluts and drudges who existed in squalor and resignation and ignorance. A rural village in the West was no breeder of feminist virtues. The equality of the frontier levelled women down to the state of the brute male. It did not elevate them into an understanding of their own courage and independence.[7]

Yet, in the safe haven of the cities, worship of the rural ideal in literature flourished. The example of the successful female writers of England, from Jane Austen and Fanny Burney to the Brontë sisters and George Eliot, spurred on American women to imitation. Lydia Maria Child, with her *Brief History of the Condition of Women in Various Ages and Nations,* pioneered in the field of popular history written about women by women. Although Lydia Child was definitely on the side of the equality of the sexes and the education of women, she was discreetly so. She seemed to prize women who were famous through their men more than those who were famed for their own work. Sappho rates only one reference in her section on Ancient Greece; Xantippe and Aspasia are given paragraphs.[8] Until she became caught up in anti-slavery work, Lydia Child in her popular novels and biographies set the pattern for the moderate lady reformer and writer, careful to work within the values of her time.

Many women were to follow the example of the young Lydia Child. The attractions of a literary life were great. The popularity of the novel was a new phenomenon, dating from eighteenth-century England. The flood tide of romanticism had made the talents of intelligent ladies peculiarly well suited to the tastes of the American reading public, which largely consisted of less intelligent ladies. Moreover, the cult of sensibility and the pursuit of the beautiful offered a psychological freedom in writing for married women, who could not get out of the home in any other way. The pen was mightier than the needle in giving the house-bound woman dignity and profits, although the writing profession was soon as overcrowded as the sewing trade. As a character in Harriet Martineau's *Deerbrook* commented, women should stick to being tutors, tailors, and hatters. There were, indeed, departments of art and literature from which it was "impossible to shut woman out." These were not, however, "to be regarded as resources for bread."[9]

Elizabeth Oakes Smith, after her early marriage to a middle-aged

Bloomers, arriving in 1850, looked exquisite on Amelia Bloomer, but they made Elizabeth Stanton look fat, Lucy Stone dumpy, and Susan Anthony angular. The fad soon passed.

Elizabeth Cady Stanton, obsessed with marriage reform, became one of the most effective propagandists of her age. Her name and face appeared everywhere.

Brown Brothers

Culver Pictures

Above: The young and the old Susan B. Anthony, saint of the woman's movement, found in it the loves and daughters she missed as a spinster. Her favorite was Anna Dickinson (left), the "Joan of Arc" of the feminists.

Culver Pictures

Women, voting in 1869 in Wyoming, the first territory with woman suffrage, were no more insulted than if they had been "visiting a grocery store or meat market." What their husbands did while they were gone is shown below.

OLD GENT. *"As Mrs. Nettlerash has gone to the Sorosis Club, I tho't I'd just come over with my Knitting. Baby not well, eh?"*
YOUNG GENT. *"No, poor thing, he requires so much Care that I really don't get time to do my Mending!"*

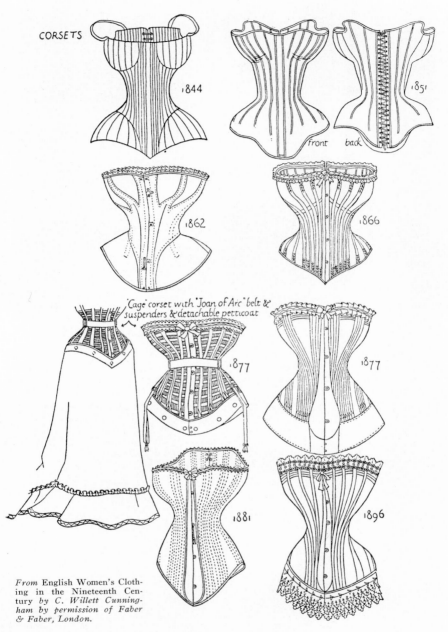

CORSETS

1844

1851

front   back

1862

1866

Cage corset with "Joan of Arc" belt & suspenders & detachable petticoat

1877

1877

1881

1896

From English Women's Clothing in the Nineteenth Century *by* C. Willett Cunningham *by permission of Faber & Faber, London.*

The history of the corset: steel ribs and whalebone dominated fashion throughout the nineteenth century.

Culver Pictures   *Culver Pictu*

Susan Anthony's successors: the Reverend Anna Shaw (left) made suffrage holy but too moderate; "Big Boss" Carrie Catt, a political realist, increased the membership of the National American Association twenty-fold; and Lucy Burns (below), incensed at injustice, dropped feminist literature over Seattle from an airplane.

Culver Pictures

Stanton's daughter Harriot Blatch set up the Women's Political Union to bring together all working women. She helped the suffragettes organize their most important march on Pennsylvania Avenue in Washington, D.C., in March, 1914. The center of feminist agitation shifted to Washington to lobby for the Nineteenth Amendment.

Suffrage achieved: August 26, 1919.

editor, felt in an extreme way the pull towards the only field open to an intelligent wife in the 1820's and 1830's. Although she loved her five sons, she had "a sad consciousness of a sweet beautiful life—buried away—smothered out—being like the statue in marble—never to be brought forth—it was not dead, for spasmodically expression sprang to the surface in the shape of essay or poem—and even grave moral and political theses, which attracted a certain local interest." She felt painfully that, had she been a boy, time and space would have been given her to fill up "this arrested, beautiful development, while marriage, which a girl must not refuse, was the annihilation of her."[10] Literature was the only way out of the wedding ring.

This yearning after the beauty and love that did not exist in many nineteenth century marriages of convenience explains the desperation with which many women wrote to each other in the private letters of the time. The 1830's and 1840's mark the age of correspondence between women. The open declaration of their love for each other was a commonplace because, according to current literary conventions, they could not express it to men—often not to their husbands. Endlessly, these women poured out their passion, confessing that they preferred "sentimental letters" from the dear friend of their hearts. Unhappy wives and lonely women found consolation in the love of one another. Although they referred to their passions with the utmost caution and in terms of sisterhood, they should, perhaps, have heeded Sir Charles Grandison's caution, "Wottest thou not, my dear, how much indelicacy there is in thy delicacy?"

As the flourishing and new ladies' novels and magazines emphasized the difference between the sexes more and more, with women representing the good and the beautiful and men the base and the brutal, so lonely women turned back towards the ideal of their girlhoods. As with Elizabeth Oakes Smith, that time became a golden age. One minister's wife with literary ambitions could write to another, "I would . . . make you a very girl with myself."[11] The greater part of contemporary popular literature yearns with longing for lost girlhood and purity in an Eden where men and sex have not yet reared their ugly heads.

There was not, however, a fixed ideal of the Victorian lady among

the good novelists of that time. These observers were continually not-
ing the vast gap between the behaviour of women in fact and in ideal.
Just as Caroline Kirkland destroyed the myth of woman's life in the
West by looking at it, so the good Victorian writers were capable of
showing a great amount of independence and perversity in their heroines. In the case of Hawthorne, he was even capable of showing his
women as evil. But then, he was not a particularly popular writer.

The more popular of the good novelists in Victorian times were
English. Yet among them, rebellious women often asked awkward
questions. Caroline, in Charlotte Brontë's *Shirley*, demanded a professional training, even if it made her masculine, coarse, and un-
womanly; for "what does it signify, whether unmarried and never-to-
be-married women are unattractive and inelegant, or not?—provided
only they are decent, decorous, and neat, it is enough."[12] Thackeray's
young women, on the whole, were sharp enough about being sold in
marriage and condemned to that state of bondage. If the author later
claimed that his freethinking girls became contented wives, his obvious happy endings did not convince those readers who had read an
opposite view in the rest of the book. George Eliot, despite her private belief that "woman does not yet deserve a much better lot than
man gives her," presented her intelligent heroines as rebels within
their narrow social framework. Only Dickens, among all the good
mid-Victorian writers, cut his heroines out of paste-board to fit the
current fashions of low-brow taste. His procession of loving and
submissive heroines are distinguished only by their similarity and
insignificance. Hardly an intelligent reader then and now could tell a
Kate Nickleby from a Little Dorrit, and forgot both completely in the
face of Micawber and Fagin. Dickens was not so much the recorder
of Victorian womanhood as the dupe or the exploiter of its ideal.

Outside the circle of good novelists, however, there was much
mediocre talent ready to exploit the stereotypes of Richardson and
Dickens. The Victorian ladies' magazines were as ready to manipulate
the mind of the American woman in the direction of home and
maternity as are the modern ones. Perhaps *Godey's Lady's Book* could
claim like its modern equivalents that it was only giving the Amer-

ican mother what she wanted. Perhaps it did run articles in favour of higher education, women doctors, domestic science, and better health, but only in a small and discreet way, exactly as the present women's magazines put an occasional "think piece" among the entertainment. The intention of the Victorian ladies' magazine was certainly more serious, moral, and religious; but its expression was as false, time-serving, sentimental, and fashion-conscious. Circulation mattered, then and now. The doctrine of woman's fulfilment in motherhood and the home, of her separate but equally valuable sphere in life, was continually preached in the words of God rather than of Freud, with duty stressed rather than gratification. The help that the feminists received from the mass magazines of Victorian times was small. The harm that was done to the cause of the single woman by preaching the virtues of the married lady with her family was enormous.

Between the hack world of the magazines and the high world of the good writers lived a "mob of scribbling women" with talent and need to earn money. Many of them wrote quite well, and were quite successful. Their very lack of opportunity in other fields forced them to express themselves in writing, and, since they were intelligent, they did so competently. In fact, because the writing of novels was a relatively new trade, social taboos did not prevent women from entering it. In the same way, when journalism became a regular profession, women found employment easily there.

The drive behind middling women writers was not so much a matter of psychological gratification as of cash. This was particularly true of the single woman in a poor family, or of widows. Sarah Hale herself, the editor of *Godey's Lady's Book,* had only become so because she had to earn a living as a widow with a large family. In this way, even the sickly literature demanded by the ladies' magazines and popular publishers gave a job to many nascent feminists who did not want to be forced into teaching. The value of books published in America increased five times between 1820 and 1850. Harriet Beecher Stowe made a fortune—if not a Civil War—with her moderate and inaccurate novel, *Uncle Tom's Cabin.* Despite a small talent fit only for a sentimental market, many feminists could earn their own bread. Thus the lady reader often kept independent those women whose lives denied the shibboleths of the lady, even if they did not dare to shock the golden goose in print.

Louisa Alcott particularly well represented the rebel with a lady's pen. Brought up in poverty by her philosopher father, she left home as soon as she could to live alone in a garret in Boston, in order to write. "I like the independent feeling," she wrote back to her father, "and though it is not an easy life, it is a free one, and I enjoy it. I can't do much with my hands; so I will make a battering-ram of my head and make a way through this rough-and-tumble world."[13] She did not marry. She began to write and eventually became rich with the publication of *Little Women*, which is an autobiographical text on how to remain genteel though poor, and how to be a young lady on nothing a year.

When a new profession opened up, that of nursing in hospitals during the Civil War, Louisa Alcott immediately volunteered for service. After a few months, she caught a disease and nearly died. She ended her life in supporting the cause of women's rights discreetly. In a letter to Lucy Stone in 1885, she wrote: "I earnestly desire to go forward on that line as far and as fast as the prejudices, selfishness and blindness of the world will let us, and it is a great cross to me that ill health and home duties prevent my devoting heart, pen and time to this most vital question of the age."[14] Her final freedom from old age and pain lay in becoming a morphine addict. Yet, to the end, she remained in the eye of the public Miss Alcott of Concord.

Thus, despite the propaganda against the feminists spread through the work of popular writers and ladies' magazines, authorship was to the middle-class woman what the factory was to the farm or slum woman, the first opportunity to earn a decent living outside the home. For teaching was vilely underpaid. Different statistical studies of eminent women found that in America and Europe up to one-third of the distinguished women in history had become famous through literature, while many of the rest had only done so through inheritance or marriage.[15] The talents of intelligent women seemed particularly suited to the form of the novel. And America was to produce, among her melancholy horde of lady poets, its own Sappho in the person of Emily Dickinson.

Emily Dickinson was never forced to live off her writing. Her greatness was hidden until after her death. The fact that the Victorian age produced no other great women writers in the United States can partially be explained by two lines of hers:

> Publication—is the Auction
> Of the Mind of Man.[16]

Too many woman writers were forced to scribble for the market. Too few were secure enough to produce a work that rebelled against popular taste. If many of the Victorian female writers were guilty of turning literature into little more than sentimental entertainment, they were not guilty of living in a society that severely limited their means of earning money. Although writing for the market does not always corrupt the best of writers, it does prevent good ones from trying to better themselves.

XVI

THE GREAT DEBATE

THE GREAT DEBATE between the feminists and their enemies was over women's work. The feminists knew that if they once had a mass of women working outside the home, they would have the vote. The anti-feminists knew that if they could influence women from working, they could hold them back from asking for more rights. This debate was, of course, a mere matter of words. Nothing that either side said changed the economic forces and needs that drove women to work. The feminists justified the professional woman and the anti-feminists the lady and mother in her home. It was a middle-class argument. Not until working women became organized in trade unions and threw their support behind the suffragettes did all American adult women receive the vote.

The feminists stated the obvious, that women did work outside the home because they had to earn a living.

If all woman's duties are to be considered as so strictly domestic, and if God and nature have really so circumscribed her sphere of action—what are we to think of the dreadful depravity of thousands upon thousands of unprotected females, who actually prefer leaving their only proper sphere, and working for their own subsistence—to starvation? . . . . Ought not such wicked creatures to be exterminated?

Either women had to be reduced to slavery as in ancient times and had to be prevented from working altogether, or they should have an equal opportunity with men in finding jobs. "Even with perfectly fair play, they will still have plenty of difficulties."[1]

The anti-feminists denied that women should work. The average woman already had an income from marriage, as she had had for thousands of years. Marriage was her trade and motherhood her duty. While there was no respect for the working woman, there was every respect for the married woman. Those females who did not marry did not wish to do so. It was their fault, if they wished to earn their bread temporarily and to be governed by the inexorable laws of supply and demand. "Woman's life and labour, mission and work, point ever homeward, and whether she serve in the store or shop, in the factory or in the home, she will be ready, whenever God's providence opens the way, to make home bright for another."[2]

Women often did not choose to remain single, the feminists replied. They had to wait to be asked by a decent man. And even if they did choose to remain single, they should not be punished. All women were not made to be mothers. "Freedom from the dogma of the child, that is the real cutting of the cord which binds the woman."[3] Moreover, no wife had an income from marriage in money; she was merely clothed and housed and fed. If society respected the wife more than the working woman, society was wrong. The working woman was degraded by the unjust tyranny of men, who paid her lower wages for the same work as a man did. "Practically, the command of society to the uneducated class is, 'Marry, stitch, die, or do worse.' "[4]

The anti-feminists answered that it was working women who caused low wages. Not only did they compete for jobs with other women, but they competed with men. "Competition must result everywhere in the degradation of woman and the pauperization of man." Most working men were fathers and had families to support; many women worked for mere pin-money. It was girls stitching in the comfortable Maine farms of their fathers who had ruined the sewing-women of New York. Any girl who could be dependent on a man and who chose to take a job was "often taking what morally belongs to another." If all women stayed at home, labour would become scarce, men would receive higher wages, and all would be happy.[5]

The feminists denied that there was always competition for jobs. The work of women expanded the economy and helped the nation. Did George Sand compete with Honoré de Balzac or George Eliot with Anthony Trollope? Men, moreover, took over women's work. They had become cooks and hairdressers and laundrymen. Work should go to the human being who could do it best. It was not a question of sex.

It was a question of sex, the anti-feminists said. Women were unfit to work outside the home. If they did, their health was ruined. Obviously no woman could compete with a man in application of mind or physical strength, and should not be protected by law if she did.

If a one-legged man should insist on being a letter-carrier, we might admire his courage and perseverance, but we should urge him to choose an occupation for which he was better suited. He might say with truth that the world is hard on one-legged men: doubtless it is. But what is hardness to the one-legged man is simply justice to the two-legged man. To make special regulations in behalf of cripples would be to create false conditions that could in the end result only in harm. To make special regulations in behalf of women could only have the same result.[6]

Women could do nearly all the jobs of men under the same conditions, the feminists replied. The factories did need regulation, but for the sake of both men and women. Of course, there was some physical labour in which women could not compete with men, but machines were doing more and more of this, and women could operate those machines. And what about the work of the home? That involved heavy manual labour and gave women ill-health.

The cook roasts slowly over the kitchen fire until her nerves become so irritable as to render her ill-temper proverbial. The parlour-girl stands on her feet month in and month out. She runs up and down, carries heavy dishes, goes out on errands when, according to the professors of sexual hygiene, she ought to be comfortably tucked up in bed, with some one to

wait upon her. . . . The seamstress, if she sews all her life, is fortunate
to escape consumption or spinal disease. Even child-bearing, upon which
such stress is laid, has not only its great suffering, but its horrible and
ghastly dangers. Where the function is exercised in excess, it destroys
health and shortens life.[7]

Had not Medea offered to stand three times in the battle-line rather
than bear a child once?

The fundamental matter, the anti-feminists replied, was a matter
of morality. Women in factories were exposed to vice and temptation.
In their homes, they would escape this exposure. Society, anyway, was
based on the family. Everything should be done to keep it together.
In colonial America, people had been better because they had held to
the family. The smallness of wages and hardships of competition
were "a blessed safeguard to civilization, and to woman herself. The
world could spare its money more easily than it could spare its love
and romance, its tender relations, its beauty, and the grace and loveli-
ness brought to it by the spiritual influence of good women."[8]

The fundamental matter, the feminists agreed, was a matter of
morality. Low wages forced working girls onto the streets. Vice was
the result of starvation and the miserable pittance paid to servants in
the homes of ladies. Factories had come to stay, as had working
women. The point was not to prevent women from getting into factories, but to make the factories fit to employ them. The family was,
indeed, the base of society, but many widows had to support their
families. High wages and fair opportunity were the only ways of
allowing women with dependents to bring them up decently. People
might have been better in colonial America, but the industrial revolution and the city and mass immigration had become facts of life. It
was the duty of a woman not to be a moral ostrich; she should go out
and help her sex. Reform would not destroy the values of the home;
it would make them possible. The anti-suffragist did not love home
more; she loved democracy and women less.

In fact, all the arguments of the anti-feminists were based on the
ideal of the lady, a state possible for everybody to attain. All could
become ladies through marriage, and ladies should not labour. In-

deed, it was sinful for a mother to go out to work and neglect her children. If she did, she would also threaten the position of her husband as the head of the family and only source of income. To save the dignity of the American father, the American mother should suffer her little indignities and claim her natural privileges. "The child is born into the lap of a covert, gladly worshipful motherhood; drinks in patience, reverence, subordination, to the one idea of the family headship, and is so to be partially configured to the grand moral headship of the Supreme Father."[9]

The arguments of the feminists were based on the fact of the working woman. By 1890, one in six of the labour force was a woman; by 1900, nearly one in five. A woman could, and indeed should, work. "Never let her say she does not *need* to labour. Disease, depression, moral idiocy, or inertia, follow on an idle life."[10] Marriage and motherhood were important, but not essential. The anti-feminist dogma was untrue which said that "all that is distinctly human is man—the field, the ship, the mine, the workshop; all that is truly woman is merely reproductive—the home, the nursery, the schoolroom."[11] Women could be original and creative through their minds and hands as well as their wombs. A single woman had the right to everything that a single man could get. Even the anti-suffragist educator Catherine Beecher wrote: "To *train* woman for her true business and *then* pay her so liberally that she can have a home of her own whether married or single—*this*—is what I am working for and I know it will come in God's good time which is the best time."[12]

The debate was also a debate on the freedom of women. The conservative wants to be free to preserve, the radical to change. For the various freedoms are contradictory; liberties war against one another. For every woman who wanted to be free from the home and children, there was another woman who wanted to be free to devote herself to nothing else. It seemed natural to a suffragist that women should be free to vote, whether they wished to do so or not. But what of the anti-suffragist who would feel duty-bound to vote if she were given the ballot? "A large majority of American women," claimed

Catherine Beecher again, "would regard the gift of the ballot, not as a privilege conferred, but as an act of oppression, forcing them to assume responsibilities belonging to man, for which they are not and can not be qualified; and, consequently, withdrawing attention and interest from the distinctive and more important duties of their sex."[13]

Of course, there were extremists on both sides of this middle-class debate, who provided the prejudices of the other side with all the wadding necessary to stuff their ears against rational persuasion. Propaganda does not appeal to sense. For every clergyman who claimed that the home was a temple and the factory the house of the Devil, there was a feminist who asserted that the home was a "monogamous harem" and a "life-long sentence" imposed on woman in a man-made world. Such assertions merely strengthened the prejudice of either side.

The debate on women's work did less to help working women than to help middle-class housewives. Trade unions were to help women in the factories; the feminist debate sharpened the minds of those who had the leisure to listen to it. The idea of equality in marriage and housework began to spread by the beginning of the twentieth century. "The woman should be in the home as much as the man is," Charlotte Gilman asserted, "no more." The time would come when "a man would no more think of having a woman become his house servant than a woman would think of marrying her butler and retaining him in that capacity." The idea that the wife earned the surplus of her house-keeping money by her labour became popular. And the right of wives to an extensive life outside the home became accepted. "A house," another feminist declared, "is as demoralizing a place to stay in all day as a bed."[14] If extreme notions of cooperative living and public nurseries did not convince most American women to give up their private care of their children and their houses, the other concepts of the feminists were accepted widely enough to make the position of the working mother acceptable in society.

The whole debate on women's work did something to make intelligent women think about their position in the home. It did make more respectable the idea of the working woman, and even of the working lady. As a leading feminist had declared in 1860, "A want of respect for labour, and a want of respect for woman, lies at the bottom of all our difficulties, low wages included."[15] But this want of respect was not to be changed, outside middle-class circles, through a battle of words. It was to be changed by women's trades unions, by strikes, by militancy. Not until the working women of America saw that they would not get better wages without a vote, did the middle-class suffrage leaders get mass support. Women who worked changed economic conditions, not women who talked. When the organizers of the working women began to talk with the organizers of the suffrage movement, something was done.

PART SIX

Allies and Enemies

They haven't th' right to vote, but they have th' priv'lege
iv controllin' th' man ye ilict. They haven't th' right to make
laws, but they have th' priv'lege iv breakin' thim, which is
betther. They haven't th' right iv a fair thrile be a jury iv
their peers; but they have th' priv'lege iv an unfair thrile
be a jury iv their admirin' infeeryors. If I cud fly d'ye think
I'd want to walk?

MR. DOOLEY

It is a plausible and tempting argument, to claim suffrage
for woman on the ground that she is an angel; but I think
it will prove wiser, in the end, to claim it for her as being
human.

THOMAS WENTWORTH HIGGINSON

XVII

WOMAN VERSUS SLAVE

THE GROWTH of enmity between North and South before the Civil War showed how no one reform could be treated singly. To the abolitionist, his crusade to free the slave had ended with efforts to keep himself free. He had had to defend his own rights of free speech and petition and jury trial and assembly and the basic right of democracy—that any person should be free to say and print and distribute what he wished without fear of bodily harm except through due process of law. Southerners, in seeking to gag propaganda, had gagged the liberty that was the right of all Americans, free or slave.

Yet, to the Southerners, the abolitionists were accessories to murder, bent on provoking another of the bloody raids led by Nat Turner or John Brown. They saw what the conservatives of the North saw, that abolition was linked to the wholesale questioning of the traditional fabric of society. The freeing of the slave was only one freedom among many demands. Did not Garrison, that anti-slavery leader, want women's rights, non-resistance, anarchy, and heaven on earth? Did not the rash call for equality mean that Irish immigrant wage-slaves would come to control the government? Were not the Mormons, free-thinkers, and atheists pulling down the pulpits of the orthodox churches? The Southerners saw that reforms did not come singly, but in a crowd. Their position seemed to them to be less the defence of slavery than the defence of the old and tried and true ways of civilization.

Particularly, the Southerners thought that they were defending the family against chaos, exactly as the anti-feminists believed. The Yankee Catherine Beecher later expressed the same Southern fears of Northern reformers, when she accused *"the woman movement,"* as they had accused the abolition movement, of uniting "all the antagonisms that are warring on the family state," such as "spiritualism, free love, free divorce, the vicious indulgence consequent on unregulated civilization, and the worldliness which tempts men and women to avoid *large* families, often by sinful methods, thus making the ignorant masses the chief supply of the future ruling majorities."[1] To the aristocrats of North and South, reforms were linked evils. For once social change had begun, no one could know where it would end.

When war between North and South became likely, the consciousness of difference between North and South grew. Radical Yankee women could once see Southern women as sisters under male oppression; now they thought of them as enemy slave-owners. Southern women thought of those of the North as infidels, who starved their servants, and they egged their men into war. "As a woman, of course," Mary Chesnut wrote with her rare candour, "it is easy for me to be brave under the skins of other people; so I said, 'Fight it out.'"[2]

Before the first battle, dreams of glory sent the Southern ladies into ecstasies of worship of the men in grey. One plantation lady presented her son, as a gift on enlistment, with a company of men to command, all outfitted in hand-stitched uniforms. The women sewed and raised funds and danced with heroes; they embroidered cases for razors; they refused to marry those who had not been wounded in the front. " 'How perfectly ridiculous!' do you say?" asked a Southern woman. "Nothing is ridiculous that helps anxious women to bear their lot—cheats them with the hope that they are doing good."[3] The South had been safely settled too long, for eighty years and four generations, to remember the savagery of Indian or British war. The fact of wounds and death was swathed in hopes of victory and chivalry.

This was not so in the West. Indians were present and ready to rise. Massacre and bloodshed were part of the reality or recent history of most communities. Every man was needed to work the land or to defend the house. There was no substitute for physical strength where there were few machines. When the men went away to fight, the women and children did as well as they could on the farms; but this was a bare existence until some of the men returned.

Mary Livermore took a trip on the railroad through Wisconsin and Iowa in 1863. She was imbued with the ancient American prejudice that women should do no field work, yet "women were in the field everywhere, driving the reapers, binding and shocking, and loading grain, until then an unusual sight." As a true Eastern-bred lady, Mary Livermore turned away in aversion. Her immediate reaction showed how much the Eastern woman continued to patronize the necessity of the life of farmers' wives. "I said to myself, They are worthy women and deserve praise; their husbands are probably too poor to hire help, and like the helpmeets God designed them to be, they have girt themselves to this work."[4] In fact, they had to bring in the harvest if they wished to eat at all.

If, in the West or the North or the South, the absence of the fighting men meant a double slavery to the land, in the cities of the North and South it meant jobs in the factories for women. At the outbreak of the Civil War, one job in four in the Northern factories had already gone to women—particularly in the mills. This number increased during the conflict; to every factory woman, the war meant more chance to get good pay and learn a skilled job in such professions as the printing trade. In the absence of men, women have both more opportunity and more drudgery.

The South, in particular, found itself cut off from the sources of manufactured goods. Factories to produce the supplies of war were conjured up in every town and city. The streets of aristocratic Richmond were filled with women, carrying lunch-pails, going to work.

Every plantation home developed from a workshop into a small manufacturing centre, which used the refuse of nature and material to produce war goods. Nearly all Southern women felt obliged to work, through patriotism and pride and necessity. The first impact of the war on the Southern lady was in the labour needed to keep it going.

For the Northern lady, the war meant an increase in the amount and scope of her charitable work. She was not pressed into service like the Southern lady; there were enough immigrant and country-women for that. The soldier took the place of the heathen or the fallen woman in her thoughts. Through the devices of fund-raising developed in the missionary societies, fifty million dollars were raised during the war for the work of the Sanitary Commission, a ramshackle but far-flung organization which sprouted in the absence of any government welfare for the troops and their families. The Commission and its many female helpers taught a generation of women how to visit the sick in hospitals, inform families of deaths, balance a diet, dispatch supplies from point to point, and the thousand details of successful and necessary volunteer service. In a real sense, Sanitary women had the opportunity to learn how to organize the multitude of women's clubs that were to spring up after the war and bring an extraordinary cohesiveness and a smattering of culture to millions of American women in the small towns.

Some of the more determined ladies in North and South did hospital work. Under Dorothea Dix, the famous reformer of insane asylums, Northern women were trained as professional nurses, or learned their trade on the job. Some of them, like Clara Barton, who was to become the power behind the International Red Cross, worked among the wounded on the battlefields. In the South, where organization among women did not exist, individual ladies went to the hospitals or turned their homes into emergency wards after local battles. War brought many ladies into direct contact with the horror of animal functions. It began to lessen the excessive delicacy and susceptibility of the early American ideal of the lady, which had been always something of an affectation in the United States outside aristocratic circles in the large cities. If, as with Jane Swisshelm, a visit to a hospital led to the sight of amputations and men dying of gangrene, "delirious, and expectorating profusely, a matter green as grass," the only alternative to fainting was practical work.[5] Jane Swisshelm brought in baskets of lemons.

As the war progressed, privation became part of the daily life of the Southern woman. The Confederate armies consumed everything. One account told of women walking twenty miles for a half bushel of coarse, musty meal. One of the chief problems of the Southern commanders was to prevent at seed and harvest time the desertion of large bodies of men, who felt that they had to help their women and children. And when Sherman marched through Georgia, occupation by the enemy added bitterness to the physical hardship endured by Southern women. His troops plundered and burned and looted, with only children and slaves and women to oppose them. They treated the South as an alien country, and they were treated as aliens in return. When Robert E. Lee surrendered at last and asked Southern women to do nothing to keep alive the war, his request was already made dumb by the brutality of the occupation.

The domination of the war over all other interests changed the priorities of the feminists themselves. Its opening years were for them a period of illusion, followed by disillusion. Elizabeth Stanton became a "full-blooded Republican and about three quarters over" in 1860.[6] Politics superseded her interest in the woman's movement, although Lincoln's later administration proved "too slow and politic" for her "straight-forward ideas of justice and vengeance."[7] The Republican Party itself began to play down anti-slavery agitation. When Stanton and Anthony went on an anti-slavery speaking tour in New York State, they were howled down by mobs. They found themselves with no useful work to do; for they had lost the ear of their audiences in the dominion of conflict.

Their reversion to an old form of reform activity was characteristic. Not for them the work of a hospital or a Sanitary Commission, the practical running of a war. They were trained agitators, with a network of contacts all over the East and West. They decided to use their talents in the one way that had become respectable in the North, after forty years of practice. They formed a Woman's Loyal League, to collect a million signatures for a petition to Congress to emancipate the slave at once. In Stanton's view, women's practical work was not their highest task; their highest service was to use their political influence to turn slaves into soldiers and thus end the Rebellion. "Work is worship only when a noble purpose fills the soul," read a joint proclamation of Stanton and Anthony. "Woman is equally interested and responsible with man in the final settlement of this problem of self-government."[8] When the war ended, Stanton and Anthony hoped to use the Woman's Loyal League to help dictate the peace. If the Loyal League's declared objective was merely the collection of signatures for a monstrous petition to free the Negro, its hidden objectives were defined later by Stanton as "the solemn lessons of the War: Liberty to all; national protection for every citizen under our flag; universal suffrage, and universal amnesty."

The Loyal League did collect more than three hundred thousand signatures, and did do some dangerous propaganda work in convincing large bodies of Northern and Western people that the Civil War was a holy crusade to free the slave and regenerate the whole of society. In war, each person is only too ready to believe that peace will bring about his own particular millennium. Reconstruction offers infinite possibilities for reform, and few likelihoods.

The shrewdness of Stanton and Anthony was to stress the work of the Loyal League for the slave, and to hold their tongues on feminism. Briefly, the anti-slavery movement seemed as single-minded as it had in its early days. Stanton noted that, in the six years that the women of the Loyal League held their claims in abeyance to those of the slaves and looked to the Republican Party, they were highly honoured as "wise, loyal, and clear-sighted." It was only with the peace, when they returned to their original position and demanded rights of their own, that "these transcendent virtues vanished like dew before the morning sun."[9] Their effort to build up a fund of gratitude among anti-slavery reformers, which would be repayable later, was a failure. After the war, each reform group returned to its own priority, even at the expense of other reforms. When a reform nears legal success, its backers become politic, ready to sacrifice any helping cause that may lose support. Reforms may grow together, but, short of a social revolution, they are victorious alone.

When Reconstruction began, the quarrel also began over what should be reconstructed. Should it be only the defeated South or all of the nation? Radical Republicans controlled Congress, and they wanted preservation in the North and vengeance in the South. The propaganda of the Loyal League was more fuel to the flames of the carpetbaggers and those who sought to occupy and humiliate the South permanently. Even the Stantons, to their discredit, used their political influence to send their eldest son as a carpetbagger to Louisiana, where he made a quick and dishonest fortune—by an irony of fate, he died unmarried and bequeathed his money to his mother, who used it for the cause of women's rights. The exaggeration of the *moral* nature of the Civil War gave full scope to the greed of self-styled avengers and prevented an expedient peace. The war had taken place to preserve the Union—not, as Reconstruction ensured, to preserve the dominance of North over South, of South over the freed slaves, and of men over women.

By occupying the South in a crass and venal and brutal way, the carpetbaggers and the scallawags saw to the Southerners' vengeance on the freed Negroes. What the North ordered by federal amendment was disobeyed in the South by social practice and state law. Here, Southern women stuck by their men in resisting Northern influence. They would not hear even the voices of their own sex, who claimed that the hated word "emancipation" should apply to their condition as well. For if emancipation of the Negroes had led to ruin and rotten government south of the Potomac, would not the emancipation of women lead to worse?

To the radical women of the North, however, Reconstruction was their opportunity to demand the suffrage, even though only nine Senators supported woman suffrage in a debate over giving the vote to the residents of the District of Columbia. They had spent thirty years in supporting the anti-slavery groups; now they expected their reward. For the ways of the slave and of women had been long associated in the minds of all reformers. Half of the freed slaves were, after all, women. "There is a great stir about coloured men getting their rights," declared the first notable Negro orator and feminist, Sojourner Truth, in 1867,

but not a word about the coloured women; and if coloured men get their rights, and not coloured women theirs, you see the coloured men will be masters over the women, and it will be just as bad as it was before. . . . I wish woman to have her voice there among the pettifoggers. If it is not a fit place for women, it is unfit for men to be there.[10]

The wording of the Fourteenth Amendment to the Constitution defined the split between the cause of women and slaves. The Constitution had never contained the word "male" before. Women had merely been excluded from voting under the laws of the states—they had once had the vote in New Jersey for nearly twenty years. The Fourteenth Amendment specifically gave "male inhabitants" the right to vote, and then referred to these people as "male citizens." To the feminist, this was the culmination of legal humiliation. The sacred document of the Constitution was now amended to include the principle of discrimination by sex, with the further implication that women could not be citizens. When the Fifteenth Amendment was added, asking that the vote should not be denied "on account of race, colour, or previous condition of servitude," the feminists also attacked it for not including the word "sex." To them, victory had been won by the dedication of women; now the peace was degrading women still more. They had lost ground since the American Revolution. For now it seemed that they could not gain the right to vote in federal elections without a new constitutional amendment.

In her speeches on Reconstruction, Elizabeth Stanton returned again and again to the Declaration of Independence, which she had always used as the basic doctrine of equality and liberty for human beings in America. She said that there were eighteen grievances of the American fathers against King George, and it so happened that women still had eighteen grievances against men. What had gone wrong with the Declaration of Independence had been the Constitution.

Our Fathers declared all men equal, then placed the power in the hands of the few. They declared no just government could be formed without the consent of the governed, then denied the elective franchise to men without property and education, to clergymen, women and negroes. They declared taxation without representation tyranny, then taxed all these disenfranchised classes. Through a century of discord, friction and injustice, these violations of the republican idea have culminated at last in a four years bloody war. And now we stand once more debating with ourselves the fundamental principles of government. From the baptism of this second revolution, with a century of added experience, shall we repeat the blunder of the Fathers and build again on the old foundation whose corner stone is class and caste?

Reconstruction only aimed to reconstruct the rooms of the South. It once seemed that the Republicans wanted to put in "new stones," but it was now evident that their chief concern was not so much the condition of the whole house as who should live in it. The abolitionists merely wanted to whitewash the walls and add a few new citizens under the roof of the house, forgetting that every extension made the weakness of the foundation more apparent. The legislation proposed for Reconstruction was too little, too sectional, and too partial.

This is not reconstruction, it is whitewashing, it is patching, it is propping up what cannot stand. This is not the negroes' hour. We have passed from him to the broader question of the life of the Republic. In the discussion of his rights we have gone back to first principles and learned that the safety and durability of a nation demand that the least right of the humblest citizen be secured. . . . The demand of the hour is equal rights to all, that the ideal republic of the Fathers be now made a fact of life.[11]

Stanton's speech on Reconstruction was the clearest statement of the drive behind early American reform, when the documents of the Revolution were still big in the minds of men. The reformers searched to turn the American ideal into the American fact. Such wholesale legislation to bring about equality in America could only come about when society was unsettled and dislocated. The years after the Civil War reproduced the conditions after the Revolution. This was the time to write the Declaration of Independence into the Constitution. "If Saxon men have legislated thus for their own mothers, wives and daughters," Elizabeth Stanton protested to Senator Blair, "what can we hope for at the hands of Chinese, Indians and Africans? . . . . I protest against the enfranchisement of another man of any race or clime until the daughters of Jefferson, Hancock and Adams are crowned with all their rights."[12]

Looking back to the principles of the past, the feminists hoped for the suffrage. An educated Anglo-Saxon woman could surely vote as intelligently as an illiterate Negro. Certainly, a majority of the American population did not support female suffrage at that time; but then, as the popular vote in Kansas showed, a majority of the population did not support a constitutional amendment to give the ballot to Negroes. Stanton and Anthony were correct to press for the vote during Reconstruction. When Congress was radical in the dislocation after the terrible war, was the only time that universal suffrage might come.

The South, and probably the majority of American voters, did not want to give Negroes the ballot in 1867. Negro male suffrage was made into law by Northern and Western legislators as a weapon to dominate the South. But no section of the nation was ready to grant women the ballot in 1867, although a Western Territory was to do so two years later. Their vote could not be used to dominate another part of the country.

There was enough residual gratitude in some of the anti-slavery agitators to form an Equal Rights Association with the feminists in 1867. Such important reformers as Wendell Phillips, Horace Greeley, and Garrison joined with Lucy Stone and Stanton and Anthony in the Association. But the emphasis of the anti-slavery supporters shifted from getting the vote for Negroes and women to pressing for the passage of the Fourteenth Amendment. In their opinion, the Negro was worse off than the white woman. Most Negroes supported their position, against the voice of Sojourner Truth. Frances Harper, who toured the South at that time, testified that when it was a question of race, she let the lesser question of sex go; but the white women all went for sex, letting race occupy a minor position. Phillips and Greeley and Garrison were all silent on the subject of women's rights when the cause of the Negro seemed in danger. Even such a staunch friend of Stanton as Frederick Douglass put his race before his championship of the other sex.

Lucy Stone, who reluctantly remained with the anti-slavery group, complained bitterly to Abby Kelley, who had married the abolitionist Stephen Foster, that all the Negroes opposed the Equal Rights Association in Philadelphia. Only one of them marvelled at the silence of women "while the great mass of the Negroes for whom they worked, would give their influence like a dead weight, against the equality of women with them." She could not understand why Abby Kelley Foster and Phillips and Garrison, who had cried for thirty years, "Let Justice be done, if the heavens fall," should now be smitten by a strange blindness, and be induced along with the nation "to accept the poor half loaf, of justice for the Negro, poisoned by its lack of justice for every woman in the land." Abby Kelley Foster and the others were making a terrible mistake. The country could only be saved by women. "The penalty for that forgetting, is not for Woman alone, or for this Country alone, but also, for that great multitude whose longing eyes are turned from all shores to our own, for an example of a government, which derives its just powers from the consent of the governed." Although Lucy Stone declared finally that she would stick to Abby Kelley Foster and kiss the hem of her garment, yet the tears were in her eyes and a nail went through her heart.[13]

Kansas, a fiercely Republican state, was holding a double referendum that year. One resolution offered to take the word "male" out of the qualifications necessary for voters; another wanted to remove the word "Negro." Lucy Stone and Henry Blackwell, Olympia Brown and Stanton and Anthony all campaigned in the months before the referendum. But the *Anti-Slavery Standard* and Greeley's *Tribune* in New York were strangely silent on the issue of women's rights, until just before the referendum, when their support came too late. An eccentric and self-made millionaire, George Francis Train, a Democrat and a Negro-hater, suddenly joined Stanton and Anthony in what he called "the great epigram campaign." His grotesque appearance and oblique phrases made a great stir and brought in the crowds. He was violently for "woman first and Negro afterward." If two wrongs could not make a right, he was surprised that the Republican Party in the state, which endorsed Negro suffrage and opposed woman suffrage, thought that two rights would make a wrong.[14] By the end of the campaign, Train had alienated all the diffident Republican and anti-slavery support of the East. But then, he suddenly offered Anthony and Stanton a newspaper of their own, to be called *The Revolution;* it was to campaign for the reforms that all three liked, such as woman suffrage, the eight-hour day for labour, an easy money policy through the issue of greenbacks, and freedom for Ireland.

The causes of both women and the Negro were voted under by the people of Kansas. Negro suffrage secured a little more than one-third of the vote, and woman suffrage a little less. Both reforms were still unpopular in the radical West. The Negro man, although he was to receive his legal and political rights in the North and the West fifty years before women, was still to be struggling a century later for the social acceptance that women had always had outside the political sphere, and for women's limited economic gains.

Stanton's and Anthony's acceptance of *The Revolution* gave them the opportunity to print their radical opinions. There is no question that they used *The Revolution* to force a break with the anti-slavery group. They printed attacks on the abolitionists, including Garrison. And the anti-slavery people were furious in return. "Oh dear a me, Olympia," Susan Anthony complained to Olympia Brown after a trip to New England in 1868,

I got so *soul sick* of the *icy faces* of Boston that I felt I could not stop another minute. . . . Not one of the *old leaders* in *Anti Slavery* now *puts himself* or *herself* in the *front ranks for Woman*—it is a *fact*—neither *you* nor *I make the fact*—we simply *state* it—no more, no less—not only do they not put themselves into the front ranks—but every one of them, so far as I can learn, most heartily wishes the Revolution *dead—dead—* *dead*—and would murder it at any minute had they the power.

In an appeal for the support of the Western woman minister, Anthony appealed to her anti-urban feelings. *"Kid Gloves and Silken Slipper* ways and means is their motto for action—Well now you and I don't believe in silver spoons and slippers."[15]

Train's contributions to *The Revolution* became more and more wild and strange. Soon he was in an English jail for Fenian activities; later he was to be confined in a lunatic asylum. Even Stanton and Anthony became apologetic about him. Although Stanton declared that she would say amen to the Devil if he offered money for a newspaper, Lucy Stone rightly commented that she and Anthony had accepted both the money and "the devil too."[16]

The next action of Stanton and Anthony provoked a final split with the anti-slavery movement. They seceded from the Equal Rights Association and called a secret meeting of their feminist friends from the Loyal League to form a National Woman Suffrage Association. Prominent Bostonians in New York at the time, such as Lucy Stone and Mary Livermore and Julia Ward Howe, were not invited to help form the National. It was a caucus of like-minded women, who felt that they had been betrayed by the Boston-led abolition movement. They felt that the cause of woman suffrage should be represented by women who put their own sex before the Negro.

The reaction of the Boston suffragists was characteristic. In the same way that conventions in Massachusetts had followed those at Seneca Falls, Lucy Stone and the anti-slavery group of feminists set up a second organization in the following year, called the American Woman Suffrage Association. If Anthony and Stanton seceded from the Equal Rights Association, Lucy Stone would secede from the National. Despite the nail in her breast because the cause of women was being advanced softly by the abolitionists, Lucy Stone accepted that God rarely gave "to one man, or one set of men, more than *one* great moral victory to win."[17] She agreed with the priorities of the anti-slavery movement, and with the sentiment of Clara Barton, who wrote: "If the door was not wide enough for all at once—and one must wait, or *all* must wait, then I for one was willing that the old scarred slave limp through before me."[18] The Negro must come first, for the Negro's cause had sparked off the woman's cause. As woman suffrage had little popular support, it needed all the friends that it could gain and keep.

Although Stone agreed with the justice demanded for women by Stanton, she could see how little the political and social situation favoured the feminists. As her friend, Thomas Higginson, wrote to Stanton, he was "haunted with the wonder why the instinct of freedom seems to be so nearly eradicated among women," when he found in the South that "no oppression could ever blunt it among the negroes." He found the progress of the equal rights principle easy among men, but among women it seemed to make scarcely any progress, "and the women otherwise most radical seem usually indifferent to the suffrage." In Worcester, "the cradle of the whole American movement, women only signed petitions as a personal favour or to please their husbands, and hardly a score of these."[19] In the opinion of the Bostonians, there was too little support of the suffrage among women, let alone men, to press for it at the expense of the cause of the Negro. Mass education, always a favourite among New England reforms, was the way to change the opinions of women.

Once a separate organization had been set up by one group of feminists, only extreme tact could have prevented the formation of another. And neither Stanton nor Anthony possessed tact. Stanton's fiery matter and Anthony's domineering manner told against them. Stone insisted that Anthony, the so-called "Napoleon" of the movement, had said at an executive committee meeting of the Equal Rights Association that she *was* the Association and the other members amounted "to shucks." In return, Anthony saw Stone as a personal enemy, bent on splitting the woman's movement rather than conceding the leadership to her and Stanton. The situation was made worse by the anti-clerical tinge of *The Revolution,* and Stanton's pushing for reforms in the marriage and divorce laws. These explosive topics annoyed the conservative suffragists of Boston, who were all for preserving the sanctities of the home and the friendship of the progressive clergy. Personal, geographical, and tactical reasons led to the forming of two suffrage organizations rather than one.

The split continued for twenty years because of the inability of Anthony and Stone to forgive or forget. The actions of each annoyed the other. Each held the other responsible for the split in the movement. When *The Revolution* foundered in debt after two years, Stone's newspaper, the new *Woman's Journal,* became the only suffrage paper in the country. At each exclusion from its columns, Anthony felt personally insulted, especially as she had to spend the next ten years of her life lecturing to pay off the debts of *The Revolution.* Basically, the split was between those women who thought that any alliance with unpopular reforms or people would hurt woman suffrage and those who thought that all pro-suffrage reforms and reformers would add strength to that weak cause. It was the difference between the exclusive and cautious temperament of the Bostonian lady and the inclusive and rash ambition of the small-town Western woman in New York.

The tactical difference between the two wings of the woman's movement was explained by Henry Blackwell in the first number of the *Woman's Journal:* "Some insist upon dragging in their peculiar views on theology, temperance, marriage, race, dress, finance, labour and capital. No one can estimate the damage . . . the cause of woman's enfranchisement has already sustained by the failure of its advocates to limit themselves to the main question."[20] It was the old argument, which Theodore Weld had used against Angelina Grimké, of pushing the main principle and not striking off until the summit level was reached. The American wing of the suffragists, like the moderate anti-slavery forces, decided to stick to the one reform of woman suffrage. It would remain single in its purpose, even if it were slow to succeed. The National, by encouraging the support of disreputable reforms and reformers, was bound to plunge into disaster.

And plunge it did. There was something fine, generous, and rash in Elizabeth Stanton's championship of her sex. It led her into her greatest error, her support of Victoria Woodhull when she spoke before a committee of Congress on women's right to vote. This charismatic clairvoyant and stock-broker and courtesan suddenly appeared on the scene of women's rights in 1871. Elizabeth Stanton immediately spoke up for her as a woman: "We have already women enough sacrificed to this sentimental, hypocritical prating about purity, without going out of our way to increase the number. Women have crucified the Mary Wollstonecrafts, the Fanny Wrights and the George Sands of all ages. . . . If this present woman must be crucified, let men drive the spikes."[21]

This infatuation of Stanton with Victoria Woodhull, which resulted in the latter's attempt to take over the National, associated the idea of "free love" with that of woman suffrage for a decade. "Never did Mrs. Stanton do so foolish a thing," Susan Anthony confided in her diary. "All came near being lost." Victoria Woodhull adopted most of the reforms of Train and ran for President of the United States, hoping for the support of workingmen, suffragists, spiritualists, and reformers of every sort and mania. Her involvement with the Beecher-Tilton scandal further tarnished the image of woman suffrage and increased the antagonisms within the movement.

Henry Ward Beecher, the first president of the American Association, was the most popular preacher in America. Theodore Tilton, whose wife he probably seduced, was a great friend of Stanton and Anthony, a well-known magazine editor, and a go-between for both wings of the suffrage movement. Mrs. Tilton confided her seduction to Anthony, who told Stanton, who told Woodhull, who, in her turn, used it to blackmail Beecher and the suffragists through her own personal scandal-sheet. Although Woodhull soon foundered in disrepute and debt, Tilton brought Beecher to trial on a charge of misconduct. At the trial, Bessie Turner, a resident of Tilton's household, accused both Stanton and Anthony of compromising conduct with Tilton, in order to discount their possible testimony against Beecher. Tilton himself was accused of misconduct with Woodhull. Although the trial ended with a hung jury and the acquittal of Beecher, the whole of America took sides for or against him, and for or against the protagonists in the case.

Willy-nilly, the American Woman Suffrage Association had to support its first president, Henry Beecher. "The Boston folks," Anthony commented spitefully, "begin to feel the kick of their Free Love gun firing quite painfully."[22] But she herself and Stanton had become personally as well as politically involved with the "free love" circle around Tilton and Woodhull. Anthony could write in her diary after the Turner testimony, "It shows the value of having lived an open above board life," but she confessed that even her own careful behaviour might be "evilly construed" in "many little moments."[23] To her enemies in the rival suffrage association, she and Stanton had committed the unpardonable sin of linking publicly the suffrage cause with "free love." Stanton confessed as much, writing sadly to Anthony, "The whole odium of this *scandalum magnatum* has been rolled on our suffrage movement."[24]

The link remained fresh in many minds and helped to explain the lack of success of the suffrage movement in the East for many decades. As late as 1885, the *Nation* was of the opinion that the suffrage cause had not yet recovered in New York. "Reformers who were at all squeamish about the company they kept began to fight shy of it, and it came to have in the eyes of the general public the air of being the first stage on the road to something in the nature of 'free love.' " In fact, only the respectability of the American Association and the success of woman suffrage in the Far West, according to the *Nation,* kept the issue alive in New York at all.[25] Four years later, a woman in Vermont told Alice Stone Blackwell that the Woodhull matter had set back the suffrage cause twenty years—to that day, the country people around her would not believe "that women want suffrage for anything but free love."[26]

In Victorian times, feminists could only get support for reforms within marriage. There was enough enlightened opinion to allow wives more rights in marriage and divorce cases. But the official women's movements had to avoid any connection with the advocates of free love outside marriage. Such an association alienated nearly all the women within the supremely middle-class movement, let alone outside it. It was the Woodhull affair that really stuck in Lucy Stone's throat and kept the two wings of the movement apart for two decades.

Elizabeth Stanton's heart triumphed over her head in 1872. She was infatuated with Victoria Woodhull. Only the jealous and supplanted Susan Anthony saved the situation from total disaster. Both Frances Wright and Victoria Woodhull set back the slow legal and political emancipation of woman because they demanded her physical freedom outside marriage too soon. If they seem merely radical now, in their time they were abominable. For marriage was near the soul of Victorian society and morality, and freedom for a woman's body hardly existed outside its laws. To be heard, the cry for bodily freedom had to be the cry of a wife and mother, as the cry of a Roman Catholic woman in 1870:

> I claim one right for woman which includes all human rights; it is that she be free to obey the Divine law of her own life that she be *not subjected to the lustful despotism of one man, or to the selfish or unwise legislation* of many. . . . I claim for the wife that she be free to bear her babes for the love of God and her husband, and that they be not *forced upon her in fear or hate.*[27]

Stanton and Anthony set to work doggedly to repair the damage that they had done. For twenty years, these two ageing women spoke and wrote wherever they could and as often as human nature would allow. Although the American Woman Suffrage Association was quite successful with those ladylike feminists, who were disgusted at the scandal around the National, the hard work and personal appearances of the two leaders of the National denied the rumors about them. They gradually won away from the American the growing group of middle-aged professional women and the organized forces of the Woman's Christian Temperance Union.

The suffrage movement remained small. It did not number more than ten thousand members in both wings of the movement. Most of these had been collected through the personal contacts built up by the suffrage leaders throughout their active lives. Occasionally, there was a splash of publicity. Anthony managed to get herself arrested for casting an illegal vote during a presidential election. Denied a jury trial, she spoke up before being fined. Her revolutionary words were traditional, "Resistance to tyranny is obedience to God." In 1876, at the Philadelphia Centennial of the Declaration of Independence, she distributed yet another version of the Declaration, that had once been the creed of the convention at Seneca Falls. This time, men were less attacked in general, and particular political and legal rights for women were more in demand.

Yearly conventions of the National in Washington built up a small group of Senators friendly to woman suffrage. "*Washington* is *the point* of attack," Anthony wrote, "and if *we are not there to make it, some others less competent surely will be.* It will not do to leave that *fortress unmanned. Reform 'Nature abhors a vacuum'* as well as physical, and we must not *suffer one at Washington.*"[28] When there was a debate in 1887 on a federal amendment to the Constitution which would remove the disqualification of sex from citizens who could vote, sixteen Senators voted for it and thirty-four against it— twenty-two members of the opposition were Senators from the South. This proposed amendment to the Constitution came to be known as the "Anthony amendment" because of her persistence in pressing for its passage.

An interesting argument that women already had the right to vote reached the Supreme Court. A lawyer from the radical Western city of St. Louis, Francis Minor, whose wife was the leading suffragist in Missouri, sued through her for her right to vote as a citizen of the United States. According to Minor's reading of the Constitution, no state law could abridge the "immunities and privileges" of citizens. The Supreme Court ruled against this interpretation of the Constitution, although it ruled in favour of the Negro citizens' right to vote despite state law.

Although suffrage was given to women in the Territories of Wyoming and Utah, the split women's suffrage associations made little progress for two decades. Stanton and Anthony had failed to win the vote for women by shock tactics in the Reconstruction period. They had failed to win it through a clever legal argument. They and Lucy Stone and their helpers had to settle down to the hard, long task of setting up permanent organizations to win suffrage state by state, which was the priority of the American Association, or by federal amendment, which was the priority of the National Association. Except in the West, the post-war decades were lean years for reform. Once the quick solution had failed, the slow solution advanced person by person and town by town. Friends had to be won and enemies placated. The very lack of success of the suffrage movement, compared with the huge success of the united organization of the Woman's Christian Temperance Union, was to bring its two wings together again.

As there could be no imposed legal and political solution through Congress, woman suffrage had to come in the good time of the state legislatures. The equality of women with men had to be emphasized more than their difference, in the mind of the public. Legislators, reflecting educated opinion, had to be persuaded of the right of women to the same treatment as men, as they had been persuaded of the right of Negroes. Clara Barton was partially right in 1869, when she wrote: "The cause is not to be hastened by quarrelling with men as men, nor with races nor with anyone. It is right and the revolving wheels of progress will gain the cause, if not another stroke is given, and possibly in less time without than with."[29] She was wrong, however, in thinking that a large suffrage organization was not necessary to agitate the revolving wheels of progress.

XVIII

⎝⎠⎝⎠⎝⎠

FEMINISTS AGAINST
THE CHURCHES

BECAUSE OF THE OPPOSITION of most clergymen to the feminists, many of the feminists opposed most clergymen. The question of anti-slavery had first split the churches, and then the question of women's rights had helped to split the anti-slavery movement. The early feminists had had to combat both their own unpopularity and the unpopularity of the extreme views of the anti-slavery Garrisonians who had supported them. "In CHRIST JESUS there is neither male nor female," the *Liberator* had proclaimed, "but all are ONE." Even so, for a single pulpit open to the feminists, twenty had been closed.

The experience of the Grimké sisters with the clergy had led them to leave the Quaker discipline and organized religion, although they had both remained very pious. William Lloyd Garrison's use of the woman's vote from Boston to take over the American Anti-Slavery Society in New York had further angered many clergymen, who had opposed both slavery and Garrison, and now opposed the supporters of women's rights. The very door of the church at Seneca Falls had been inexplicably locked when the first women's rights convention had met there.

The religious question was seriously debated at the women's rights convention at Syracuse in 1852. The debate lasted for two days, and almost split the young movement. Antoinette Brown introduced a long resolution, claiming that women's rights were upheld by the Bible. She was opposed by the rationalist, Ernestine Rose, who saw the dangers of basing women's demands on Holy Writ rather than on natural justice. There were too many hostile texts, such as "Thy desire shall be to thy husband and he shall rule over thee," or "The head of every man is Christ; and the head of every woman is man." If the authority of the Bible were admitted, the Book would have to be rewritten, in order to defend the cause of women.

Although Antoinette Brown offered to do the rewriting, Ernestine Rose pointed out that her view was only as good as that of any other minister, and all had their different opinions of the Bible. A revolution did not need the Book. "When the inhabitants of Boston converted their harbour into a teapot rather than submit to unjust taxes, they did not go to the Bible for their authority."[1] This neutral point of view won, and the resolution was dropped. The attitude of the feminists to the churches remained divided, however, and was one cause of the twenty years' split in the movement. Eventually, the agnostic Elizabeth Cady Stanton did produce a Woman's Bible, which was not so much an interpretation of the Bible as an attack upon it. The Bible was too contentious a document to help the feminists. They might draw their private inspiration from it, but they had to edit it or deny its authority to present a convincing case in public.

When Lucy Stone and the Boston wing of the suffragists split from Stanton and Anthony and the New York wing, religion was one of the hidden causes. Although Lucy Stone had been anti-clerical when young, marriage and motherhood made her severely respectable and a believer in a "Guiding Influence." The leading Boston feminists and their male supporters were mainly God-fearing. Because of the Woodhull affair, Lucy Stone continued to accuse Stanton and Anthony of immorality and godlessness until her organization merged again with theirs. "As men are known by the company they keep," she wrote darkly, "so are societies."

Elizabeth Stanton was always anti-clerical and led the anti-clerical forces in the women's rights movement. She was another who had been put in a spiritual turmoil by Finney; but, like the young Lucy Stone, she rejected the tortures of spiritual doubt for the firmness of moral doing. Although she was careful never to avow herself an atheist, since most of her supporters in feminism were members of the churches, she was always outspoken against organized religion, even if she stopped short of attacking God Himself. There was a heretic flavour to everything she wrote. She enjoyed asking the embarrassing religious question. As she wrote in *The Revolution* during its brief career, "The female communicants of several large American churches are asking whether they also have not souls; and, if so, why they are excluded from choosing their minister? It will be very difficult to answer that question, more especially as the average woman in America knows more theology of a kind than the average man, and subscribes quite liberally." Or, as she dared to ask still again in a head-line, "Why Should We Not Pray To Our Mother Who Art In Heaven, As Well As To Our Father?"[2]

This question of a female God continued to preoccupy Elizabeth Stanton. Although she did not want to become a female God herself like Ann Lee or Mary Baker Eddy, she wanted God to become female, or at least man to accept the female in God. "Every form of religion which has breathed upon this earth has degraded woman," she wrote. "Man himself could not do this; but when he declares, 'Thus saith the Lord,' of course he can do it." She ran ahead of Freud in emphasizing the connection between religion and sex. "The love of Jesus, among women in general," she wrote in a private letter to her daughter, "all grows out of sexual attraction. The Virgin Mary appeals in the same way to her male worshippers."[3] A clergyman friend of hers could not appease her wrath by trying to persuade her that Christianity "kicking out Paul" had helped women, and that "Christ mingled the woman with the man."[4] She was bent on her own way.

Try as she would, she could not escape religion. Her preoccupation with it increased, until she took upon herself and some chosen feminists the task of writing a Woman's Bible. For the Bible was the source still most quoted against women, and it galled her terribly. The more discreet feminists refused to cooperate in the task, especially those who were members of Lucy Stone's rival suffrage society. Mary Livermore warned against an attack on the Bible, "except as the facts make war upon it." For, whatever the result, the Woman's Bible would be assaulted with the "mad-dog cry of 'atheist,' 'infidel,' and 'reviler of holy things,' " all couched in "pious billingsgate."[5]

Yet Elizabeth Stanton went ahead and produced her Woman's Bible, based on a translation from the Hebrew made by a feminist, Julia Smith. She denied divine authority, although her views were not shared by some of the more moderate feminist commentators. For her, the Bible was a body of writings "wholly human in their origin and inspired by the natural love of domination in the historians." Woman's subjection to man grew out of giving the Bible too holy a source. Her social and political degradation was but an outgrowth of her status in the Bible and in the codes of the churches, all written by fallible men.

As for the episodes of the Old Testament itself, those which were used by the anti-feminists were treated with contempt. The creation of man was obviously at the same time as the creation of woman. The myth of Eve was the mere allegory of "a highly imaginative editor." The removal of Adam's rib was "a petty surgical operation." The Jewish Lord, "guiding and directing that people in all their devious ways, and sanctioning their petty immoralities," was now out of place. The Old Testament was the "mere history of an ignorant, underdeveloped people," without special inspiration; in fact, it needed expurgation before it could be placed in the hands of women and children. The text of Lot's daughters was omitted as unworthy of a place in the Woman's Bible. "A humane person reading these books for the first time, without any glamour of divine inspiration, would shudder at their cruelty and blush at their obscenity."

As the Bible grew towards the New Testament, Elizabeth Stanton's objections calmed. Although she still complained that "injustice to woman is the blackest page in sacred history," she liked the story of Ruth, who "believed in the dignity of labour and of self-support."

As for Christ himself, she had no criticisms, except for those clergy-men who removed the story of the woman taken in adultery from their texts. She forgot to reproach herself for her own omissions and distortions.[6]

The Woman's Bible did little but harm to Stanton's cause. It was a factor in the disastrous anti-suffrage vote in the Massachusetts referendum of 1895, and was quickly disowned by the official move-ment, now that the National and the American wings of the Woman Suffrage Association were joined. Before its publication, an anti-cler-ical resolution had been rejected at the annual convention of the Association. "Is there any of you that think we can ever succeed in the woman suffrage movement without the religious men and women of this country?" a questioner had asked, and was not answered.[7] The rationalism and anti-clericalism of the old leaders were giving way to the devout politicking of the new. The explosion came at the conven-tion of 1896, after the appearance of the Woman's Bible. Antoinette Brown finally won her debate with Ernestine Rose, and Elizabeth Stanton, still much the same after some fifty years of struggle, was repudiated.

The two women who were to lead the feminist movement after the retirement of Susan Anthony, Carrie Chapman Catt and the Reverend Anna Howard Shaw, supported a resolution which declared that the official woman's movement had no connection with the Woman's Bible. Although Susan Anthony had thought Elizabeth Stanton's comments on the Bible "flippant and superficial," she rallied to the support of her old friend. She was, in her own opinion, "born a heretic." In a moving speech, she said that this denial of Stanton would set back the cause of reform. "A Christian has no more right on our platform than an Atheist. When this platform is too narrow for all to stand on, I shall not be on it. . . . Who is to set up a line?"[8] But the line was set up and the vote went against her and soon Elizabeth Stanton and she wholly retired. The middle-aged and the believers had taken over from the aged and the rationalists, and the wooing of the churches had begun.

The Reverend Anna Howard Shaw was the only minister to head

the national suffrage organization. Even as a child in Michigan, she had stood on stumps to "address the unresponsive trees." She had heard a woman minister preach and had decided to become one herself. After years of struggle, she had been ordained by a small Methodist sect; but she had then decided that the cure of bodies was as important as the cure of souls. So she had followed the example of Elizabeth Blackwell and had qualified as a doctor. Joining the forbidden ranks was always more interesting for an aggressive woman than marching with them.

She settled in the East and turned to reform, a respectable occupation for a woman by the end of the nineteenth century. By training and belief, she naturally was attracted to the most successful women's organization of its time, the Woman's Christian Temperance Union. She then met and began to worship Susan Anthony, and transferred her efforts to suffrage reform; but she could never swallow Elizabeth Stanton, who disliked both temperance and church workers. In a private letter, Anna Shaw declared that she would not work under and would work to defeat Susan Anthony's long-time friend.

Feminine jealousy formed part of her dislike, for the unmarried Anna Shaw revered Susan Anthony and felt herself to be the older woman's apostolic successor. Although Susan Anthony preferred the more politic Carrie Chapman Catt as the next leader of the woman's movement, she was not displeased when Anna Shaw superseded her rival at the end of four years. For she knew that the woman doctor and minister would follow in her footsteps. Even four years after Susan Anthony had died, Anna Shaw was writing at Easter that she wanted to sit beside her dead leader's grave, "though she too, if Christ arose from the dead, is risen and is here with me now."[9]

Anna Shaw made the suffrage movement holy. She founded a religious department within the organization that worked with local ministers for suffrage; but she also made the movement dull. While the progressive and the prohibition movements flourished, the decade of Anna Shaw's leadership of the women's crusade was the doldrums of the suffragettes. In an age of belief in evolution and of social ferment from top to bottom of society, Anna Shaw seemed too moderate, too middle-class, too safe and sound. She never believed in fighting churches or men. "We will never win the battle by bully-ragging." And she could not organize well, as could her rival and supplanter, "the Big Boss," Carrie Catt. She was the pale shadow of the past, without its fire and iconoclasm. As Elizabeth Stanton's daughter declared, her loyalty was to a rut worn deep and ever deeper.

When the suffrage movement was young, anti-clericalism was a lusty element in its growth. But this was in an age when only one American in seven was a church member. Nearly three in seven were by the end of the century. Although it was easier for Elizabeth Stanton to blaspheme and rewrite the Bible in the relaxed social atmosphere of the 1890's, it was harder for her to find support among the feminists. As the women's organization grew in numbers, it grew in religious members and in the support of ministers. God had once kept woman down; now He seemed to be doing all He could to help her up. The real problem of the woman's movement, as Anna Shaw said in her speech of resignation, was "ethical and religious. Freedom, true freedom, must come from within."[10] In this quest for spiritual freedom, for which Anne Hutchinson had fought, the vote could not help.

XIX

৩৩৩৫২৫

THE LIBERTY OF THE WEST

"THERE SEEMS SOMETHING conservative in the soil of the Atlantic coast," a suffragist wrote to Susan Anthony in 1884. "The far West is infinitely more alive than we are; just think of having Woman Suffrage in Three Territories and not even in one of our little Eastern States! One would suppose that perseverance and eloquence were of no avail whatever; it must be that tornadoes, blizzards, and geysers are absolutely necessary to make human vision clear."[1]

From the earliest days of the settlement of the West, observers had noticed that "a real liberty" was to be found there, apart from American political theories. "The practical liberty of America," a pioneer wrote in 1817, "is found in its great space and small population. Good land, dog-cheap everywhere, or for nothing, if you will go for it, gives as much elbow-room to every man as he chooses to take."[2] But this "practical liberty" of owning acres for men meant slavery for their wives, who had to live on those acres. A man might feel free in his domain, his own extensive fields; but a woman in her domain, her shack, felt bound by dirt or mud.

The promise of the migratory West held out for men a sense of infinite freedom in moving on to better lands, but each new journey meant the sacrifice by their wives of a house, where they had been free to exist in comfort. The opportunities of one sex to make money

ensured the loss of opportunities of the other sex to make a decent
home. As Margaret Fuller noted on an early trip to the West, the
great drawback upon the lives of the settlers was the unfitness of the
Eastern women for their new lot. "It has generally been the choice of
the men, and the women follow as women will, doing their best for
affection's sake but too often in heart-sickness and weariness. Besides,
it frequently not being a choice or conviction of their own minds that
it is best to be here, their part is the hardest and they are least fitted
for it."[3]

Virgin land usually spelt to a woman isolation, disease, and hope-
lessness. According to their historian, Walter Webb, the Great Plains
"repelled the women as they attracted the men. There was too much
of the unknown, too few of the things they loved."[4] Once the emigrants had moved from the shelter of the forest to the prairies,
women were condemned to lose every freedom in a waste of wind,
sun, grass, and sand. The verdict of another historian of the Texas
Panhandle was equally bleak: "The lives of women were associated
with dirt floors, dirt walls, dirt roofs, a pallet or homemade bunk for
a bed, homemade furniture of all kinds, a few dishes, insufficient
cooking utensils, every inconvenience of living."[5]

Even the journey West was hard for women. When there was no
room on a waggon, they would walk for hundreds of miles, carrying
a child in their arms. If there were mountains to cross, the waggons
were raised and lowered by ropes, while the women climbed. Often
an epidemic came on the migrant trains, and killed the husbands who
had started the family West. One traveller found a bereaved group of
a woman with five children in the Plains in 1852:

An open, bleak prairie, the cold wind howling overhead, bearing with
it the mournful tones of that deserted woman; a new made grave, a
woman and three children sitting near by; a girl of fourteen summers
walking round and round in a circle, wringing her hands and calling upon
her dead parent; a boy of twelve sitting upon the waggon tongue, sobbing
aloud; a strange man placing a rude head-board at the head of the grave.

Often there was not even enough wood on the Plains to make a coffin,
since death was so frequent and wood so scarce. The dead were

buried quickly in a hole in the ground. As an early Kansas woman pointed out, "The graveyard is one of the first apportionments and the soonest to be thickly inhabited."[6]

The only event more frequent in the West than death was birth. White women were so rare that they were not allowed the luxury of being spinsters or widows. In 1850, men outnumbered women by three to two in the frontier states and territories. In 1860, there were twenty men for each woman in Colorado. In 1872, Abigail Duniway declared that there were virtually no unmarried women in all the Northwest. A typical case was that of Malinda Pound of pioneer Indiana. Married at the age of sixteen, she had fifteen children in the next twenty-one years, of whom twelve lived. She was rarely without "one porch child, one cradle child and one a-coming." She became a grandmother by the age of thirty-four, married twice, and died at sixty-three without writing a word. Her life lay in children and cleared soil.[7]

If suffrage for American women came from the West, it did not come from the demands of toiling women in isolated farms. Occasionally, an Easterner, blinded by a Jeffersonian belief in the independent virtues of the farmer, praised the life of those women who worked farms on their own. According to Henry Blackwell in 1870, many women had used the terms of the Homestead Act to set up as independent farmers in Nebraska, and some had cultivated forty or more acres "with such business tact and womanly grace as to win the respect of their male neighbours."

A letter to the *Woman's Journal* in the same year gave another picture of a hut in Iowa, isolated in the dirt and burning sun. Its woman occupant said that life there was "mighty easy for the men and the horses, but death on *oxen and women.*" Indeed, "While the men went abroad often, in the necessary discharge of business, the women were almost as constant to their homes as real estate itself. Often, a woman and a dog had to guard the growing crops, forming a sort of live fence, in the absence of boards or rails, and they must be constant as posts, or the crops would be destroyed." The letter concluded that suffrage for women was a hopeless proposition in rural

Iowa because of the great distances. "The church had not yet found them out, and there was nobody to lead them in any efforts to hold meetings."[8]

The true picture of the independent woman on her farm was that of a widow with children, who had to survive and knew no other trade. There were only about a quarter of a million women running farms on their own in 1890, although half of the total female population of America still lived on farms. Of these, some were mere speculators. "All over the thickly settled parts of Dakota," a contemporary account ran, "hundreds of women live alone in their own shack and garden patch." These women were establishing a period of six months' residence, which would give them the title to their land. Then they hoped to sell out to neighbouring farmers, and to return to their small towns or to the city with a nest-egg. In fact, they used virgin land as their dowry. The account ended by saying that only a few women worked the land themselves, and existed barely "by unspeakable labour."[9] The total failure of many Eastern reformers, who tried to persuade factory girls and prostitutes to lead a healthy and independent life on their own Western farms, should have convinced them that most women knew that a decent life might be found anywhere rather than on the land. As Frances Willard's mother said, when asked about the culture of farm life, "If one wants culture she should pack up her duds and go where folks live."

The Western supporters of women's rights rarely came from the farms. They came from the small towns, and particularly from among women allowed some leisure by the fact of their husbands' small wealth. It was noticeable that interest in women's rights never sprang up in the first days of the pioneers, but only after a network of small towns covered the wilderness of the new Territories. The Western States, when they were admitted to the Union, all had a high urban population for the times—on the average, one in four of the population already lived in towns of between five thousand and twenty-five thousand inhabitants. The West, particularly, was civilized from the town in its earliest days.

Harriet Upton of Ohio, who became the treasurer of the National

American Woman Suffrage Association and a power in the Republican Party after 1920, had no illusions about the lives of pioneer women in the Western Reserve in the earliest days. She based her account on family memories, for she was already in the third generation of small-town life. "Most of the forefathers had two or three wives. Women could not stand the hard work, the hardships, the child bearing, and early succumbed. Many a gravestone in this northern Ohio read: '——— beloved wife of ——— died ——— aged thirty-two' or thereabouts, 'leaving eight' possibly ten, 'children to the tender mercy of God.' "[10]

Not until some town life began did the anti-slavery movement reach Ohio. In 1843, Abby Kelley visited Salem, and seven years later the radical town spawned a fully fledged convention on women's rights. The feminist movement spread through the small towns, until it collapsed in the Civil War. It had little political influence, however, for it did not know how to lobby at the state legislature. Another small town, South Newbury, revived the movement after the war, as the poor sister of the great reform crusade of Western townswomen in the late Victorian period, temperance. Throughout the history of the suffrage movement in Ohio, the small towns were to give more support for woman suffrage than the homes of the "rum power," Cincinnati and Cleveland.

Suffrage sentiment moved westward across the Plains with the small towns and the new Western cities. Wyoming was the first Territory to adopt woman suffrage in 1869. The history of the passing of that law is a microcosm of the forces behind the passing of similar laws in the new West. It was not so much due to the scarcity of white women, although there was only one adult woman for every six men in 1870, as to the power of a single radical woman, the influence of the famous early feminists, the skill of a pro-suffrage politician, and the fact of the small communities in Wyoming.

The moving spirit behind the measure was an aggressive woman from western New York, Esther Morris. She had been converted by another woman from western New York, Susan Anthony, at a lecture at the town of Peru, Illinois, where she had lost an inheritance in land because of being female. She drummed up support for votes for women at a series of tea or dinner parties, held in the gold-mining community of South Pass, before its first election campaign. South Pass had a population of some six thousand, and was the largest community in Wyoming. It also held the largest number of white women, who represented the only island of morality outside the brutishness of the mining camps. In South Pass, both candidates were in favour of woman suffrage, for fear of losing the strong influence of the few local women over respectable voters.

A friend of Esther Morris, a Virginian ex-colonel named Bright, was elected; his wife happened to be a suffragist as well. As a Democrat, he supported woman suffrage because the ballot had just been given to the Negro, and it galled him to keep it from his wife. Moreover, he had "a strong feeling that it was just." He introduced a suffrage bill when the Democratic State Senate met; the bill was drafted by the influential Secretary of the Territory, E. M. Lee, who had worked on a defeated suffrage bill in Connecticut two years previously. Along with other measures providing for equal pay to teachers of both sexes and for the property rights of wives, the bill passed both Houses of the tiny legislature. Although anti-suffrage feeling had time to put pressure on the Republican Governor of Wyoming, he signed the bill. For, as luck would have it, his home town was Salem, Ohio. He had attended a meeting on women's rights there, and was also married to a suffragist.[11]

In this way, a small-town Western woman, a Governor, an experienced suffrage politician, and a Southerner angry that the Negro had been granted the vote, gave Wyoming suffrage. There was a direct line of apostolic succession from the propaganda work of the pioneer suffragists in the young towns of the Middle West to the success of suffrage in the Far West; Anna Dickinson herself spoke in Cheyenne in 1869. The contacts necessary to drum up interest in the measure could only be made in the largest community in the state. Distance was the bugbear of all Western reformers. The lack of men in the legislature meant that there were few to influence; only twelve votes were necessary in all to pass the measure. The early legislators were also ignorant of the prejudices of settled lawmaking bodies; they had not represented others so long that they could feel sure that their own opinions were those of the voters; they were open to intelligent persuasion. Moreover, they were certainly conscious of the fact that Wyoming's lead in giving women the vote would attract good publicity *and settlers' wives* to develop the Territory. "Women," wrote a local humorist, "can give this Territory a boom that will make her the bonanza of all creation."[12] When male prejudice was later aroused, and the arguments of Eastern anti-suffragists became known, it was already too late; the enemies of the measure in the legislature did not know of the delaying techniques which would have held up the bill. With its final passage, the theories of what women would do with the vote could be put into practice, in the very worst of conditions, in the violence and rowdyism of Western elections.

The anti-suffragists always claimed that decent women would not as well as should not vote; even the Wyoming lower house had proposed that the vote should be given only to "ladies," not to "women." The polls were dirty and full of dangerous and drunken men. A wife who voted against her husband would question his natural leadership. "If the woman agrees with the man, her suffrage is useless. If she does not, the difference is fatal to the family."[13] Ladies and "the best women" would refuse to soil themselves with politics, and only "the bad women" would go to the polls, thus increasing the dominance of undesirable elements in American life. Women would neglect the home if they engaged in politics. Anyway, they did not know enough to vote. As the lack of support for the suffrage movement in the East showed, most women simply did not *want* to vote. Finally, city women could get to the polls more easily than countrywomen, thus increasing the influence of the home of European vice against the home of American virtue.

The answer of the suffragists was a complete denial. They said that women would "purify politics and elevate the standard of morality." They would clean up the polls because of the respect which the anti-suffragists always claimed that all men had for them. If a woman voted against her husband, it was as reasonable as her worshipping in a different church—already acceptable in American society. If she voted in the same way as he did, there would be no quarrel. "The best women" were sure to vote, because they had a sense of responsibility. "Bad women" might vote, too, but so did bad men; they might well vote with the good women, for "the worse women are, the more they will counterfeit virtue, when they come to vote."[14] If women were too busy in the home to vote, were not men too busy in the office? Men always claimed they did the harder work. As for women being too uneducated to vote, that was the fault of men. And what about all the illiterate or immigrant males allowed to vote? Most women did really want to vote; they were too scared of the opinion of society to say so. Even if most of them did not, they should be given the vote as a matter of human justice, as the Negro man had been given the vote before he was ready for it. The city woman could, indeed, vote more easily than the countrywoman, but the answer was to reform electoral procedure and have many polling-places equally accessible to all.

The experience of Wyoming satisfied neither suffragist nor anti-suffragist. The polls were cleaned up, and elections grew to be even quieter than in respectable Vermont. When ladies appeared to cast their ballots, they were no more insulted than if they had been "visiting a grocery store or meat market." Although the divorce rate in Wyoming was high, this did not seem to be the result of political quarrels—and political differences were not a ground for divorce. "The best women" did vote, because the largest section of women voters were married women living in small towns. There were too few "bad women" in Wyoming to influence politics. Homes were not neglected because of voting, which was an infrequent affair, and women seemed to vote along the same partisan lines as men. Outside the larger communities, women did not use the vote very much. "In the smaller and more rural places the women take little interest in it, as indeed the men do."

As for "purifying politics," the women hardly changed the situation at all, except "in favour of temperance and good schools." For the two years in which women in Wyoming served as jurors, however, they were more severe than men on drunkards and sexual criminals and murderers. Esther Morris herself was appointed the first woman justice; none of the forty cases which she judged was overturned in a higher court. In fact, as Lord Bryce summed up the experience of Wyoming and Colorado, nothing showed "that politics are in the Woman Suffrage States substantially purer than in the adjoining States, though it is said the polls are quieter. The most that seems to be alleged is that they are no worse; or, as the Americans express it, 'Things are very much what they were before, only more so.' "15

The fears of the anti-suffragists and the hopes of the suffragists were no more confirmed in that most suspect of states to the Eastern mind, Utah, the only Western state where there were as many women as men. There, the elders of the Mormon Church saw the utility of granting the suffrage to women. In 1869, the Cullom Bill was introduced into Congress; it made polygamy illegal in the states and territories of the United States. The Mormon leaders saw that the gift of the vote to women in that most patriarchal of all communities would show how plural wives desired their position. Women in Utah, already organized in Female Relief Societies to urge each other on by example and to help the poor, were given the suffrage the following year.

The vexed question of plural marriage in Utah gave many curious insights into the liberties possible for men and women in the America of the nineteenth century. Joseph Smith and Brigham Young and their followers were not free to have many wives in the settled East or Midwest, because of attacks by offended local mobs. They had to trek to the wilderness to be free to enjoy their own religious and social ideas. Round the Great Salt Lake, the Mormon religion flourished. Single women freely emigrated there from the East and from Europe—they were not "mesmerized," as some enemies of the Mormons claimed. Nor, as their relative contentment showed, were they deceived about their prospects.

The Mormon apologists said that plural marriage was not a sin, but a virtue. No women were allowed to remain single in Utah; no virgin could enter the Mormon heaven; she would be annihilated upon death without the intervention of a husband. Thus, in theory, there were no prostitutes and no old maids forced to work outside the home in Utah. Thus there was no double standard, as practiced in the Eastern cities, and none of the vice and misery of the Sodoms and Gomorrahs on the Atlantic Coast. Each plural wife was meant to have a house of her own, and was meant to be a sister to the other wives of her husband. In fact, plural wives were freer than single wives. "A plural wife," said one woman State Senator in Utah, who had defeated her own husband in an election in 1908, "isn't half as much of a slave as a single wife. If her husband has four wives, she has three weeks of freedom every single month."[16]

Moreover, the plural wife was free from the excesses of male lust, and thus could live the Victorian sexual ideal in marriage as the monogamous woman could not. Sir Richard Burton found that, in Utah, "all sensuality in the married state is strictly forbidden beyond the requisite for ensuring progeny,—the practice, in fact, of Adam and Abraham. During the gestation and nursing of children, the strictest continence on the part of the mother is required—rather for a hygienic than for a religious reason." Mormon women, through plural marriage, could achieve the marriage reform advocated by the young Lucy Stone and Elizabeth Stanton. Thus, for some women, plural marriage could mean freedom of their bodies from too much interference by their husbands. They could have a small and well-spaced family, as the Eastern woman could not.

No pioneer woman in the wilderness could be free from work. "Life in the wilds of Western America," Burton continued, "is a course of severe toil: a single woman cannot perform the manifold duties of housekeeping, cooking, scrubbing, washing, darning, child-bearing, and nursing a family. A division of labour is necessary, and she finds it by acquiring a sisterhood."[17] Plural marriage was the rational answer to frontier life, a cooperative of women to share labour, as in the Old Testament.

Children were also needed desperately to help in the building up of the wilderness and in the spreading of the Mormon religion. Polygamy seemed an efficient and eugenic way of ensuring regular and healthy babies, according to the sexual theories of the time. Certainly, the system was vigorously defended by most Mormon women against the United States government. They did not want their children to be declared legal bastards by any law annulling plural marriage. Even if Mormon society was excessively patriarchal, so were all rural pioneer societies—and the fact was that a plural husband had to work himself to death to support more than one wife.

Yet there were apostate Mormon women, who fled in horror from the system and made Utah stink in the nostrils of the nation. Not all of these women were paid propagandists for those Gentiles who wanted to take over the government of Utah through the disenfranchisement of the Mormons. Some had wanted to remain single, and had found that they could not, for there were no jobs available in Utah for single women. Some rebelled against the dogmas and patriarchalism of the Mormon Church, and the subordinate position of women on earth and in heaven. These found woman suffrage in Utah merely a device to strengthen the power of Brigham Young and to perpetuate theocracy and polygamy. "When Mormon women vote it is simply duplicating the male vote over and over again, for they all vote the same ticket—the one given them."[18] Indeed, one of the chief arguments of the anti-suffragists elsewhere against woman suffrage was that the depraved female nature of the Mormon women had prevented them from voting themselves out of polygamy, even though they outnumbered their men by three to two.

The enemies of the Mormons claimed worse. They said that polygamy bred vice, incest, forced marriages, sexual slavery, degenerate children, and unbridled male lust. The situation of Mormon women was as bad as the position of female slaves under Southern planters. The morality of the Mormons was a fiction. The men did not work themselves to death; they married often so that they could live off their wives and work them to death. Polygamy was merely instituted to gratify the lechery and avarice of the Mormon leaders and to perpetuate their power. With the system of the harem came the vices of Turkey and Asia.

The fidelity of Mormon women to their husbands and the prosperity of Utah made their case more reasonable than that of the
apostates. Plural marriage was open to abuse, but only one in thirty
Mormons was rich enough to support more than one wife. Polygamy
was a rich man's privilege; it really ensured that the wealthy had
more children. Thus it offended the democratic ideal of the United
States, although the Mormons could maintain that any American had
the equality of opportunity to become a Mormon and marry often.
Most plural wives probably accepted their situation, even if they did
not wish it for their daughters. One of them declared that, if she
chose, her daughters "would each be the one wife of a good husband,
but that must be as God pleases."[19]

Once the Mormon women had been given the vote, Anthony and
Stanton welcomed them, because they were manifestly respectable,
and the ageing Lucy Stone rejected them, because monogamy was a
passion to her with a husband so much younger than herself. The
acceptance of Mormon women in the National Woman Suffrage Association was another reason for Stone to brand it as "unclean."
Congress agreed with her that plural marriage was intolerable. In
1887, another Act reinforced the provisions against polygamy with
strong penalties. It also took away the vote from Mormon women
because of their failure to emancipate themselves from their degradation.

Congress was, however, not bare-faced enough to insist on the
removal of suffrage from women, when Wyoming applied to be
admitted to the Union. In 1890, both Houses barely passed a measure
to make the territory a state. "It is the beginning of the end," Anthony said in the Senate gallery. And when the Mormon Church
finally bowed to pressure and gave up the doctrine of plural marriage
in 1896, Utah was also admitted to the Union and women were
immediately given back the suffrage.

Utah was, however, the third state to adopt woman suffrage. Three
years before, the vote had come to women in Colorado. The state was,
as a pioneer woman noted, "a country of extremes. Whenever it
undertook to do anything, it acted in the most wholehearted way."
The wind blew so hard that people could not go out for three days at

a time; hailstones were so large that they killed chickens; grasshoppers ate whole harvests; rivers inundated towns. The very excess of nature, according to this witness, made Colorado adopt woman suffrage.[20] Indeed, it was the first state in which men went to the polls in a referendum and gave women the vote. The radical Populist Party briefly controlled the state legislature, and radicalism was rampant everywhere because of severe economic depression.

As Walter Webb pointed out, there was a connection between geography and radicalism. The pioneer ranchers were not radical because they were few and struggling wholly with nature. But when the farmers came, they collected in groups on arable land. They also confronted terrible obstacles. "They were far from markets, burned by drought, beaten by hail, withered by hot winds, frozen by blizzards, eaten out by the grasshoppers, exploited by capitalists, and cozened by politicians. Why should they not turn to radicalism? When men suffer, they become politically radical; when they cease to suffer, they favour the existing order."[21] It was the same with Western women. As Mary Ellen Lease declared in Washington in 1891, "After all our years of sorrow, loneliness, and privation, we are being robbed of our farms, of our homes, at the rate of five hundred a week, and turned out homeless paupers, outcasts and wanderers, robbed of the best years of our life and our toil. Do you wonder that women are joining the Farmers' Alliance and the Knights of Labour?"[22]

Certain other factors helped the victory of woman suffrage in Colorado. There were many small towns, which could easily provide audiences for the suffrage speakers. These tended to give their votes against the saloons and the large corporate interests in Denver and the mining camps. As the woman's vote was still supposed at the time to "purify politics," the reform impulse of the small towns extended to woman suffrage. The corporations and the liquor interests did not campaign seriously against the measure because they did not believe that it would pass. The chief organizer of the suffrage campaign was not an alien and aged Easterner, but the aggressive young Westerner, Carrie Catt. Colorado adjoined both Wyoming and Utah, and had many emigrants from both states, where women had long had the vote. And the economic depression lasted long enough among the farmers and the small towns that supplied them to shake rural people from the conservatism of prosperity. If the results of woman suffrage did little to change the partisan and corporate control of the state in the long run, it did seem an immediate victory for reform. There were few who had the wisdom and coolness of the Denver business-man who later stated, "I did not expect the enfranchisement of women to work a revolution in our government, and I have not been disappointed."[23]

In the same year that Utah became a suffrage state, Idaho also adopted woman suffrage. As with Colorado, it was flanked by Utah and Wyoming, and received the benefit of emigrants and their ideas. Again Populism was rampant during economic depression, again radicalism swept the farms and the small towns, again Carrie Catt ran the suffrage campaign there. But it was the radical surge for William Jennings Bryan that really won the measure. Idaho went for Bryan and woman suffrage together in the November of 1896. Bryan found national defeat, but woman suffrage remained in the state constitu-tion. One Western newspaper pointed out that Idaho and Colorado had won their suffrage referenda because Westerners had employed Western methods. Where Easterners had come to help in the woman suffrage campaigns of Kansas and California, their "blundering in-terference" had lost the measure.

At the end of the nineteenth century, the four states with votes for women were all part of the Great Plains and their bordering mountains, some of the most difficult and bleak farming country in the continent. All except Utah were peopled by a majority of native-born Americans with American parents, under the influence of the reforming Protestant churches. In Wyoming, a special and personal situation had given women the vote early; after they had the vote, partisan politics could not deprive them of it, for fear of throwing their vote to another party. Utah's decision to give women the vote had been religious. The other two states had briefly contained a ma-jority of radicals because of the slump, and the anti-suffrage interests of the corporations and the saloons had not been prepared. Above all, these were states without large cities, with the exception of Denver. They depended for their prosperity on the land and the trade of farmers in small towns.

In Kansas in 1894, Susan Anthony found that "the *lowest* voters of the slums" had combined with the Republicans and the whiskey Democrats in an "unholy alliance" to defeat the Populists and the country vote and woman suffrage.[24] There also, the fact that prohibition had been adopted in the state since 1867 had antagonized many men from supporting woman suffrage, because it was popularly supposed that a woman's vote was a dry vote. Yet in none of the early four suffrage states was prohibition adopted for twenty years after the coming of votes for women, thus seeming to disprove the belief about woman suffrage meaning the immediate end of the saloon.

The defeat of woman suffrage in California in 1896 showed how the liquor vote in large cities could cancel the pro-suffrage vote in small towns. There, after an intensive campaign, the measure just failed to pass, because of the "purchasable and slum vote" of San Francisco, Oakland, and Alameda. With the growth of large seaboard cities in California, and with the rising prosperity of the farmer all over the West, radicalism declined. For fourteen years, no states in the Union followed the example of the first four suffrage states, where human vision had been made clear by the excesses of "tornadoes, blizzards, and geysers."

Only temperance made gains in the West, because states could be dried up county by county outside the mining towns and cities. Suffrage, however, could only come through the state legislature or through a state-wide referendum. Moreover, the religious leaders of the small towns made temperance a priority for their women followers. If they supported the vote for women, it was only in the hope of using that vote against the saloon, on the principle that "women's vote would be to the vices in our great cities what the lightning is to the oak." As a Wisconsin woman wrote to the Ohio suffrage newspaper, *The Ballot-Box*, "Just as much as I want to do my own praying, do I want to do my own voting."[25] Unfortunately for the suffragists, the support of the drys was frequently luke-warm or totally lacking.

For a reform which is near success denies its connection with any other reform that may lose it support. Despite the fact that both drys and suffragists believed that their chief opponent was the organized saloon vote, they were leery of each other. "Enmity against a common foe," an acute observer wrote of them, "does not always result in an alliance between two crusaders, but it cannot fail to produce a feeling of benevolent neutrality."[26]

XX

UNEASY ALLIANCE

In 1889, Henry Blackwell made a trip to the Northwest to try and influence the area to adopt woman suffrage. His first visit was to North Dakota, which was to be the third state to adopt prohibition in that same year. "The trouble is," Blackwell wrote back to Lucy Stone, "that all who would be friendly [to suffrage] are more friendly to Prohibition and to link the two questions together would be fatal, for prohibition is being bitterly fought and many prohibitionists are strongly anti-suffrage." In Montana, he found that a woman suffrage meeting had never been held. Again, it was "the Prohibition alliance that hurts us most—Both parties are utterly opposed to that and the fear that Woman Suffrage means prohibition is the greatest obstacle."

In Washington Territory, even former friends of woman suffrage, where it had been in effect from 1883 until 1887 until voided by the State Supreme Court, had lost their enthusiasm. As one said, "The women led by the preachers have set every neighbourhood by the ears," because of temperance and opposition to immoral candidates for election. "And so for their very virtues," Blackwell commented sadly, "independence, discrimination of character, love of Temperance and good morals—the women are politically slaughtered." In South Dakota, prohibition had been put into the state constitution, but it was on the point of being put out. There, Blackwell wrote that "we shall meet the full force of this ebb tide against prohibition—and the prohibitionists themselves will oppose Woman Suffrage for fear it may lead to a revolt against both and put the State into the hands of the Democrats who are opposed to both."[1]

Abigail Duniway, who battled almost alone for woman suffrage in the Northwest for fifty years, found the same dangerous connection between prohibition and women's rights. She was one of the few feminists who refused to endorse prohibition, for fear of losing the vote of the drinkers who were also suffragists. In her early days as a farmer's wife, she had been an ardent dry. She was converted to the cause of women's rights by the knowledge of other wives whose husbands "would go on occasional sprees, and spend the wives' 'butter money' for whiskey and tobacco."[2] But her priorities shifted from the wrongs caused by the saloon to the wrongs caused by the oppression of women. Like the prohibitionists, she disassociated herself from the secondary reform to press her own favourite. She hated the meddling of the Eastern suffrage leaders and of the Woman's Christian Temperance Union in Oregon. She once threatened to have the dry suffrage leader, Anna Shaw, arrested if she came into the state. It took six referenda to carry Oregon for woman suffrage, all due, in Abigail Duniway's opinion, to the fears of men that woman suffrage meant prohibition. Indeed, when the measure finally carried the state in 1912, the women's vote helped to put through state-wide prohibition two years later.

This uneasy, and often unwilling, alliance between the two reforms in the rural Northwest was complicated by urban factors in other states. There, as Blackwell pointed out, the prohibitionist strategy of drying up the small towns individually through local-option elections proved conclusively to the big cities that the small-town woman was interested in voting dry. It was useless to show by the example of the four woman suffrage states that votes for women did not bring about prohibition; the wets did not believe this, even though they put placards in rural areas to persuade dry voters that woman suffrage had failed to affect saloons.

Local and upstate example proved threatening to the voters in the large cities. Woman suffrage seemed a mere weapon of the drys, in their fight to impose their rural morality on the cities. As a Denver minister declared, "I will utterly despise woman suffrage and curse the day I voted for it if the women of Denver are not alive to the necessity of voting as one, for local option."[3] Until the cities began to worry about reforming themselves rather than resisting the influence of reforming ministers and evangelical small towns, votes for women seemed less human justice than rural bias. When, however, professional women and factory women demanded the vote, that was an urban affair.

Another factor making for an uneasy alliance between the drys and the suffragists was the disproportionate success of the early temperance workers. The Woman's Christian Temperance Union was founded in 1869, the very year that the tiny suffrage movement split apart. It had adopted the political techniques used by the anti-slavery reformers, to lobby for temperance education bills. By the beginning of the twentieth century, its members outnumbered the suffragists by more than ten to one; by 1912, it had more than a quarter of a million members. Any self-styled lady in a small town felt free to join the movement, for it was the most respectable and religious reform of all, demonstrably for purity and the home and against drunkenness and vice. The Devil it fought was a visible one, the saloon, not an intangible concept, oppression by the male sex. As one suffragist commented, "It is so much easier to see a drunkard than it is to see a principle."[4]

Cooperation between the two causes was a personal matter. Susan Anthony, scarred by her experiences with dress reform and Train and Woodhull, refused to endorse temperance officially, although she had been an early worker in that cause. On the other hand, Frances Willard, an early supporter of the ladylike American Woman Suffrage Association, was converted by Anthony to the policy of the federal suffrage amendment. Brought up in Ohio and on the Wisconsin prairie, with her father an agrarian reformer and her mother an Oberlin student, Frances Willard knew from childhood the radical reform movements of her time. Although temperance was her first concern, she was also interested in any measure that could help women and the poor. She was elected president of the Woman's Christian Temperance Union, and used that enormous organization to advocate many humanitarian reforms, largely connected with the prohibition of the liquor trade. More than any other person, she was responsible for awakening tens of thousands of women in small towns into social consciousness—the first condition of becoming aware that they wanted the vote.

Frances Willard did more for the suffrage cause. She had the national convention of the Woman's Christian Temperance Union endorse woman suffrage in the 1880's. Anna Shaw made her reputation as the organizer of the new suffrage department of the Union, but it was Frances Willard who was responsible for getting many of the state branches of the Union to work actively for votes for women. It was she who, as the *Woman's Journal* said, bridged the chasm which separated the women of the churches from the suffrage cause. In one day, nearly one hundred dry women preached from the pulpits of St. Louis—a place where they had hardly been allowed to stand since the days of the Grimké sisters. By 1902, clergymen, even in orthodox Massachusetts, were supporting woman suffrage in a proportion of six to one.[5] After the death of Frances Willard, Anna Shaw continued the Midwestern alliance between the evangelical churches and temperance and votes for women, when she came to lead the national American Woman Suffrage Association.

The success of the Woman's Christian Temperance Union in attracting members explained the failure of the Victorian suffragists. Willard's genius was to claim continually that the temperance movement was only to protect the home and the child. She appealed to that very ideal to which the anti-suffragists appealed. And because, among politically minded women, the respectable were many and the radical were few, the Woman's Christian Temperance Union prospered. The supreme cleverness of Willard was to use this conservative organization to advocate woman suffrage and child labour laws and other progressive legislation, always in the name of purity and the home.

She called the ballot "a necessary weapon for home protection." She coined a motto for the Union, "Do Everything," when it had been formed to do one thing.

Yet Willard could not do more than give the suffrage cause the hypothetical backing of the largest body of organized women in the world. Depending on whether the dry women were conservative or radical by nature, they would help the local suffragists. Some felt with the woman who wrote to *The Ballot-Box,* "Prohibition, Woman Suffrage, and Education shall bring to us a new heaven and a new earth."⁶ More thought that prohibition alone would bring a new heaven and a new earth. The actual suffrage department of the Woman's Christian Temperance Union, however, produced five million pages of suffrage literature a year, more than the suffragists did. Although Willard's conversion to socialism before her death in 1898 put her even more out of touch with her followers, during her life she was a force of influence behind the cause of women and of labour. After her death, however, the Woman's Christian Temperance Union reverted to a predominant concentration on the dry cause.

If there were some dry women who were also suffragists and many suffragists who were also dry, relations between the two groups remained, on the whole, neutral. The situation which Henry Blackwell had discovered in the Northwest in 1889 continued, with local variations. Despite frequent pronouncements of the separation of the causes, they remained linked in the public mind, as the causes of the rights of women and of Negroes remained linked in the mythology of the South. While prohibition helped woman suffrage in one area, it hindered in another. Votes for women did the same service for the drys. While some would argue that the drys were a "stalking horse" for the suffragists, others would claim that the suffragists were "parasites on temperance." A Massachusetts anti-suffragist summed up the situation with the remark, "They have mixed those babies up, and woman suffrage and temperance are not merely foster brothers but twins and look so much alike you don't know which is which."⁷

The prohibitionists, however, did manage to close most of the saloons in small towns and villages, and to dry up most of the continent outside the cities and mining towns. Although the suffragists had won partial suffrage in such matters as school elections in twenty-one states by the turn of the century, they had received full suffrage in only four. The basic method of the drys was superior to that of the suffragists. They could close the saloons one by one in the rural areas of each state, once they had lobbied a local-option bill through the state legislature. But the suffragists could not get full suffrage county by county; they had to win the whole state either through a referendum or through legislative command.

In the South, moreover, the drys could and did separate themselves successfully from the suffragists. Southern ladies would crusade for them in their role of defenders of the home and the family. The centre of prohibition success in the states shifted to the South, when Oklahoma, Georgia, Mississippi, North Carolina, and Tennessee, all adopted state-wide prohibition between 1907 and 1909, the period of the doldrums of the suffrage movement. In the South, conservative and racial propaganda was on the side of the drys, for prohibition was an instrument to keep liquor from Negroes and to buttress the purity of the home.

If the suffragists were glad of the local support of the Woman's Christian Temperance Union, where it was available, they also took from the Union the upper middle-class leadership which had given it power and prestige. In the Victorian period, the Union was led by the wives of men with local status. These dry chiefs did not, on the whole, work for a living; more than one in two of them had husbands, who were in professional or managerial jobs. By 1910, little more than one in three of the dry women leaders was the wife of a professional or an official.[8]

At the same time, the suffrage movement was increasingly led by women of wealth, such as Mrs. O. H. P. Belmont, and professional women in their own right as well as the wives of professional men, such as Carrie Catt. One study of twenty-six major suffrage leaders between 1890 and 1920 found that sixteen of them had a college degree, while the same number had worked in a professional job. Those born before 1859 tended to be members of the Woman's

Christian Temperance Union, those born afterwards tended not to be. All but one were Protestants, all but two of old American stock.[9] Suffrage took over from temperance work as the reform priority of the educated girl at the turn of the century. She tended to study social sciences rather than evangelism, and to be fired by statistics on poverty rather than the Sermon on the Mount. The girl who fifty years before had wanted to be a missionary in China now wanted to be a social worker in the Lower East Side of New York.

The social prestige of suffrage rose, until, in the decade of the First World War, it became socially *smart* in the large cities to be a suffragist. At this moment, millions of middle-class women joined the suffrage movement, so that by 1916 its membership easily topped that of the Woman's Christian Temperance Union. The dry movement depended for much of its appeal on the anti-urban and evangelical feelings of women in small towns, but the suffrage movement eventually drew its mass support from women in the cities and from those women in the small towns who looked to the cities for social leadership.

In this manner, the priority of women reformers between the Civil War and the First World War correctly reflected the possibility of reform in a nation where most of the population dwelt on farms concentrated round small towns, which were interested in the reforms backed by the local churches. But when a revolution in communications and the growth of cities had shifted the attention of reformers to urban problems, the priority of women reformers changed to suffrage, as an urban and social solution divorced from the religious crusade against the saloon. Nothing showed this shift of emphasis better than the Women's Organization for National Prohibition Reform, which flourished between 1929 and 1933. This mushrooming group collected three million members in the cities to oppose the Eighteenth Amendment to the Constitution, which was finally repealed. The organization was led by smart urban socialites. Its huge influence and success showed how much and how quickly social leadership had left the pulpit of the small town for the example of the city lady. In the widespread women's club movement, a similar change in focus and leadership took place; in its most extreme form, this change turned the Daughters of the American Revolution from a radical group of women into a reactionary clique of ladies.

Yet the prohibition movement was successful nationally before the suffrage movement was. This success was due to the efficiency of a new organization founded in Ohio in 1893, the Anti-Saloon League. It took over the leadership of the dry crusade from the Woman's Christian Temperance Union through its efficient use of the evangelical churches, where the principle of male leadership was more acceptable to local ministers. In Ohio, the suffragist Harriet Upton found the League "long on promises but short on fulfilment." Purley Baker, the chief of the League, might declare, "The antidote that is to meet the saloon opposition to American citizenship is to be found in the enfranchising of American womanhood"[10]; but the League tended to turn the matter of suffrage support over to the Woman's Christian Temperance Union. "To a woman," Harriet Upton declared, "we were prohibitionists. Dry men were for prohibition and not opposed to woman suffrage, but they watched us with a jealous eye. It was the dry men outside of the dry organization who believed women were being unjustly treated by law and by customs who were our main supporters."[11]

Thus, even without official support, the believers of one cause could count on the support of the majority of those who backed the other cause—except in the South. And once the second wave of woman suffrage gathered momentum in the West with the rise of the Progressive movement, the drys began to gain from the suffragists. The Woman's Christian Temperance Union had educated two generations of women in social consciousness and in the techniques of reform agitation. Temperance had been to the later suffragists what anti-slavery had been to the pioneer feminists. Dry women were treated as badly as abolitionist women by state legislatures, and they began to want the vote to punish their legal representatives. One California suffragist explained the support of the drys in Southern California by telling the story of a delegation of dry women in front of the Committee of Public Morals in Sacramento. The women, as the representatives of fifty thousand others in the state, were pleading with their political representatives for protection for young girls. The chairman of the Committee laughed and said, "Well, you are no more than fifty thousand mice! How many votes can you deliver?"[12]

A comparison between the states which adopted both woman suffrage and prohibition before the passage of a federal amendment shows that, in the Progressive era, woman suffrage helped prohibition more than prohibition helped woman suffrage. Although the first four suffrage states did not enact state-wide prohibition for two decades, six of the following woman suffrage states put through prohibition within four years of women getting the vote. Only in Michigan, however, did the passing of state-wide prohibition precede the granting of suffrage to women by less than a decade. In the surprising case of Kansas, it took forty-five years for the dry state to endorse woman suffrage, because of the alienated wet vote of the cities there.

Carrie Catt had an intimate knowledge of the connection between the prohibition movement and woman suffrage in the West. It was her opinion that "had there been no prohibition movement in the United States, the women would have been enfranchised two generations before they were. Had that movement not won its victory, they would have struggled on for another generation."[13] In fact, her judgement seems to be faulty. Even without prohibition it is unlikely that many women in the East and South would have been enfranchised sooner than they were. The suffragists were fond of exaggerating the degree to which their unpopular cause was blocked by the organized liquor trade. Moreover, if the passage of the dry Eighteenth Amendment removed one of the chief objections to the passage of the suffrage Nineteenth Amendment, it is doubtful whether Congress could have delayed much longer in granting women the suffrage, once the victorious British Empire had generally done so after the First World War.

More true would be the statement that the dry women's organization trained up generations of women in political and reform activity, and made them question their traditional place in society. Had there been no prohibition movement in the United States, fewer women would have known that they wanted the franchise. But the passage of the Eighteenth Amendment was one of the last victories of the evangelical morality of the small town, while the passage of the Nineteenth Amendment was one of the first victories of the social morality of the new cities and suburbs. For Southern lawmakers, in a body, supported the first and opposed the second, because the South by this time was the most predominantly rural area in the nation.

PART SEVEN

The Birth of the Modern Woman

Freedom is demanded to do good; if some use their freedom to do evil, that is the unavoidable friction of the machinery, the bad investment which goes to profit and loss in the business of progress; but freedom nevertheless is the watchword of truth.

ELIZABETH CADY STANTON

Americans are by definition free and equal; if then anyone talks or acts as if he were not free and equal, he must have been born somewhere else.

HAROLD STEARNS

XXI

❦

UPON THEIR LOINS

AFTER THE CIVIL WAR, the turbulent Atlantic seaports and the flood of immigrants within their slums made the native-born Americans concerned with holding onto power. Although all Americans had once been aliens, except for the Indians, those born in the New World felt that the land was particularly theirs. It was their birthright, not merely their chosen refuge. Their children should inherit the earth, not the children of alien people pouring out of the ships in Boston and New York. Yet, at that very moment, the birth-rate was falling among the native-born Americans. The Civil War had killed many of their best men. "All the fruitfulness of the present generation, tasked to its utmost," warned a Boston doctor in 1868,

can hardly fill the gaps in our population that have of late been made by disease and the sword, while the great territories of the far West, just opening to civilization, and the fertile savannas of the South, now disinthralled and first made habitable by freemen, offer homes for countless millions yet unborn. Shall they be filled by our own children or by those of aliens? This is a question that our own women must answer; upon their loins depends the future destiny of the nation.[1]

The prevalent worry among native-born Americans about their declining fertility was contradicted by the feminists' demand for marriage reform and fewer children, thus adding to the differences between the conservatives and the radicals. "When the relations of the sexes are regulated by the enlightened conscience and sound judgement of woman," *The Revolution* declared,

and not by the morbid appetites of man, her whole life will not be devoted to one animal function, at the expense of all other enjoyments. When we apply the same laws of science to the propagation of the human family as to the lower animals, women will not marry before twenty-five, nor have children but at intervals of four or five years, nor under any circumstances unless both parents are possessed of sound minds in sound bodies, without moral or physical weakness, or taint.[2]

In this war between those who clung to the traditional belief that they should multiply at all costs to replenish the empty earth and those who thought that they should only multiply wisely and replenish well, *The Descent of Man and Selection in Relation to Sex* of Charles Darwin gave a scientific background to their dearest prejudices. Nothing shows better than the controversy over evolution and eugenics how social fears influence the choice of arguments to allay them, and how the conservative or the radical temperament sees the same theory as a proof of opposite conclusions. Darwin persuaded few of the truth of his own observations. He persuaded many of the truth of theirs.

Elizabeth Stanton, with her eye for the fashionable argument, immediately pressed Darwin into service to buttress her case. "Science has alienated the right to discuss freely whether our ancestors were apes," she declared in 1870. "Let it be as free to ask whether our posterity shall be idiots, dwarfs, knaves and lunatics; and if not, by what change, if any, in our social institutions, such wretched results may be avoided."[3] Good breeding, if necessary by the prohibition of law, was necessary to produce the higher type of man and woman. Even without the change of social institutions, people should choose their mates carefully and procreate thoughtfully. Self-control was all. The race could only be purified and improved by the abstinence of the educated and the good.

The controversy over Darwin's and Huxley's works further strengthened the feminist cause, because both seemed to attack the literal truth of the Bible. If Genesis were biologically wrong, what was the force of God's curse on Eve? The infallibility of the Word of God was badly shaken by the theory of apes and men, and women were freed to question the religious taboos laid on their mothers. Yet, as a suffragist warned, Darwin and Huxley were not on the side of the feminists. They seemed "to make woman simply a lesser man, weaker in body and mind—an affectionate and docile animal, of inferior grade. That there is any aim in the distinction of the sexes, beyond the perpetuation of the race, is nowhere recognized by them." Huxley in 1865 had denied even the natural equality of the sexes, and had declared "that in every excellent character, whether mental or physical, the average woman is inferior to the average man, in the sense of having that character less in quantity and lower in quality."[4] In fact, the very popularity of Darwin and Huxley in conservative American circles was due to their emphasis on motherhood as woman's vital role, as well as to their implied justification of the rich with the theory of the survival of the fittest.

Anthropology, however, was ready to give new ammunition to the feminists. Increasing study of primitive tribes in the late Victorian period made it clear that matriarchy was the normal condition of many peoples. Women could be superior and dominant in the laws and customs of society. Indeed, the King of Dahomey had a royal guard of Amazonian women. These stout soldiers drank and cursed and fought better than the men of Dahomey. When one of the women ran away in battle, the rest of them would accuse her bitterly of fighting just like a man.

If women were superior to men in some societies, then their subordinate position in evolved Western society was artificial, not natural. The position of women could be changed, as well as should be changed. In fact, according to the Victorian ideal that woman was morally better than man, did not the proper ordering of society in America involve a matriarchy? Should not woman's dominance in the American home become her dominance in the whole of the vast home

of the United States? Was she not the natural head of the family of
the nation, as Queen Victoria was of the British Commonwealth of
Nations? Biology supported anthropology in such an idea. As Matilda Gage declared in 1884,

Through biology we learn that the first manifestation of life is feminine.
. . . Science also proves that a greater expenditure of vital force is requisite for the production of the feminine than for the masculine. . . . Male
infants are more often deformed, suffer from abnormal characteristics,
and more speedily succumb to infantile diseases than female infants. . . .
It is manifest that woman possesses in a higher degree than man that
adaption to the conditions surrounding her which is everywhere accepted
as evidence of superior vitality and higher physical rank in life; and when
biology becomes more fully understood it will also be universally acknowledged that the primal creative power, like the first manifestation of life,
is feminine.[5]

When Weismann proved the continuity of the germ plasm at the
end of the nineteenth century, the arguments about the influence of
heredity seemed conclusive, as opposed to the arguments about the
change possible in children under a good environment. Such emphasis
on heredity explained, to a certain extent, the swing of the leading
suffragists from the idea of votes for all women to the idea of votes
for some educated women—and some educated men. Their fears began to coincide with the fears of most old-stock Americans that they
would be swamped by the flood of new immigrants from Southern
and Eastern Europe, although the population of foreign-born people
in eighteenth-century America had been double what it was to be in
the opening decades of twentieth-century America. As a conservative
suffragist declared, "An oligarchy of class, where the refined govern
the uncouth; of learning, where the educated govern the ignorant; of
race, where the Saxon rules inferior people, is natural and can be
endured; but an oligarchy of sex is the most odious aristocracy under
the sun."[6]

Thus, while anthropology and biology provided arguments that
women could be superior to men and therefore should be treated as
their equals, immigration and eugenics provided reasons to old-stock

Americans to keep women in their place as wives and mothers in the home, even if they were given the vote. The loins of American women were never more necessary, in order to preserve the destiny of the nation. "The female is biologically dominant," declared *Woman and Social Progress* in 1912. "Woman is the race . . . is at the top of the human curve from which the higher superman of the future is to evolve. . . . Her whole soul, conscious and unconscious, is best conceived as a magnificent organ of heredity."[7] Thus eugenicists merely stressed, what the early Victorians had once stressed and the later Neo-Freudians were to repeat, that the soul of woman lay in her womb. Reproduction was the true duty and fulfilment of the female sex.

The answer of the suffragists to this eugenic argument was, on the whole, a qualified agreement. Since most of the leading suffragists were married and mothers, they supported the eugenic argument. They claimed, however, that wives should reserve the right to have few children. They agreed with the influential Havelock Ellis that birth control was "the only available lever for raising the level of our race." Because the unfit did not check the number of their children, there was no need for the fit to lower themselves to their level. They should realize their "responsibility for the coming race" by having fewer and better children. "We generate the race," Havelock Ellis declared; "we alone can regenerate the race."[8]

Despite the hysterical attacks of such traditionalists as Theodore Roosevelt, who considered that a marriage with one or two children was "wilful sterility" and led to "every hideous form of vice," eugenic reasons favoured the spread of birth-control and the power of women to choose the size of their families. Such influential, although conservative, eugenicists as C. W. Saleeby went so far as to advocate woman suffrage solely because of eugenic reasons. The vote would lead to the reform of marriage and divorce in the eugenic sense. It would also serve the cause of "preventive eugenics," such as the adoption of laws against "racial poisons" like venereal disease and alcohol.[9]

The vote for women was increasingly presented by suffragists as well as eugenicists as the only method of raising a pure and healthy family. Woman suffrage was a moral measure, to ensure the rights of a wife and her children. "Perhaps in no clearer light is the rising ideal of family life revealed," wrote a male suffragist,

than in woman's fierce revolt against the ancient, man-made standard of the sex relations. She righteously resents commercialized prostitution, the low legal age of consent for girls, the "conspiracy of silence" regarding venereal disease, and the whole "double standard of sex-morals" as degrading to her personality. It is in this connection that the new movements for sex education, sex hygiene, and eugenic marriage disclose their chief meaning. Hence they are invariably an accented part of the equal suffrage programme.[10]

Yet this appeal to eugenics was dangerous. For it denied other freedoms that some unmarried women were seeking. It emphasized the sanctity of the mother in the home at the expense of the single woman outside it. By doing so, it claimed not so much equality of women with men as more control for wives over husbands. It emphasized matriarchy in the house rather than equality on the job. Acceptance by suffrage leaders of the virtues of motherhood sounded like the arguments of the Victorian anti-suffragists. By choosing not to educate women to see a meaning in the vote beyond the protection of the home, the suffragists were partly responsible for many of the frustrations which wives continued to feel after they had been given the suffrage. The vote solved none of the problems of motherhood, which had more to do with lack of liberty than lack of the ballot.

The anti-suffragists, of course, used biological and evolutionary arguments to buttress their case in the same way that their enemies did. To them, women were condemned to inequality by nature and heredity. That is why they should never seek to compete with men. In the most influential work on anthropology of its time, *The Passing of the Great Race,* Madison Grant denied that women were higher up the scale of evolution than men:

Women in all human races, as the females among all mammals, tend to exhibit the older, more generalized and primitive traits of the past of the race. . . . It is interesting to note in connection with the more primitive physique of the female, that in the spiritual sphere also women retain the ancient and intuitive knowledge that the great mass of mankind is not free and equal but bond and unequal.[11]

Such consciousness should lead women to remain where they were, the mothers of mankind. For in that position they would do the greatest good to humanity. Indeed, feminism was immoral, in the opinion of another contemporary work. Not only did it preach a false equality between the sexes, but it encouraged educated women to have fewer children, when the race demanded that they should bear the most children. For morality meant now, as it was a relative affair, "that course of conduct which will lead to the greatest common good."[12]

Even the giving of the vote to women, according to the anti-suffragists, was not a progressive step demanded by evolution, but a step backwards. As was usual in anti-suffrage propaganda, the few feminists who advocated complete equality with men in all areas of life were wrongly equated with the mass of the suffragists. "To treat women exactly as men," Mrs. Arthur Dodge declared, "is to deny all the progress through evolution which has been made by an increasing specialization of function. Woman suffrage in its last analysis is a retrogressive movement toward conditions where the work of man and woman was the same because neither sex had evolved enough to see the wisdom of being a specialist in its own line."[13] The doctrine of separate spheres for male and female distinguished civilization from savagery. Sexual equality would mean the death of the lady.

Thus those women, like Stanton and Gage, who wished to feel superior to men picked from anthropology whatever suited their preference. Those "Anglo-Saxon" suffragists who wished to feel superior to immigrant women also chose eugenic arguments to fit their ideas of limited suffrage. Those politicians among the reformers who wished to attract the support of the conservative majority of American wives emphasised even more the eugenic virtues which would flow into the home from the ballot. All sorts of suffragists, outside the radical fringe, were guilty of hallowing the virtues of motherhood at the expense of the virtues of the free and single woman.

This policy was good tactics, for the majority of American men and women were married and had families. Yet it was a betrayal of those single women who were suffragists because they believed in the ideal of absolute equality with men. On these unrepresentative suffragists, the anti-suffragists directed their fire. They used the vocabulary of eugenics to damn the single state as a crime tantamount to that committed by the Victorian "old maid." At a memorial service to Frances Willard, a Senator went so far as to declare that her life's work was less than that of the least American mother.

Meanwhile, the increasing tide of immigration and the fertility of immigrant women worried all the middle-class women of old American stock, who led and joined the organizations that supported or opposed reforms. The best people were choosing not to breed. Phi Beta Kappa girls from Wellesley had fewer children than their sister alumnae. Only one-fifth of American women with doctorates were married and had children. After two hundred years, a thousand Harvard men could only expect to have fifty descendants, while a thousand Rumanians would have one hundred thousand descendants. Extinction was the price of rising on the scale of evolution. The Great Race would Pass beneath the Rising Tide of Colour unless the problem of the immigrant and the inferior was solved.

Immigration made eugenics and evolution a passion in American life, until emigration laws cut down the fascination of the topic in the 1920's. When Carrie Catt went to college, she "got Evolution in every class room and laboratory." A whole generation of middle-class girls was taught to mouth the language of Darwin. When the "new immigration" rose to its peak, the language of eugenics was added to that of evolution. The struggle for the survival of the fittest in conversation was really joined. Even after the First World War, a French traveller found that he never got out of his depth if he carried two talismans, a treatise on eugenics, and a Bible.[14] And for once Mencken was ignored, when he puffed, "Eugenics is the theory that charm in a woman is the same as charm in a prize-fighter."[15]

XXII

THE NEW WORLD
AND THE IMMIGRANT

"WE ARE ALL ALIENS," declared Frederic Howe in 1922.

And what is less to our liking we are almost all descended from the peasant classes of Europe. We are here because our forebears were poor. They did not rule over there. They were oppressed; they were often owned. And with but few exceptions they came because of their poverty. For the rich rarely emigrate. . . . Only those who came in the *Mayflower* made their own laws and their own fortunes. Those who come to-day have their laws made for them by the class that employs them and they make their own fortunes only as those aliens who came first permit them to do so.[1]

Such considerations did not influence the treatment of the immigrant to America between the coming of the Irish before the Civil War until the closing of the gates to the New World in 1924. Even the Negro sometimes seemed more American and preferable to the despised Irishman. "Every man woman and child of them," Susan Anthony wrote to Elizabeth Stanton of the free Negroes in Kansas after the Civil War, "is brimful of good common sense, and knows more than any ten of the same class of Irish population."[2] In Boston particularly, where the main weight of the Irish descended, the change of attitude towards the suffragists showed how much the new immigrants were hated.

Massachusetts had once been receptive to radical and feminist ideas, before the coming of the Irish. And yet after the Civil War, the home city of Margaret Fuller and the anti-slavery movement became the stronghold of the anti-suffrage movement. Such a turn in sentiment reflected more than the growing conservatism of an ageing city, which had always preferred evangelical to social reform. It was a desperate clutch at threatened traditions. "With woman voting," said a Boston clergyman, "the country is given up to Romanism. The priest loses the man, but keeps the woman. Give him the control of the vote of the thousands of servants in the great cities, and there is an end to legislation in behalf of the Sabbath, the Bible, the school system, temperance, and morality."[3] In a private letter to a friend, even the judicious Oliver Wendell Holmes could say that, while he had refused to sign a petition against woman suffrage at the request of the president of Harvard, "as our households are constituted, I do not care to see the basement arrayed in greater force against the drawing room (which it nearly governs already) by adding Bridget and Hanna to the list of voters."[4] Considerations of caste and class had made the middle classes of the Eastern cities rigid in their defence of their slipping power.

Nothing showed the rise of feeling against the new immigrant women and, by implication, against the suffragists more than the controversy over the Boston schools in the 1880's. Bostonian women had been given the right to vote in elections to the school board. Some nativist women with a talent for organization had massed the middle-class Protestant women's vote at the polls to put in the Republicans and sweep the Irish Catholic Democrats off the school board. This action coincided with the attacks of the American Protective Association against the immigrants. The partisan and prejudiced use of the vote by Bostonian women harmed the cause of the suffragists, especially in the minds of their liberal supporters. The Irish Democrats were naturally hostile, especially since tradition prevented them from allowing their own womenfolk to go to the polls. They found the idea of a woman voting morally repugnant.

In answer to this hostility in the slums of Boston, Lucy Stone and other Protestant middle-class suffragists began to shift to a demand for municipal suffrage—a right which widows and single women with property had held in England for twenty years. This extension of the vote to property-owning women would increase the voting power of the middle class against the slums. Boston could be cleaned up through the principle of "enlarged housekeeping." In fact, Lucy Stone had drifted so far out of contact with the life of the poor that she blamed the Homestead strikers for not setting up in business on their own with their savings if they did not like the conditions of their job. She and the rest of the Protestant middle-class suffragists still lived in a rural and early Victorian world of the mind, where the caste system of the city had not yet destroyed equality of opportunity.

Hostility to the immigrant and the conservative reaction of the middle-class lady proved to be powerful factors in Massachusetts in the disastrous referendum on woman suffrage held there in 1895. By a unique clause, women were allowed to record their own vote on the proposition. Only four in one hundred did so; the rest abstained from voting. Of that small proportion, twenty-five in twenty-six were in favour of woman suffrage. But, on the whole, public opinion and apathy and the abnormality of the proceeding had kept the would-be lady and the immigrant woman in her home. "They were afraid of their husbands," Mary Livermore explained. In the whole state, few more female votes were cast on the issue than in Boston alone during the school elections. Education remained the prior reform among the women of New England. The vote was too abstract an issue to engage their enthusiasm. Radicalism had largely left the women of the towns of New England for the newer towns of the West. The conservative lady had become the ideal of social life in bourgeois Massachusetts, while the subservient peasant woman had remained the fact of social life in the Boston slum. Only a small group of professional middle-class women wanted the vote, in order to set the seal of victory on their long fight for economic and educational equality with men.

The men of Massachusetts, however, only voted the suffrage measure down in a ratio of two to one. They split along the old rural and urban lines that had been set up in the days of the anti-slavery movement. Twenty-eight small towns in the state cast a majority in favour of woman suffrage, chiefly in the areas where Garrison had once been strong. All fourteen cities in the state voted against the measure, with Boston itself turning it down by three votes to one. The school issue had alienated the Catholic wet immigrant vote. Even Thomas Higginson admitted that if the object of some of the suffragists was to detach from their cause "every Democrat, every Catholic, and every foreigner," they could not have acted more wisely. If suffrage was to be carried in Massachusetts, its advocates would have to make a wider appeal.[5]

Except in the settlement houses and the working women's clubs, the suffragists continued to deny that they needed the help of the immigrant women. Until the end of the suffrage crusade, most of its supporters prided themselves on their position in society, which was neither aristocratic nor proletarian. Mary Wollstonecraft herself had addressed her *Vindication,* not to the lady or to the poor, but "to those in the middle class, because they appear to be in the most natural state."[6] The official magazine of the National American Woman Suffrage Association agreed more than a century later, when it declared that the suffrage movement was "bourgeois, middle-class, a great middle-of-the-road movement; evidence of a slow-come mass conviction; representative of that most coherent, tightest-welded, farthest-reaching section of society—the middle."[7]

Of course, the middle class was not so tightly welded that it did not have its geographical and social divisions, particularly over matters of votes for women. "It is impossible at present to know whether the 'effete' East will take to us as kindly as the 'middle class Middle West,'" wrote an Ohio suffragist in 1914. "Massachusetts will be a hard nut to crack. I often find so-called cultured people the most cynical and difficult to impress."[8]

Some middle-class women, however, were prepared to save the suffragists from the consequences of their own exclusiveness. They saw the need to convert the new immigrant men and women to the suffrage cause, difficult as the task was. The leader of these women was Jane Addams. Brought up in rural Illinois, she was educated at Rockford, known as the "Mount Holyoke of the West." Her father was a rationalist, a State Senator, and a personal friend of Abraham Lincoln; as a child, she had a "doglike affection" for both of them.

Jane Addams spent her twenties in a drift of purpose, travelling round the Midwest and Europe. The view of the poverty of the East End slums of London first gave her a horror of her status as a lady tourist. In Europe, "the form of heavy-laden market women and underpaid street labourers [was] gibing her with a sense of her uselessness." On her return to America, she visited some Western farms on which she owned mortgages. Life there was as bad as in the slums of Europe. The image that remained in her mind was of a herd of starving pigs, which had turned to eating each other. Finally, after seeing a bloody Spanish bullfight with indifference, she realized that her vague plan of setting up a settlement house in the slums of Chicago would have to be done, or she could not continue to live with herself. She had overcome the curious period of inertia which riches had inflicted on the middle-class girl before marriage. Jane Addams decided to remain single and to become active, thus escaping the uselessness of "the snare of preparation."9

At Hull-House in Chicago, which she founded, Jane Addams was to set an example that was imitated by hundreds of small-town and suburban girls. Most of these avoided "the snare of preparation." They could go directly from college into social work at one of the hundreds of settlement houses that were to spring up in the major cities of America. Social work in the slums was to the girl at the beginning of the twentieth century what the support of missionary work abroad had been to her grandmother. For the barbarian had come to the shores of the New World. By pioneering in the contacts of lady reformers with union and immigrant women, Jane Addams broke through the caste barrier that had prevented the suffragists from getting a mass following.

Her voice always spoke for a minority opinion in the suffrage

conventions. Her immense authority in social work gave her a prestige, if not always a following. She opposed the middle-class acceptance of the concepts of eugenics and evolution to excuse their defence
of the existing economic system. To Jane Addams, environment was
the most important thing in life; heredity was little. It was the slum
that made the bad American woman, not the fact that she was an
immigrant or a Catholic. "The statement is sometimes made," she
wrote, "that the franchise for women would be valuable only so far
as the educated women exercised it. This statement totally disregards
the fact that those matters in which woman's judgement is most
needed are far too primitive and basic to be largely influenced by what
we call education."[10] Matters of pure food and water, of children's
schools and clothing, of protection against fire in factory and tenement, of decent wages and low rents, of garbage collection and electricity, depended on every woman's vote against the indifference of a
city administration. It was interesting that Jane Addams, who had
found the Western farm as badly in need of reform as the urban
slum, should have thought that the main effort of reformers and
suffragists should be concentrated on the city rather than the country,
where the most virtue was popularly thought to reside. She revelled
in the city as the hope of democracy and social improvement. She
wanted Chicago to prove as fertile as the Greek city-states. By her
example, she did much to explain how those late Victorians who
reacted against small-town evangelism turned to social reform in the
slums as their natural duty in life.[11]

Although the thousands of workers in the settlement houses were
an essential bridge between the middle classes and the new immigrants, they did not prevent enmity between the social groups. They
found that most bourgeois ladies were indifferent to any feeling of
solidarity with their sex. They would rather be respectable than
women. They were happy with things as they were, and they prided
themselves on their moderation. One social worker and suffragist
complained bitterly of

the luke-warm very comfortable middle-class rich women. They are dis-
gustingly calm because there is nothing troubling them, and they always

THE NEW WORLD AND THE IMMIGRANT   [247]

excuse their lack of interest by saying that the rest of us are *"hysterical"* about the conditions of working women, and that somebody must be "moderate." A moderate interest in the working women is almost as bad to me as being a mugwump in politics, for a man who cannot work inside his own party lines is not any good anywhere.[12]

Outside the Scandinavians and the radical Jews, the new immigrants cordially returned the dislike of the middle-class suffragists. Most of them came from peasant backgrounds in Ireland, and in Eastern or Southern Europe. There, equality with women had been unthinkable. Their patriarchalism was as absolute as that of the early American labourers in the wilderness, and had as strict religious taboos against women. Rural societies tend to adopt the rule of the Father, in heaven and on earth. The fact of meeting slum conditions rather than the uncleared wilderness did not make the reaction of the new immigrants any different from that of the early American colonists. To stop their children from adopting the savagery of hunters in the streets, they stressed the values of God and the home which they had brought over from Europe. The only defence of the new immigrant against the squalor of the American tenement was a desperate re-creation of his European past. This re-creation, with its strange and imported sounds and sights and smells, further widened the gulf between the new immigrants and the old-stock Americans, who became more convinced that such alien behaviour threatened the traditions of their own past.

An acute commentator on the immigrants in Boston at the end of the Victorian period noticed how "the immigrant tended to blur the memory of the clay on his boots with a vision of the rolling green hills of Ireland, or obscure the memory of a broken-down farm with the vision of the forests and shores of Maine or Nova Scotia. Russian Jews, Italians, Germans, Scots, Canadians, Englishmen, and Americans all shared a knowledge of a past era prior to industrialization." As the years went by, the reality of the past diminished, and the "old country" took on the qualities that were missing in the squalor and slum living of the American city.

In this blend of fact and fancy, life was less disciplined and more leisurely, and men lived in simple communities where all spoke the same language, went to the same church, and shared a common life. Friends were true and wealth unimportant, the girls prettier and the cooking better, honest craftsmen laboured for love to make things of beauty, not cheap machine shoddy, and when a man came home at night it was to a neat cottage and a family of healthy happy children.[13]

In fact, the mythology of the old American pioneers and the new ones was exactly the same.

Thus the nostalgic sentimentalism of the new immigrants agreed with many of the arguments of the Victorian anti-suffragists, who also believed in the family virtues of a golden age. The peasant who migrated from the land of Europe into the American city, the home-steader driven by the hardship of the frontier back into the factory, and the middle-class conservative from a rural town, all had much in common. With the brutality of urban fact before them, they gilded the brutality of rural or small-town life behind them. It took a gener-ation of children, native and immigrant, brought up in the city, to allow virtue to be found in the city. We hallow our roots, whether asphalt or grass. Only this new urban generation of workingmen and professionals could begin to be persuaded by some of the suffragists to give up traditional masculine beliefs and vote for woman suffrage, in order to clean up the corrupt cities that had always been their home.

The position of the peasant European woman in the Eastern Amer-ican city was particularly brutal. Another founder of a settlement house, Lillian Betts, found that the concept of a home centring on the mother was practically non-existent in the slums. Apathy, drunk-enness, sloth, and ignorance made slum women incapable of the smallest household task. Children were largely ignored by their mothers after they could walk. None of the slum mothers could cook properly, nor sew, nor clean, nor concentrate on any task which might have turned their tenement rooms into a cheerful place for living. The dreariness of their family surroundings explained why the im-migrant men preferred the saloons and the children the streets. The mothers themselves preferred to sit in the halls and on the steps, and were reluctant to give up each other's company for household work.

The women in the alleys had married, it was found, at about eighteen. They knew absolutely nothing of housekeeping. Many of them acknowledged that they had never made a fire before they married. . . . A pot and a frying-pan were the only cooking utensils the most lavish closet revealed. . . . Over seventy per cent of the women drank to the point of unconsciousness. All used liquor. . . . Not one influence is at work to raise the general moral tone of this community, the voting power of which outnumbers four to one regions where every influence in and out of the homes tends to develop moral standards and political intelligence in the same political unit.[14]

The only salvation in these conditions lay in the gregariousness of the women. When the social workers began to arrive from the settlement houses, the mothers' clubs and the working girls' clubs were a great success. The other way out of the tenement for the young immigrant women lay in their jobs. Their wage-earning period meant emancipation. Like the first American factory girls, they had money of their own, which their mothers had never had. Although there were dangers in the unrestricted freedom allowed to immigrant girls in finding work, yet these girls learned to escape the bad conditions of their families. Indeed, freedom for them came to mean leaving the traditions on which their parents depended for survival. They adopted briefly the current manners of the urban American girl, even if marriage within their ethnic group returned them to the tenement life of their mothers. At least, they could speak English and knew a little of life outside the block and the ghetto. For them as for the early Americans, freedom meant a rebellion against that European past which still ruled their parents. Thus some of them became good material for suffrage propaganda.

For those immigrant peasant families who emigrated out of the seaboard cities onto the farms of the West, life was not so different from that of Europe, except for the problems of climate and distance. Village life could be found in the American small town, at least at the lower levels of the American small town. While the suffragists always noticed how the German farmers would cast their votes against woman suffrage, they could get some support from the Scandinavians. And by their very application to the land, the peasant farm families of Europe made the virgin soil the frontier of opportunity, which was denied to them by the low wages of the city. Willa Cather noticed how the willingness of the women in the family group to "work out" and send home their wages made the foreign farmers the first to become prosperous in Nebraska. "After the fathers were out of debt, the daughters married the sons of neighbours,—usually of like nationality,—and the girls who once worked in Black Hawk kitchens are to-day managing big farms and fine families of their own; their children are better off than the children of the town women they used to serve."[15]

Thus, while the frontier of opportunity for the middle-class American woman lay in escape from the small town into the professional jobs of the city, the frontier of opportunity for the European peasant woman lay in escape from the city slum into the opportunity of the land. The ideal of becoming a lady made the Victorian girl unfit for doing manual labour on the earth. The fact of European peasant experience fitted the immigrant slum-dweller for few other ways of making a comfortable living. It so happened that many European peasants never raised enough money to leave the slums, and many American girls married before they left the small towns. Both groups longed for escape, and both were not given the opportunity.

The savagery of the frontier was removed, by the terrible conditions of life in the immigrant slums, from the settled farming areas into the expanding cities. It was Henry Adams, that dispossessed urban aristocrat, who first saw how industrialism and its alien working hordes had taken away the social and political power that was his birth-right. The machine, and the principle of the Dynamo, had remorselessly taken over America. Nothing could be done to control this. In New York,

power seemed to have outgrown its servitude and to have asserted its freedom. The cylinder had exploded, and thrown great masses of stone and steam against the sky. The city had the air and movement of hysteria, and the citizens were crying, in every accent of anger and alarm, that the new forces must at any cost be brought under control. Prosperity never before imagined, power never yet wielded by man, speed never reached by anything but a meteor, had made the world irritable, nervous, querulous, unreasonable and afraid. All New York was demanding new men, and all the new forces, condensed into corporations, were demanding a new type of man—a man with ten times the endurance, energy, will and mind of the old type.[16]

For Henry Adams, the pioneer had come again with a vengeance into the frontiers of the city. The qualities described by Frederick Jackson Turner as necessary to hew a home out of the wilderness had passed to the new peasant immigrants on the land, and were even more vital for those Americans of old stock who wished to hack out a fortune in the jungle of cities. For Henry Adams, the frontier struggle now lay in the city street, and he was not equipped to fight because of his upbringing as a Bostonian and a gentleman. The current belief in social Darwinism offered further evidence that the struggle for the survival of the fittest had been transferred by the machine and factory from wilderness to urban strife. The war between the superior and the inferior, or the war between the classes of poor and rich, had replaced the primitive struggle between settler and Indian. Horatio Alger's heroes were the new frontiersmen. For their daughters, the city and its suburbs alone would mean freedom to find a good job and a good husband and a good life.

In another way, the frontier of the slums freed the settled farmers and their wives. If the factory system meant cripples among the immigrant men and women workers of the city—there were one million industrial accidents in 1913 alone—the goods from the factories meant less cripples bent over the ploughs and wash-tubs of the farm. Railroads, highways, tractors, automobiles, radios, washing-machines, chemical fertilizers, telephones, often produced at great human cost in the cities, did much to free the farmer and his family from loneliness and stagnation. The price of certain freedoms in the Corn Belt was the imposition of certain slaveries on the conveyor belt. The struggles of the first farmers to achieve the American dream of individual liberty in the wilderness are almost holy. The struggles of the new immigrants to achieve more freedoms for the first farmers' children and grandchildren are not hallowed and should be.

The solution of the problem of living for those rural immigrants who had to work in the city was to be solved by the suburb, connected to the city by train or streetcar. This represented, for American wives, the happy compromise between a healthy country upbringing for their children and the pleasures and culture of urban life for themselves. At first, the suburbs of the late Victorian age seemed the best of all worlds for the growing groups of educated wives, who could find stimulating company among many people of the same background as themselves—a rarity in the small town. And they did not lose touch with city life, while being spared its inconveniences. A letter from a suburban wife in New England in 1880 to the *Woman's Journal* prophesied the society that was to grow up around every large city in the land:

As I look from the window where I write, upon the suburban village in the valley below, I see a multitude of neat houses, each set in its little garden or orchard, and almost exclusively occupied by a population of New England birth and descent. Of almost every one of these little households it may be said that a woman is the mainspring; the men are away all day, and it is the wife or mother who gives tone and character to the house. These women vary greatly in education, refinement, enlightenment, but certain qualities they have all in common; they are, with scarcely an exception, energetic, practical, and "smart" . . . these executive qualities are rarely wanting. You see it in the look of their houses and dinner tables, in their children's dress and their own, and in the standing of these children at school.[17]

The early suburbs, like the early small towns, represented an opportunity for middle-class wives rather than a prison. They meant freedom to bring up children well, freedom to dominate the home in the absence of the commuting father, and freedom to acquire the graces of the lady. American girls had already begun the pattern of moving from the small town into the city to find work and a husband, and then moving out to the suburb to rear children. Thus they brought to their final home a rural ethic and a city polish, which explained both the conservatism and the radicalism of the suburb. They were to supersede the women who remained in the small towns as the hard core of moderate movements for reform, especially over matters of schooling and hygiene. Moreover, they were to be much more occupied with social, rather than religious, improvements.

The suburb did, after all, return to the ideal of the first American cities, which were countrified towns with green spaces between the houses. And as the suburb increasingly represented the chosen way of life of married American women, it also came to settle the quarrels that divided them, as it had settled the quarrel between city and country life.

Although some suburbs remained as exclusive as the first ones in New England or as any slum ghetto, they came to include an economic middle class of white skin. The small-town girl who married well found herself the neighbour of a family of new immigrants' children, who had also made good. The way out of the small town and out of the slum seemed to point in the same direction of the suburb. There, slowly, the traditional ideas of ethnic group and caste would change to meet the suburban fact. The ideas of the small towns and farms of the Midwest and of Europe began to mingle with the influences of the city.

If it took generations to turn the suburb from the small town writ large into the city writ small in terms of culture and tolerance and education, it was because generations of children had to grow up in the suburb before that way of life could seem as *natural* to them as life on the farm had seemed to their parents, or urban life had seemed to the old families of Boston or Philadelphia. Only the slow progress of the years could make the suburb into the true melting-pot of America, and mould its immigrants into sharers of the same joys and frustrations and freedoms and bondages of life in the no-man's land between races and classes, country and city.

XXIII

༄

INFERIOR ANIMALS
AND SUPERIOR BEINGS

A REVOLUTION feeds on hatred, a reform on compromise. Some of the more aggressive feminists preached the hatred of men, some preached their conversion. All suspected that women were superior in essence, although often inferior in behaviour.

Before the romantic revolution of the 1830's, clergymen had usually stressed the sinful nature of woman. Her flesh was weak; she must be shielded from temptation. It was such discrimination of sex which Sarah Grimké had denounced. "Man has inflicted an unspeakable injury upon woman, by holding up to her view her animal nature, and placing in the background her moral and intellectual being." By pretending to save woman from her weaknesses, man had taken the opportunity to tyrannize her. "Ah! how many of my sex feel in the dominion, thus unrighteously exercised over them, under the gentle appellation of *protection,* that what they have leaned upon has proved a broken reed at best, and oft a spear."[1]

Yet in the decades before the Civil War, there was a change in attitude towards women. Their animal nature was no longer stressed by men, but their spiritual. They were excluded from politics not because of their inferiority, but because of their superiority. They were not so much sinful as too good for this world. Their moral worth put them above the nasty business of money-getting and politics.

This argument was, of course, a dangerous one for those who preached masculine control. The early feminists were quick to put it to their own use. Elizabeth Stanton, who began her life as a believer in the equality of mankind after the style of the rationalists of the eighteenth century, soon switched to Victorian ideas of the moral superiority of women. It was a more convenient reason for demanding the vote. By 1848, she was saying that man was "infinitely woman's inferior in every moral virtue, not by nature, but made so by a false education. In carrying out his own selfishness, man has greatly improved woman's moral nature, but by an almost total shipwreck of his own. Woman has now the noble virtues of the martyr."[2]

Stanton quickly developed her ideas into a consciousness of the war between the sexes. She was revolutionary by nature, but in a way, she was right in accusing men. They did not so much oppress women deliberately as cause them to feel extremely conscious of their sex. By emphasizing the separate sphere of the home, men encouraged aggressive women to think of themselves as apart from men. When matters of culture and learning and the rearing of children were turned over to wives by husbands, women were encouraged to consider that their sex gave them a distinct function, different from and better than the mere getting of money. Indeed, the anti-feminist propaganda of the "high and holy sphere for which both nature and the God of nature intended woman" encouraged women to think of themselves as superior creatures.[3] Like the doctrine of the segregation of the Negro, the doctrine of separate spheres for men and women encouraged both sexes to see themselves as responsible only to their own kind. A certain solidarity of sex, like that of race or class, was the result.

At each woman's step forward and downward from her pedestal, the feminists who thought themselves the crusaders for their sex were thrilled. When Stanton first heard Anna Dickinson speak in public, she found her life-long hopes and prayers realized. "For whatever any woman does well, I feel that I have done it. Just as any poor negro listening to Douglass loses himself in the pride of race, so do I in womanhood."⁴ As the barriers between the sexes were broken down, so those women who felt solidarity with their own sex rejoiced. But as equality with men approached, they did not give up the idea of their own superiority.

Most Victorian women, however, would not or could not see that they were oppressed by the male sex. They had been helped throughout their lives by fathers and husbands and brothers, and they were grateful. As Elizabeth Blackwell wrote after reading the report of one of the first conventions on women's rights, "I cannot sympathize fully with an anti-man movement. I have had too much kindness, aid, and just recognition from men to make such attitude of women otherwise than painful; and I think the true end of freedom may be gained better in another way."⁵

In such a spirit, her beloved brother, Henry Blackwell, wooed and married the man-hating Lucy Stone, who had found nothing but meanness in her own father. "Believe me," he wrote, "the mass of men are not *intentionally* unjust to women, nor the mass of women *consciously* oppressed."⁶ He spoke the truth, as the small following of the radical feminists showed. The concept of a war between the sexes seemed ridiculous in an age where men voluntarily gave women and children protection and shelter and food and clothing. Henry Blackwell himself converted Lucy Stone within marriage, until she become one of the leading defenders of the cooperation of the sexes.

The concept of male oppression was yet another factor in the split in the suffrage movement in 1869. The vocabulary of anti-slavery did encourage radical women to put themselves in the position of the slave and see themselves as bent under the lash of their male masters. Yet most of the anti-slavery leaders were men, and many of these supported woman suffrage. Not all men could be bad. It was when Stanton and Anthony reacted against the caution of the abolitionists after the Civil War that they denied the principle of cooperation with men. In their eyes, the male sex had shown solidarity and betrayed the cause of women for that of the male Negro. The language of *The Revolution* cried aloud the war of the sexes: "Society, as organized to-day under the man power, is one grand rape on womanhood, on the highways, in our jails, prisons, asylums, in our homes, alike in the world of fashion and of work."[7]

Lucy Stone and the supporters of the Boston wing of the suffragists replied correctly that votes for women could only come through votes by men, and it was no good provoking a sex war. Such moderates as Julia Ward Howe declared themselves opposed to "the unkind suggestions made and entertained concerning the opposite sex." She did not want to hear abuse of her father, grandfather, uncles, and male relatives in general, nor of her husband "hinted at as a Satan behind the scenes." Henry Blackwell cautioned Anthony against bullying and threatening politicians. Women could persuade men; they could not scold them into compliance. "Try to combine men and women as far as possible," he advised. "Do nothing to antagonize the sexes."[8]

Despite his advice, the National Woman Suffrage Association had no men in leading positions. When negotiations began for the coming together of the two wings of the suffrage cause, Alice Blackwell asked Anthony whether there was a by-law excluding men from holding office in the National. Anthony replied that she could not say that there never had been, although the law had been out of use for a long time. "We have not elected any men to office," she stated, "simply because no men have offered us much help. We have treated them as they treat us."[9] Indeed, when the suffrage movement did unite, men disappeared rapidly from high positions in its ranks. As Stanton had claimed at the inception of the movement in 1848, "Woman herself must do this work—for woman alone can understand the height, and the depth, the length and the breadth of her own degradation and woe. Man cannot speak for us—because he has been educated to believe that we differ from him so materially, that he cannot judge of our thoughts, feelings and opinions by his own."[10]

This was the crux of the idea of the sex war. Were men and women so different that they could not understand one another? Was there no possible equality between the sexes as human beings? Were women superior to men as moral beings and inferior as physical animals? The Victorian woman never solved the problem, and it has not been solved today. When the men of Wyoming drank to the women on the evening that they gave them the vote, the toast was, "Lovely ladies, once our superiors, now our equals." As political and social equality with men came to women, however, they were not prepared to act equally with men. Victorian tradition and social custom preserved their image of themselves as the better half and the weaker sex.

Julia Howe early pointed out in 1883 the difficulties of equality for women. It was easy to cast all the blame on men while women were still deprived of the vote.

In the Old Testament account of the fall of man, Adam pleads in excuse for his offence the influence of his wife. "The woman whom thou gavest me" and so on. Women to-day for much of the mischief that they do, and for more of the good which they leave undone, may well plead "the man whom thou gavest me did lead me to this." But, in the redemption of society which we hold to be near, this excuse, which did not avail the man, shall be taken away from the woman. She shall become a free, an instructed agent.[11]

The increasing liberties of women gave them no one to blame except themselves. And the concept of the sex war lost even more credibility as women could increasingly choose or reject the ways of men. By the end of the Victorian age, many commentators had begun to stress the similarity of the sexes, not their differences. Some judged by capacity as Wendell Phillips had judged—"The best and greatest thing one is capable of doing, that is his sphere." Some emphasized that equality between the sexes did not mean competition for jobs, but cooperation within them. As Olive Schreiner wrote, feminism was essentially a movement of the woman towards the man, of the sexes towards closer union.[12]

Still other compromisers adapted the environmentalism of such thinkers as Herbert Spencer to prove that most differences between the sexes were the result of artificial training. "Much that we now

call feminine is really unfeminine, since it is a perversion of nature."[13] If nature were allowed to assert itself, the sexes would become very like each other. In fact, if Havelock Ellis was right and the
female body and brain were higher on the scale of evolution than the
male, then equality would lead more to the feminization of man
than the masculinization of women. Biology further showed that female organs remained in the male in a rudimentary form, and male
organs in the female. The sexes were, in capacity and nature, little
different.

Under this attack, conservatives preached the message that they still
do. Woman was different from man because only she could be a
mother. Against such preaching the early feminists had particularly
rebelled. As Angelique Martin had written from Warren, Ohio,
she did not want men to treat women "as mere hatching and breeding
machines whom they scornfully send back to their nurseries and
kitchens, forbidding them to aspire to anything else."[14] Stanton had
voiced the same complaint at the end of her maternity period in
another Western small town: "So long as man continues to think and
write, to speak and act, as if maternity was the one and sole object of
a woman's existence—so long as children are conceived in weariness
and disgust—you must not look for high-toned men and women
capable of accomplishing any great and noble achievement."[15]

The later suffragists were more politic, for they wished to appeal to
the conservative majority of women who did marry and have children. Indeed, radical feminists in the early twentieth century did not
so much preach the right of a woman to have childless affairs outside
marriage as her right to have a child outside marriage. The most
notorious of these was the Swedish feminist, Ellen Key, who wanted
large families for single women. Her works were rightly attacked by
Rebecca West as "the first appearance of the Victorian aunt as a
philosopher." For they did not escape from the traditional idea that a
woman's most satisfactory and creative act was to have a baby.

In a curious way, this new maternal demand was an outgrowth of
the Victorian woman's attack on men through the concept of the
"double standard" for the sexes. The crusaders for the purity of

women and men had been worried by the rising rate of illegitimacy in America. As they thought in terms of women being ruined by men, they held men responsible for having bastards. It was they who should be punished for the illegitimate child. "Let us wipe out of our vocabulary the term illegitimate child," one crusader said, "there can be no such thing. Let us begin to talk about illegitimate fathers, and treat them as such."[16] When a bill came up in the Colorado legislature to set up a segregated vice area in Denver, a woman asked that "fallen men should be segregated the same as fallen women." When the sponsor of the bill agreed to this clause, the woman replied, "But there would be no men left." The bill was laughed down.[17]

In their work of driving vice and the "double standard" from America, the crusaders for purity thought that they would get bad husbands to act as purely as good wives. In fact, by preaching a single standard for men and women, they were also encouraging good wives to imitate bad husbands. Equality can both level up and level down. When the crusade for purity declined in the twentieth century, it was because many women chose to imitate men in sexual freedom rather than many men choosing to imitate good women in self-restraint.

The feminists who preached a woman's right to natural motherhood were latter-day Victorian moralists. Women, and not men, should fix the standard in sex, wrote Ellen Key in the language of the Victorian lady, for women had to play the chief part in racial life.[18] If, as the anti-feminists said, woman's chief role was motherhood, if all women could not get married because of the selfishness of men, and if there should be a single standard between the sexes, then every woman had the right to bear a child whenever she wished. The sex war would be ended by the equality of men and women in the pleasures of the body and the fulfilment of the race. If the state took over the economic role of the father, marriage would be unnecessary for women who wished to become mothers. "Frankly I do not know just what is meant by 'sex freedom' and 'sex war,' " wrote one militant suffragist. "I do not know whether it means freedom and war for denial or freedom and war for the gratification of the fundamental impulse of life. . . . Sex intercourse is as natural as breathing, and while not as necessary for life to the individual, here and now at this minute, is a necessity for the creation of future generations."[19]

Of course, when the radical fringe of the woman's movement shifted from preaching a sex war for the preservation of the purity of womanhood to preaching sexual equality for the gratification of both men and women, the majority of Americans were equally shocked. Marriage still remained the most holy institution in America; even the rising rate of divorce seemed chiefly to be for the purpose of remarriage. The leaders of the suffragists, fearful of another Woodhull affair, refused to back the ideas of maternity outside marriage. Indeed, their support of maternity within marriage was slanted against the single woman, who wished to remain childless. She alone, by finding discrimination against her in her profession and through the social pity of others, kept alive the idea of the war of the sexes.

The adoption of men's dress by women showed up something of the change of their ideas. Some women had put on men's dress during wars and during the westward migration, in order to fight and live beside their men. Some had adopted male dress within a particular profession. The notorious Dr. Mary Walker wore men's clothes all her life; she believed so much in the equality of the sexes that she even founded a female colony called "Adamless Eve" to prove that the anatomy of women was similar to that of man.[20] In terms of travelling and studying without annoyance, male dress was a positive advantage. Both of the medical Blackwell sisters seriously thought of putting on men's clothes in order to work at the Sorbonne. As Stanton wrote in *The Revolution,*

The true idea is for the sexes to dress as nearly alike as possible. We have seen several ladies dressed precisely like gentlemen, who appeared far more elegant and graceful than any real man we ever saw. A young lady in Fifth Avenue dressed in male costume for years, travelling all over Europe and this country. She says it would have been impossible to have seen and known as much of life in woman's attire, and to have felt the independence and security she did, had her sex been proclaimed before all Israel and the sun. . . . When we have a voice in legislation, we shall dress as we please, and if, by concealing our sex, we find that we too, can roam up and down the earth in safety (not seeking whom we may devour), we shall keep our womanhood a profound secret.[21]

Elizabeth Stanton prophesied the assumption of trousers by women correctly in time. Yet women did not seek anonymity in male dress. They adopted the elements of it that suited them to make themselves not only more elegant and graceful than any real man, but also more recognizably and indubitably real women. While men, on the whole, kept their dress sober and did not use it as an erotic ornamentation, women stole from a man's wardrobe what would increase their powers of enticement. The early dress reformers had complained that women's skirts were a red rag to male lust. Later reformers were to say the same thing of men's trousers adapted to the taste of women. Until the American woman would succeed in feminizing the American male, the equality of the sexes in dress would provide none of the male anonymity desired by some feminists, although it would provide many women with even more bodily freedom within their clothing than the average man could boast.

By choice, most American women freely adopted or rejected whatever they pleased among the privileges of the male. They did not compete for jobs in slaughterhouses or down mines; they did not dress in boiler-suits or work-boots; they did not refuse the privileges offered to them by the continuance of the tradition of male chivalry. They took equality when it suited them, and retained a feeling of some moral and social superiority. Although they could no longer blame men or lack of education for their physical inferiority, they could rail in the psychologist's ear against the discrimination of nature.

XXIV

A VERY AMERICAN TALE

"I WISHED TO WRITE a very *American* tale," Henry James wrote of *The Bostonians*, "a tale very characteristic of our social conditions, and I asked myself what was the most salient and peculiar point in our social life. The answer was: the situation of women, the decline of the sentiment of sex, the agitation on their behalf."[1] That James should have thought so in 1883 was a tribute to the propaganda of the few feminists of the time. His success was to display most of the attitudes of the lady feminists of Boston. His failure was to explain the women behind those attitudes, for he thought in the terms of humorous scepticism of the anti-feminists.

The Bostonians is the only Victorian novel of merit written about feminism, yet the picture it gives is false, and geographically confined to a conservative city in America at a conservative period. James's subtlety was to mock at his anti-feminist hero, the Southerner, Basil Ransom, as much as he did at his feminists. But this was a clever mask of impartiality to hide a real partiality. James did not like the feminist cause; his book is intended to attack it as well as to describe it.

The main characters of the book are little more than basic caricatures, taken from current feminist figures and stereotypes. No feminist is allowed to possess breasts; all of them have shapeless and masculine figures. Verena Tarrant, for whom the feminist Olive Chancellor fights with Basil Ransom, is a pale copy of Victoria Woodhull, who also came from a poor background and mesmerist circles, also married an old-fashioned Southerner, and also supported free love. Even so, James denies Verena the fire and force and passion that were in the character of the true Victoria; her charm is passive, while that of Victoria was active and charismatic. Olive herself is a stereotype of the spinster lady reformer, fastidious, snobbish, man-hating, theoretical. James chose to ignore the obvious fact that most of the leading feminists in Boston were married, had children and breasts, and defended men. He preferred the stereotype of the urban, spinster, Northern Olive against the patriarchal Southern Basil, in conflict for the body, heart, and soul of the innocent Verena, just returned from the West. Only the minute social observance of James's style has disguised his facile choice of main characters.

The social interest of *The Bostonians* lies in James's description of the changes taking place in the city during the late Victorian period. Its merit is to show how the centre of militant anti-slavery work could become the centre of anti-suffrage work. The minor characters of the book, although jeered at with little sympathy or understanding, do show the change of feeling among middle-class reformers and ladies in the city. Miss Birdseye in particular, although made a figure of fun, does represent what Olive cannot, the faith of the pioneer reformers in contrast with the cautious delicacy of their followers. "She belonged to the Short-Skirts League, as a matter of course; for she belonged to any and every league that had been founded for almost any purpose whatever. . . . She looked as if she had spent her life on platforms, in audiences, in conventions, in phalansteries, in *séances;* in her faded face there was a kind of reflection of ugly lecture lamps."

The difference between Miss Birdseye and Olive is the difference between generations, between the woman reformer and the lady reformer, between a relatively classless Boston and a city of castes, between the idealist and the materialist with ideals. Miss Birdseye "had never had a penny in her life. No one had any idea how she lived; whenever money was given her she gave it away to a negro or a refugee. . . . Olive had been active enough, for years, in the city-missions; she too had scoured dirty children. . . . But she reflected that after such exertions she had the refreshment of a pretty house, a drawing room full of flowers . . . whereas Miss Birdseye had only a bare vulgar room." In fact, even Olive realized that "this frumpy little missionary was the last link in a tradition, and that when she should be called away the heroic age of New England life—the age of plain living and high thinking, of pure ideals and earnest effort, of moral passion and noble experiment—would effectually be closed."[2] Not until the lady could be persuaded to go and *live* in the settlement house would the dialogue between Miss Birdseye and the urban poor be resumed.

In his later novels, James was to show the same mixture of dislike for assertive women cloaked by an exact observation of their habits. His anti-feminism was masked by an unending concern for the new woman. In *The Portrait of a Lady,* which claims to show a lady's inner self, the birth of her child and his death is covered in a few lines, while the whole novel revolves around the lady's reactions to men. Such a display of feminine callousness may be intentional, but it seems to be a misunderstanding of how a woman works. Even a lady can feel.

Yet his observation of social behaviour always rescues James. If he often misses the truth of a woman's character, he does not miss the social reasons that guide her actions. *Daisy Miller* provides both evidence and condemnation of the inability of American parents to control their children "in the age of obedient parents." If death comes to Daisy as the price of disobedience—as to any wilful Victorian heroine —yet the reasons for her disobedience are an acute commentary on the dangers in the American tradition of being too nice to children. James is often good material for the social historian, although rarely for the seeker after the nature of women.

A commentator on the American girl in fiction in the late Victorian period found James's attitudes widespread. The ideal of the past remained in the portrayal of the American girl as dainty and delicate, pretty and pure; but Eve had begun to eat the apple. A malaise slowly afflicted the American heroine. She possessed amazing frivolity, no parental influence, and—curiously enough—"no ideal of home life." American girls were all, apparently, middle-class and no longer trained in the kitchen; they only wanted a good time. They expected and were taught to expect life to be one long round of parties, trips, and social amusements. This gave them a lack of direction, an avidity for "having fun," which made them go to excess.

This change in literary fashion pointed the way to the coming ideal of the giddy girl and the flapper. But behind the gay girl stood the frightful figure of the mother that she was to become. "As surely as the girl herself is brilliant and charming, so surely is the mother, or elder female relative, or friend who accompanies her, silly and ridiculous . . . exasperatingly foolish, exasperatingly vague, helpless, senseless, and addle-pated."[3] In the grotesque and silly type of older womanhood, the late Victorian novelist showed his American girl what she would become. The cult of youth had overtaken the novelists by the turn of the century. It was to attack both the anti-feminist ideal of home and mother and the feminist ideal of the single professional woman.

American fiction remained preoccupied with women from the time of Henry James until woman suffrage became the law of the land. Its emphasis seemed to shift from disapproval of feminism into praise of rebellious girlhood, and from that, in the progressive era, into a brief approval of feminism. A group of distinguished *women* novelists appeared for the first time in American literature, Willa Cather and Edith Wharton and Gertrude Atherton and Ellen Glasgow. They defended feminism from the woman's point of view. They made the crusaders of their sex into sympathetic women instead of the usual stereotypes of male authors. "I sometimes wish I were a suffragette," said one of Glasgow's characters. "The only natural human beings seem to be those who are making trouble."[4] These women writers were both intelligent and popular, and did much to make the cause of women's rights seem reasonable to their time.

The mass magazine and the popular novel began to reflect the swing in intelligent opinion in the East and West. Woman suffrage became a commonplace in the progressive and liberal press. The collective sense of sin, which Beatrice Webb found in the English middle class in late Victorian times, seemed to affect the American middle class in the decade before the First World War. Reform became the fashion, and feminism was one of many desirable reforms. No one quite knew how far the change of society would go, but all change seemed to be for the good.

Articles on the Coming of the New Woman were printed everywhere; these pieces did not so much explain her as forecast what she would be. In them, ideal was stressed as the answer to rotten social fact. Radical women became muckrakers, or filled the bohemias in the large cities in search of personal freedom. If early Victorian magazines concentrated on the lady, pre-1917 ones concentrated on the rebellious female and her defiance of a man's world. It was a restless time, in agitation and literature, with much expected and little known. The ferment of the post-war twenties was already seething in the pre-war decade in the pioneer bohemias in the cities. In fact, the Jazz Age seems something of a frenzied wake to celebrate the death of the serious rebellion of women before the war.

Another gentleman from Boston, Henry Adams, summed up the changed attitudes of women in the early twentieth century. He was bitter about the social and moral changes that had excluded him from the political power which should have been his by birth. Yet he, too, saw in the rise of women "a very *American* tale." He saw the two new principles in society as the Virgin and the Dynamo. Once, the energy of the inertia and submission of women had carried on the race. Women had been content to breed; but now men had given up their interest in sex and the family to concentrate on the machine and work, and women were no longer content to rotate round the cradle and the family. They wanted equality with men in the service of the Dynamo.

Already the American woman, in Adams's opinion,

had no illusions or ambitions or new resources, and nothing to rebel against, except her own maternity; yet the rebels increased by millions from year to year till they blocked the path of rebellion. . . . From the male, she could look for no help; his instinct for power was blind. . . . She was free; she had no illusions; she was sexless; she had discarded all that the male disliked; and although she secretly regretted the discard, she knew that she could not go backward. She must, like the man, marry machinery. Already the American man sometimes felt surprise at finding himself regarded as sexless; the American woman was oftener surprised at finding herself regarded as sexual.[5]

In point of fact, the futuristic fears of Henry Adams were to prove as baseless as the nostalgia of Henry James. Both thought, in the stereotypes of anti-feminism, that the emancipation of women and the equality of the sexes would mean a sexless horde of working men-women, unwilling to have children. In fact, the American woman was to think of herself as more and more sexual, while only the man was still surprised sometimes to find himself regarded as sexless. After the great depression, the birth-rate was to rise for twenty years, as machinery provided riches even for the large family in the middle class. The American woman was to continue to rotate around the cradle and the family, like any Victorian woman in the golden age of James and Adams. The rebels would continue to increase by millions from year to year till they blocked the path of rebellion, but only because they did not feel they should rebel against the fact of their own maternity.

Women still had illusions, fostered by their education. They were not yet free, for their minds had not been trained by social custom and education to make an independent choice. They could rarely think outside the stereotype of marriage and children, like their foremothers. They were the New Victorians.

XXV

〰️

THE HEIRS OF
ANNE HUTCHINSON

Two women completed the rebellion which Anne Hutchinson had begun in search of spiritual freedom. Mary Baker Eddy founded the most successful religion ever set up by a woman in America, and even wrote her own full-length bible. Charlotte Perkins Gilman disproved to her own satisfaction everything said by any authority before her, and freed her spirit utterly. She lived and died answerable only to herself, "above reason and Scripture," as Governor Winthrop had once feared, "not subject to control."

Mary Baker Eddy founded an enduring church. After a neurotic and wandering youth, she became a disciple of the faith healer, P. P. Quimby. In a time when the ideas of magnetism and spiritualism and water cures were declining, faith healing was becoming more popular, as it seemed to have a Christian foundation. Mary Eddy added to and copyrighted many of Quimby's ideas after his death. She published the first edition of her own bible, *Science and Health,* in 1875. She claimed, as all the women prophetesses had claimed, that she was inspired directly by God in the many revised editions of the book, even though Mark Twain pointed out that a foreigner at that time could not own a copyright in the United States.

Mary Eddy's beliefs in the superiority of mind over matter and in the possibility of healing by religious understanding spread. It was an age, as all previous ages had been, of great and unremediable disease; the first antibiotics were not invented until after Mary Eddy's death. Perhaps religious understanding could cure the sick where medicine could not. By the first decade of this century, Mary Eddy had attracted some sixty thousand people to her Churches of Christ Scientist. She had genius as an organizer. Many believed that she, in her careful retirement, was a female Christ, as they had believed of Ann Lee and Jemima Wilkinson.

Mary Eddy even believed that she was Godlike herself, although she trimmed her claims to deity under the ridicule of her critics. As she wrote to her chief worshipper, Augusta Stetson, late in her life: "Jesus was the man that was a prophet and the best and greatest man that has ever appeared on earth, but Jesus was not Christ, for Christ is the spiritual individual that the eye cannot see. Jesus was called Christ only in the sense that you say, a Godlike man. I am only a Godlike woman, God-anointed, and I have done a work that none others could do."[1] Mary Eddy's use of the word "only" in this letter hardly shows that she admitted the superiority of the "Godlike man" to herself. At other times, she talked of the prophecies in Daniel which foretold of the Second Coming of Christ in the year that she discovered Christian Science. At one time, she even referred to herself in letters to her congregation as "Mother Mary," claiming some of the worship of the Virgin Mary in the Catholic religion as due to herself.

After Mary Eddy's death in 1910, her church grew steadily. She had founded a slowly expanding religion, and had become a saint—if not a God. Some of her success came from the position of women in the nineteenth century, still a prey to the terrors of death from childbirth or disease and still frustrated by political inaction. Christian Science, which was neither particularly Christian nor at all scientific, provided both an emancipation through faith from fear of illness and an outlet in organization and adoration for active and confined women. Followers such as Augusta Stetson, who raised more than a million dollars to build the First Church of Christ Scientist in New

York, could be priestesses and powers in Mary Eddy's church. They were excluded from most high positions in the Protestant and Catholic churches. Mary Eddy thought herself a Godlike woman. Those women and men who agreed with her thought a woman could and should be Godlike, too.

The complement of Mary Eddy was the self-willed, self-taught, self-believing Charlotte Perkins Gilman. Born in the East at the time of the Civil War, she was brought up poor and vagabond; her father deserted her mother, and she could not forgive him. "The word Father, in the sense of love, care, one to go to in trouble, means nothing to me." Her faith, and the fact of her life, was a world run by and for women alone. She took to gymnastics, cold baths, and questioning. She studied every social science, and reduced them to quick, certain, and simple answers, "strengthened by an innate incredulity which refused to accept anybody's say-so, even if it had been said for a thousand years. If a problem was said to be insoluble, I forthwith set out to solve it." She solved the problem of evil by equating it with death. "Death is the essential condition of life, not an evil."

At the age of twenty-one, she had reached the condition where freedom was possible. Her strength of will set her a working day of sixteen hours, with exercise playing a large part in the remaining eight. Her autobiography read:

My own mistress at last. No one on earth had a right to ask obedience of me. I was self-supporting of course, a necessary base for freedom which the young revolters of to-day often overlook. This freedom never meant self-indulgence. From sixteen, I had not wavered from that desire to help humanity which underlay all my studies. Here was the world, visibly unhappy and as visibly unnecessarily so; surely it called for the best efforts of all who could in the least understand what was the matter, and had any rational improvements to propose.[2]

In trying to reform the twentieth century, Charlotte Gilman spoke as the true daughter of the improving nineteenth.

Marriage put an end to this life of perfect freedom through perfect dedication. Although her chosen husband was a charming artist, housework and the birth of a baby daughter plunged Charlotte Gilman into a nervous depression, which prevented her from doing anything. She felt sick in the house and well outside. The memory of her spinster freedom allowed her no satisfaction in the small slavery of marriage and motherhood.

She and her husband divorced by mutual consent and with mutual good-will. But her "laboriously built-up hand-made character" totally collapsed. Occasional nervous depressions plagued her for the rest of her life, which she spent in California. She reproached herself for writing only twenty-five books in the next forty-two years, as well as doing much work for suffrage and socialism. Yet her beliefs were strong enough to allow her to remain on good terms with her past husband, even though he married her best friend. Although she herself married again, it was a matter of such little importance that she hardly refers to her second husband in her autobiography.

Charlotte Gilman was the greatest writer that the feminists ever produced on sociology and economics, the Marx and the Veblen of the movement. She always asked the brutal question, and was never satisfied by the easy answer. Two of her books, *Woman and Economics* and *The Home: Its Work and Influence,* should be classics of social study. The case for woman against man was never presented in a more stimulating, witty, or pointed form. If Charlotte Gilman was sometimes unfair, it was because life had sometimes been unfair to her. She represented the finest part of that iconoclasm which some other American pioneer women had showed. She was even prepared to pull down that holy of holies, the American home, in her quest to free her sex. "The home, as our oldest institution, is necessarily our lowest. . . . To eat, to sleep, to breathe, to dress, to rest and amuse one's self—these are good and useful deeds; but are they more hallowed than others?"

Mary Eddy ended the search for women to become God. Her later imitators failed. Even the successful Aimee Semple Macpherson was only a passing and gaudy phenomenon among revivalists. But with Charlotte Gilman the new woman was born—the woman answerable only to herself, and to herself before God. Charlotte Gilman knew that she was the future, and that if she could be wholly free, other women might be able to follow her example. Although she was made by her time, she wanted to escape it. "It will be a great thing for the human soul when it finally stops worshipping backwards."[3] She lived to see the legal and political emancipation of women, and she was disappointed by their apparent failure to use their new freedom to develop their minds and spirits.

The riches of modern America have diminished the hunger of woman's search for spiritual liberty. The rabbit that Eliza Hard's cat brought to her on her knees in the wilderness is now an heirloom, engraved in silver on a tureen. The wealth and abundance of the land have soothed the fierce quest of those who once built it to be the New Jerusalem, paradise on earth. As those women who broke into the male churches discovered, becoming is always more satisfying than being on arrival. To build a future and set a precedent fulfils a need more than to enjoy an inheritance. Women cannot be gods now, but only women. And the search for the freedom of the human soul within a comfortable female body is a slippery business.

PART EIGHT

The English Example

I found about ten, wretched degraded-looking women crouching round the fire—one especially I noticed who hid her disfigured, diseased face from me. I went up to them, laid my hand on a shoulder and said, "My poor woman, is it true that if I offer to come in and see you now and then you would treat me with abuse and coldness? Can this be true of English Women to an English Lady?"

EMMA SHEPPARD

XXVI

THE ENGLISH EXAMPLE

IF AMERICAN MEN fought with English men, the women of both countries helped each other against their men. Curious parallels as well as personal contacts linked the two movements for women's rights. The English example provided both a stimulus for and a commentary on American feminism. For in England the struggle of classes and sexes was more defined. The aristocracy and the male were more powerful there. As one English feminist wrote, "American women do not dislike men as much as English women do."[1]

The fact of royalty and the peerage in England early brought up the question of woman suffrage. As in colonial America, there was more equality between men and women in the aristocracy than between the aristocrats and the rest of society. In the absence of sons, daughters could inherit thrones, titles, and large estates. Moreover, as voting in England was limited by property qualifications until the twentieth century, distinctions of sex continued to seem less important than those of wealth and rank. Unlike in America, there was always a body of conservative opinion in England which denied its traditional prejudices about the position of the lady in the home because of the political advantage of giving the vote to single women of wealth. As Acton wrote, "Girls and widows are Tories, and channels of clerical influence."² This fear of increasing the Tory vote, however, kept many Liberals from supporting woman suffrage, although by temperament they approved of the measure.

The large estates owned by some women in England gave them real political power. Occasionally, they could nominate Members of Parliament in rotten boroughs. Their own right to stand for parliament was shrouded in medieval precedent; but no lady, in fact, seems to have done so, although the law did not expressly forbid her. Social custom excluded single women from active participation in politics, although it encouraged them to vote in church matters, and sometimes in municipal matters. In these respects, English women were more politically free than their American sisters before the Victorian age.

Anti-slavery work first brought middle-class, dissenting English women to form groups for political action. The movement spread to some circles of the established Church of England. It became so respectable that even the conservative Hannah More was a worker for the cause of the slaves, however much she refused to see the bondage of her own sex. The movement, in its turn, provided the first stimulus for like action on the part of American ladies. In another respect, there was a curious similarity between the two countries. Abolitionism in England, as suffragism was to be, was something of a protest of the Northern and Western cities against London. Slavery had been much the local problem of Bristol and the ports on the Irish Sea. The first anti-slavery societies had grown up there, and the first slum social work by women was to begin there. Through local Members of Parliament, the campaign against the slave trade was carried to London. As in America, the radical reform movements to free the slaves and women were to flourish more in the Puritan North and West than in the more apathetic Eastern great city. The difference between the countries was that both social and evangelical reform in England was always an urban affair, while, in the Victorian period, evangelical reform was chiefly a small-town affair in the United States.

The issue of feminism sprang up earlier in England than in the United States because of the fact of female aristocrats with great social power. There was also a large dissenting middle class in the Northern manufacturing towns of England, which resented its exclusion from political power and was ready for radical solutions. Although only the extreme fringe of this group listened to such writers as Mary Wollstonecraft, its social existence allowed her opinions to be read, even if they were denied. It was noticeable that the first large reform movement outside the major parties in England, that of the Chartists, at first included votes for women in its demands. The Chartists numbered their supporters in millions in the industrial cities of the North, compared to the tens of thousands of Locofocos in the small American cities. In early Victorian times, feminist ideas in England had a greater chance of spreading in all groups of urban society.

The First Reform Bill of 1832 was to the few English suffragists of the time what the Fourteenth and Fifteenth Amendments were to the American suffragists after the Civil War. In that Bill, which extended the franchise to sections of the middle classes and which represented the new industrial cities with moderate fairness, the world "male" first appeared in the English Constitution. Although the extreme radical, "Orator" Hunt, presented a petition from a wealthy Northern spinster that single women with property should be allowed to vote, the suffrage was limited to "male persons" with property. Somewhat as in the case of the American male Negro, the English middle classes received the vote at the expense of the legal exclusion of women.

Before its impetus faded away in England with the successful abolition of the slave trade, the female abolitionists passed on the message of feminism to the unseated American women delegates at the world convention of 1840. Harriet Martineau, Anna Jameson, Amelia Opie, and Mary Howitt were met and read widely by American radical women; Lady Byron was pitied and copied. There were many contacts between the Quaker and Unitarian circles that fostered societies for women's rights in both England and America. Both Stanton and Anthony were complimented by English suffragists for knowing most of the active English workers in the cause, although

Frances Power Cobbe misjudged their temper when she wrote to them that nearly all the leaders of the suffragists in both countries "would far rather that women should remain without political rights to the end of time than that they should lose those qualities which we comprise in the word 'womanliness.' "[3]

The English example was even more important for the pioneer American feminists because English women were actively engaged in politics in the 1840's. Not only were some of them a force in the Chartist movement, although its leaders had dropped their original demand for woman suffrage; but they were also powerful in the Corn Law League, which successfully pushed for the repeal of the protective tariff in favour of English farmers and for free trade. The agitation for the movement centred in Manchester, as it was intended to reduce the price of bread for city workers. It was no accident that also from Manchester both the respectable and the militant suffrage movement was to spread.

In Victorian times, Manchester rapidly grew to be the second city of England and the capital of the industrial North. It was distinguished for its wealth, its Puritanism, its pride, and its hatred of London. As the country hated the city in America for its luxury and vice, so dissenting Manchester loathed governing and profligate London. The North of England did not even have the satisfaction of state law and states' rights to protect it from the commands of Westminster. The political parties largely ignored geographical divisions. Thus the dislike of the South by the North could not be represented politically; there was no Northern bloc in one party. Only through reform movements could the rest of England impose something of its morality on dominant London.

At the same time as the first women's rights conventions in America, small female suffrage organizations were founded in Manchester and the nearby industrial city of Sheffield. Although the Sheffield society petitioned the House of Lords, these first attempts at suffrage organization were local and soon lapsed. In 1867, however, the English suffrage movement found its Susan Anthony in the person of Lydia Becker. Fired by the debate on woman suffrage during the passage of the Second Reform Bill, she founded the Manchester Women's Suffrage Committee. In the following year, she organized more than five thousand Manchester women householders to demand the vote. In 1869, unmarried women householders did, indeed, receive the right of voting in local elections. Following the lead of Manchester, other woman suffrage committees were founded in abolitionist Bristol, in Edinburgh, and in London, before any national suffrage organization had been founded in America. The good fortune of the English suffragists was to have as their champion in parliament the greatest philosopher of his time, John Stuart Mill.

The Second Reform Bill, which extended the limited franchise to the lower sections of the middle class, had dropped the words "male person" in favour of the word "man," at the same time that the word "male" was being included in the American Constitution. And, by a contemporary legal decision, all laws relating to "man" were held to apply to "woman." In the case of voting, however, something more specific had been needed to break down the barriers of social custom. John Stuart Mill had proposed that the word "person" should be substituted for the word "man." This would have given women the vote if they had owned property. Mill had been converted to the cause of woman suffrage by his wife, an ardent feminist. She had followed the reports of the early women's conventions in America with interest, and had commented on them favourably in the influential *Westminster Review*.

Although Mill soon lost his seat in parliament, Lydia Becker kept the question of woman suffrage alive in England for the next twenty years. On her own, she edited the *Woman Suffrage Journal,* which came to a stop with her death. She corresponded with many of the Members of Parliament, and, like Anthony in Washington, she never allowed the representatives of limited democracy to forget that they had excluded a whole sex from the ballot. Nearly every year for the remainder of the nineteenth century, woman suffrage was debated in the House of Commons. Three times, a bill to enfranchise propertied women won a majority vote, but the bill never reached a second reading because of government indifference.

Lydia Becker, as persevering and plain and dominant as any Anthony, was even more independent, for she had no Elizabeth Stanton to help her. With few and occasional helpers, she fought for woman suffrage against widespread apathy. Even the current gibe at her, "There are three sexes, Male, Female, and Lydia Becker," paid tribute to her lonely eminence. Only among a few aristocratic or middle-class ladies, such as Barbara Bodichon, the co-founder of Girton College, and among working girls, did Lydia Becker find support. At one meeting in Manchester where she spoke amid the cheers of the factory girls, she felt that communion with her own sex which also gave fulfilment to the spinster Anthony. "I can't tell you how my heart went out to those women," she wrote, "and to see them look at me—oh, it was really sacred—awful: it was as if I received a baptism."[4]

If the late Victorian period was the doldrums of the suffrage movement in England because the suffragists could not win England county by county as the West of America was being won state by state, yet single women with property were becoming used to voting. Elizabeth Blackwell wrote back to her brother Henry in high glee about being able to vote in English municipal elections, while his wife Lucy Stone could not do so in Boston. "What will you say to *'the effete civilization of the old world,'* when you realize that it has laid upon me the burden of a vote!" She had voted in a local election for a friend of hers, a woman doctor. "I walked off in the conscious dignity of a voting citizen, persuaded that the responsibilities of a mighty empire rested upon my shoulders and with stern resolves always to be a rate payer and never to hide my grandeur behind a husband! . . . It is rather funny that I by coming to England, should be the first woman of the family to vote."[5]

This use of the vote in a limited way made many middle-class women in England politically conscious. In Lord Bryce's opinion, American women talked less about politics than English women—but then, he was used to conversation in aristocratic circles in England, where politics was a normal subject. Indeed, it had been the aristocratic Lady Amberley's public demand for the vote which had sparked off Queen Victoria's famous diatribe against the early feminists. "The Queen is most anxious to enlist everyone who can speak or write or join in checking this mad, wicked folly of 'Woman's Rights' with all its attendant horrors, on which her poor feeble sex is bent, forgetting every sense of womanly feeling and propriety. Lady Amberley ought to get a *good whipping."*[6] Jealousy of feminine rivalry for her position of pre-eminence may have made the Queen choose this masculine remedy for stopping women's rights by flogging. Yet there is no doubt that the majority of her subjects of both sexes agreed with her dislike of the feminists. Victorian England remained more traditional than Victorian America, outside the Eastern cities and the South. Supporters of women's rights in parliament were ahead of those they represented and of their Queen, who was royal before she was a woman.

If the example of the ageing Queen was a great deterrent to the English suffragists, yet the blatant class system of England and the party organization there encouraged those women who wanted the vote. The Liberal Party with its core of support based on middle-class dissenters made use of women canvassers through the Primrose League and the Women's Liberal Federation. In these groups, Liberal women learnt all the arts of applying political pressure within a party—training that only a few American women in the Western states were allowed to acquire. This political experience encouraged the growth of the middle-class National Union of Women's Suffrage Societies, which was almost the same in social membership and policy as the National American Woman Suffrage Association. At the end of the Victorian age, most suffragists on both sides of the Atlantic wanted a limited suffrage for middle-class women, in order to increase the decent vote in society.

The rise of the Labour Party in England at the turn of the century, however, added the militancy of the class struggle to the English suffrage movement. England was far more highly industrialized than America, and in a small country the fight of labour against capital was more obvious. As Jane Addams commented in 1914, before the English-trained militants had begun operations in America, "This world-wide entrance into government on the part of women is happily a bloodless one and has been without a semblance of violence save in England where its manifestations are not unlike those of the earlier movement among English workingmen."[7]

Again the new impetus behind the English suffrage movement came from radical circles in Manchester. As in America, suffragists tended to be bred, not converted. Richard Pankhurst had been an early supporter of woman suffrage, an extreme Republican, and one of the founders of the Labour Party. Upon his death, his radical widow, Emmeline Pankhurst, decided to work for woman suffrage within the Labour Party, aided by her two daughters, the violent Christabel and the socialist Sylvia. They were joined by Annie Kenney, a local mill-girl, who carried the message for them to the working girls in the factories. Although they were supported by the Labour Party leader, Keir Hardie, he could not convince his working-class followers that votes for a limited number of middle-class women, who would probably vote Tory or Liberal, should precede universal suffrage in Edwardian England. The Pankhurst women, disappointed with the policy of the Labour Party, founded the Women's Social and Political Union in 1903. This organization was to make the name of the "suffragettes" fearsome throughout the world.

The Pankhursts were not only inflamed by the militancy of the English labour unions, which, in fact, behaved much less violently than their American counterparts. They were also spurred on by the example of the Irish revolutionaries. The aristocratic Gore-Booth sisters, one of whom became the first woman Member of Parliament as a Sinn Feiner, filled the middle-class Pankhursts with ideas of revolution outside normal political methods. The sense of superior birth often frees people to act against convention. Some of the militancy of the English lady can be explained by her sure knowledge that she was a lady—while her American sister was often not sure enough of her status to behave unlike a lady.

In the decade before the First World War, the Pankhursts led hundreds of militant women to mass imprisonment and physical assault on the representatives of English government and law. While the main suffrage organization, as in America, pressed more quietly for votes for women chiefly in middle-class circles, the militants led professional women and factory girls from the slums of the East End of London into stone-throwing, the hitting of policemen, the slashing of pictures, suicide in front of racehorses, the chaining of themselves to railings, and hunger strikes. In this way, they hoped to gain huge publicity and to awaken the government to the danger of continuing to withhold the vote from women.

The reaction of most American and English people to the tactics of the militant suffragists was one of shock and horror. At last, the concept of the sex war, in which few believed, seemed to have become a fact. "It is no longer a joke," declared an English Member of Parliament to a group of American anti-suffragists. "It is a sex war. . . . The whole movement is but part of the effeminate superficiality of this generation. This superficiality finds its consummation in the present masculine abasement now witnessed in America."[8]

In England, at least, the government and the police were masculine enough to deal brutally with the militant suffragists, in return for the violence demonstrated towards themselves. Chivalry in England was often shown only to women who behaved themselves and belonged to a high social class. No female servant in England was protected by the fact of her sex, nor was any radical woman. Not only Queen Victoria advocated brutal methods against demands for the vote. This lack of courtesy between classes and between partisans of ideas made the English more ready to treat their women as guilty human beings and less ready to protect them as superior angels.

Harriot Stanton Blatch saw the importance of the difference between the attitudes of American and English men towards their women, when she first began to import militant tactics into the United States. "We are up against a hard proposition in the American man," she declared in an interview.

Now, in England, it's different. There, they take us seriously. They deny us our rights, but they don't put us away as if we were spoiled children, or indulgently lie to us as if we didn't know what we want. Why, in England they bar us from parliament; the police puts us off the streets; they send us to jail!

And what do we get in America? Why, they blandly admit us before the legislative committees, listen to all we have to say, treat us with perfect courtesy, even tell us they will vote for us, and then never so much as bother to answer our arguments. As for voting on our measures, they simply pocket them without a word. They won't bar us from the streets. They won't so much as put us in jail. It's distressing, I tell you. Yes, highly insulting!

Emmeline Pankhurst corroborated Harriot Blatch's words, when she herself crossed the Atlantic to spread the gospel of militance. "All the American men I met," she declared, "seemed to regard the movement as something of a joke. They did not seem to think that there was any great demand for the vote on the part of American women. We have had definite opposition to encounter on the part of the English male, and I don't know but what it is preferable to this half-amused indifference which I see in the men of America."[9] Nothing annoyed the serious suffragists more in both countries than to be taken lightly.

At the height of their activity before the First World War, the militant suffragists made the idea of the sex war believable in England. Their indiscriminate attacks on friend and foe among the Liberals in power drove many moderate suffragists from their ranks. For total war against all men seemed to be imminent. The winning of the vote seemed to be merely an excuse for female aggression against the male. Sometimes, the whole militant movement seemed to be a mere glory train for Emmeline and Christabel Pankhurst. Their chief lieutenants, the Pethick-Lawrences, split from them; and even Sylvia Pankhurst formed her own union of working women in the East End, when her mother and sister began to flirt with fashionable Tory circles in their search for political allies in getting the vote. Yet, although the militant movement was divided and open to criticism, it did break the conspiracy of silence over the activity of the suffragists that seemed to exist in the English press, and it did cause many women to join the moderate wing of the suffrage movement, led by Millicent Fawcett.

In America, as an acute suffragist noticed, the general lack of militancy was not due

to American women, but to American men. In every country it is the men who should be held chiefly responsible for the tone and conduct of the suffrage movement, as the government is in their hands, authority and power are theirs, and they are able to make the task of the feminist comparatively easy and pleasant. Englishmen have chosen to make it very difficult. In England the militant movement is like a slave insurrection; it presents characteristics of the uprising of a servile class; the bitterness of those who have been treated unjustly, the determination of the downtrodden to rise and at all hazards to themselves to conquer respect and consideration for their sex; and the arming of the one part of the community—women—against the other part.[10]

Despite the right of municipal suffrage, English married women were far behind American women in legal rights. They suffered from many of the Victorian inequalities under the law that the pioneer American feminists had successfully lobbied to repeal. The very revolt of some English women was all the more violent because the feminine ideal there under Victoria had been "semi-oriental." In a society dominated by the masculine club, where educational opportunities for women were still scandalously inadequate, English women had more reasons for rebellion.

Violence had not always been considered wrong in the British Isles. Historically, the suffragists asked, what of Bodicea?

If it was praiseworthy for English people to cut off the head of Charles I when he tried to act the tyrant, why is it damnable for Miss Annie Kenney to break a window? . . . . If Irishmen, who incited to riot, arson, cattle driving and even manslaughter, were rewarded by gaining sympathy and assistance from Gladstone and the Liberal Party, why are the women who, under great provocation, resort to much milder methods, treated like the worst of criminals and their just demands for the franchise waved aside?[11]

The coming of the First World War provided a curious justification for the policy of the militants in England and America. "Why all this tenderness and delicacy about militancy in the form of banner-bearing," asked Mrs. Belmont, "when the Governments of all nations are conscripting their men, including our own nation, to be militant?"[12] Both of the main suffrage organizations in England and America immediately used their forces to help in the war effort by staffing hospitals and raising funds for the government. Although the militants in both nations refused to cooperate with their governments, Carrie Catt hoped that the war had "knocked the *militant* movement into a sky hat."[13] The bloody massacre of men abroad filled the daily newspapers, not the minor war of the sexes at home.

The militant movements in both nations were, strangely enough, full of pacifists. Sylvia Pankhurst, who alone in her family had kept up contacts with the socialists, went to jail as a pacifist, as did other socialist suffragists in America. Pacifism had long been a part of the feminist movement in both countries, while militancy was recent. As Julia Ward Howe had declared, "Peace and woman suffrage go together, masculine government being founded upon the predominance of physical force."[14] It was in the hope that the votes of women would bring about universal peace that some suffragists equated the ballot with the millennium. The bitterness of moderate suffragists against the extreme militants was often based on a sincere feeling that women ought to remain peaceful at all costs. "Women never show up their real weakness," Anna Shaw declared, "so much as when they attempt force."[15]

Yet Anna Shaw and like-minded suffrage leaders in both countries swallowed their pacifism when the call to arms came. They served their country first and their principles afterwards. Few of the suffragists, as few of the male pacifists, were imprisoned because they stuck to their principles; but those who were jailed under the Defence of the Realm Act in England and the Sedition and Espionage Acts in America displayed the deep political divisions that already separated the suffragists before they had the vote. There were few who put their personal or humanitarian faith above their patriotism, especially when patriotic work was politically expedient in order to gain the vote.

As in America, most of the English suffragists gave up the pursuit of other social reforms for the single-minded chase of the ballot. When the government offered the vote to all women over thirty years of age, the suffragists accepted the offer, although it deprived most of the young female munition workers of the ballot. Equality with men in voting was not to come until 1928. The suffragists were also fortunate that the pro-feminist Lloyd George replaced the anti-feminist Asquith as Prime Minister; they did not have to convince an unwilling Woodrow Wilson as in America. They asked for nothing but the vote, as the Americans did. In return, they received nothing but the vote. There was no reconstruction of English society after the war. Indeed, Emmeline and Christabel Pankhurst ran unsuccessfully for parliament as Conservative candidates. As in America, humanitarian aims and sexual solidarity were forgotten in partisan politics, once the vote was won. The only advance was in women's legal and economic status, which was brought up to a rough equality with that of men—a position that American women had won without the vote.

Thus the English example was similar to the American experience. Both moderates and militants helped the suffrage movements in their different ways. Both suffrage organizations were unable to manipulate the women's vote as a sex after they had been given the ballot because of their support of partisan politics before. Even the concept of the sex war died in England with the actual war deaths of a million British men, especially in the upper echelons of English society. With too few men to go around middle-class and aristocratic women, those that survived were flattered rather than condemned. When women became superior in their numbers in the land of the living, the equality of the sexes in England became a more feasible idea.

The English example had led the American feminists in anti-slavery work, in municipal voting, in national organization, in militant action, and in the granting of the vote to women over thirty years of age. Even more galling for the American suffragists was the example of the British Dominions. Women in New Zealand received the vote in 1893 and in all Australia in 1902. Even in neighbouring Canada, woman suffrage progressed faster than in America, although on the

American pattern. The Canadian suffragists won the West, province by province, although Quebec was not to give full suffrage to women until the Second World War. By 1918, all the Canadian provinces but three had given women the vote, because of the feeling of democracy bred by the war. "How long," asked the National American Woman Suffrage Association in despair, "will the Republic of the United States lag behind the Monarchy of Canada?"[16]

The similarities of the movements for women's rights in the English-speaking world, geographical and social, with their cross currents of thought and personal contact, were brought to an apt success by the First World War. That struggle made it clear to all farsighted people that the human race lived in one world, linked and joined and international. The women of one country would be stirred by the example of the next. From the experience of Scandinavia and revolutionary Russia and the English-speaking peoples, the doctrine of the legal and political equality of the sexes would slowly spread across the world, without any more need for the militant action of women. Yet in no instance did the ballot in women's hands bring about the reconstruction of a society. Except in rare cases, men continued to rule, and voting women to be a conservative force.

PART NINE

Nothing but the Vote

Why cannot reformers labour together side by side, each in their own speciality, knowing that each is helping the other? As I see the human race, we are all one vast *chain-gang*, and no person or clan can advance one step without moving the whole body.

A Letter to *The Revolution, 1869*

XXVII

❧❧❧

THE CONTINUING DIVISION

THE TWO WINGS of the suffrage movement, led from Boston and New York, came together again. A new generation of leaders did not feel the personal enmities of the old. The growing state organizations in the West found the quarrel of the East incomprehensible. The American Woman Suffrage Association was rapidly losing its supporters, while the National was gaining all the time, stealing state organizations from its rival. Anti-suffrage forces had begun to organize, particularly in Massachusetts. There was need for a vast educational campaign to combat their propaganda, as well as to increase support for woman suffrage. And the powerful Woman's Christian Temperance Union, whose members in Massachusetts alone outnumbered the suffragists by forty to one, was led by Frances Willard, who pressed for a union of the suffrage organizations.

The daughter of Lucy Stone, Alice Stone Blackwell, brought about the union. The chief difficulty lay in getting Lucy Stone to accept either Stanton or Anthony as the president of the united society. After Anthony and other National delegates had shaken hands with the President of the United States, the self-confessed father of a bastard, Grover Cleveland, Stone was sure that "the unclean side" was still uppermost with them. She felt the two organizations were "different

in essence," and she found, in Anthony, "her old grasping spirit
. . . just as fully alive as ever."¹ But in the end, the merger was
arranged in 1890, with Stanton as president, Anthony in her usual
position of *éminence grise,* and Henry Blackwell and Alice Blackwell
powerfully placed with the *Woman's Journal* still under their control.

The united movement, the National American Woman Suffrage
Association, did not heal the geographical split in the movement.
Every convention saw a quarrel between the Westerners and the Easterners. And there was a new sectional interest added, that of the
Southerners. The suffrage movement began to grow below the Potomac. On a holiday in Georgia in 1887, Lucy Stone found that all the
women wanted the vote, but they were afraid. "They said it was here,
as it was at the North forty years ago, that they could not do anything."² Yet pioneer suffragists were rising up, such as Laura Clay of
Kentucky, who declared in 1893 that the South could not be left out
of the suffragists' calculations. "You have worked for forty years and
you will work for forty years more and do nothing unless you bring
in the South."³

Anthony succeeded Stanton at the head of the organization after
two years. As a Westerner through home and an Easterner through
work, she could mediate between two of the sections of the movement. The centre of the movement had been the Stanton house in or
near New York City; it now moved West to the Anthony home at
Rochester. Anthony even thought—amid the universal flattery she
now enjoyed—that she was revered in the South. Her successor, Carrie Catt, did not think so. In her opinion, Anthony had "little idea
how those old 'Confeds' hate her." It was beautiful in her old age that
Anthony should feel so satisfied, but she should not go South.⁴ Indeed, Anthony was never forgiven by Southerners for having been an
abolitionist, and for supporting a federal suffrage amendment on the
lines of the Fourteenth Amendment, rather than a solution which
would preserve states' rights.

The battle against Eastern dominance was fought and won at the
suffrage convention of 1894. The debate opened with a quarrel over

whether the meagre funds of the organization should be spent on helping to carry Kansas for suffrage or New York. A Kansas Populist said the liquor interests were so strong in New York that a campaign there would be trying "to climb to the moon." Kansas had already gone for prohibition, and would soon go for suffrage. The funds went to Kansas. "Our *best work for the cost,*" Anthony pointed out later, "is to get suffrage in the West."[5] Anna Shaw agreed with her when she took over the leadership of the woman's movement. Under her orders, fully nine-tenths of the money raised for campaigns was raised in the East and expended in the West. Even so, the Westerners thought that any money spent in the East was wasted, while the Easterners insisted that they were as important as their Western sisters.

The second quarrel in 1894 was over the site of the next convention. Under Anthony's guidance, the National had held its convention every year at Washington, in order to put steady pressure on Congress and the President. She had been successful in doing so, and had secured the debate of her federal amendment in the Senate. But the Westerners resented the expense of travelling East year after year, and they wanted the propaganda of holding a national convention in the Middle West. One Western delegate threatened a new Western association "if the convention remains in Washington and if the policy of this association remains to be conducted entirely by Eastern people." She thought rightly that a Congressman was "a green toad on a green tree and a brown toad on a brown tree." If his home district and state approved of woman suffrage, he would vote for it in Congress. When the matter finally reached the ballot, the Westerners and Southerners triumphed, backed by Easterners from the old American society who disliked Anthony's policy. Atlanta was chosen as the site of the next convention, with Cincinnati a close second, and Washington a poor third.[6]

When Anthony resigned from the presidency of the Association in 1900, she was succeeded by the efficient organizer, Carrie Catt. Catt tried to set up a permanent headquarters in New York, but she could not raise enough money to do so. With Stanton's withdrawal, there had been no New York base for the movement. In fact, the leaders of the organization were so split apart by geography that the official centre was the small town of Warren, Ohio, which happened to be the home town of the treasurer, Harriet Upton. Catt's incursion into New York provoked the hostility of the New York residents, led by Lillie Devereux Blake. They combined with the Southerners, who disliked Catt's backing of the Anthony federal amendment, to force the resignation of the new Western president in 1904, after the national organization had been weakened through the adoption of a policy of states' rights. The malleable and weak Anna Shaw was elected to be the new president. She could be trusted to rule through a cabinet system, and, as she lived near Philadelphia, the organization would remain decentralized. More power was given to the state groups, and different policies were followed in East and West and South.

Geographical rivalries continued to shake the loose Association. In the South, Laura Clay and the aggressive Kate Gordon from New Orleans pushed the argument of Henry Blackwell in the days of Reconstruction—that woman suffrage in the South would bolster white supremacy, not weaken it. Even if all women were given the vote in the South, white women would outnumber black women by two to one. In fact, white Southern women alone outnumbered the whole of the Negro population below the Potomac. Anyway, since the black man had been enfranchised, did not that make him the political superior of the white woman? As Anna Shaw declared in New Orleans, "Never before in the history of the world have men made former slaves the political masters of their former mistresses! . . . There is not a colour from white to black, from red to yellow, there is not a nation from pole to pole, that does not send its contingent to govern American women."[7]

This dominance of inferior breeds incited Southern suffragists to demand the vote. "How can I," asked a woman from Florida, "with the blood of heroes in my heart, and with the free and independent spirit they bequeathed me, quietly submit to representation by the alien and the negro?"[8] Kate Gordon agreed with these arguments, and added the most telling one. Political expediency demanded the vote for women. For if all women got it, Negro women could be excluded from voting as easily as Negro men, through state laws. Then the forces of white supremacy in the South would be doubly strong.

Yet political expediency was no argument against the conservative passions of the defeated South. Although the National American Association finally declared in 1899 that the causes of woman and the Negro were separate, the South continued to see them together. Anthony was the living embodiment of the connection of the causes. Laura Clay could beg the suffragists in the South not to press for "dress reform, or bicycling, or anything else," but to ask "the simple question why the principles of our forefathers should not be applied to women."[9] Yet the majority of Southern men and women persisted in seeing all change advocated by Westerners and Northerners as bad. To them, woman suffrage could not come alone. It would bring the whole complex of extreme feminist demands, from easy divorce to the right of mixed marriages.

The fact that Southern women were forty years behind in their demands for the vote put them in the position of women in the North in the 1840's, when the factories were only beginning to free them from the home. At that time, the causes of anti-slavery and women's rights were inextricably linked. So they were in the South in the decades before the First World War. Although political expediency dictated that woman suffrage would increase the white vote, the patriarchal tradition was stronger. Moreover, political myth allowed anti-suffrage Southern politicians to obscure the issue by claiming that Negro women would get the vote, when in fact Negro men had been excluded from voting by state laws. As a Southern correspondent, who believed in the political myth, warned Anthony in 1884, "The very existence of slavery put the South in a condition opposed to progress, and the fact of negro women voting, if the ballot be given to women, will cause our men to fight every inch of ground."[10]

Although much of the anti-suffrage propaganda in the South was demagogic and appealed to racial prejudice, there were genuine political fears at the base of that propaganda. Congress had tacitly accepted the Southern States' exclusion of the Negroes from the polls through state laws. But the Force Clause still existed in the Fourteenth Amendment, and, if woman suffrage re-opened the whole question of Negro suffrage, the Southern States might be totally disenfranchised by the votes of the North and the West. Moreover, federal amendments were anathema in the South, which had gone through a period of Negro and carpetbag rule because of federal amendments. "Remember," said a shrieking pamphlet in Alabama, "that *Woman Suffrage* means a re-opening of the entire *Negro Suffrage* question; loss of State rights; and another period of reconstruction horrors, which will introduce a set of female carpet-baggers as bad as their male prototypes of the sixties."[11]

The later militancy of some of the suffragists provided more reasons for conservative Southerners to distort the effect of the vote on the Southern lady. Once it had been proved by the vote of Western women that women did not vote as a group and would not punish a party for withholding the vote from women in the South and the East, there was even less reason for Southern Congressmen to listen to the suffragists. Even so, however hopeless the situation, the few suffragists of the South were correct in insisting that all American women could not get the vote without the support of some Southern legislatures. Sectional prejudices would have to be accommodated within the movement, or else there was no hope of finding thirty-six states to ratify a federal amendment.

The undisguised racism of the Southern suffragists such as Kate Gordon and Laura Clay—two of the seven most powerful officers in the National American Association after Anthony's retirement—worried the suffragists from the North and the West. Although Carrie Catt and Anna Shaw had to be diplomatic to gain some Southern support for suffrage, they lost the crusading spirit of the old abolitionists. "It is such a pity," the retired Anthony declared, "for the Northern women—*just like politicians*—to succumb to the Southern prejudice—but I suppose they will."[12] The vocabulary of the movement changed from the language of human rights to that of expediency. Negro women in the North were excluded from some suffrage parades, for fear of offending the South. As one Negro leader wrote to another about the suffragists, "All of them are mortally afraid of the South and if they could get the Suffrage Amendment through without enfranchising coloured women, they would do it in a moment."[13]

Although the Northern and Western leaders of the suffragists tried to deny the link between the cause of the Negro and that of women outside the South, they had their own reason for supporting the idea of a restricted vote for women. Much of the anti-suffrage feeling in the North was directed against the thought of new immigrant women getting the vote, thus doubling the corrupt machine vote of the large cities. What the Negro was to the Southern anti-suffragist, the immigrant was to the Northern. While the suffragists endlessly repeated that Anglo-Saxon women should have the vote to counterbalance the immigrant vote, the anti-suffragists were prepared to fight to the end not to increase the alien vote.

The language of the Northern suffrage leaders, even that of Elizabeth Stanton, increasingly shifted towards the expedient of educated suffrage for women. In 1902, she declared,

The popular objection to woman suffrage is that "it would double the ignorant vote." The patent answer to this is to abolish the ignorant vote. Our legislators have this power in their own hands. There have been various restrictions in the past for men. We are willing to abide by the same for women, provided the insurmountable qualification of sex be forever removed.[14]

The promise of the American Revolution in terms of human equality and liberty was forgotten in an effort to win the vote for a limited number of white, Anglo-Saxon women, in the same way that the terms of the Constitution had once denied the principles of the Declaration of Independence. As a woman journalist noticed in 1900, a complete change in the style of suffrage dress had taken place during the decade. "Everything is being worn à l'aristocrate, with the repeated assertion that too many people are voting already."[15]

But Eastern and Southern ideas of restricted suffrage were less popular in the egalitarian West, where there were few Negroes and new European immigrants. Moreover, it was unlikely that the Supreme Court would uphold a measure so contrary to the ideal of American constitutional law. Thus, while Easterners talked of educated suffrage and Southerners of white suffrage, Westerners continued to talk the language of human rights and liberty and equality.

The next major geographical quarrel in the suffrage organization resulted in the defection and secession of much of the East. First, the daughter of Elizabeth Stanton, Harriot Blatch, returned to New York after twenty years in England. She had observed the beginnings of the militant suffrage movement led by the Pankhursts, and realized the propaganda value of dramatic suffrage tactics. She had not, like her mother, lived the early part of her life in a small Western town; most of her experience lay in the suburbs or cities of the East Coast of America or of Europe. She could see what was lacking in New York, for it was the same in London. Suffrage must get the support of factory women. College girls needed to get together with union organizers, as they were beginning to do through the settlement houses. Disgusted with the middle-class and ladylike leadership of the National American Woman Suffrage Association, which was flirting with the aristocratic idea of educated suffrage, Harriot Blatch set up her own Women's Political Union.

The object of the new organization, founded in 1907, was to bring together all working women, both the new women pioneers in the professions and the factory women. Instead of ladies repeating the platitudes of human rights to legislative committees, she brought forward factory girls to shock with raw accounts of sweatshop conditions. She organized the first mass suffrage parade in New York. In fact, she injected the new enthusiasm of the rebellious English suffragists in London into a similar social situation in New York. She was a true daughter of her mother in her love of spontaneity and dislike of organization. To one observer, the Women's Political Union was "the free lance type," did "brilliant, spasmodic, unsystematic work," was good "at pulling off great publicity stunts," but was "quite disorderly and difficult to deal with."[16] Until Harriot Blatch met Alice Paul, she did not find her Anthony.

The second Eastern rebellion began with the conservative and wealthy Mrs. O. H. P. Belmont. She decided to give her financial support to the suffragists, but she wanted personal power as well. She offered the National American Association a permanent headquarters in Fifth Avenue in New York. At the convention of 1912, hostility to her broke out. Anna Shaw, associated with Mrs. Belmont and other Eastern women, forced the resignation of two of the leading officials from the Middle West, who seemed likely to make a bid for the leadership. This created a hostile Western faction in the movement, which led a Western and Southern counterattack on Mrs. Belmont, over her proposal to locate national headquarters in New York.

The quarrel worsened when the same group supported Jane Addams, who had personally endorsed Theodore Roosevelt and the Progressive Party for the election. She was vice-president of the suffrage organization, which was pledged to a strict non-partisan policy. Susan Anthony had laid down the non-partisan gospel. "My *one article of party creed*—shall be that of *woman suffrage*—All other articles of party creeds shall be with me as a drop in the bucket. . . . We are beggars of each and all."[17] Despite this long-standing article of faith and the fury of Mrs. Belmont—a staunch Republican—Jane Addams's action was upheld, as a *personal* action that did not involve the suffrage movement. In a fury, Mrs. Belmont withdrew her support from the National American Association and looked for another. Private and geographical feuds had again split the movement apart.

The caution of Anna Shaw in pressing for a federal suffrage amendment, for fear of antagonizing the Southern suffragists, led to another secession. The National organization had always kept a lobby in Washington to press for the "Anthony amendment," but this lobby was almost moribund. It had been so unsuccessful that Congress, which had at least bothered to lock up the suffrage amendment in committee during the decades before 1896, hardly considered the question again until 1913. Once Anthony had given way to Western pressure to hold the annual conventions of the National American Association outside Washington, some of the pressure on the legislators slackened, and they were only too happy to let sleeping bitches lie.

The arrival in Washington, however, of two suffragists, the

Quaker Alice Paul and her friend Lucy Burns, put life into the agitation of the Congressional committee there. Both were Eastern college graduates and urban social workers, both had joined with the British militants and had been in jail and on hunger strike. "Alice Paul had a more acute sense of justice," a member of their organization said, "Lucy Burns, a more bitter sense of injustice. Lucy Burns would become angry because the President or the people did not do this or that. Alice Paul never expected anything of them."[18] Both women decided to apply some of the tactics of the militants against the British parliament to the American Congress. With a brilliant flair for publicity, they organized a suffrage parade of five thousand women just before Woodrow Wilson's inauguration, when the streets of Washington were full of curious visitors. Luckily for them, the suffragists were mobbed and insulted by the crowd, and became martyrs, just as the female abolitionists had once been. Huge and favourable publicity was the result, for American men had been wounded on their sore spot, their claim of invariable chivalry to women.

Talented at raising money and support with her terse activism, Alice Paul set up her own organization, the Congressional Union, to campaign solely for the passage of the "Anthony amendment." At first, Anna Shaw included the new organization within the loose structure of the National American Association, but immediately the priorities of the two groups clashed. Alice Paul wanted all effort to go behind a campaign for the federal amendment; Anna Shaw knew well that each state where a suffrage referendum was due wanted help and money. The old clash between the American and the National Associations flared alive again. Was suffrage to be won in the states or at Washington? This time, the new Congressional Union found itself in the position of the old National, working for pressure at Washington. In this way, Alice Paul could claim that *she* was the true heir of Susan Anthony, not her apostolic successor, Anna Shaw.

The successful militancy and enthusiasm of Harriot Blatch's and Alice Paul's organizations—soon to merge in the Woman's Party— proved attractive in the West. They would have again played the role of the old National in stealing the support of their conservative rival had not Anna Shaw been pushed out of the leadership of the main suffrage organization and Carrie Catt been elected president for the second time. She was to increase the membership of the National American Association twenty times in two years, from one hundred thousand to two million.

In the eleven years that she had been away from the Association, Catt had become a power in the international and in the New York suffrage movements. She had run an organization which pooled the experience of the suffragists in all nations, and she had been one of the master-minds behind the unsuccessful, but significant, attempt in New York in 1915 to pass woman suffrage by referendum. In the referendum campaigns of that year in the four Eastern States of New York, New Jersey, Pennsylvania, and Massachusetts, woman suffrage had received two votes in five. Even in Massachusetts, which had defeated the proposal so decisively twenty years before, more than one in three votes went to the women. It was obvious that with an efficient and strong leader like Carrie Catt the Eastern States could follow the Western ones into the suffrage column.

Catt was a political realist. She did not hate those who could be useful to her. As an old friend of the "Anthony amendment," she approved of what the Congressional Union and the later Woman's Party were doing. In the convention of the National American Association in 1913, she had openly supported Alice Paul against Anna Shaw, saying that all pressure should perhaps be put on Congress, as it had been in Reconstruction days. Alice Paul's criticism of the inefficiency of the Association had helped Catt to make Anna Shaw resign. Even so, once she took over the Association, Catt kept spies in Alice Paul's organization, and she let Woodrow Wilson know in advance of any embarrassing plans of the militant women. She revived the effectiveness of the National American Association's lobby at Washington, which, led by such tireless workers as Maud Wood Park from Massachusetts, kept up a dual pressure on Congress. While the Congressional Union tried to defeat Woodrow Wilson in the election of 1916, Catt refused to take sides, knowing that she

would need the support of the victor in getting the federal amendment.

Catt's strategy proved correct, for without Wilson's influence in the
Democratic state legislatures of the South the Nineteenth Amendment would have had an even more difficult passage through the few
Southern legislatures which passed it. Catt saw the need of both
militancy in the movement—to bring publicity and the support of the
aggressive trade unions—and of respectability—to attract the backing
of more conservative ladies and men. In fact, Catt made the split with
the Woman's Party a useful thing. The National American Association could get the benefit of militance for the cause, while disclaim-
ing responsibility for that militance. Both work in Washington and
in each state was needed, for both a federal amendment and ratification by thirty-six states was needed. As Alice Blackwell wrote, anybody who was digging away at either end of the ditch was hastening
the coming of suffrage.

To win in the West and even in the East was not enough; some of
the Southern States had also to be won. This practical consideration
made Carrie Catt evolve a master plan, by which the tactics of the
members of the Association in each individual state were made
subordinate to national strategy. Aided by the fortunate legacy of
more than a million dollars, Catt imposed an over-all control on the
movement and gave a sense of national purpose to each suffragist.
Although she took over the leadership of the main suffrage movement at the time when woman suffrage was most likely to succeed—
after the outbreak of the First World War in Europe—yet she was a
true president of the enormous organization of some two million
members in that she seemed to represent all and each. Even if both of
the old Southern suffrage leaders, Kate Gordon and Laura Clay, split
off from the movement in defence of states' rights, when the federal
amendment neared ratification, Catt did impose a brief psychological
unity on the main suffrage movement and did persuade its members
that freedom for women to vote lay in obedience within a pressure
group.

XXVIII

⁓⁓

UNIONS FOR WOMEN

WOMEN WORKERS and trade unions have never got along well together. The first women who worked in the factories thought of their jobs as casual affairs. Bad working conditions were part of the natural order of things; low wages were better than unpaid labour in the home. Although there were small Female Labour Reform Associations in some mill towns, the first case of widespread organized agitation by women was during the Pittsburgh strikes of the 1840's. The result of six years of agitation was the passage of ten-hour laws in New Hampshire, Pennsylvania, and New Jersey. These acts limited the working week of women to sixty hours, although manufacturers avoided their provisions by making special contracts with their employees. Yet strikes and organized protest throughout the East had led to legislative action. It was an important precedent, although the laws only protected women in factories, not human beings.

Early women's trade unions were temporary affairs. Wage-cutting might cause a spontaneous walk-out, but this quick union split apart when conditions returned to normal. Only the women shoemakers had a permanent union, the Daughters of Saint Crispin, for several years after 1869. Two of the male trade unions, the printers and the cigarmakers, also admitted women during the reform ferment after the Civil War. Yet, on the whole, workingmen like professional men did not want the competition of women for their jobs—especially as a woman's wages for the same work could be as low as one-quarter of a man's. Most trade unions excluded women altogether. Even the printers took care that their women members should not rise above the position of compositors to the higher grades of their profession. The early Victorian union was a closed shop for qualified men.

When the Knights of Labor set up the nucleus of a national union in the 1880's, women were invited to join them. At one time, more than a hundred "assemblies" of women were attached to the organization. The Knights of Labor supported the equal rights of the sexes. They even hired a woman organizer, the widowed Leonora Barry, "to go forth and educate her sister working-women and the public generally as to their needs and necessities." If she failed to do much education during five years of continual effort, and if she took refuge in a second marriage, the fault lay more with her audience than with herself. As she declared, she found among working women "the habit of submission and acceptance without question of any terms offered them, with the pessimistic view of life in which they see no ray of hope." Women who were receiving reasonable wages would not combine with women who were being sweated. Again, many women were deterred from joining unions "by foolish pride, prudish modesty and religious scruples; and a prevailing cause, which applies to all who are in the flush of womanhood, is the hope and expectancy that in the near future marriage will lift them out of the industrial life to the quiet and comfort of a home."[1]

Farm women in the West, however, were more ready to join the farmers' unions. They were equal with their men in work, they marketed their eggs and butter equally, and they were equal in protest. When the Grange movement rose in the 1870's, its charter read, "No Grange should be organized, or exist, without women." Although the rise and fall of the movement was swift, women outside the abolition movement got their first taste of political work and agitation in its ranks. The Greenback movement imitated the rise and decline of the Grange. But when the Populists rose in the 1890's, three women were among their leaders. One of these, Mary Ellen Lease, was the greatest demagogue of her time. She was Irish, vindictive, passionate, imperious, under the sway of "a hidden power," driven on by "a Great Force." She fanned the whirlwind of the debtor farmers of Kansas. When this "female Old Hickory" spoke, the parades were a mile long, and her rich contralto voice had a hypnotic effect on her audience. Her phrase, "What the farmers need to do is raise less corn and more hell," became the battle-cry of her cause. If Populism sank with the new prosperity of the farmer and other causes, it had bred the first powerful woman politician in the United States.

Other leaders of women were thrown up in the industrial wars of the cities. Factory conditions at the turn of the century stank in the nostrils. Laundresses worked, stripped to the waist, for twelve hours a day in temperatures above one hundred degrees Fahrenheit. Machines were unguarded and could amputate fingers or hands. Poisons fouled the air in many industries; women breathed brass and glass dust, naphtha and paint fumes, and the exhalations of lead and phosphorus. The jawbones rotted off girls who made matches. There were hardly any washrooms in the factories. Pools of oil and grease lay on the floors, inviting tragedies such as the Triangle Shirtwaist Fire and its murder of one hundred and forty-five girls. Everywhere, there was din, dirt, and danger.

Yet if the factory was bad, the tenement workshop was worse. The slums had taken over some of the functions of the farm in home industries. Many regulations could be enforced in the factories, but few in the tenements. The competition of the sweatshop homes kept the markets flooded with goods and wages low. Contagious diseases were passed on, unchecked. In one tenement, a visitor found a dying consumptive making cigarettes by licking their tips. Above all, tenement industry allowed a husband to accept low wages, because his wife and children could earn at home the difference between starva tion and subsistence.

The American Federation of Labor, which rose on the ruins of the Knights of Labor, followed its forerunner's policy of organizing women. The fact that most of the women organizers were Irish or

Jewish showed how women in the new immigrant groups had not yet found America the land of opportunity. The middle-class feminists were led by women of old American blood; working women were led by new immigrant stock. The middle-class woman had time to worry over the vote, to confirm her status; the Irish or Jewish woman wanted a job at a decent wage. "There is no harder contest," said a woman unionist, "than the contest for bread." When the suffrage movement produced its militants, they only imitated on the political scene what had been practiced by women labour organizers during the strikes of eighty years. If most of the middle classes found militancy shocking, working women found it a fact of life. For they had often been treated brutally by their employers, and had to reply with violence.

Mother Jones was called by Clarence Darrow "the Wendell Phillips of the labour movement." She was born in Ireland in 1830. She came to America, and worked as a teacher and a dress-maker in Chicago. She married an iron-moulder, but her husband and four children all died in an epidemic. She became an organizer for the Knights of Labor and for the mineworkers. For fifty years she was in the thick of all the bitter and bloody mine strikes. She was shot at, mobbed, beaten, and jailed, an old woman armed only with a hatpin. When deputies with rifles beat back striking men, she led forward armies of women, brandishing mops and brooms, against the bayonets. With them, she chased away scabs and strike-breakers, and organized the miners.

Once, when Mother Jones was jailed with her women's army for disturbing the peace, she made them bring their babies into the courtroom and the jail. For five days, the women sang patriotic songs and the babies howled until they were let out. Yet, although Mother Jones was a radical about economics, she was a social conservative. This was why she was so successful among the peasant wives of the new immigrants. She thought their traditional thoughts; she was even against careers for women. "If men earned money enough," she wrote in her autobiography, "it would not be necessary for women to neglect their homes and the little ones to add to the family's income."

On one occasion, she shocked a meeting of wealthy women suffragists, after she had become a legend in her old age. She told them
that women did not need the vote to raise hell like her; they needed
convictions and a strong voice. In Colorado, the women had had the
vote for two generations, and men and women were still bound in the
slavery of the mines. Politics was the servant of industry. For working women, economic justice came before the vote. Suffragists should
help the unions first, and get the vote afterwards. "No matter what
your fight," Mother Jones concluded magnanimously, "don't be ladylike!"[2]

Other women who were powerful in the trade unions were brought
over to the side of the suffragists by middle-class women, who went
into the slums to meet them. The settlement house opened a small
bridge between the lady and the working woman. When Jane Addams and Lillian Wald and Margaret Dreier Robins went out to meet
women in the factories, they found out the leaders of those women
and taught them to organize better and hate less. When the Irish
union leader, Mary Kenney, first went to Hull-House and met the
ladies there, her impression was that "they were all rich and not
friends of the workers."[3] Later, Jane Addams let her use the place
for union meetings and had her educated. In the end, she came to like
the wealthy women who founded with her the National Women's
Trade Union League in 1903. This League helped working women in
some major strikes, but, by 1910, not more than one woman factory
worker in twenty had joined any union.

Leonora O'Reilly was another of the Irish workers from the slums
who was educated by middle-class reformers into organizing unions
and opposing the idea of the class struggle. She was invaluable to the
suffragists, for she could talk the language of the union people and
get mass support for suffrage parades. While a middle-class woman
offended by her words and accent, Leonora O'Reilly knew the terms
of her job, which were a foreign language to the ladylike suffragists.
"For the sake of the kiddies in the White Goods Trade," she wrote in
1913 to all the women labour organizers in New York,

those of us who believe in Votes for Women ought to make as big a showing as possible this year to prove to the politicians that the Working Girl has arrived and that she knows that she has rights as well as duties, and means to fight for them. When she isn't fighting she can stand up and be counted at least.

So please will you help Mother O'Reilly to put the fear of God if not of Votes in the Politicians' hearts.[4]

The many settlement houses which sprang up at the turn of the century brought the young feminists into contact with working conditions. This contact was invaluable for the suffrage movement. Through the houses, college girls learned of the need of high wages for working women, and working women learned of their need for the vote. The suffrage movement had begun in the cities of Boston and Philadelphia in the crusade to free the slaves. Its leadership had shifted to women from Western small towns, until, under the leadership of Anna Howard Shaw, the movement lay becalmed in its doldrums. There had been no understanding of the pressing need for factory reform. But once the Socialist Party—which polled a million votes in 1912—backed woman's suffrage, the leaders of the women's trade unions began to work for the vote. Labour organizers stirred up support in the slums, where the suffragists had never penetrated. And the new, militant Woman's Party applied strike tactics to the political scene. In doing so, it attracted mass support from aggressive working women, who liked militancy.

The centre of power of the suffrage movement shifted back to the Eastern urban cities just when the suffrage issue had been won in the West and needed new states to conquer. The small town, during its period of evangelical radicalism, had reformed the West; the slum and the factory, in their first period of agitation for social reform, were to provide the impetus behind suffrage in the East. The city had founded the small towns, which rebelled against the city. Now the city was to end what the city had begun, the crusade for women's rights, just at the time when more women began to live in cities than in the country.

No one was more important than Margaret Dreier Robins in establishing contact between the leaders of the working women and the suffragists. Daughter of a rich German-American family, she married Raymond Robins, a Klondike millionaire and preacher of the Social Gospel. She organized the National Women's Trade Union League in New York, and financed Hull-House in Chicago. She employed Leonora O'Reilly, and through her made the women unionists interested in the vote. She also made the suffragists and the Progressives work to pass laws protecting working women, who felt at last that middle-class people were helping them with more than charity. Yet she was more concerned with protecting the weak than with bringing equality to mankind. She was to fall out with those suffragists who wanted an Equal Rights Amendment to the Constitution, that would repeal many of the laws which Margaret Robins had helped to put through in order to bring the eight-hour day to women workers.[5]

Some of the organizers of the women's unions were not won over by the settlement workers. Like Mother Jones, they resented ladies. They wanted a classless society, not one where every woman had the right and opportunity to imitate a lady. In this way, they rejected the American dream, and Americans came to call them "reds," who looked to other countries for their ideals. Yet, in some measure, they were yearning after the oldest American dream of all, that of true equality. They wanted every woman to be the social equal of every other woman, even if the process involved levelling down. Their prized equality was more than equality of opportunity; it was equality in all parts of life. They thought that the freedom of all people to be on equal terms with their own kind involved the stopping of the freedom of some people to grow rich. In this belief, they were good socialists and seemed bad Americans.

Ella Reeve Bloor was one of the few labour organizers who came from a middle-class, old American family. Her first wish was to be a foreign missionary; but she married a labour lawyer and a progressive, and joined the suffrage movement through Quaker contacts. Soon she was converted to revolutionary socialism, divorced her husband, and married a labour organizer. Like many other middle-class women, she came to her profession through her husband. She herself began to organize unions in Delaware, in the intervals of rearing six children. She went to the Chicago stockyards for Upton Sinclair to verify his material for *The Jungle*. In 1912, backed by the conservative state suffrage organization, she campaigned all over Ohio for votes for women. Yet she was proud of campaigning for something else. "All my suffrage speeches," she wrote, "were class struggle speeches. I did not mention the word 'socialism' but I handed out good, strong socialist doses. I always tried to make clear that the object of our campaign was not alone to get the vote but to prepare women to use the power of the ballot to get decent pay and decent conditions for women and so to strengthen the position of the whole working class."

Ella Bloor's priority was better working conditions, while that of the suffragists was the vote. They did not understand each other's point of view. In one strike, Ella Bloor had seen seventy-three children suffocated to death in a crush, probably caused by deputies or scabs. She could not forget such episodes, and she could not explain them to the suffragists. "For many of the secure middle class ladies the suffrage movement was a mere feminist fad. I tried to make them see the really vital importance of suffrage to the working women, as a weapon against economic inequality. And I tried to make them see that not the vote alone was important, but its proper use in building a better society." When the militant English suffragist, Emmeline Pankhurst, came to see Ella Bloor, she scolded her for working for the "man's party" of the Socialists. Ella Bloor thought the English woman had the "narrow feminist idea . . . of working for women alone," while she wanted to work for mankind and for the workers before the vote. In their priorities for freedom, the feminists disagreed.

Once women did get the vote, political differences split the labour leaders from the middle-class suffragists. In Ella Bloor's opinion, the splendid and militant Woman's Party degenerated to "a narrow, anti-labour sect."[6] In fact, most of its members had merely reverted to the American middle-class ideas of what freedom and equality meant, the opportunity to become a lady. Ella Bloor, in disillusion, turned to the new Communist Party, at the age of fifty-seven. In its ranks, she found "the fullness and richness" of her life. To nearly all American women, her political choice made her into an enemy and something of an alien. If she had once fought for the vote for women, now she had joined a party which wanted to make that vote useless.

Elizabeth Gurley Flynn was another labour organizer who also was to turn from socialism to Communism. Her mother, who was "lace curtain Irish," was an early suffragist. Her father, who was "shanty Irish," was a labourer who bettered himself by becoming a civil engineer. He was a socialist, and socialism became the religion of the young Elizabeth Gurley. "We hated the rich, the trusts they owned, the violence they caused, the oppression they represented."[7] Her early heroine was Molly Malone, who organized the Harlem Equal Rights League in 1905. A year later, at the age of sixteen, Elizabeth Gurley became a street-corner speaker. Soon she joined the International Workers of the World, the Wobblies; she was called "The Rebel Girl" by Joe Hill himself. She married a Western miner and labour organizer, left him, and spent a decade with the Anarchist leader, Carlo Tresca. She carried on the fire of the early women labour leaders into the twenties and thirties, despite bouts of legal persecution. She did not join the Communist Party until 1937; eventually she became its national chairman. Even so, her radicalism remained an emotional and personal thing, and she seemed to sit ill at the head of that small and ineffective party until her death.

Freedom within the factory system was impossible; but the system could be bettered. Most reformers believed in reform through law and political pressure; they also believed that the votes of working women could apply that political pressure. Some women believed in reform through social revolution; in a curious way, they looked back to the days of the utopians who had sought to build a paradise in the New World. It was no coincidence that Mary Eddy, who wanted to regenerate the earth through Christian Science, called herself Mother Mary, in the same way that Mother Jones called herself Mother to lead her striking children. The socialist idea of paradise was merely the old American idea of an Eden in the wilderness; but it could never become a powerful idea, because most American women had always wanted individual liberty to rise in the civilized world rather than a social equality forced upon them by government.

Curiously, Emma Goldman attracted few followers to her own wild brand of freedom. The nineteenth century had abounded with anarchists in all but name; the official Anarchist movement had been very powerful at the beginning of this century. And Emma Goldman was the freest of the free. Perhaps she failed to attract mass support because anarchy, by definition, can have no party and no leaders. Perhaps the fact that she was a Jewess from Russia and no lady told against her. Perhaps she was too brutal when she made it clear that "women need not always keep their mouths shut and their wombs open." Perhaps she was too much the atheist and free-thinker and mocker of the law in an age terrified of the red bogey.

Yet all she wanted was what Anne Hutchinson had wanted, freedom of the spirit from government and oppression. Only her method was not by the acceptable way of individual religious freedom, but by the dangerous path of the radical change of society. Freedom of the soul for Emma Goldman could only come through freedom of the body. If Anne Hutchinson spoke up two hundred years too soon, Emma Goldman's gospel was "about eight thousand years ahead of her age." She had no wilderness to flee into during her century; no society could satisfy her. Revolutionary Russia proved as disappointing as capitalist America for this visionary in search of liberty. As she once declared in court, "Where shall I go? Everywhere on earth the laws are against the poor, and they tell me I cannot go to heaven, nor do I want to go there."[8]

The quest for women's freedom from the Victorian factory led to various postures of liberty. The conservatives merely wanted to feel free to deny that anything was wrong. Middle-class reformers wanted to better working conditions with the help of union leaders, but they did not want to alter the basic structure of society. In their view, women should be free to enjoy what they could earn; they should, however, be allowed to earn more. Even the socialists wanted to keep the factory system; they thought wrongly that, if working women owned their factory, they would feel more free when they worked within it. Only the anarchists wanted to put an end to factories, as far as possible, and to free women from work, motherhood, the home, and all the chains of society.

The moderate reformers were successful because, in the first two decades of this century, they had the support of many Americans. Factory work remained a casual affair for most of the female sex; for every woman who worked her whole life in a factory, many worked there at intervals, while they were not doing the jobs of wives and mothers. A women's trade union seemed unnecessary to a temporary worker. The class war seemed silly to the prospective wife, who hoped to rise in the world with the right sort of husband.

The militant feminists failed to make women hate men. The militant socialists failed to make women hate ladies. The sex war, like the class war, never became a popular concept in America, although both concepts were widely discussed. A revolution in society demands a fierce belief in justice, allied with the hatred of a sex or a caste or a class. There was no revolution in America because there was not enough hatred. Few believed the American militants who said, "There is a sex-war, just as there is a class-war." There was only gradual reform in the factories, and the gift of the vote to all adult women.

XXIX

༄ ✦ ༄

THE PROGRESSIVE ANSWER

THE SUFFRAGISTS and the Progressives made the same miscalculation, that the vote of the majority of the people would cure most of the ills of society, because most people would vote for the good. Their belief in democracy made them also believe that the reform of the techniques of representation would mean the reform of the nation. They underestimated the cleverness of professional politicians in manipulating the new techniques and the new voters, and they overestimated the ability of those techniques and voters to judge well and do good.

The Progressive movement was distinguished from preceding reform movements by gathering together a large urban following as well as support from the small towns and rural areas of America. The Populists and William Jennings Bryan had failed to capture the big cities; but Robert La Follette in Wisconsin and Hiram Johnson in California could get backing from the Western cities. The very success of the Progressives, in seeming to heal the split between urban and rural reformers in the years before the First World War, has misled many commentators into thinking that it was a cohesive movement. In fact, it was not, although the urban and rural wings of the movement had some common aims. As in all reform movements, the split between East and West and South, and between city and country, remained.

Nothing showed better the deep division in the movement than the behaviour of Hiram Johnson to Charles Evans Hughes in the election of 1916, when he refused to throw the support of the Californian Progressives behind the Eastern candidate for the presidency of his own party. Again, the Eastern Progressives turned on the Midwestern neutralist Progressives with the First World War; Theodore Roosevelt thought that Robert La Follette should be hanged. The Progressive Party itself showed a complete change of appeal and nature between the Eastern Roosevelt's campaign in 1912 and the Midwestern La Follette's campaign in 1924. After the Progressive cause collapsed in the East with the boom of the 1920's, it was the Western Progressives who continued to fight on alone for what Western radicals had always wanted since the days of the Grange.

Over matters of peace, prohibition, finance, and tariffs, the Progressive movement in the West diverged from that in the East. If, briefly, the two wings agreed over the need to bust the trusts, preserve equality of opportunity, improve representative techniques, control immigration, and give the suffrage to women, the alliance was one of means, not of fundamental ends. While the country reformers still thought that all virtue resided on the farms, the city reformers began to consider that virtue might be found in the regulated power of the growing cities.

The problem of appealing to these new cities made those reform politicians successful who, like La Follette, could talk both the language of the farm and small town and that of the middle-class residential district. For Senators especially, outside the South, it became essential to appeal in both city and country. In a similar way, some of the suffragists had for a long time tried to win over the urban and suburban ladies, with their conservative reforming zeal, to the side of the more radical women in the small towns. These diplomatic women had preached, as the divided Progressives were to preach, the harmony of all reasonable reforms.

"I recognize the fact that we can work for peace and for temperance," Julia Ward Howe told the National Council of Women in 1891, for social purity, for civil service reform, without calling ourselves suffragists. Many work for those causes to whom the name is almost abhorrent. And yet, I believe that the principle which is slowly bringing the political enfranchisement of women is identical with that which we recognize in the accepted measures which I have just named. It and they are only features of that better state of society towards which we are not drifting, but marching. The whole new Christian scheme holds together.[1]

It was the talent of the Progressive movement to use the diplomacy of Julia Howe and Frances Willard to persuade middle-class ladies in city and town to support social reform and woman suffrage, in order to save the home. Their argument was a persuasive one. The community, they said, was only an extension of the home. Women had saved the morals of men and children within the house; now they must do so without. "One after another," wrote a Progressive and a suffragist,

the duties that formerly belonged exclusively to the individual households have become the common duties of the community—the care and protection of children; their schooling and physical training; the regulation of morals and health and cleanliness; the supervision of food, the inspection of buildings, the prevention of disease, the regulation of drainage and sanitation, and a score of other like duties. All of these are essentially domestic. . . .

When the anti-suffragists declare that the woman's place is the home we grasp them by the hand and say amen most earnestly. The woman's place is the home. But to-day would she serve the home she must go beyond the house. No longer is the home compassed by four walls. Many of its most important duties lie now involved in the bigger family of the city and State.[2]

Caught by the very progress of society that the Victorians had believed inexorable, even the conservative woman had to go outside the house to preserve what was inside. The fashionable language of evolution gave the Progressive argument added force. Did not the world-wide aspect of the suffrage movement, Jane Addams asked in 1914, make it "part of that evolutionary conception of self-government which has been slowly developing through the centuries?" Just as "industrial changes took spinning out of private houses, so political changes are taking out of the home humanitarian activities, not to mention the teaching of children."[3]

With large areas of national life controlled by the trusts and political machines, women had to form themselves into large groups to fight for their own interests. "People are everywhere finding out," said the president of the National Consumers' League,

that their single strength is too weak. They have to group themselves and make certain regulations for protection; and that is politics. Are women less concerned than men in having clean streets, decent sewers, untainted milk, good schools, charities properly administered, hospitals put on a proper footing? Yet we cannot have to do with any of these things without taking part in politics, pure and simple.[4]

The Progressive argument had a further appeal, because a great many women's organizations had grown up in the late Victorian period in the small towns and cities. These were the women's clubs. The reason for women organizing themselves so much in America lay partly in pioneer traditions of visiting, partly in the social leadership of the churches, partly in the "good neighbour policy" of an immigrant society, partly in the habit of organizing taught by the Civil War and the lyceum movement, and mostly in the fact that a growing body of middle-class women found themselves with new leisure, brought about by labour-saving machinery, Irish servants, and the wealth of their husbands. They had the habit of activity, and had long been trained in church work. As they were supposed to acquire the culture for the family and pass it on to their children, they set up week-day clubs to acquire knowledge of the earth, in order to supplement the Sunday clubs where they acquired knowledge of heaven. By 1900, a Senate Committee on Woman Suffrage was told, "Well, gentlemen, wherever there are two women nowadays, there is a club. The remotest hamlet is no exception to this rule."[5]

The mushrooming women's clubs were set up for every purpose under the sun. Many of them did join, however, the General Federation of Women's Clubs, which claimed a membership of one and a half million women by 1914. Through these busy groups of middle-class women, the Progressive movement turned its ideology into fact. An official of the General Federation paid tribute to this fury of local activity:

> Thousands of towns, cities and hamlets can bear testimony to the work of these organized women: there are more sanitary and better ventilated schoolhouses; there are more numerous parks and more cleanly streets; there are district nurses who visit the sick poor in their homes and give instruction in the simple rules of wholesome living; there are sanitary drinking fountains for man and beast; there are vacation schools and play-grounds; there are juvenile courts and equal guardianship laws; there are cleaner markets; there are many free public libraries and thousands of travelling libraries; there is a lessening of objectionable bill-board orna-mentation; there is a determined campaign, nation-wide, against the housefly; there is a more intelligent knowledge of the prevention and care of tuberculosis; in short, there is scarcely any movement for the better-ment of living conditions or for the social and moral uplift of the Ameri-can people that has not received a helping hand from the club woman.[6]

By this time, there was nothing more dangerous for a politician than an attack on women's organizations. When Grover Cleveland, once he was safely out of the White House, wrote in the *Ladies' Home Journal* that the "best and safest club" for a woman was her home, all hell broke loose. He was reminded that hordes of women and children were forced to work in terrible conditions outside the home. The bitter fact was that many of the clubwoman's fellow countrywomen were "the helpless prey of the greed, the lust, and the neglect of unbridled men." The official bulletin of the Federation quickly went on to say that the organized women's clubs were not a political nor a suffrage nor a social organization—only a religious and philosophic one "in the fullest sense of these words." The fullest sense of the words, of course, meant that the Federation was a polit-ical and social organization, and that it did officially support woman suffrage.[7]

The huge success of the Progressive movement lay in the revolt of the middle classes in city and town against their loss of prestige and status to the machine politician and the managers of the trusts. They were not used to government by big business and corrupt politics. The good fortune of these people was to have large reform organizations already in existence, which were trained to agitate for and carry through many of the petty details of improved government. There were millions of women with energy and time enough, longing to do political or reform work. Suddenly, such work became socially acceptable, except among extremely conservative and aristocratic groups. Women were free to take part in reform activity outside the house, where before they had been free only to do so within the house or the church. This involved them necessarily in political activity. The result was the cleansing of thousands of little things in urban and town life.

Nothing made this new crusade of women more clear than the support of the women's organizations for the Pure Food and Drug Act of 1908. Led by Dr. Harvey Wiley, the clubwomen fought against adulterated and badly preserved foods. This fight became a crusade, because it was a defence of women's temple, the kitchen, and of their nostalgia for the taste of fresh farm food. In Mark Sullivan's opinion, these women, by the pressure they brought to bear upon Congress, "without votes, without ever thinking they needed votes, did a work greater than anything that women accomplished or attempted during the eight years after women got the suffrage."[8]

The success of the women organized against adulterated food and drugs, showed again the subtlety of the Progressives in stealing the anti-suffragists' thunder by taking women outside the home in order to preserve the home, by converting them to the idea that social change was necessary for social conservation. The Progressives played on the remnants of Victorian feeling, that it was the duty of the lady to help the unfortunate; they used this aristocratic ideal to persuade middle-class women that it was also their duty to solve the problems of a new urban society. When the Women's Clubs of California campaigned for factory laws for working women, their slogan was:

"Let us be our sisters' keepers." The educated lady was no longer free to despise the factory girl; it was her duty to help her through political, not charitable, work. In this way, social reform came to be the heir of evangelical reform. Thus the anti-suffragists were forced to retaliate with new arguments, which began to seem silly, as they contradicted those that the anti-suffragists had used in Victorian times and the Progressives were using now.

The subtlest of the anti-suffrage arguments used the old suffrage argument about priorities of reform. Now that the suffragists had begun to identify themselves with the successful Progressives, the anti-suffragists claimed that an interest in suffrage would drive out an interest in social reform. Instead of saying that a woman should not engage in political reform work at all, the anti-suffragists said that she only had the leisure to engage in one reform at a time. They quoted the opinion of a leading English suffragist, Mrs. Pethick-Lawrence, that she had never seen so many women working for social betterment as she had in the American cities, but in England women had turned their attention to politics and had accomplished nothing like so much in civic reform. The machine bosses, in fact, *wanted* woman suffrage, because the women's vote was even more easy to manipulate than the mens'. Conditions in the sinful Western cities of San Francisco and Reno and Denver and Seattle showed this conclusively. Indeed, "the way to do away with the moral influence of women in public life is to give the vote to all women."[9]

More hysterically, the losing anti-suffragists cried red revolution, and tried to link woman suffrage with the new fear of middle-class America—industrial strife. "Woman Suffrage," stated one pamphlet, "is sprung from Socialism in the first place, and towards Socialism it tends."[10] The turncoat suffragist, Annie Bock, told the Senate Committee on Woman Suffrage that she had become disillusioned by finding that women in politics were worse than men. The Socialists had brought woman suffrage to California; she knew, because she had worked in the campaign. "When I say Socialist," she continued,

I do not mean only those people who hold the red card and pay their regular dues to the Socialist Party, though they were the prime movers, but

I mean all the people, men or women, who advocate or work for any or all of the measures that tend to State paternalism and the weakening of the Nation, I care not whether they denominate themselves near Socialists, humanitarians, sympathizers, reformers, Fabian revolutionists, opportunists, industrial unionists, Christian Socialists, progressives, or what not. They are all working intentionally or unintentionally to the same end— *a worse than French Revolution.*[11]

By this rag-bag accusation of all and every reform, the anti-suffragists hoped to preserve the exact state of society forever as it was, like a fly in amber.

Yet the Progressive wave swept across the West and into the East before the First World War. The excitement of a revived belief in democracy, the fervour of the cleansing of the corrupt cities, the renewing of the American promise of equality of opportunity, all these forces pushed on woman suffrage. It was part of the basic Progressive faith in city and town that the more people who voted, the better government would become. "The extension of suffrage to women," the suffrage organization declared in 1905, "is needed to check the growing corruption of politics by creating a voting constituency too numerous to be controlled by mercenary considerations."[12] Numbers would swamp the special interests.

In addition, there was a tendency "to exalt direct popular sovereignty and disparage representative government," through the devices of the initiative, referendum, and recall.[13] These devices needed the votes of women, which were still popularly supposed to be mainly on the side of morality and good government. Such a consideration made heavy drinkers like the Californian Jack London vote for their own reform through woman suffrage.

I voted that women might vote, because I knew that they, the wives and mothers of the race, would vote John Barleycorn out of existence and back into the historical limbo of our vanished customs of savagery. . . . The women are the true conservators of the race. The men are the wastrels, the adventure-lovers and gamblers, and in the end it is by their women that they are saved. . . . The women know.[14]

Even the rigidly masculine Mr. Dooley was made to confess, "I wudden't mind at all havin' a little soap an' wather, a broom an' a dusther applied to polyticks."[15]

The Progressive wave split the major party organizations in the Far Western States. In a bid for Progressive support, one or other of the major parties helped to enact woman suffrage in Washington, California, Oregon, Arizona, Nevada, and Montana, between 1910 and 1914. Kansas also went for woman suffrage at long last. Except for Nevada, all these adjoining states already had a large urban population outside the small towns, ranging from three in ten city people in Kansas to more than six in ten in California. To the generally pro-suffrage vote of the declining small towns of the Western States was added the educated middle-class vote of the growing cities and suburbs. Some of the vote of the workingmen of the cities also went to the suffragists in order to protect their wives and daughters. For the labour unions and the Socialists had been slowly working to change traditional patterns of thought into a demand for a voice in the regulation of the new cities.

The successful alliance between Western small town and urban middle class made the woman's vote an important factor in Congressional and presidential elections. This was first shown by the attitudes of the major party candidates in the presidential election of 1912, the election that put the most varied choice before the American voters in the twentieth century. Two of the four candidates, who were to poll the most votes, supported woman suffrage. Two did not, although one was to be converted while in the White House.

The leading supporter of suffrage was Theodore Roosevelt. He had been an early feminist; his Harvard senior dissertation was called "The Practicability of Equalizing Men and Women Before the Law."[16] He believed that the race could only be bettered through its mothers; but, as with other dangerous topics like prohibition which divided party lines, he was politic about the timing of his declaration of support. While still in the White House, he wrote to Harriet Upton, "Personally I believe in woman suffrage, but I am not an enthusiastic advocate of it because I do not regard it as a very important matter."[17] His successor in the presidency, William Howard Taft, did not even approve of woman suffrage personally. And Roosevelt, out of office, remained canny on the subject.

When in Norway in 1910, Roosevelt showed how he was not yet ready to espouse a cause that might lose him party support. In answer to the Norwegian leader of the suffragists, he replied at his conservative and eugenic best:

The prime duty of the average woman is to be a good wife and mother, just as the prime duty of the average man is to be a good husband and father, a good and efficient home-maker. Whenever this woman, the good woman, the woman who is really the most important citizen in all the State, feels that to the vital and exhausting duties which she already performs, she can with wisdom and profit add yet another duty, that of the suffrage, why, I shall be most glad to see her assume it; but I wish to be certain that this is her real feeling.[18]

In fact, he was saying exactly what every other politician was saying outside the woman suffrage states, that they would not give women the vote until those women threatened the political future of the representatives of the people. They would change their mind, as a Senator once said, not because they saw the light but because they felt the heat.

In 1912, however, Theodore Roosevelt failed to win the nomination of the Republican Party, and became the presidential candidate of the new Progressive Party. He had no organized Republican machine to bring him to the White House by a comfortable majority. So when the Progressive convention supported votes for women, he went along with the party platform. There were six states in the West where a million women already had the vote. These women did not, however, vote in the election of 1912 as a bloc vote for the Progressive candidates, although both California and Washington went for Roosevelt. They seemed to split their votes on usual party lines; their vote could not be distinguished from the votes of the men. Roosevelt ran second to the Democratic nominee, Woodrow Wilson, although he did beat the Republican candidate, Taft, into third place. The other supporter of woman's rights, Eugene Debs, the Socialist candidate, polled a million votes, only one in fifteen cast in the election. For, although he alone supported the complete equality of women and men, he wanted the radical reconstruction of society—a solution to which most American men and women were totally opposed.

By the mid-term elections of 1914, however, there was a militant organization of women, the Congressional Union, ready to put the women's vote to use in the West for the suffrage cause. By this time there were nine woman suffrage states. Because Woodrow Wilson and the Democratic majority in both Houses of Congress stood firmly against the federal suffrage amendment, Alice Paul and the Congressional Union decided to campaign against all Democrats in the suffrage states of the West. In this way, they could punish the "party in power" for not putting through woman suffrage, even if individual Democrats who supported votes for women suffered for their party's fault. The whole Democratic Party was named as the enemy of the "Anthony amendment," and an attack on it could only be mounted through the states of the Far West.

The Congressional Union sent out its speakers from the East. In forty-three elections in the suffrage states where the Democrats ran a candidate, only twenty Democrats were elected—fewer than expected. The aggressive policy of the Congressional Union seemed successful, if the normal mid-term swing against the party in power were discounted. The Democratic majority of the Rules Committee of the House of Representatives immediately moved the federal suffrage amendment onto the floor of the House, where it was defeated, securing seventy-eight votes short of the two-thirds majority needed for its passage. The Congressional Union had scared Democratic politicians enough to make them push the bill to the vote, thus involving anti-suffrage Republicans in the blame of its defeat.

This action of the new militant wing of the suffrage movement precipitated the old quarrel of the suffragists over the question of partisanship. At the time of the original split between the National and the American Woman Suffrage Associations, Stone had accused Stanton and Anthony of working with the pro-slavery Democrats against the anti-slavery Republicans, in order to push through woman suffrage at the expense of the Negro. Later, the re-united suffrage leaders had adopted a strict policy of non-partisanship, aiming to work with all friends of suffrage in either major party. They did not wish to be led astray by supporting minor parties, like the Prohibition Party, which bid for their support with a plank advocating votes for women.

In a paper circulated among the branches of the National American Woman Suffrage Association in 1915, the policy of non-partisanship was justified:

1. Because it holds individuals responsible. Every man must answer for himself to the women of his constituency.

2. A Democratic vote is as good as a Republican vote for suffrage.

3. Suffrage is not a partisan question but one of fundamental justice and can be considered by individuals regardless of party.

4. The policy of the National Congressional Committee is to oppose those men who by their vote clearly disregard the wishes of their constituents in opposing suffrage. This makes their defeat a practical possibility and does not make the National amusing by making empty threats.

5. It is obviously absurd to attempt to defeat men because they belong to the majority party. Suffragists must depend upon their suffrage supporters to defeat any member of Congress, and it is doubtful whether even in the suffrage states the women can be induced to vote against a man because he is a Democrat. Moreover, the majority party, being in the saddle, is the most difficult party to defeat.

6. It makes suffragists ridiculous to attempt to defeat the best friends they have in the Senate. For example, Senator Chamberlain, of Oregon, who is a Democrat and up for re-election in 1916, introduced the suffrage amendment.

Despite these general justifications of a non-partisan policy, the main suffrage organization had practical objections to the policy of the Congressional Union. It rightly claimed that the Union was trying to do impossible things, given the party structure of the country. The Union was trying to apply the example of the English militants to a completely different political situation:

1. "The party in power" is an English term and does not apply to American politics. We have a "majority party" which becomes such by chance rather than by the unified intent of every section of the country.

2. No suffrage amendment has passed in any state without both the Democratic and Republican parties. How can a suffrage organization consistently oppose its friends of the past? Many who voted for us in the suffrage states are here in Congress now.

3. The women in the suffrage states are no longer primarily suffragists, but voters, and belong to all three parties. They will not unite as a body to oppose any party, while the suffragists in other states have no vote.

4. Many Democrats who oppose suffrage are fairly representing their own constituencies. We would be amusing to threaten to defeat such men. . . . The militant policy of suffragists in attacking members because they belong to the "party in power" is an incitement to members of that party to oppose suffrage.[19]

Such a divergence of policy between the two wings of the suffrage movement could only be settled by the test of the election of 1916. Then, Woodrow Wilson, leading a party which usually lost presidential elections, faced the united Republican Party led by the progressive Easterner, Charles Evans Hughes. They were so similar in policy that Theodore Roosevelt referred to Hughes in private as a pink-whiskered Wilson. In the campaign, Roosevelt proved more important than his party's nominee. He made an issue of what was uppermost in the people's mind, whether America should or should not enter the First World War. Roosevelt spoke up for a strong foreign policy against Germany and for universal military training, while Hughes carried on an ineffectual campaign against Wilson's so-called inefficiency in government. Wilson's answer was to point out the many progressive measures put through under his administration. While Roosevelt made the Republicans seem the war party despite Hughes's moderation, Wilson spoke up for peace and progressive reform, despite his entangling foreign policy and failure to regulate big business.

There were twelve woman suffrage states, and the Congressional Union, now the Woman's Party, led a determined campaign against Wilson and the Democratic candidates in all of them. While Wilson stuck to his party's platform of support for woman suffrage through the action of the individual states, Hughes was persuaded to come out ahead of the Republican platform in support of the "Anthony amendment," in order to put an end to "sex antagonism." To the Democratic slogan about Woodrow Wilson, "He kept us out of war," the Woman's Party added the slogan, "He kept us out of suffrage."

The Woman's Party seemed to have some success in Illinois, the most eastern of the suffrage states, where the votes of the sexes were counted separately. There, seventy thousand more women voted against Wilson than for him, more than the proportion of his male opponents. Yet the Woman's Party alienated the Western women by its stupid tactics. Particularly annoying was the sending of a train to the West, known as the "Golden Special," which had been hired by Mrs. Belmont, "the Mark Hanna of the Suffrage and the meal ticket of the Anthony amendment." She filled it with a load of Eastern socialite suffragists, who were carried in luxury from city to town. Once, the train was picketed by a Western suffragist carrying a placard, saying, "Which Goose Laid The Golden Egg?" Westerners were always ready to resent Eastern interference in their affairs, particularly by such obvious representatives of successful Eastern capital. "Instead of arousing sympathy and enthusiasm," one correspondent noted, "the sables and emeralds with which some of the 'Hughesettes' decked themselves, provoked antagonism and envy."[20] Most of the women were, anyway, associated with the Republican Party, which did not endear Democratic women to them. After the election, the Republicans thought that the Golden Special had done more harm to Hughes than anything or anyone, except for the belligerent Roosevelt.

Wilson just scraped through against Hughes in the election. While the industrial East on the whole voted for the high wages associated with rearmament, the West added its vote to the Solid South in defence of peace and isolation. Ten of the twelve woman suffrage states went for Wilson; he lost only Illinois and Oregon. In California, the women's vote was supposed to have given him the state and the election. The Democratic Party in the suffrage states did even better than their leader. The real factor in the surprising result was not the suffrage vote, but the German-American vote, which turned away from its normal Republican allegiance to support the "peace party."

Although the Woman's Party claimed that its campaign had been effective in taking the women's vote from Wilson and his party, it was disbelieved. If its claim had been true, Wilson would have had to have won the united male votes in the suffrage states. The failure of the Woman's Party in the campaign of 1916 held up the granting of woman suffrage for another two years. As the acute Louis Seibold commented after the election, members of Congress agreed that the result had "effectively removed Suffrage as a cause of Congressional irritation. Hence it is that members of both Houses will not be thrown into a state approaching hysterics by the rustle of a skirt; fear to meet militant advocates face to face; or sidestep every time a female of the species arises at a public meeting with blood in her eye intent on heckling a candidate." The only triumph of the suffragists, according to Seibold, was the election of the first woman to Congress, Jeanette Rankin of Montana.[21]

The political commentators, however, underrated the persistence of the suffragists. The untainted National American Woman Suffrage Association set out to convert Wilson and Congress slowly to the measure, while the Woman's Party redoubled its militance. With Wilson's declaration of war in the spring of 1917, new social factors entered the situation. Personally, the suffrage cause suffered a blow when Jeanette Rankin, true to her feeling for peace, voted against the war. This vote kept her out of the House of Representatives for twenty-two years. It was her bad fortune to be elected again in 1940, when she was the sole person to cast a vote against war after the Japanese attack on Pearl Harbour. She was never again elected as a representative of the people of Montana. An anti-suffragist summed up the prejudice against her in 1917, "While Miss Rankin may represent the suffragists by her vote, she does not represent the true women of the country."

Carrie Catt took care to show that the suffragists did represent the true women of the country. She pledged the support of the National

American Association to the war effort. This helped her in what she claimed as her greatest triumph, the carrying of New York State for woman suffrage in 1917. As well as volunteer war service, the suffragists there imitated Anthony's example in the Civil War, and collected a signed petition from over a million women of the state. This time, they asked for the vote for themselves. Their success in getting the million signatures put an end to the anti-suffrage claim that Eastern women did not want to vote.

The example of New York showed how the newspapers, like the ministers before them, had changed their minds on the suffrage issue for fear of displeasing their readers. Of the fifteen major dailies in the state, ten were for woman suffrage, three were neutral, and only two against. Even the upstate rural press backed the measure by three to one. Only the foreign-language press, respectful as always of the conservative traditions of the new immigrant groups, opposed woman suffrage—except for the Scandinavian and radical Jewish newspapers.

The measure carried the state by a majority of one hundred thousand votes, which was gathered in New York City, where the Tammany machine was persuaded to remain neutral. The fact that the vote of the largest city on the Atlantic seaboard could favour woman suffrage showed how much the suffragists were gaining support among urban middle-class men and some factory workers. During the same year, industrial Rhode Island and Midwestern Michigan and Nebraska gave women the right of voting in presidential elections. Thus, in one year, women had doubled the power of their vote in terms of representation in the electoral college. Their support could no longer be antagonized, even if it could not be delivered as a block vote against any major party.

The war gave this impetus to the suffrage cause because of the good example that most women set. Their patriotism could even be excessive. Some put on military uniforms, even before the declaration of war, and drilled in female camps; others denounced German neighbours as spies. Yet, as in the Civil War, the opportunities of women increased in those jobs that were usually reserved for men. In armament factories and behind the plough, women were regularly seen. Wilson's own declaration that the war was to make the world safe for democracy seemed to hold out a promise to the suffragists. At a time when the United States was looking beyond its own frontiers, the example of Canada and England was decisive.

Wilson's own conversion to the suffrage cause was a cautious one. He kept up, during the war years, a correspondence with Carrie Catt, whom he appointed to a post on the Women's Committee of the Council for National Defence. Like Theodore Roosevelt, he temporized on the exact moment when he would throw his support of the federal amendment into the fight in Congress. "I candidly do not think," he wrote to Catt on May 8, 1917, "that this is the opportune time to press the claims of our women upon the Congress. The thought of the Congress is so much centred upon the matters immediately connected with the conduct of the war that I think the general feeling would be that the time was not well chosen."[22] Catt, conscious that his support would be necessary to gain a few votes from the Southern Senators opposed to woman suffrage, deferred to him over his choice of "the opportune time." In her estimation, a year more or less made little difference to a cause that had struggled for seventy years.

The militant Woman's Party was not, however, so patient. It instituted a constant picket of the White House, based on the strike tactics of unions. Many of its members were Quakers who opposed the war. They heckled "Kaiser Wilson" during his speeches, claiming that he did not rule a democracy at home while he fought in the name of one abroad. Senators were continually harassed, until some of them were disgusted by these "Bolsheviki of America." About a hundred women were arrested by the police; when they went on hunger strike, they were forcibly fed, as the English suffragettes had been. Yet these instances of brutality were limited, because Wilson was being warned by Catt of the hostile demonstrations. In one letter, she actually praised the President for his "serene and tactful handling of the recent 'picket crisis.' "[23] She was no Anthony or Stanton, to put the cause of the solidarity of women above the political use of conciliating the man in the White House.

The Republicans swung more and more to the support of the

suffragists in a bid for the women's vote in the elections of 1918. They wished to embarrass the Democrats through the solid anti-suffrage vote of the Southern Democrats. On January 10, the House of Representatives voted on the "Anthony amendment." The measure passed by one vote more than the required two-thirds majority. Despite Wilson's declaration that at last he favoured the federal amendment, the Democrats were split evenly on the issue while the Republicans voted for it by five to one. Congressmen from six states voted solidly against the measure; except for Delaware, all were in the South. They were joined by a majority of the Congressmen from conservative Massachusetts, Pennsylvania, New Jersey, and Ohio. Indeed, nearly every Congressman was a green toad on a green tree and a brown toad on a brown tree. The New York delegation had changed its mind over woman suffrage with the passage of the measure in the state. State action, as the National American Woman Suffrage Association had always claimed, was necessary to win votes in Congress for the federal amendment. The Western Congressmen were practically solid for suffrage, and even Congressmen from Florida, where the suffragists showed surprising strength, were politic enough to vote the way the wind was blowing.

On October 1, the "Anthony amendment" reached a vote in the Senate. It failed by two votes to reach the required majority of two-thirds. Again the Republicans supported the measure, in a ratio of three to one, while the Democrats only did so in a ratio of three to two. Just before the Senate vote, Wilson himself was persuaded to break constitutional precedent and to intervene in the Senate. The mid-term elections were approaching in November, and he was afraid that the onus of resisting the "Anthony amendment" would fall upon the Democratic Party in the suffrage states. Thus he followed the advice of his son-in-law, William McAdoo, that he should address the Senate before its vote, on the grounds that suffrage was a war measure necessary to make the world safe for democracy. As Wilson told the Senate, "Old governments like that of England, which do not profess to be democratic," had given the vote to women, while America, the champion of democracy, lagged behind.

Wilson's intervention met with "an air of hostility, a frigid atmosphere," which did nothing to change the opposition of the Southern Senators or the outcome of the roll call.[24] Yet it made enough good propaganda to prevent the suffrage vote from swinging away from the Democrats. In fact, in the key state of Illinois, the women's vote favoured the Democratic candidates.

The election of 1918 as a whole, however, favoured the Republicans, who took over control of Congress. Even the National American Woman Suffrage Association campaigned against four anti-suffrage Senators, and helped to secure the defeat of two of them. The result of the election made it clear that the new Congress would pass the "Anthony amendment" as the Nineteenth Amendment to the Constitution, to succeed the dry Eighteenth Amendment. If this happened, the Republicans could claim the credit for giving women the vote. For the Democrats would have failed to do so while they had a majority in Congress.

In the "lame duck" session of the old Congress, the Democrats outside the South laboured to convert the Southerners in time. The "Anthony amendment" came up to the vote again on February 10, 1919. It failed to pass by one vote, leaving the responsibility for blocking it on the Democrats. When the new Congress was installed, the federal amendment again passed the House with a vote of more than three to one in its favour. In the Senate, it at last secured the necessary two-thirds majority, with the Southerners obstructive to the end, sure of the support of their one-party states.

The opposition of the Deep South to the Nineteenth Amendment can only be explained by its habit of resisting to the last ditch any law which seemed to be an interference with its internal affairs. It disliked the principle of federal amendments; it was the stronghold of rural partriarchalism; it foresaw the difficulty of maintaining the idea of Southern chivalry while excluding Negro women from the polls; and it had already seen, in the Illinois election of 1918, that Northern Democratic Senators would not be punished by women for the obduracy of their Southern brothers. Moreover, despite the growing numbers of suffragists in the Border States and Florida and Louisiana, many Southern women were vocally opposed to the vote. As

THE PROGRESSIVE ANSWER   [335]

Ellen Glasgow wrote of the Southern woman of the time, she "was capable of dying for an idea, but not of conceiving one."[25]

The ratification of the Nineteenth Amendment by thirty-six states was a rapid affair. As with the Eighteenth Amendment, the state legislatures tended to feel that where Congress led they should follow. The difficulties of the suffragists lay in the attitudes of the hard core of the anti-suffrage movement, the conservative Northeast, with its fear of immigrant female voters, and the South, with its fear of all female voters. The prompt ratification of the amendment by the Massachusetts legislature, prodded by both major parties in order to get the suffrage issue off the stage before the election of 1920, broke the Northeastern resistance. All of the Western States and most of the Northern ones ratified, until the number stood at thirty-five states. The Solid South remained opposed to the measure; either one of the Border States or Vermont had to be won. Soon, due to the delays of the other states, the attention of the suffragists became fixed on Tennessee.

In Memphis, every anti-suffragist or liquor interest congregated to oppose the lobbies of the National American Woman Suffrage Association and of the Woman's Party. The old Southern suffrage leaders, Kate Gordon and Laura Clay, joined the opposition to defend states' rights, "appealing to Negrophobia and every other cave man's prejudice." The legislature was made drunk by the issue of free liquor. Finally, the Senate of Tennessee approved of the amendment easily, and the House, after cliff-hanging suspense, also approved by a majority of two votes. On August 26, 1919, the Governor of the state signed the proclamation, and the Nineteenth Amendment was adopted in the Constitution. Twenty-six million adult American women were free to vote in all American elections—if they were allowed to register freely under state law.

By keeping the main suffrage organization out of party politics, Carrie Catt had achieved what she wanted. She did not want a repetition of the fiasco of Reconstruction, which had made the male Negro voters support the Republican Party for sixty years and the South support the Democrats for a century. "If woman suffragists had agreed to espouse one political party or certain popular questions," she conceded in 1915, "it is not impossible that their cause might have been swept in the haven of victory long ago. But with what result? That party would have had a moral hold upon the woman vote which would have robbed it of the 'free will' which should be the right of every citizen."[26] Carrie Catt wanted to leave the woman voter of 1920 free to choose her partisan candidate, as all Northern and Western white men were free to choose theirs. She did not question whether, under the party system of that year, many voters were free enough from propaganda and family tradition to make any significant choice between two major parties, so similar in policy.

The example of the early suffrage states had shown that women would vote along party lines. In Colorado, although the result of the women's vote appeared small in the legislative scale, it weighed heavily in the psychological scale. It tended "to cultivate intelligent public spirit among the women of Colorado," declared a study in 1909.

Many have not been aroused; many have become discouraged and lost interest after the failure of their early efforts; comparatively few have taken an active part in political life; but thousands vote, and to every one of these thousands the ballot means a little broadening in the outlook, a little glimpse of wider interests than pots and kettles, trivial scandal, and bridge whist.[27]

Above all, the new women voters in the West were shaken from the assumptions of the centuries, that men should have a total control over public affairs. Some women could feel, as one Western woman did after her first visit to the polls, "I voted, but when I returned from the polls I returned to my room and fell upon my knees and begged my Creator to forgive me."[28] Yet repetition made for normality. When women could vote legally, they learned how to vote casually, and took another step towards a feeling of psychological equality with men.

Herbert Croly emphasized this gain to a woman's ego in a shrewd article in the Nation in 1915. He said that it was obvious that the women's vote would change little, and here the anti-suffragists had a case. If the vote would change little, why work for it? If it would change much, it was dangerous. In Croly's opinion, however,

The truth of the matter seems to be that while the winning of the vote will itself change nothing very radically, it will register one of the greatest changes in the world. The mere right to mark a ballot for or against (two candidates) is a small advance. Yet enlightened men and women will fight for it because it is a convenient symbol of a new outlook upon life and a new position in the world.

This is the real strength of the suffragists. They need have no illusion that votes will bring about a quick regeneration in society. They have only to point out the enormous changes which machinery and education have brought to them. They live in a world which is a different world from that which conventional males and sheltered antis dangle before them. And because the world is different, it is impossible to amble along through it with platitudes about chivalry and protection and the gray hair of grand-mothers and the sweetness of young wives.[29]

Social and economic change, bringing new opportunities for women, had made the insolent demands of 1848 seem the reasonable request of 1919. "The revolving wheels of progress" had done much of the work of the suffragists for them. Women did not get the vote in America before society, outside the South, was prepared to give it to them.

Even if the leaders of the suffragists knew that votes for women would not bring about the millennium, they could not stifle hope in their hearts. For them, as for the Progressives that had helped them, the vote was more than a convenient symbol; it was the totem of an ideal democracy. The cool-headed Carrie Catt arranged that the final victory convention of the National American Woman Suffrage Association should become the first convention of the new League of Women Voters. In her presidential speech, she veered between ideal hopes and factual fears. She mirrored the confusion and disappointment that the suffrage chiefs were to feel with their hardly won right, and with the diminished forces of organized women prepared to follow their call. As with all the Victorian pioneer feminists, the excitement of the struggle for a right was to be dulled by its use.

"Arise, women voters of East and West, of North and South," Carrie Catt declared, "in this your union together; strong of faith, fearless of spirit; let the nation hear you pledge all that you have and all that you are to a new crusade—an American crusade, a national crusade; a crusade that shall not end until the electorate of the Republic is intelligent, clean, American." Yet this cry for action was immediately succeeded by words of caution. The brutal facts of politics were pointed out. "The only way to get things in this country is to find them on the inside of the political party," for the powerful major parties saw to the making of laws. "It is not a question of whether they ought to be powerful or ought not to be powerful; they are. It is the trend of the present political development and instead of appealing to them for the things you want, it is better to get on the inside and help yourself to the things you want."

By this realistic reasoning, Catt was condemning women to the very fate that the anti-suffragists had always claimed would be brought upon them by politics, the dirty rough and tumble of partisan strife. "Women must not be content," Catt continued, "until they are as independent within the party as men are, which isn't saying much." She looked round the convention hall in her pessimism and saw the rifts that partisan politics had already begun to cause among the old suffragists and the new women voters. Was this the result of the gift of a "free will" vote to women?

Partisanship, Catt warned, meant nothing unless it was chosen freely. It should not be inherited from a family or a husband. If so, "you don't know the antecedents of your party, but you know they were right. You don't know what is your platform or what your party stands for, but you are for it. Partisanship is a brand-new emotion to some of our women and they are working it pretty hard." Already sister suffragists had discovered that they were no longer suffragists, but primarily Republican or Democratic or Socialist voters. Each began to look as if "the other had some kind of contagious epidemic" that they never suspected before. Would class or party loyalty claim the first attention of women voters, rather than loyalty to their own sex?

Catt finished her speech by acknowledging her own mistake. By concentrating wholly on the winning of the vote in the last five years, she had forgotten about the humanitarian impulses that had formerly made the Progressives and the suffragists work together. Her winning plan for the vote had excluded other plans to help in the improvement of society. It had been "a very in-growing time" for the suffragists. For they had known that they would win, if they made no mistakes.

This policy had kept them clear of unpopular alliances, but it had also kept them clear of moral commitments. It had kept them exactly in line with sentiment in the major parties, for fear of offending a Republican or a Democratic friend. It may have made the suffrage woman "too rigid and too conservative"; but the new League of Women Voters, Catt declared in hope, had to be "five years ahead of the political parties." The Women Voters must regain that progressive and humanitarian drive that had led to their first victories in the West.[30]

Such was the mixture of despondency and hope with which the leader of the suffrage cause met the question of what women would do with their votes. They were at last free to choose whatever political party they wished. But had not their vote been reduced to a mere "convenient symbol" in their minds, by the slow and politic method of its getting?

PART TEN

The New Victorians

If the nineteenth century is to be governed by the opinions of the eighteenth, and the twentieth by the nineteenth, the world will always be governed by dead men.

Elizabeth Cady Stanton

XXX

❧

CHANGING PATTERNS

WITH THE NINETEENTH AMENDMENT, the feminist movement reached its apogee. Never again could organizing women persuade millions of their sex to protest against their position in society, nor could they organize a block vote against a particular social wrong. With their own success, American women chose to repay the Negro man for ignoring them after the Civil War by ignoring him after the First World War. Decade by decade, Victorian women had won more liberties and more equalities with men, each in their due order of importance and possibility of success.

Those women who hoped for the millennium when women entered politics were quickly disappointed. Although a quantity of special laws for women were passed in the first two years after the Nineteenth Amendment, the fear and the interest of legislators in the feminist pressure groups declined rapidly, once it was clear that these pressure groups hardly influenced the women's vote at all. Fewer women than men voted in elections for three decades. For women were still in their political infancy, as commentators pointed out, and they still relied on male advice. In the first two decades of female voting, the married women's vote duplicated that of their husbands. Even after the Second World War, a detailed study found out that only one wife in twenty-two said that she cast a different vote from her husband. In most cases, the husband was dominant in the choice of how the two votes would be cast.[1]

In point of fact, the grip of the political machines on the cities was tightened in the 1920's, because, "from the boss clean to the bottom," the female relatives of every man in the machine were registered and voting female relatives. To these early city bosses, the vote for women was merely a "multiplication table."[2] Women refused to vote against anti-feminists in Congress, and sent them back with increased majorities as their representatives. The League of Women Voters was in despair. As Alice Stone Blackwell wrote bitterly to Carrie Catt in 1929, "Mrs. Poyser's immortal saying about the women being fools because God made them to match the men, is proving itself true."[3]

Yet the feminists expected too much too soon from the ballot in the hands of women. They had become the victims of their own propaganda and of the fears of their opponents, that women were better than men and not their equals. They had believed the American sociologist Lester Ward, when he put forward the idea of the natural superiority of women, and the thesis of the Vaertings, that power would make women free at last and make them dominant over the other sex.[4] They were deceived into too great expectations by the doctrine of the differences of the sexes, for they had forgotten the early feminist emphasis on the sameness of human reason. They were doomed to quick disappointment.

In one sense, however, they could have expected that disappointment. For women had been given the vote in a man-made world. Men had set up the political parties and the political system badly. Women were expected to work within that bad system. It would take them a generation to learn how to penetrate the political parties and to agitate within them, for they could not overturn the parties by a social revolution. In time, women would change the political system to suit some of their own goals and needs. Not until they understood it could they change it more than superficially.

This argument was to prove increasingly correct. There were noticeable changes in the goals and the structure of the political parties over four decades. The first changes were symbolic, the representation of docile women on the national committees of the parties, and the cleaning-up of polling-booths. Soon other changes became more evident. The open bribery and corruption of the spoils system had to be pushed out of sight, because of male scruples in the presence of females. By the decade of the thirties, with the coming of the ideology of the New Deal and with the erosion of the power of the city machines because of federal welfare, radical women became a powerful factor in reform politics.

Although little new special legislation for women was passed, Frances Perkins was one of the important figures in the New Deal. In Texas, the formidable Minnie Fisher Cunningham was a power in reform politics for forty years, and the terror of the local Democratic bosses. By 1964, Senator Margaret Chase Smith of Maine could be a serious contender for the Republican presidential nomination. If women hardly penetrated to any of the important decision-making levels in either of the political parties, they did take over much of the making of policy at local levels and in educational matters, in that sphere of "enlarged housekeeping" for which the suffragists had demanded the vote.

Few women were sent to Congress. As Mr. Dooley's friend Hogan said, "I care not who casts th' votes iv me counthry so long as we can hold th' offices. An' there's on'y wan way to keep the women out iv office, an' that's to give thim a vote."[5] To be a woman still meant to be unavailable as a political candidate, because conservative men and women in both major political parties did not wish to be represented by a woman. The relative failure of women, after getting the ballot, was also the relative failure of men to live up to the ideal of the equality of the sexes.

Women were elected occasionally to the Senate, inherited governorships on the death of their husbands, and reached minor positions in the Cabinet. Yet the exception was still the rule. Although women were often dominant at the local level, they were largely absent at the national level.

Their preferences did, however, both change the image and the availability of those politicians whom the major parties chose to fight elections. Although women remained, on the whole, less informed about political matters than men, they had learned by 1960 to vote in equal numbers with men and to vote independently. New pollsters now found that two-thirds of married women voters denied that their vote was dictated by their husbands' preferences; at least, if wives were still influenced by their husbands in political matters, they *said* that they were not. After the Second World War, political equality became more of a fact for the woman voter.

While men still seemed to judge candidates on their party label and political experience, women seemed to judge by the candidate's personal characteristics and background. That their criterion was worse than that of men is open to question; it was merely different. A new breed of respectable male politicians rose up to meet the demand. Outside parts of the South, the local political machines, already badly damaged by the New Deal, split into more and more fragments.

Thus there has been a rise of the "independent" within the major party system, who owes his career to the "personal" vote of women in his state or district. The women's vote, where measurable, has usually proved to be more conservative, more Republican, and more against foreign commitments than the vote of men. If its power increases, both federal aid and foreign aid will be under more fire in the future. The influence of the woman voter has mainly been cast in favour of local concerns. On the national scale, it is inward-looking. On the matter of world peace, however, pressure for the settling of foreign differences has grown on Presidents and Congresses. This pressure has mainly been women's pressure, and their representatives are beginning to feel the heat and, perhaps, to see the light.[6]

If women's freedom to vote affected little in politics for some time, their freedom to work saw to important changes in the family. The great depression, after the Revolution and the Civil War, was probably the most important event in American life, in terms of changing traditional patterns of thought. As the analysers of Middletown discovered, women were better adapted to ride out the depression than men. For they were less affected.

The narrowed role of the male, so largely confined to moneymaking, took the brunt of the shock. . . . For an occasional woman the depression may have been almost a relief, akin to a time of serious illness in the family; a time when all worries as to alternative lines of action are laid aside and one does the single, obvious task immediately at hand. For other women, forced to work at earning the family's living, the heightened tolerance of such work on their part in the depression has eased something of the sharp emotional ambivalence often involved in such work in more normal times.[7]

In fact, since women were cheaper to hire in the depression, they got the lioness's share of what jobs there were available. The female labour force grew faster in the thirties than it had done in the previous two decades, while men in their millions were forced to stay at home with the children and fret at their woman's role. The depression did much to bring equality in work and home-making to the sexes, by putting women in the factory and men in the house. Followed as it was by the Second World War, when full employment was offered to any woman who cared to work, the idea of the working wife finally became an accepted part of social belief. Although the employment of wives by industry was deplored by many people, their numbers in the factories grew, particularly those of middle age who no longer had babies at home. More than one-third of adult women were at work or looking for work by 1962. Three in five of these were married, and two in three married women worked full time.

Of course, more poor women worked than middle-class women. While one married white woman in three had a job, one Negro woman in two had a job. The patterns of change applied less to minority groups. Society among the Negroes and the Indians and the new immigrants and the poor whites resisted change in the status of women, although that change inevitably came, as patriarchal societies crumbled before economic opportunities for women.

In areas of the South and the Border, poor white women still lived like the pioneers on the farm and in the early mill towns. A study of *Mothers of the South* at the end of the depression found that the majority of Southern mothers were farm tenant women. They lived in a cotton dress, a ragged sweater, and old shoes. They produced the most children and endured on the edge of subsistence, reproducing the bare and bleak existence of the Pilgrim Fathers and the Western pioneers. Only emigration by their many children kept whole families from starvation. Curiously enough, the women showed their pride by preferring field work to housework, thus breaking the old American taboo against women's outdoor work on the farm. All members of the large sharecropping families worked during spring and summer and fall, in the same way that all the family provided labour for the spindles in the Southern mill villages.[8] Large areas of the South, in fact, lived in agricultural and industrial conditions that dated from before the Civil War. For once fantasy matched fact in the South. Only in the growing Southern cities did women find many of the opportunities of their Northern and Western sisters.

Lower on the social scale than the sharecroppers and workers in the mill villages were the two or three million migrant agricultural labourers. These people lived, and continue to live, a life of squalor and poverty without opportunity. American democracy does not apply to them. Not one of their children of either sex has ever graduated from college. This is not because of bad biological inheritance, but because they do not have enough money to complete their schooling. The opportunity of the womenfolk of the migrant labourers does not exist. Their life until death is and will be spent in drudgery on the land, although the soil has already been cleared. That drudgery will not be for their own profit, but for the profit of others.

Among the new immigrant groups in the urban slums, women were kept in subservience, for that was the peasant tradition, as it had always been among peasant immigrants to America. From the first British pioneers through the Irish to the Puerto Ricans, generations had to experience the American wilderness of nature or slum before the immigrant women could free themselves from masculine control. With the decline of the settlement houses and of the contacts between

middle-class and slum women, however, the feeling of apartness between ghetto and suburb increased. Yet those who were successful in
the ghetto continued to move to the suburb, where all continued to
mingle in a middle-class ethic. The rich of different ethnic groups
usually have more in common with each other than the rich with the
poor of the same ethnic group.

Two groups in society remained outside the suburban melting-pot,
one by choice and one by exclusion. These were the Indians and the
Negroes. The Indians, despite their own savagery, were the most ill-
used people in American history. If their answer to American society
has been withdrawal, it has been the only answer which has saved
their pride. Although most Indian women were kept as drudges and
near-slaves by their men, as is usual in primitive peasant or hunting
societies, yet some tribes had set an admirable example to the early
Americans.

The Navajos, for instance, treated their wives as equals. Navajo
husbands had to pay for their brides. Married Navajo women kept
control of their possessions, and in case of divorce they received an
equal share of common property and the custody of the children.
Work was shared between men and women, both sexes ate together,
and men even carried babies on their backs from time to time. Navajo
husbands never struck their wives, consulted them on all important
decisions, and even worshipped a female God.[9] If their attitude towards women was rare among Indians, the Quaker attitude towards
women was even rarer among white people.

Only now, with the popularity of sociology, are many Americans
interested in why Indian women seem relatively content, in face of
the poverty and mistreatment of their people. The tribal yearnings of
middle-class Americans have even made the Indians relatively popular, as preservers of ancient wisdom. The lucky discovery of oil and
compensation for broken treaties has also made some of the Indian
tribes rich. These new riches seem more ready to break up their
traditional way of life than any other cause. If it is bad to live poorly
but with roots, it may be as bad to live comfortably but without roots.
If the Indians through wealth or through lack of opportunity on their

barren reservations become Americans at last, they will accept the fact of their likely future and deny the ideal of their past.

The Negroes, however, turned from the beginning towards the ideal of becoming good Americans rather than of reverting to the life of good Africans. The institution of slavery changed their conditions of life until they had forgotten their tribal roots. The plantation destroyed customs, while the reservation preserved them. The particular effect of slavery was to make Negro society a matriarchy. Where marriage was casual and even husbands could be sold away, the only family link was between mother and child. The father's presence was infrequent. In fact, the father's role was partially played by the overseer or the plantation owner, even when he had not sired the child.

The condition of matriarchy continued after the end of slavery. When the feminist Frances Gage visited the South Sea Islands, she found that the freedwomen refused to marry the freedmen, who were trying to force marriage upon them. The freedmen were saying that "in the present state we cannot control these women. They go where they choose; keep their own wages and spend them as they choose, but if married we should be their masters." The freedwomen resisted such a change, for they said that they knew the brutality of their would-be husbands. "We know these men better than the government, just let us take care of ourselves."[10]

Negro women did begin to marry more frequently, but economic conditions conspired to continue the matriarchy in Negro society. For black women were not considered a threat to white society, while black men were. The Victorian Negro woman could find a job fairly easily as a domestic or as a factory worker, while the Negro man found it difficult to get employed. The stereotype of the wage-earning mother of children doling out money to her gambling, feckless husband was established in Negro myth, and was a reflection of social fact. As an authority on the position of Negro women wrote, "Emancipation only tended to confirm in many cases the spirit of self-sufficiency which slavery had taught."[11] Only in the small but expanding Negro middle class, particularly among the families of Negro ministers, was the beginning of a Victorian patriarchal pattern set up.

The tradition of matriarchy has persisted until modern times. By 1963, Negro women not only outnumbered Negro men, but were better educated and often had better jobs. The relationship of the Negro male to the Negro female, according to social studies, was the direct opposite of the white stereotype of the dominant Negro man. In fact, the wife was usually dominant over the husband and the children and the finances, while the man played the role of the resentful dependent. Although increasing opportunities for jobs for Negro men have appeared, the tradition of matriarchy is dying slowly among poor Negroes, however much middle-class Negroes have developed equal relationships within marriage. The relative success of the Black Muslims among the poorer segments of Negro society can be explained as much in terms of the Negro man's revolt against the dominant Negro woman as by his revolt against the white man. The excessive patriarchalism of the male Black Muslims and the submission demanded from female Black Muslims are signs of the growing self-importance of the Negro male, both in his own society as well as in American society.

The principles of the priority and the geography of reforms have been demonstrated yet again by the recent Negro revolt. Negro men received the vote before the majority opinion of America was prepared for it, and before any American woman had received that right. The result was that they could salve something of their pride and dignity by feeling that they belonged to a superior sex, at least in political terms. Once all American women got the vote, however, the Negro man became increasingly conscious that he was the least favoured group in society. Even Negro women had the chance to find jobs when he did not. Migration from the South increased, until half the Negro population had left Dixie. As for the American woman, the city was the frontier of opportunity for the rural American Negro. Yet in urban conditions the Negro man felt particularly denied, for there is no way in the slum—as there is on the sharecropping farm—of existing without money.

The surprising thing is that the Negro revolt has been so long in coming—fully four decades after the emancipation of women. Part of the reason has been the principle of matriarchy in Negro society. Negro women, like all women, tend to conservatism and opposition to violence. But once the Negro revolt for economic and legal equality did gather strength in the early sixties, exactly the same geographic divisions and tensions appeared in that protest movement which had once split apart both the anti-slavery and the feminist causes.

There was a split between various militant splinter groups and a main moderate wing. There were small groups that preached violence and large groups that preached passive resistance. There were extreme reformers that hated church influence and reformers that used the churches as the spearhead of protest. Negro groups in the Northern and Western cities disliked the moderate leadership of Martin Luther King, while the Southern Negro often feared the retribution from white society which might descend upon him in revenge for Northern militance. The comfortable middle-class Negro could wash his hands of the reform movement altogether, except in its moderate manifestations, for any change might make him worse off.

As with the anti-slavery and the suffrage movements, the Negro movement was only successful *legally* because it could exert political pressure in terms of votes. Nothing makes propaganda more powerful than the backing of the ballot. And as in the previous reform movements, fear of the militant Negro reformers gave the moderate Negro reformers backing among progressive Americans and among labour unions, although they received little support from middle-class white women or the diminished forces of the drys. Two new patterns of reform agitation emerged in the Negro revolt, the borrowing of the tactics of non-resistance from India and the use of students as the shock troops of protest—a group of people that, outside Oberlin, had played no major part in American reform movements, although Karl Marx had considered them as the revolutionaries *par excellence* of Victorian Europe.

The Negro cause will succeed slowly, both legally and socially. It will break out into sporadic riots, because the fact of a black skin cannot be changed; but it is more likely that Negro men will achieve increasing equality with their own womenfolk and with American society. Except for the Black Muslims, they have clung to the ideal of integration rather than of withdrawal like the Indians into reservations. Thus they cannot easily resist the social and industrial trends which are slowly making the United States into a congeries of suburbs grouped around cities and manufacturing centres. In these suburbs lies the true melting-pot of America, for all are being reduced in the crucible of middle-class behaviour and values. Because of the silly fears associated with skin-colour, the Negro will be the last to be accepted into the suburban way of life; but, short of a revolution, he will be, for he has already begun to be. Economics will make him accepted. The middle class is a group of wealth. The future of American society lies in the great majority of the urban and suburban middle class. Integration means joining this group.

When women received the vote, many of them wondered whether they were, in fact, more free. The suffrage movement had concentrated all its energies into the narrow range of the getting of the ballot. The exercise of this occasional right made few women feel more free. As a critic pointed out in 1924, "The libertarian movement has been such a dismal affair, not because it has been too free, but because it has not been free enough. The democracies and the women of the world have been potentially liberated; but not so very long ago they were slaves, and they have still a slave's idea of freedom."[12] In the growing leisure of the growing suburbs, inhabited by the growing middle classes of growing America, dwelt a race not so much of free women, but of New Victorians.

XXXI

⟡

THE NEW VICTORIANS

WE ARE THE NEW VICTORIANS. Dead men still rule the twentieth century. Otherwise most American women, who have reached the material conditions that make freedom possible, would not still feel bound.

Equality and liberty are states of mind. Even the slave can *feel* free and equal to his master. In point of fact, however, equality is usually measured by the position of one's sex or race or group in relation to the most favoured group in one's society. As one's condition approaches that of the favoured group, one feels more equal. If, as in America, the opportunity to become powerful or rich—although not to become white-skinned—is held to be within the capacity of every child, then reform will aim at keeping open equality of opportunity for all, not at imposing economic equality upon all. "True republicanism," declared *How to Behave* in 1856, "requires that every man shall have an equal chance—that every man shall be free to become as unequal as he can."[1]

Although the industrial structure of the twentieth century has effectively denied equality of opportunity to most of the poor in their search after riches, the Victorian myth still rules, that American men and women have equal opportunity to become the presidents of their chosen corporation or of their country. Yet the fact is that, as in Europe, the sons of the rich are increasingly succeeding the sons of the rich, even in the White House. Their opportunity alone is equal to that of their fathers, or better.

As for liberty, the freedom of getting as much money as one can has been curtailed by the federal government. This has led to a clinging onto Victorianism. For income tax is, indeed, a partial denial of the American promise in the unamended Constitution of "life, liberty, and property." Of course, that promise was itself a denial of the original promise of the Declaration of Independence, the promise of "life, liberty, and the pursuit of happiness." Once the pursuit of happiness had been changed to the possession of property, the ideal of being was changed into the fact of having, or the ideal of getting. Only now, when the ideal of getting has been limited by the large defence and welfare budget of the federal government has the ideal of being begun to flower again. And even here, because most Americans cannot see the contradictions between the freedom to be and the freedom to get, they feel restricted.

For women, particularly, their freedoms are confused. If freedom meant for them freedom to be equal with men and to have the same opportunities, it meant freedom to get as much as a man did. In point of fact, women did not enter the labour market as much as men because many of them believed that they should stay at home and raise children. For every two men that work, more than one woman does. Yet for those that do work, their chances of reaching the top in business or politics are small; men fill seventeen out of twenty of the leading professional and technical jobs. Victorian traditions still rule the proper place of women in business and in the home. The exception remains the rule.

Yet women do own now two-thirds of the wealth in private hands in the country. They have not earned it; they have married it, and have been left widows. In 1960, there were eight million widows compared to two million widowers. The new widows were as rich and independent and powerful as the only free women in colonial days, the first American widows. Their numbers were augmented by a horde of divorcées, whose alimony gave them all the freedom of the widow before the death of their husbands. Indeed, as the death-rate declined, divorce rose as the solution of an unhappy marriage.

As in Victorian days, men continue to work too hard and too long. The difference is now that many of them earn too much money. The success of feminism has, in a curious way, freed men by lessening their responsibility for the upkeep of a tribe of female dependents, like the fifteen people looking for support to the father of the Blackwells. False necessities, such as bigger houses and cars, and clothes, have replaced real necessities, such as mouths to feed and roofs to find. The need of men to overwork has become their excuse. To get as large an income as possible still seems better than to have more time for being, on a smaller income.

The rich wives and widows are Victorian in another way. They have never claimed equality with men in business. A feminist noticed in 1930 what had been noticed in 1830, that Europeans found the idleness of the wives of American businessmen a strange phenomenon.[2] The Victorian heritage was the idea that a man's work alone should support his family, and that the self-respect of his wife should depend upon *his* status, not upon her own. This idea was, in fact, a new one in terms of human history—that one sex should support the other entirely. It was strange, as Veblen pointed out, that men should allow women to consume for them, and should like women to be useless.

Yet most wives of rich Americans accepted their position thankfully. They wanted to be superior in their sphere, in the home and in cultural matters. As Count Keyserling once pointed out,

The American woman originally *feels* superior; this *feeling* is the basic reason of her actual superiority and supremacy. For feeling is the immediate expression of being on the subjective plane, and it is actually impossible to feel what is not real. Thus she has developed those very qualities which have been characteristic of every ruling race. She wields immediate, direct authority; she need not prove her superior position, it is accepted as a matter of course.[3]

When Victorian men allowed their wives to do nothing very much outside the home and gave them power over spending and consumption, they gave them the feeling of being superior at the art of living. And thus, for more than a century, the majority of adult American women, those who have remained in their homes, have been moderately free to be, because they have had little need to get.

The fact is that most American women have done little with the leisure of the home, in terms of developing themselves. Their superiority there has made them put too much emphasis on their jobs there, rather than on their opportunities to be. They have made too much of the work of mothers and housewives, too little of the quest to become free in mind and spirit. As their opportunity for leisure and self-improvement has increased, they have expanded their care of their children and their homes to take in the slack of the superfluous hours. They have cultivated their progeny more than their own gardens, their rooms more than their own brains. They have remained Victorians in their concentration on the duties of the house and the family, when much of their work has been removed by public schools and machines and supermarkets. The very move of the American family from the urban apartment to the huge suburban house seems to be more a woman's drive to find more floors to clean than an urge to find more space to live in. For breadth of view can well exist in a narrow room.

American wives have also imitated the Victorians in their urge to have children to justify their position. The American population growth in the decade before 1960 was four times that of Great Britain, three times that of Italy, one and a half times that of Japan, and nearly that of India. Twenty-eight million new Americans reached the land of the crowded living—only a little fewer than the total American population before the Civil War. The difference between the new American mothers and the Victorians was that wives now had efficient contraceptives and *chose* to have families ranging from two to four children. The eugenicists were pleased to discover that the educated bred as much as the ignorant for the first time in recorded history. The suburban birth-rate was higher than that of the slum, and equal to that of the farm. After a steady decline for a century, which had become precipitous after 1920, the growth of population rose for twenty-five years after 1935 until it reached the point where it had been when women got the vote and discovered the accessible contraceptive.[4]

The late Victorian fears of race suicide through having too few children "of good stock" were now replaced by the fear of race suicide through having too many children of any stock. By remaining Victorian in seeking the meaning of life in motherhood, American women seemed set on making all life impossible by multiplying too fast and replenishing the earth which was already too full. Demographers had hoped that riches would lead to people having fewer children; it seemed to lead to them having more. Children were no longer needed to till the soil, but to consume the unnecessary money made by overworked fathers and the useless time in the hands of underworked mothers. American wives, in search of the fulfilment promised to them by psychologists once they would have children, did not reflect that each child they produced for their own pleasure might prevent a child *already born* from fulfilling himself or herself. Opportunity of work was already restricted and was becoming more so because of automation; opportunity of being was threatened by the overcrowding of the desirable places on the earth's surface. The birth of more and more children was taking away the opportunities and liberties of those already alive.

America remained the most pioneer of all Western countries in its customs of courtship and early marriage. The Yankee system of bundling continued in the teen-age system of petting. Every inducement for early marriage was still put forward, until the average age of marriage in America dropped to the youngest in the Western world, two years lower than it had been sixty years before. Even to the girl who completed college—and half dropped out of those that entered college—marriage took priority over professional work. While in Europe in the past twenty years, women have nearly doubled their number in the professions, fewer American women in proportion now hold professional jobs than in the 1940's, and fewer take doctorates. In the 1870's, two college girls in five from Vassar had married before the age of twenty-seven; in 1920, it was three in five; by 1960, four in five.[5] Curiously, as marriage had once seemed to be freedom for the Puritan girl, so it seemed freedom to the modern girl.

The difference was that the Puritan girl had not been free to find a job outside the family, while the modern girl feared to find a job outside the family. Opportunity, like lack of opportunity, can lead to the same choice. By the 1960's, ninety-three American women in each hundred had married before the age of thirty-four. Spinsters had become rare birds. The early feminist ideal of the single professional woman had almost disappeared in the New Victorian culture of the habitual wife.

The propaganda in the ears of American women, which urged them to marry early and to breed often, remained the most Victorian theme of all. Psychologists replaced clergymen as authorities, sociology replaced revealed truth, the emphasis on function replaced the emphasis on ideal, tribal models of the content replaced heavenly commands to be content. Yet Victorian prejudice and judgements of value remained exactly the same. It was still held better for a woman to become a mother, not because God said so, but because Freud said so and because most women did become mothers. It was bad to remain single and childless, not because the Bible said so, but because ideals were only frustrations at the best, and because most women did not remain single.

The jargon of the bickering schools of psychoanalysts joined the measured cadences of the Old and the New Testaments, and buttressed religious judgements. They were to a whole generation of modern women as important as the mesmerists and phrenologists had been to a generation of Victorian women. In fact, those that had seemed to deny God joined those that supported God in praise of motherhood, and all opposition to the ideal of the home and family was nearly stifled. For the great majority of American women were wives and mothers, and the praise of the majority seemed to be the praise of democracy. Curiously enough, the success of the Middle

European schools of psychology in America was the final victory by the European urban refugee over the American rural ideal of self-reliance and independence of judgement. Vienna superseded London and Paris as the model for urban American life.

Although the good psychologists limited their treatment to the measurably insane and did more for that forgotten tenth of the human race than had ever been done before, the bad psychologists tried to allay the discontent of the sane by explaining that any questioner of majority rule was merely a sufferer from emotional or physical disturbance. In the land of the equal, the superior is a deviant. One text of the twenties accused Tolstoy of partial impotence, John Stuart Mill of small genitals, and Ibsen of inadequate capacity in sex; this, of course, explained their feminism for "there is nothing so potent as male impotence as a magnifier of female virtue."[6] Another influential text of the forties, *Modern Woman: The Lost Sex,* claimed that most of the pioneer feminists were driven on by "penis-envy," and that the shadow of the phallus lay at the back of all rational judgement. The essential Victorianism of the text, which naturally was all for home and mother, was nowhere better shown than in the old demand to tax bachelors for being selfish. Indeed, it demanded that they should attend sessions in psychotherapy. To wish to be single was demonstrably to be a deviant. The book even went so far as to recommend the dismissal of spinster teachers, both to urge them to get married and to stop them from perverting the young.[7] This was Victorianism carried to excess, all in the name of Freud, who had been himself a tolerant man. Such anti-feminist claptrap was merely another version, in sexual terms, of the old anti-feminist vilification of reforming women as "she-males." It is the fate of all those who wish to change society to be assailed by the mediocre jargon of their time.

"Phrenology," said the best-selling women's magazine of 1839, "although a science of comparatively recent date, we take to be absolutely necessary. Every mother should be able to make a scientific examination of her own children's craniums, whereby she may discover with precision the peculiar bent of their genius."[8] If the word "psychology" is substituted for "phrenology," and "psyche" for "cranium," the injunction remains the same today. The mother is now the home psychologist, because her time has trained her to be so. In fact, she is the heir of the Victorian mother phrenologist, whose time trained her. We are the victims of contemporary beliefs and of present times. It is lucky for our children, if we choose to have them, that they can be so little harmed by our influence. There is no evidence, after all, to show that children are harmed by *little* parental attention. It is the quality of parents' care which affects children.[9]

The mass ladies' magazines naturally followed the demographic curve and the current fad. Circulation for them was still all. While the birth-rate declined and feminism was popular, they preached the virtues of the career woman with a small family. When the birth-rate rose and fulfilment through the family and sex became the fashion, they preached this new doctrine. They returned to the statement of the *Ladies' Home Journal* in 1890, that "the one great destiny is to be a mother of the Republic, and outside of this glory other careers are exceptional."[10] If this doctrine was set out less in terms of destiny and glory than in terms of pleasure and gratification, it was merely because the catch-words of psychology had taken over from those of imperialism.

In yet another way, the dominance of some of the concepts of psychology over the American woman showed her essential Victorianism. This had been first shown by the success of Freud in the United States rather than Havelock Ellis; the praiser and explainer of sex in family terms was triumphant over the praiser and explainer of sex in individual terms. While Havelock Ellis had urged the similarity of the two sexes and the falseness of the distinction between "masculine" and "feminine," in the style of the old rationalists, Freud had urged the difference of the two sexes and the importance of male dominance, in the style of the early Victorians. Freud won the argument, because most Americans still thought in Victorian and family terms.

The result of Freud's victory has been the repetition of the Victorian emphasis on the different roles of the sexes and on the different sphere of women. Through psychological language, as once through the language of romanticism, women have become more conscious of being women than of being human beings; but they are worse off than the early Victorians, for their bodies have been exalted at the expense of their minds. Thus in sexual fulfilment rather than in sexual restraint, modern women have sought to imitate their fore-mothers. The modern failure to emphasize a common humanity has, indeed, made the sexes conscious not only of their differences, but of races and groups. The psychology of difference easily becomes the psychology of hatred. It is the ideal of the equality and similarity of humanity in the face of the fact of its inequality and differences that brings together the sexes and the classes and the races in hope. Human beings are born unequal. By believing that they can be equal, they become more equal.

Every study has shown the increasing frequency of orgasm and the increasing sexual demands of American women. If in Victorian times it was considered "a vile aspersion" that women were capable of having an orgasm, it was considered in modern times a vile aspersion that any woman was incapable. Of course, women would and did demand freedom of their bodies in sexual experimentation, for the efficient contraceptive divorced sexual pleasure from the need to have children. With the advent of the secure contraceptive pill for women, those who could get it and were not prevented from using it by religious scruple had the right to choose between those they slept with and those they wished to be the fathers of their children. If, at this time, many women seem to be taking advantage of their new sexual freedom, it is only because psychology and opportunity have allowed them to do so. The French feminist who declared, *"Après le droit du vote le droit de l'orgasme,"* was correct, for technology made her so.

Yet the very use of the orgasm as casually as that of the job may well dull its pleasure, until it becomes a normal part of life. A new freedom usually results in an excessive use, before its repetition becomes something of a slavery. The search for the orgasm may well follow the original feminist search for work, which, as a feminist complained in 1930, "has lost the glamour which surrounded it in the days when women had to struggle against odds for this means of self-expression. It is no longer the ultimate aim of life, but has taken a subsidiary place."[11]

The finding of economic and legal and social and now bodily freedom for women has left them with the most difficult freedoms to find, those of the mind and of the spirit. Much of the discontent of American women is, indeed, because the *easy* freedoms have been gained. The psychology of freedom for a woman depends on her being *more* free than her mother; but what if the mother is already free in body and opportunity? Much of the present nostalgia for the gay twenties is part of a wish to be born in the time of the pioneers of freedom of the body. And much of the new push towards experimentation in sex and drugs is an urge to find an ultimate freedom. The rejection of parents demands a new liberty.

Many American women have already reached the life of relative leisure, for which their husbands work all their lives and achieve only in old age. Of course, these wives continue to do some housework until they die, while their husbands often find their retirement intolerable because they have the habit of steady work. Yet the leisure-time of men also grows. The machine and the computer have made some men work even harder, but, on the whole, they have made most men and women work less. Automation is destroying jobs and shortening the working week for nearly all. It is giving back to modern men the leisure that the pioneers and the Victorians could not afford. It has also given to women the strength, through electrical power, that their bodies have not been trained to have. In this way, the machine has given the women something of the strength of the man, and the man something of the leisure of the woman.

Other industrial trends point towards the growing equality of the sexes and to a lessening of the differences that divide them. Pioneer Americans usually employed themselves, and thus they made a virtue, called "masculine," out of assertion, dominance, aggression, and independence. Few women were able to employ themselves at this time. They were employed without pay by men; and thus they had to make virtues, called "feminine," out of humility, meekness, and obedience. Now the growth of large corporations has led to the employment of most Americans by other Americans, at the same time as American women can easily work outside the home for wages. Thus while American men have had to give up their independence to become wage-earners, American women can give up their dependence on men and become wage-earners themselves, if they so wish. The transition of women from an agricultural to an urban and organized society has been easy, for they have gained in freedoms all the way; the type-writer represents a high standard of living where the needle ensured a low one. But the transition of men has been difficult, for they have lost some of their freedoms and independence. The result has been the growing psychological equality of the sexes as wage-earners.

Despite the trends of industrialization, Victorian patterns of be-haviour have persisted. Many households imitate that of Mr. and Mrs. Catt, where he did the business work and she did the reform work. The school boards and local government have become very much the concern of suburban women. The equal marriages of some of the pioneer feminists, where both husband and wife worked in order that both might have equal leisure for self-improvement, are still rare. The wasteful organization of families in separate homes has not given way to cooperative nurseries and kitchens. The American wife still puts privacy before more freedom from her children and her housework. Two in three American women, indeed, still seem to prefer not to work until necessity makes them work. This may also be true, of course, for many American men, who are driven to their jobs by the fetish of social custom rather than the inclination of their minds.

The long leisure of married American women is bound to lead to long leisure for all human beings in a rich society, when automation has reduced necessary social work for most people to a few hours a week. Until this state of affairs becomes a fact, the problem is whether men should continue to earn money while women continue to stay in the home, or whether both should earn the same amount of money by working half of the time and looking after the home half of the time. The emphasis on sexual differences has made it seem odd for men to look after children, even if they enjoy doing so. Why, asks

Brigid Brophy, should all the home-making talent inside male bodies be wasted, or the business talent inside mothers' bodies?[12] As the working week of the man shortens, so his role in the home will increase. And women will be displaced from their Victorian position of total control of the home, which the overwork of the Victorian men gave to them. The feminist will continue to insist that such an equality in the role of the sexes is good, while the traditionalist will see nothing but evil in this confusion of "masculine" and "feminine" roles. Yet it will come.

In fact, as the husband acquires leisure at last in the prime of life, and his wife learns how to use the leisure that she already has, they will either make new and often unnecessary work for themselves around their children and their house, or they will turn to the improvement of their minds and spirits. Education has already become a national priority in American reform, not the mere speciality of Yankee reformers. And in the Far West—so often the innovator of radical practice—the search for the spirit is everywhere under way, through all the religions of East and West and through some new ones.

It is noticeable that in California, where drugs are available to take people to the land of beatific vision, it is housewives who usually apply to use them. Of course, the drug is the easy way to free the spirit, as psychoanalysis is the easy way to find an understanding friend: anyone can buy either. The very comfort of American life and the Eldorado of the average middle-class home has made only the easy way attractive; but the road to the improvement of the mind or of the soul is hard. Dieting for the sake of the body is not the same as fasting for the sake of the soul. Yoga to strip fat off the flesh is not the same as yoga to free the spirit. For those radical women who wish to withdraw to the wilderness like Anne Hutchinson in order to seek for or to be God, the habit of comfort keeps their bodies in a split-level ranch. Seekers after truth are no longer capable of leaving civilization or of existing without other people. Thus they must put up with the discontents of society and its laws.

A comfortable body usually houses a comfortable soul. In this way, those millions of housewives who demand adjustment to an unsatisfactory way of life are demanding that they should be made to see the virtues of their bodily habits. They want the still, small voice of divine discontent to be called wrong. And it often is.

God is not real any more, in the way that He was to the pioneers. He is not present in daily striving, only in a social meeting with fellow human worshippers on Sundays. He is a comfortable God, whose blessing is invoked on comfortable folks in comfortable congregations. He no longer draws utopians into the wilderness; He settles suburban couples into their rocking-chairs so that they move while sitting still. The alliance of the home and the church, so necessary for women in face of the savagery of the frontier, has remained as a social convenience for making the suburb seem to be the chosen paradise which it is not.

The Victorian fear of death still exists, although it has been largely translated into the fear of old age. The cult of heaven has been replaced by the cult of youth. Most people seem to prefer to seem younger and sillier than they are, rather than wiser and older as the Victorians wished to be. To live to old age is to live to a period of loneliness and separation from one's family, in a community of old people. Only among them, in the booming suburbs of the soon-to-die, does the Victorian dialogue on death and disease still flourish. For now that the expectation of life for an American white woman has reached nearly three-quarters of a century—more than double that of her Victorian sister—death only seems a likely event in her closing days.

In this age of the leisured woman, faced with the solution of the important material problems of life, and frightened at the hard work and uncertainties of improving the mind and the spirit, a reversion to Victorianism can be expected. That was a time when work seemed a practical good, that was a time when God seemed a reality, that was a time when the family was thought to be enough. In this reversion, however, the American woman is less well placed than her foremothers. The home is no longer solely her province, for her husband has more time to spend in it and her children have more opportunity to escape from it. Many Victorian wives could expect to die before they had finished rearing their brood; now wives can expect to live through to a lonely widowhood.

Some wives, unable to use their leisure to improve themselves, have gone back to work in their middle age. The large female labour force is chiefly composed of the married and the divorced and the ageing, those who work only part of their lives. Nearly equal with a man in work, when she wishes to work, and becoming more equal in looking after the home and family, the American woman can no longer claim to be the better half. Her problems are not so much those of her sex as those of humanity. Even if she retains one important biological difference from men, that of possible motherhood, she can deny the difference. She can have complete control over whether she wishes to have a child or not. In terms of free choice—if any choice can be called free—the American woman is at last as free as the American man, and his equal in all essential ways.

The four decades since the official granting of the vote to women are too short a time to judge what women will do with their new freedom and equality. Traditions lag up to three generations behind a change in the law. In that sense, we are all Victorians. If most women continue to see themselves chiefly as reproductive females, they will live and work within the limitations of the weaker sex and the better half. If they choose to see themselves chiefly as human beings, they will live and work as human beings for the better whole.

NOTES

I have not included a bibliography in this work, as any adequate bibliography of the history of women in America would take another book to compile. All scholars in this field should begin at the Radcliffe Women's Archives or at Smith College. I have, however, tried to include in my notes most of the material which I have found relevant in the writing of this book.

My thanks are particularly due to the librarian and staff of the Widener Library, Harvard University (HU); the Radcliffe Women's Archives (RWA); Columbia University Library (CU); the New York Public Library (NYPL); the Library of Congress (LC); and the Huntington Library (HL). In the interests of brevity, I have used the above-mentioned initials to identify the source of letters and manuscripts, and I have only used the name of a specific collection of papers when a quoted letter is catalogued under another name than the recipient of that letter.

I have further referred in the notes to the National American Woman Suffrage Association as N.A.W.S.A. I have also, in the quoted material in the text, tried to make the spelling consistent throughout. As American spelling altered between the eighteenth and the twentieth centuries, and as many of my sources were letters scribbled in haste, I have further taken the liberty of editing slightly some of the letters quoted in the text. I have a horror of the word [*sic*], which merely serves to point out the illiteracy or carelessness of the original writer and the smartness of the commentator. Should anyone wish to verify my slight editing of the quotations, a note will identify the original source.

My gratitude goes to David Potter, whose hospitality and insight have greatly helped this work. I am also grateful to those who have read all or part of this work, and have criticized it for my benefit. These critics include Carl Degler, Oscar Handlin, Richard Hofstadter, Keith Melder, David Morgan, Marianne Sinclair, Barbara Solomon, and William R. Taylor. The faults are my own; the generous gift of their time is theirs.

Finally, I wish to thank the American Council of Learned Societies. Without its generous and nomadic grant, this book could not have been written.

INTRODUCTION

Frederick Jackson Turner's famous essays on the frontier and the work of David Potter and Richard Wade have been vital for my thinking on this section. I am also much indebted to an unpublished paper by Frank Thistlethwaite, "The Origins of the Woman's Movement in the United States."

1. Ralph Waldo Emerson, "Man the Reformer," *Works* (11 vols., Boston, 1883–1887), I, p. 218.
2. Elizabeth Neall to Elizabeth Pease, June 18, 1842, Gay papers, *CU*.
3. MS Autobiography of Elizabeth Oakes Smith, pp. 329–335, *NYPL*.
4. Julia Howe, *Reminiscences, 1819–1899* (Boston, 1900), p. 376.
5. Lydia Child to Ellis Loring, April 11, 1843, *NYPL*.
6. Benjamin Thomas, *Theodore Weld, Crusader for Freedom* (Rutgers University, 1950), p. 114.
7. Lydia Child to Ellis Loring, February 15, 1842, *NYPL*.
8. *Letters of Lydia Maria Child* (Boston, 1883), p. 26.
9. Lydia Child to Louisa Loring, April 30, 1837, *RWA*.
10. Benjamin Thomas, *op. cit.,* p. 110.
11. See Elizabeth McCracken, *The Women of America* (New York, 1904), p. 392.
12. Lucretia Mott to Sydney Gay, April 13, 1850, Gay papers, *CU*.
13. Elizabeth Stanton to Henry Stanton, October 9, 1867, *LC*.
14. Lucy Stone to Samuel J. May, July 25, 1850, Blackwell papers, *LC*.

15. Lucy Stone to Susan Anthony, January 10, 1854, Blackwell papers, *LC.*
16. For an understanding of prohibition, see J. A. Krout, *The Origins of Prohibition* (New York, 1925), and A. A. Sinclair, *Prohibition: Era of Excess* (Boston, 1961). See also Anna Shaw, *The Story of a Pioneer* (New York, 1915), and Mary Peck, *Carrie Chapman Catt* (New York, 1944).
17. Willa Cather, *My Antonia* (London ed., 1943), p. 118.
18. Susan Anthony to Jessie Anthony, July 19, 1898, *HL.*

I. EARLY CONDITIONS

The authorities on marriage and the American family are George Howard, *A History of Matrimonial Institutions* (3 vols., University of Chicago, 1904), and Arthur Calhoun, *A Social History of the American Family from Colonial Times to the Present* (3 vols., Cleveland, 1917–1919). There is an excellent bibliography on the position of women in the American colonies by E. Leonard, S. Drinker, and M. Holden, *The American Woman in Colonial and Revolutionary Times, 1565–1800: A Syllabus with Bibliography* (University of Pennsylvania, 1962). Perry Miller's various works are, of course, seminal on the Puritan mind. I have further used William Sweet's valuable works on early American religion, *Revivalism in America, Its Origin, Growth and Decline* (New York, 1944) and *Religion in the Development of American Culture, 1765–1840* (New York, 1952). Also essential are the famous work of Chastellux, *Travels in North-America in the years 1780, 1781, and 1782;* Crèvecoeur, *Letters from an American Farmer;* and Harriet Martineau, *Society in America.* Among other familiar sources, the Journal of Nicholas Cresswell and the diaries of William Byrd II of Westover give spirited pictures of life in the eighteenth century.

In the section on the home, I have also used Joseph Folsom, *The Family and Democratic Society* (New York, 1943); H. and E. Hart, *Personality and the Family* (New York, 1935); and Bernhard Stern, *The Family, Past and Present* (New York, 1938). Lucy Salmon, *Domestic Service* (New York, 1897), is invaluable. The letters in the nineteenth-century ladies' magazines, particularly *Godey's Lady's Book,* the *Woman's Journal,* and *The Revolution,* give intimate insights into women's life during the century.

The books of Carl Bridenbaugh, *Cities in the Wilderness* (New York, 1955) and *Cities in Revolt* (New York, 1955), are seminal on the early American city. I was also helped by an unpublished paper of Barbara Solomon, "The New England Culture and the Nineteenth-Century Woman."

1. George Fitzhugh, *Sociology for the South* (Richmond, Va., 1854), p. 86.
2. Sweet, *Revivalism in America, op. cit.,* p. 3.
3. W. Blane, quoted in William Sprague, *Women and the West* (Boston, 1940), p. 73.
4. Elizabeth Oakes Smith, *op. cit.,* pp. 245–249, *NYPL.*

5. *The Whole Duty of a Woman: Or, an Infallible Guide to the Fair Sex* (London, 1737), p. 45.
6. Alfred Hamer to Abner Hamer, December 20, 1856, *RWA.*
7. Calhoun, *op. cit.,* I, p. 138.
8. *Letters of Rebecca Gratz* (Rabbi David Philipson, ed., Philadelphia, 1929), pp. 206–207. Reprinted by permission of Jewish Publication Society.
9. *Ladies' Miscellany,* October 20, 1830.
10. K. Blake and M. Wallace, *Champion of Women: The Life of Lillie Devereux Blake* (New York, 1943), p. 24.
11. A. de Tocqueville, *Democracy in America* (Vintage ed., 2 vols.), II, p. 194. Also valuable as a contemporary account of American society is Mrs. Trollope's *Domestic Manners of the Americans.*
12. Eliza Farnham, *Life in Prairie Land* (New York, 1846), p. 38.
13. Crèvecoeur, *op. cit.* (Original ed.), p. 70.
14. Samuel Hopkins, *Memoirs of the Life of Mrs. Sarah Osborn* (Worcester, Mass., 1799), pp. 8–9.
15. *Memoir of Ann Eliza Starr of Connecticut* (Philadelphia, 1827).
16. Calhoun, *op. cit.,* pp. 109–111.
17. Diary of Betsey Capen, September 30, 1838, *RWA.*
18. *Samuel Sewall's Diary* (M. Van Doren, ed., New York, 1963), p. 138.
19. Diary of Sarah Ripley Stearns, August 20, 1802, *RWA.*
20. Diary of Eunice Callender, December 31, 1815, *RWA.*
21. See Sweet, *Revivalism in America, op. cit.*
22. Mrs. Trollope, *op. cit.* (Vintage ed.), p. 110.
23. Quoted in Morton and Lucia White, *The Intellectual Versus the City* (Harvard, 1962), p. 31.
24. Diary of Sarah Watson (Sunday), 1833, Dana papers, *RWA.*
25. See Mary Livermore, *The Story of My Life* (Hartford, Conn., 1897).
26. Lydia Child to the editors of *Life Illustrated,* December 30, 1855, *RWA.*
27. Martineau, *op. cit.* (Anchor ed.), p. 337.
28. Sweet, *Religion in the Development of American Culture, op. cit.,* p. 192.
29. Lewis Tappan to Benjamin Tappan, May 14, 1825, *LC.*

II. THE FIRST REBELS

Alice Felt Tyler's *Freedom's Ferment* (University of Minnesota, 1944) gives the best general account of the religious sects and utopias in America before the Civil War. Robert Baird's *Religion in America* (New York, 1844) gives the point of view of the mid-nineteenth century.

1. See H. and M. Green, *The Pioneer Mothers of America* (3 vols., New York, 1912), I, pp. 371–373.
2. John Knox, *The First Blast of the Trumpet Against the Monstrous Regiment of Women, 1558* (E. Arber, ed., London, 1878), pp. 15, 17.

3. See Emery Battis's excellent account of Anne Hutchinson, *Saints and Sectaries* (University of North Carolina, 1962), pp. 116, 242, 286.
4. Baird, *op. cit.*, pp. 38–39.
5. Elizabeth Vining, "Women in the Society of Friends," Ward Lecture (Guildford College, N.C., 1955).
6. F. W. Evans, *Ann Lee, the Founder of the Shakers, a Biography* (4th ed., New York, 1858), p. 146.
7. *Familiar Letters of John Adams and His Wife Abigail Adams During the Revolution* (New York, 1876), pp. 149–150.
8. See E. R. Turner's thorough article, "Women's Suffrage in New Jersey: 1790–1807 (*Smith College Studies in History*, Vol. I, No. 4, July, 1916).

III. WOMAN OR SLAVE

Keith Melder's thesis, *The Beginnings of the Women's Rights Movement in the United States, 1800–1840* (Ph.D., Yale University, 1963), is excellent on the connection of the woman's movement with the churches. It is generally the best single account of the origins of the movement for woman suffrage.

Of the many works on slavery, I have relied most on Louis Filler, *The Crusade Against Slavery, 1830–1860* (New York, 1960), and Gunnar Myrdal, *An American Dilemma: The Negro Problem and Modern Democracy* (2 vols., 6th ed., New York, 1944). Filler's book has a valuable and up-to-date bibliography. Also useful were Alice Tyler, *op. cit.;* Arthur Schlesinger, Sr., *The American as Reformer* (Harvard University, 1950); and Russell Nye, *William Lloyd Garrison and the Humanitarian Reformers* (Boston, 1955).

1. See A. Perkins and T. Wolfson, *Frances Wright: Free Enquirer* (New York, 1939), pp. 193, 296. Also useful is W. Waterman, *Frances Wright* (Columbia University, 1924).
2. Henry Blackwell to Lucy Stone, September 17, 1855, *LC.*
3. Quoted by K. Melder, *op. cit.*, p. 189.
4. *The Lily*, May, 1852. This was Amelia Bloomer's temperance sheet in Seneca Falls, which Elizabeth Stanton turned into a women's rights newspaper.
5. Letter of Harriet Martineau to the Woman's Rights Convention, Worcester, Mass., October 15–16, 1851.
6. Filler, *op. cit.*, p. 21.
7. Abby Folsom, *A Letter from a Member of the Boston Bar to an Avaricious Landlord, with an Expression of Sentiments* (Boston, 1851), p. 10.
8. Margaret Thorp, *Female Persuasion* (Yale University, 1949), p. 196.
9. Lydia Child, *An Appeal in Favour of that Class of Americans called Africans* (Boston, 1833), p. 19.
10. See Catherine Birney, *Sarah and Angelina Grimké* (Boston, 1885), pp. 81, 147, 165, 172.

11. Sarah Grimké, *Letters on the Equality of the Sexes, and the Condition of Woman* (Boston, 1838), p. 122. See also Angelina Grimké, *Appeal to the Christian Women of the South* (Boston, 1836) and *Appeal to the Women of the Nominally Free States* (Boston, 1837).

12. *Letters of Theodore Dwight Weld, Angelina Grimké Weld and Sarah Grimké, 1822–1844* (G. Barnes and D. Dumond, eds., 2 vols., New York, copyright 1934 by the American Historical Association), I, pp. 415, 429, 434–6, 454. Reprinted by permission of Appleton-Century-Crofts. See also Benjamin Thomas, *op. cit.*

13. Henry Blackwell to Lucy Stone, June 13, 1853, *LC.*

14. *Ibid.,* August 24, 1853, *LC.*

15. E. S. Miller to Charles Miller, August 27, 1843, *NYPL.*

IV. THE FEMINIST BIBLES

I have used here the main texts mentioned in this section—particularly accessible is the Everyman edition in one volume of Mary Wollstonecraft and John Stuart Mill on the subject of women's rights. I have used the Boston edition of 1860 of *Woman in the Nineteenth Century.* Also helpful were Emma Clough, *A Study of Mary Wollstonecraft and the Rights of Women* (London, 1898); the definitive study by Ralph Wardle, *Mary Wollstonecraft, a Critical Biography* (University of Kansas, 1951); and Mason Wade, *Margaret Fuller, Whetstone of Genius* (New York, 1940).

1. Mary Wollstonecraft, *Maria or the Wrongs of Women,* in her *Collected Works* (W. Godwin, ed., 4 vols., 1798), II, p. 153.

2. *A Vindication of the Rights of Woman, op. cit.,* Introduction, pp. 18, 57, 63.

3. *Woman in the Nineteenth Century, op. cit.,* pp. 38, 122, 176.

4. Harriet Taylor, "The Enfranchisement of Women," *Westminster and Foreign Quarterly Review,* July, 1851.

5. *On the Subjection of Women,* see Introduction, viii.

6. *Woman in the Nineteenth Century, op. cit.,* p. 327.

V. THE FIRST SUFFRAGISTS

Otelia Cromwell's *Lucretia Mott* (Harvard University, 1958) is the definitive biography. Also useful to me were Anna Hallowell, *James and Lucretia Mott* (Boston, 1884); *William Lloyd Garrison, 1805–1879: The Story of His Life Told by His Children* (4 vols., New York, 1885–1889); *Slavery and "The Woman Question"; Lucretia Mott's Diary of Her Visit to Great Britain to Attend the World's Anti-Slavery Convention of 1840* (F. Tolles, ed., Supplement No. 23 to the *Journal* of the Friends Historical Society); and Volume 1 of *The History of Woman Suffrage* (E. Stanton, S. Anthony, and M. Gage, eds., New York, 1881).

Lucy Stone has had two biographers bent on praising her, her daughter Alice Stone Blackwell, *Lucy Stone, Pioneer of Woman's Rights* (Boston, 1930), and Elinor Hays, *Morning Star, a Biography of Lucy Stone, 1818–1893* (New York, 1961). The bulk of her papers are to be found among the Blackwell papers in the Library of Congress.

Elizabeth Stanton wrote an exuberant autobiography, *Eighty Years and More* (New York, 1898). There is also a carefully edited collection of her letters along with a re-issue of her autobiography done by her son and daughter, Theodore Stanton and Harriot Blatch, *Elizabeth Cady Stanton* (2 vols., New York, 1922). Alma Lutz has written a flattering biography, *Created Equal* (New York, 1940). The Stanton papers in the Library of Congress preserve the letters of husband and wife.

There is a vast amount of writing on Susan B. Anthony, most of it eulogistic. The most judicious picture of her is to be found in R. Riegel's collection of analyses of Victorian radical women, *American Feminists* (University of Kansas, 1963). Of the favourable biographies, Alma Lutz, *Susan B. Anthony* (Boston, 1959), is the best. Also useful for its material is Ida Harper, *The Life and Work of Susan B. Anthony* (2 vols., Indianapolis, 1898–1908). Katherine Anthony, *Susan B. Anthony* (New York, 1954), overpraises her subject, and Rheta Dorr, *Susan B. Anthony* (New York, 1928), debunks her in a partisan way. Although the literature is large, Anthony remains a remote personality. Her papers are mainly at the Library of Congress, the Huntington Library, and Smith College.

1. See Lucretia Mott to Elizabeth Stanton, 16 March, 1855, *LC.*
2. See *William Lloyd Garrison, op. cit.,* II, p. 372.
3. See Elizabeth Stanton, *op. cit.,* p. 82.
4. See O. Cromwell, *op. cit.,* pp. 103, 128.
5. Mary Bull, "Woman's Rights and Other Reforms in Seneca Falls," *Good Company,* 1870, Stanton papers, *LC.*
6. Rheta Dorr, "The Eternal Question," *Collier's,* October 30, 1920.
7. Lucretia Mott, "Discourse on Women," December 17, 1849.
8. See Elizabeth Stanton's scrapbook of press comments on the convention at Seneca Falls, *LC.*
9. *Proceedings of N.A.W.S.A.,* 1898, p. 76.
10. See *Proceedings of the Woman's Rights Convention,* held at Worcester, Mass., October 15–16, 1851.
11. *Proceedings of the Woman's Rights Convention,* held at the Broadway Tabernacle in the City of New York, September 6–7, 1853, p. 30.
12. Lucy Stone to Lucretia Mott, undated, 1850(?), Lutz papers, *RWA.*
13. Elizabeth Stanton, "Address to the Legislature of New York," February 14–15, 1854.
14. *The Lily,* May, 1852.
15. Lucy Stone to Francis Stone, August 31, 1838, *LC.*
16. Lucy Stone to Mrs. Stone, March 14, 1847, quoted in Alice Stone Blackwell, *op. cit.,* p. 66.

17. Sarah Stone to Lucy Stone, November 28, 1846, *LC.*
18. Frank Stone to Lucy Stone, June 6, 1847, *LC.*
19. Luther Stone to Lucy Stone, June 1, 1847, *LC.*
20. Lucy Stone to Susan Anthony, November 2, 1855, Blackwell papers, *LC.*
21. Alice Stone Blackwell, *op. cit.,* p. 145.
22. Lucy Stone to Henry Blackwell, October 8, 1854, *LC.*
23. Henry Blackwell to Lucy Stone, February 12, 1854, *LC.*
24. Lucy Stone to Henry Blackwell, January 30, 1855, *LC.*
25. Henry Blackwell to Lucy Stone, January 10, 1855, *LC.*
26. Henry Stanton to Elizabeth Stanton, autumn, 1843, *LC.*
27. Elizabeth Neall to Abby Kimber, December 11, 1841, Gay papers, *CU.*
28. Elizabeth Stanton to Susan Anthony, March 1, 1853, *LC:* see also an edited version of this letter in Stanton and Blatch, *op. cit.,* II, pp. 48–49.
29. Lucy Stone to Elizabeth Stanton, August 14, 1853, *LC.*
30. Undated, in the Stanton papers, *LC.*
31. Elizabeth Stanton, *op. cit.,* pp. 232–233.
32. Susan Anthony to Martha Wright, July 6, 1856, *HL* (copy of a letter in the Sophia Smith Collection).
33. Susan Anthony to Elizabeth Smith Miller, February 15, 1892, *NYPL.*
34. See Susan Anthony to Anna Dickinson, February 19, 1868; March 18, 1868; January 15, 1869; and November 5, 1895. These letters are contained in the Dickinson papers, *LC.* See also Giraud Chester, *Embattled Maiden: The Life of Anna Dickinson* (New York, 1951).
35. Susan Anthony to Elizabeth Stanton, June, 1856, *LC.*
36. *Ibid.,* September 29, 1857, *LC.*
37. Lucy Stone to Susan Anthony, March 25, 1856, Anthony papers, *LC.*
38. Susan Anthony to Anna Dickinson, February 22 and March 22, 1870, *LC.*
39. Susan Anthony, "Speech to the Farmers at Yates County Fair, Upper New York State, 1858" (MS in the Anthony papers, *LC*).

VI. THE REVOLT AGAINST CIVIL DEATH

Richard Morris, *Studies in the History of American Law* (New York, 1958), is seminal on women's rights in early American law. Also helpful were George Howard, *op. cit.;* the first volume of the *History of Woman Suffrage, op. cit.;* and K. Melder, *op. cit.*

1. See William Blackstone, *Commentaries on the Laws of England* (4 vols., Philadelphia, 1771–1772).
2. Courtney Kenney, *The History of the Law of England as to the Effects of Marriage on Property* (London, 1879), pp. 14–15, quoted by K. Melder, *op. cit.*
3. See Yuri Suhl, *Ernestine L. Rose* (New York, 1959), pp. 49–65.
4. Clarina Nichols, "On the Responsibilities of Woman," *Woman's Rights Tracts,* No. 6, from a speech delivered at Worcester, Mass., October 15, 1851.
5. Ernestine Rose, "An Address on Woman's Rights" (Boston, 1851).

6. Lydia Child to Ellis Loring, February 24, 1856, *Letters of Lydia Maria Child* (Boston, 1883), p. 74.
7. Mark Twain, *More Tramps Abroad* (London, 1897), p. 208.
8. See "Equal Rights Amendment to the Constitution Proposed," *Hearings before a Subcommittee of the Committee on the Judiciary,* U.S. Senate, 71 Cong., 3 Sess., S.J.Res. 52.

VII. THE ALPHABET OF REFORM

I am much in debt to Merle Curti's excellent *The Social Ideas of American Educators* (new ed., New York, 1959). K. Melder has also pertinent things to say on the question. See also Carl Bode, *The American Lyceum* (Oxford University, 1956), and Mary Benson, *Women in Eighteenth-Century America* (Columbia University, 1935).

1. *Arguments before the Judiciary Committee of the House of Representatives by a Committee of the Sixteenth Annual Convention of N.W.S.A.,* Washington, D.C., March 8, 1884.
2. Quoted in Carl Holliday, *Woman's Life in Colonial Days* (Boston, 1922), p. 92.
3. *Free Enquirer,* October 31, 1829.
4. Quoted in Curti, *op. cit.,* p. 177.
5. Hannah Crocker, *Observations on the Real Rights of Women* (Boston, 1818), p. 51.
6. Catherine Beecher, *The Evils Suffered by American Women and American Children: The Causes and the Remedy* (New York, 1846), pp. 3–4. See also Alma Lutz, *Emma Willard, Daughter of Democracy* (Boston, 1929), and Beth Gilchrist, *The Life of Mary Lyon* (Boston, 1910).
7. Lyman Stowe, *Saints, Sinners and Beechers* (Indianapolis, 1934), p. 55.
8. See *Ohio State Archaeological and Historical Quarterly,* July, 1954, p. 282.
9. Letter from Harriet Martineau, *op. cit.,* October 16, 1851.
10. *Woman's Rights Advocate,* No. 1. (Salem, Ohio, 1852).
11. Madame T. Blanc, *The Condition of Woman in the United States* (Boston, 1895), p. 177.
12. Quoted by Eleanor Flexner, *Century of Struggle* (Harvard University, 1959), p. 127. Flexner's book is the best general work on the factual history of American feminism.

VIII. A SWEET ORDER IN THE DRESS

There is an excellent description of American colonial dress in Alice Earle's *Two Centuries of Costume in America* (2 vols., New York, 1903). Useful on nineteenth-century dress reform is R. Riegel, "Women's Clothes and Women's Rights," *American Quarterly,* Autumn, 1963.

1. Harriot Hunt to Elizabeth Stanton, June 30, 1852, Stanton papers, *LC.*
2. See A. Earle, *op. cit.,* II, pp. 473, 500, 766, 772, 785.

3. See Titus Blunt, quoted in Thomas Branagan, *The Excellency of the Female Character Vindicated* (New York, 1807), p. 17.

4. Mary Livermore, *What Shall We Do with Our Daughters?, Superfluous Women, and Other Lectures* (Boston, 1883), p. 28.

5. Abba Woolson, *Woman in American Society* (Boston, 1873), p. 221.

6. See C. Willett Cunnington, *Feminine Attitudes in the Nineteenth Century* (New York, 1936), p. 187.

7. Gerrit Smith to Elizabeth Stanton, December 19, 1853, *LC.*

8. Elizabeth Stanton to Gerrit Smith, January 5, 1851, *LC.*

9. B. R. Hall, quoted in W. Sprague, *op. cit.,* p. 137.

10. Susan Anthony to Lucy Stone, May 25, 1852, Blackwell papers, *LC.*

11. Mary Bull, *op. cit.*

12. Elizabeth Stanton to Lucy Stone, February 23, 1854, *LC.*

13. Abba Woolson, "The Relation of Woman to her Dress," *Papers and Letters Presented at the First Women's Congress of the Association for the Advancement of Woman* (New York, 1873), p. 109.

14. F. P. Dunne, *Mr. Dooley in the Hearts of His Countrymen* (Boston, 1899), p. 154.

15. D. C. Bloomer, *The Life and Writings of Amelia Bloomer* (Boston, 1895), p. 76.

IX. THE OSTRICH GAME

The literature on the Southern lady is vast. The best introduction to the ideas behind her creation lies in Rollin Osterweis, *Romanticism and Nationalism in the Old South* (Yale University, 1949). Ulrich Phillips, *Life and Labour in the Old South* (Boston, 1929), and F. Simkins, *A History of the South* (New York, 1953), treat the Southern lady with great courtesy. Wilbur Cash, *The Mind of the South* (New York, 1941); J. C. Furnas, *Goodbye to Uncle Tom* (New York, 1956); and Edmund Wilson, *Patriotic Gore* (New York, 1962), treat her with less courtesy.

1. Reminiscences of Elizabeth Perkins Cabot, p. 29, *RWA.*

2. See the *Universalist and Ladies' Repository* of 1836.

3. Barbara Bodichon, *Women and Work* (New York, 1859), pp. 18–19.

4. Frances Kemble, *Journal of a Residence on a Georgian Plantation in 1838–1839* (J. Scott, ed., New York, 1961), Introduction.

5. Mary Chesnut, *A Diary from Dixie* (B. Williams, ed., Boston, 1961), pp. 21–22, 44.

6. Gail Hamilton (Mary Dodge), *A New Atmosphere* (Boston, 1865), p. 63.

X. THE MAKING OF THE LADY

The sources of this chapter are many and are based on Victorian etiquette books, novels, diaries, and magazines. These include Mrs. Sanford, *Woman, in Her Social and Domestic Character* (6th ed., Boston, 1844); Madame Celnart, *Book of Politeness* (5th ed., Philadelphia, 1847); *Miss Leslie's Behaviour Book* (Philadelphia, 1859); Gail Hamilton, *op. cit.;* and Florence Hartley, *The Ladies' Book of Etiquette and Manual of Politeness* (Boston, 1873). I am particularly indebted to Arthur Schlesinger, Sr.'s brilliant *Learning How to Behave* (New York, 1946); Foster Dulles, *America Learns to Play* (New York, 1940); and J. A. Banks, *Prosperity and Parenthood* (London, 1954).

1. George Burnap, *Lectures on the Sphere and Duties of Woman* (Baltimore, 1841), pp. 73, 82.
2. Frances Wright, *Views of Society and Manners in America* (P. Baker, ed., Harvard University, 1963), p. 219.
3. Thomas Hamilton, *Men and Manners in America* (London, 1833), and Francis Grund, *Aristocracy in America* (New York, 1839), both quoted in *The Happy Republic* (G. Probst, ed., New York, 1962), pp. 186–187.
4. MS of an address delivered before the lyceum of Seneca Falls, *circa* 1850, Stanton papers, *LC.*
5. Horace Bushnell, *Women's Suffrage; the Reform Against Nature* (New York, 1869), p. 142.
6. Alexander Walker, *Intermarriage* (New York, 1839), pp. 74–76.
7. George Napheys, *The Physical Life of Woman* (5th ed., Philadelphia, 1870), p. 29. See also Edward Dixon, *Woman and Her Diseases, From the Cradle to the Grave* (10th ed., New York, 1857).
8. Walker, *op. cit.,* p. 92.
9. Lorenzo Fowler, *Marriage: Its History and Ceremonies, with a Phrenological and Physiological Exposition of the Functions and Qualifications for Happy Marriages* (New York, 1847), p. 125.
10. See Banks, *passim.*
11. From "Our Young Girls," Elizabeth Stanton's most popular lyceum lecture in the 1870's, *LC.*
12. Edward Clarke, *Sex in Education, or, A Fair Chance for Girls* (5th ed., Boston, 1874), p. 30. It was answered by *Sex and Education: A Reply* (Julia Howe, ed., Boston, 1874).
13. A. Hughes Bennett, "Hygiene in the Higher Education of Women," *Popular Science Monthly,* February, 1888.
14. Reminiscences of Marion McFadden, Poole papers, *RWA.* See also T. Shannon, *Perfect Girlhood* (Marietta, Ohio, 1913).

XI. THE UNMENTIONABLE FEARS

All investigation here begins with Oscar Handlin's brilliant chapter on "The Horror" in *Race and Nationality in American Life* (Boston, 1957). There is an interesting catalogue of the ideas of pioneer American sexual reformers in Sidney Ditzion, *Marriage, Morals, and Sex in America* (New

York, 1953). Norman Himes, *Medical History of Contraception* (New York, 1936), is the standard work on that subject. H. Woolston, *Prostitution in the United States* (New York, 1921), is adequate.

1. Samuel Jennings, *The Married Lady's Companion, or Poor Man's Friend* (2nd rev. ed., London, 1808), pp. 28–30.
2. P. Dunne and A. Derbois, *The Young Married Lady's Private Medical Guide* (4th ed., Boston, 1854), p. 12.
3. *Godey's Lady's Book,* March, 1852.
4. Diary of Harriet Robinson, October 6, 1854, *RWA.*
5. Frederick Hollick, *The Matron's Manual of Midwifery, and the Diseases of Women during Pregnancy and in Child Bed* (47th rev. ed., New York, 1850), pp. 87, 284, 410–411.
6. Robert Dale Owen, *Moral Physiology; or, A Brief and Plain Treatise on the Population Question* (5th ed., New York, 1831, and 10th ed., Boston, 1875), pp. 49, 76 of 1875 ed. See also Charles Knowlton, *Fruits of Philosophy* (New York, 1833).
7. See *The Malthusian,* January, 1881.
8. Thomas Bull, *Hints to Mothers, for the Management of Health during the Period of Pregnancy, and in the Lying-In-Room* (3rd ed., New York, 1842), p. 123.
9. See the *London Medical Gazette,* July, 1849.
10. See Dio Lewis, *Chastity, or Our Secret Sins* (New York, 1871). Also useful is Carl Bode, "Columbia's Carnal Bed," *American Quarterly,* Spring, 1963.
11. *Proceedings of the National Purity Congress,* Baltimore, October 14–16, 1895.
12. John Jones, "The Social Evil" (Washington, D.C., 1871).

XII. THE FREEDOM OF THE FACTORY

For a general survey of the American industrial revolution, T. Cochran and W. Miller, *The Age of Enterprise* (rev. ed., New York, 1961), is excellent. I have also used Lucy Salmon, *op. cit.;* Ernest Groves, *The American Woman* (rev. ed., New York, 1944); *America Through Women's Eyes* (Mary Beard, ed., New York, 1933); Edith Abbott, *Women in Industry: A Study in American Economic History* (New York, 1918); and *Women's Work in America* (Annie Meyer, ed., New York, 1891).

Invaluable on conditions at Lowell are Harriet Robinson, *Early Factory Labour in New England* (Boston, 1889), and Lucy Larcom, *A New England Girlhood* (new ed., New York, 1961).

William Sanger's *The History of Prostitution* (New York, 1858) provided much of the ammunition of the moral reformers in the late Victorian period.

1. Quoted in *America Through Women's Eyes, op. cit.*, p. 133.
2. Harriet Robinson, *op. cit.*, pp. 11–12.
3. Orestes Brownson, quoted in T. Cochran and W. Miller, *op. cit.*, p. 23.
4. Annie Quinby, in *Proceedings of N.W.S.A.*, 1884, p. 89.
5. W. Sanger, *op. cit.*, p. 526.
6. Elizabeth Stanton to Robert Ingersoll, March 20, 1880, Stanton papers, *LC*.
7. *The Revolution*, January 29, 1868.

XIII. THE PROFESSIONAL WOMAN

This analysis of Victorian professional women has been worked out from *A Woman of the Century* (Frances Willard and Mary Livermore, eds., Buffalo, N.Y., 1893).

1. *Godey's Lady's Book*, December, 1862.
2. Diary of Elizabeth Blackwell, July 18, 1837, *LC*.
3. Elizabeth Blackwell, *Pioneer Work for Women* (London ed., 1914), pp. 22–24, 49, 56, 69.
4. Elizabeth Blackwell to Barbara Bodichon, September 25, undated, *CU*.
5. *Ibid.*, May 25, 1860, *CU*.
6. Diary of Emily Blackwell, June 20, 1858, *RWA*.
7. Elizabeth Blackwell to Barbara Bodichon, June 3, 1856, *CU*.
8. Helen Morton to Mary Hopkinson, July 24, 1872, *RWA*.
9. Frances Kemble to Charles Sedgwick, May 12, 1849, *CU*.

XIV. THE REVEREND SUFFRAGISTS

1. T. D. Stone, *Biography of Mrs. Rebecca Gair Webster* (Boston, 1848), p. 204.
2. *Memoirs of the late Mrs. Susan Huntington of Boston, Massachusetts* (Boston, 1826), pp. 51–52.
3. See the papers of Harriot Boynton Thompson, *RWA*.
4. See Almond Davis, *The Female Preacher, or Memoir of Salome Lincoln* (Providence, 1843).
5. See MS of the autobiography of Antoinette Brown Blackwell (C. U. Gilson, ed.), pp. 46–47, 51, 66, 73, *RWA*.
6. Antoinette Brown to Lucy Stone, undated, 1848, Blackwell papers, *RWA*.
7. *Ibid.*, August 4, 1852, *RWA*.
8. *Ibid.*, June 8, 1853, *RWA*.
9. Antoinette Brown to Horace Greeley, September 6, 1854, Greeley papers, *NYPL*.
10. *Ibid.*, January 8, 1855, *NYPL*.
11. Susan Anthony to Antoinette Brown Blackwell, April 22, 1858, *RWA*.
12. See the Olympia Brown papers in the *RWA*.
13. See an undated interview with Augusta Chapin in the Soulé papers, *NYPL*.

XV. BOOK-MAKING PROPENSITIES

I am much indebted to four excellent studies: W. Neff, *Victorian Working Women* (Columbia University, 1929); J. Hart, *The Popular Book* (University of California, 1961); Dorothy Dondore, *The Prairie and the Making of Middle America: Four Centuries of Description* (2nd ed., New York, 1961); and P. Thomson, *The Victorian Heroine, a Changing Ideal, 1837–1873* (Oxford University, 1956).

1. Lavius Hyde to Sarah Hyde, May 12, 1852, Bradley-Hyde papers, *RWA*.
2. Lucy Larcom to Harriet Robinson, February 3, 1857, *RWA*.
3. See *The Works of Anne Bradstreet* (J. Ellis, ed., Charleston, 1867).
4. Katherine Anthony, *First Lady of the Revolution: The Life of Mercy Otis Warren* (New York, 1958), p. 163.
5. See J. F. Cooper, *The Last of the Mohicans* (London ed., 1938) and *The Prairie* (London ed., 1938), p. 158.
6. Timothy Flint in the *Western Monthly Review* of 1828, quoted by Logan Esarey, "The Literary Spirit Among the Early Ohio Valley Settlers," *Mississippi Valley Historical Review*, September, 1918.
7. See Mary Clavers (Caroline Kirkland), *A New Home—Who'll Follow* (New York, 1839).
8. Lydia Child, *Brief History of the Condition of Women in Various Ages and Nations* (New York, 1832).
9. Harriet Martineau, *Deerbrook* (2 vols., New York ed., 1839), quoted by Thompson, *op. cit.*, p. 15.
10. MS of Elizabeth Oakes Smith, *op. cit.*, pp. 283–284, *NYPL*.
11. See W. Taylor and C. Lasch, "Two 'Kindred Spirits': Sorority and Family in New England, 1839–1846," *New England Quarterly*, March, 1963.
12. Charlotte Brontë, *Shirley* (London ed., 1875), p. 203.
13. See Marjorie Worthington, *Miss Alcott of Concord* (New York, 1958), p. 83.
14. Louisa Alcott to Lucy Stone, August 31, 1885, Lutz papers, *RWA*.
15. See Cora Castle, *A Statistical Study of Eminent Women* (New York, 1913); also H. Cairns, "The Woman of Genius," in S. Schmalhausen and V. Calverton, *Woman's Coming of Age* (New York, 1931).
16. *The Complete Poems of Emily Dickinson* (T. Johnson, ed., Boston, 1960), p. 348.

XVI. THE GREAT DEBATE

Robert Smuts, *Women and Work in America* (Columbia University, 1959), is generally useful on the position of working women at the end of the Victorian age, and on the theories behind that position.

1. Marion Reid, *Woman, Her Education and Influence* (New York, 1848), pp. 57–58.

2. Justin Fulton, *The True Woman and Woman Vs. Ballot* (Boston, 1869), pp. 198–199.

3. Lorine Pruette, *Women and Leisure* (New York, 1924), p. 207.

4. Caroline Dall, *Woman's Right to Labour: Or, Low Wages and Hard Work* (Boston, 1860), p. 104.

5. Charles Elliott, "Woman's Work and Woman's Wages," *North American Review*, August, 1882.

6. Elinor Whiting, *Woman's Work and Wages* (pamphlet), Massachusetts Association Opposed to Further Extension of the Suffrage to Women, *HU*.

7. Julia Howe, "The Industrial Value of Woman," *North American Review*, November, 1882.

8. Elinor Whiting, *op. cit.*

9. H. Bushnell, *op. cit.*, p. 171.

10. Caroline Dall, *op. cit.*, p. 62.

11. Grant Allen, "Woman's Place in Nature," *Forum*, June, 1889.

12. Catherine Beecher to "Lizzie," July 24, 1867, Lutz papers, *RWA*.

13. Catherine Beecher, *Woman's Profession as Mother and Educator, with Views in Opposition to Woman Suffrage* (Boston, 1872), p. 7.

14. See Charlotte Gilman and Henrietta Rodman, quoted in *Anti-Suffrage Essays by Massachusetts Women* (Boston, 1916), p. 142.

15. Caroline Dall, *op. cit.*, pp. 6–7.

XVII. WOMAN VERSUS SLAVE

1. Catherine Beecher, *Woman's Profession, op. cit.*, p. 1.

2. Mary Chesnut, quoted by M. Beard, *op. cit.*, p. 195.

3. Mrs. Roger Pryor, *Reminiscences of Peace and War* (New York, 1905), quoted by M. Beard, *op. cit.*, p. 205.

4. See Mary Livermore, *op. cit.* and *My Story of the War* (Hartford, Conn., 1887).

5. Jane Swisshelm, *Half a Century* (Chicago, 1880), p. 244.

6. Speech of Elizabeth Stanton at an Anti-slavery meeting, 1860, *LC*.

7. Elizabeth Stanton to Martha Wright, August 10, 1862, *LC*.

8. *History of Woman Suffrage* (New York, 1881), II, p. 53.

9. *Eighty Years and More, op. cit.*, pp. 236, 240.

10. *History of Woman Suffrage, op. cit.*, II, p. 193.

11. Speech of Elizabeth Stanton on Reconstruction, 1867, *LC*.

12. Elizabeth Stanton to F. Blair, October 1, 1868, *LC*.

13. Lucy Stone to Abby Kelley Foster, January 24, 1867, Blackwell papers, *LC*.

14. George Train, *The Great Epigram Campaign in Kansas* (Leavenworth, Kansas, 1867).

15. Susan Anthony to Olympia Brown, July 20, 1868, *RWA*.

16. Elizabeth Stanton to Olympia Brown, March 23, 1868, quoted by Elinor Hays, *op. cit.,* p. 201.
17. *Ibid.,* p. 203.
18. Clara Barton to Mary Norton, October 15, 1869, Lutz papers, *RWA.*
19. Thomas Higginson to Elizabeth Stanton, December 22, 1866, *LC.*
20. Invaluable on the split in the women's movement is Lois Merk, *Massachusetts and the Woman-Suffrage Movement* (rev. thesis, Radcliffe Library, 1961). The quotation comes from Merk, p. 372.
21. Elizabeth Stanton to Lucretia Mott, April 1, 1872. There is an edited version of this letter in T. Stanton and H. Blatch, *op. cit.,* II, p. 137.
22. Susan Anthony to Martha Wright, May 30, 1871, *HL* (copy of a letter in the Sophia Smith Collection).
23. See the Diary of Susan Anthony, May 6–9, 1872, and August 25, 1874, *LC.*
24. Quoted by Robert Shaplen, *Free Love and Heavenly Sinners* (New York, 1954), pp. 131–132. Shaplen, along with Paxton Hibben, *Henry Ward Beecher: An American Portrait* (New York, 1927), gives the case against Beecher. Lyman Stowe, *op. cit.,* gives the case for him. Emanie Sachs treats Victoria Woodhull in *The Terrible Siren* (New York, 1928) in a breathless way.
25. Quoted by Merk, *op. cit.,* p. 374.
26. Alice Blackwell to Lucy Stone, June 12, 1889, Blackwell papers, *LC.*
27. Mary Nichols, quoted in Paulina Wright Davis, *A History of the National Woman's Rights Movement for Twenty Years* (New York, 1871), p. 34.
28. Susan Anthony to Martha Wright, January 1, 1873, *HL* (copy of a letter in the Sophia Smith Collection).
29. See note 18.

XVIII. FEMINISTS AGAINST THE CHURCHES

In an unpublished thesis, Helen Horowitz writes well on the religious beliefs of Elizabeth Stanton and Anna Shaw. The religious debates are particularly interesting in the proceedings of the women's rights coventions of 1852 and 1893 and 1896.

1. Yuri Suhl, *op. cit.,* p. 129.
2. *The Revolution,* May 7 and July 30, 1868.
3. Elizabeth Stanton to Harriot Stanton, April 17, 1880, *LC.*
4. William H. Channing to Elizabeth Stanton, October 10, 1884, *LC.*
5. Mary Livermore to Elizabeth Stanton, September 1, 1886, *LC.*
6. See *The Woman's Bible* (2 vols., New York, 1895–1898). It is an interesting as well as a contentious document.
7. *Proceedings of N.A.W.S.A.,* 1893, p. 96.
8. *Ibid.,* 1896, p. 92.

9. Anna Shaw to Lucy Anthony, Easter Day, 1910, *RWA*. See also Anna Shaw, *The Story of a Pioneer* (New York, 1915).
10. *Proceedings of N.A.W.S.A.,* 1915, p. 17.

XIX. THE LIBERTY OF THE WEST

1. Letter of Sarah Hallock, *Proceedings of N.W.S.A.,* 1884, p. 134.
2. George Flower, quoted in Alice Tyler, *op. cit.,* p. 18.
3. M. Fuller, "Summer on the Lakes," *The Writings of Margaret Fuller* (M. Wade, ed., New York, 1941), p. 44.
4. Walter Webb, *The Great Plains* (New York, 1931), p. 505. Webb's work is seminal and illuminating.
5. L. Hamner, *Short Grass and Longhorns* (Norman, Oklahoma, 1943), p. 11.
6. Quoted in Dee Brown, *The Gentle Tamers* (New York, 1958), pp. 37, 38. See also the diary of Louise Peeler, 1851, *RWA*.
7. Elizabeth Hayward, *A Woman Named Malinda* (Salem, Indiana, 1954).
8. *Woman's Journal,* May 21 and July 30, 1870.
9. Emma Haddock, "Women as Land-Owners in the West," *Papers Read Before the Association for the Advancement of Women* (Louisville, Ky., October, 1886).
10. MS of the autobiography of Harriet Taylor Upton, *RWA*. See also F. Allen and M. Welles, "The Ohio Woman Suffrage Movement," *RWA*.
11. See Miriam Chapman, *The Story of Woman Suffrage in Wyoming, 1869–1890* (M.A. thesis, University of Wyoming, 1952); T. A. Larson, "Petticoats at the Polls," *Pacific North-West Quarterly,* April, 1953; and F. D. Stratton, "Early History of South Pass City," pamphlet, University of Wyoming. Also useful are Grace Hebard, "How Woman Suffrage Came to Wyoming," and the relevant passages in Eleanor Flexner, *op. cit.*
12. Bill Nye, quoted in W. Sprague, *op. cit.,* p. 152.
13. *Address of Cassius Marcellus Clay, before the Alumni of Yale University,* June 28, 1887.
14. Thomas Higginson, "The Nonsense of It," (A.W.S.A., Boston, 1889).
15. James Bryce, *The American Commonwealth* (rev. ed., New York, 1918), pp. 606–607.
16. Martha Cannon, "Significance of the Woman Suffrage Movement," *Session of the American Academy,* February 9, 1910, p. 20. See also L. Arrington, "The Economic Role of Pioneer Mormon Women," *Western Humanities Review,* Spring, 1955.
17. Richard Burton, *The City of the Saints* (F. Brodie, ed., New York, 1963), pp. 478–493.
18. *The Ballot-Box,* August, 1880.
19. Quoted in W. Sprague, *op. cit.,* p. 168.
20. Lucy Fosdick, "Across the Plains in '61," *RWA*.

21. W. Webb, *op. cit.*, p. 505.
22. Address of Mary Ellen Lease in *Transactions of the National Council of Women in the United States,* Washington, D.C., February 22–25, 1891, p. 216.
23. See the judicious examination of the effects of woman suffrage on Colorado by Helen Sumner, *Equal Suffrage* (New York, 1909), p. 219.
24. Susan Anthony to Elizabeth Miller, July 25, 1894, *NYPL;* and Susan Anthony to Thomas Bowman, September 7, 1894, *HL.*
25. *The Ballot-Box,* July, 1880.
26. L. Ames Brown, "Suffrage and Prohibition," *North American Review,* January, 1916.

XX. UNEASY ALLIANCE

I found highly useful Abigail Duniway's *Path Breaking* (Portland, Oregon, 1914), because it describes the rare case of a farmer's wife becoming a suffrage leader. Also essential were P. Odegard's seminal *Pressure Politics* (Columbia University, 1928), the history of the Anti-Saloon League, and the chapter on "The West and Suffrage" in Mary Earhart's *Frances Willard* (Chicago University, 1944), although it exaggerates slightly the influence of the Woman's Christian Temperance Union on the suffrage movement.

1. Henry Blackwell to Lucy Stone, July 8, 18, 22, 1889, and August 23, 1890, *LC.*
2. A. Duniway, *op. cit.,* p. 28.
3. Quoted in P. Odegard, *op. cit.,* p. 85.
4. Quoted by M. Earhart, *op. cit.,* p. 194.
5. See the *Woman's Journal,* March 5, 1898, and January 24, 1903.
6. *The Ballot-Box,* August, 1876.
7. Quoted in L. Merk, *op. cit.,* p. 148.
8. See Joseph Gusfield, "Social Structure and Moral Reform: A Study of the Woman's Christian Temperance Union," *American Journal of Sociology,* no. 61, 1955; and Janet Giele's penetrating *Social Change in the Feminine Role: A Comparison of Woman's Suffrage and Woman's Temperance, 1870–1920* (Ph.D., Radcliffe, 1961).
9. See Aileen Kraditor's excellent and stimulating *The Ideas of the Woman Suffrage Movement, 1890–1920* (Ph.D., Columbia University, 1962), pp. 264–265.
10. See P. Odegard, *op. cit.,* p. 85.
11. MS of Harriet Upton, *RWA.*
12. Selina Solomons, *How We Won the Vote in California* (San Francisco, 1912).
13. C. Catt and N. Shuler, *Woman Suffrage and Politics* (New York, 1923), p. 279. See also Charles Neu, "Olympia Brown and the Woman's

Suffrage Movement," *Wisconsin Magazine of History*, Summer, 1960; and Ella Stewart, "Woman Suffrage and the Liquor Traffic," *Annals of the American Academy*, November, 1914.

XXI. UPON THEIR LOINS

I have again found useful Oscar Handlin's *Race and Nationality in American Life, op. cit.*, which is fertile in suggestions in this field.

1. Horatio Storer, *Why Not? A Book For Every Woman* (Boston, 1868), p. 85.
2. *The Revolution*, February 10, 1870.
3. *Mrs. Elizabeth Cady Stanton's Address at the Decade Meeting of the National Woman's Rights Movement*, New York, October 20, 1870.
4. See Thomas Higginson, *Common-Sense About Women* (Boston, 1881), pp. 11–14.
5. *Proceedings of N.W.S.A.*, 1884, p. 70.
6. Kate Woolsey, *Republics Versus Woman* (London, 1903), p. 27.
7. Scott and Nellie Nearing, *Woman and Social Progress* (New York, 1912), pp. 14–17. See also G. Hall, *Adolescence* (New York, 1908), pp. 561–562.
8. Havelock Ellis, *The Problem of Race-Regeneration* (New York, 1911), p. 51.
9. C. W. Saleeby, *Woman and Womanhood* (New York, 1911), p. 24.
10. George Howard, "Changed Ideals and Status of the Family and the Public Activities of Women," *Annals of the American Academy*, November, 1914.
11. Madison Grant, *The Passing of the Great Race* (New York, 1918), p. 27.
12. See S. H. Halford, in *Population and Birth-Control* (E. and C. Paul, eds., New York, 1917), p. 230.
13. Mrs. Arthur Dodge, "Woman Suffrage Opposed to Woman's Rights," *Annals of the American Academy*, November, 1914.
14. André Siegfried, *America Comes of Age* (New York, 1927).
15. H. Mencken, *A Mencken Chrestomathy* (New York, 1949), p. 626.

XXII. THE NEW WORLD AND THE IMMIGRANT

1. Frederic Howe, "The Alien," in *Civilization in the United States* (H. Stearns, ed., New York, 1922). Reprinted by permission of Harcourt, Brace & World, Inc.
2. Susan Anthony to Elizabeth Stanton, February 14, 1865, *LC*.
3. *The Revolution*, quoting the Reverend J. D. Fulton, December 17, 1868.
4. Oliver Wendell Holmes to J. E. Pfeiffer, March 22, 1885, *RWA*.
5. See L. Merk, *op. cit.*, and *Anti-Suffrage Essays by Massachusetts Women, op. cit.*

6. Mary Wollstonecraft, *Vindication, op. cit.,* Introduction.
7. *Woman Citizen,* July 7, 1917, quoted by A. Kraditor, *op. cit.,* p. 237.
8. Ethel Vorce to Harriet Laidlaw, December 24, 1914, *RWA.*
9. See the chapter "The Snare of Preparation" in the most candid of the autobiographies of the pioneer feminists, Jane Addams, *Twenty Years at Hull-House* (New York, 1911).
10. Jane Addams, "The Modern City and Municipal Franchise for Women," Address to N.A.W.S.A., Baltimore, February, 1906.
11. For a brilliant examination of the psychology of Jane Addams and of her role in contemporary American life, see Jill Conway, "Jane Addams: An American Heroine," *Daedalus,* Spring, 1964. The whole issue concerns American women.
12. Louise Leeds to Harriet Laidlaw, September 20, 1913, *RWA.*
13. Sam Warner, *Streetcar Suburbs* (Boston, 1962), p. 11. Reprinted by permission of Harvard University Press.
14. Lillian Betts, *The Leaven in a Great City* (New York, 1902), pp. 14–16, 57. Reprinted by permission of Dodd, Mead & Company, Inc.
15. Willa Cather, *op. cit.,* p. 118.
16. Henry Adams, *The Education of Henry Adams* (Boston, 1918), pp. 499–500.
17. *Woman's Journal,* September 25, 1880.

XXIII. INFERIOR ANIMALS AND SUPERIOR BEINGS

1. Sarah Grimké, *op. cit.,* pp. 21, 24.
2. MS of the speech by Elizabeth Stanton read at the Waterloo convention of August 2, 1848, Stanton papers, *LC.*
3. Albert Bledsoe, "The Mission of Woman," *Southern Review,* October, 1871.
4. Elizabeth Stanton to Martha Wright, April 22, 1863, Stanton papers, *LC.*
5. Elizabeth Blackwell, *op. cit.,* p. 145.
6. Henry Blackwell to Lucy Stone, June 13, 1853, *LC.*
7. *The Revolution,* January 14, 1869.
8. Quoted by L. Merk, *op. cit.,* pp. 374–375.
9. *Woman's Journal,* May 5, 1888.
10. See note 2.
11. Address of Julia Howe, in *Papers Read Before the Association for the Advancement of Women, op. cit.,* 1883, p. 42.
12. See Olive Schreiner, *Woman and Labour* (New York, 1911).
13. Abba Woolson, *Woman in American Society* (Boston, 1873), p. 213.
14. Angelique Martin, *Essays on Woman's True Destiny, Responsibilities and Rights, as the Mother of the Human Race* (Warren, Ohio, 1851).
15. Elizabeth Stanton to Gerrit Smith, December 21, 1857, Stanton papers, *LC.*
16. *Proceedings of the National Purity Congress,* 1896.

17. *Vigilance*, May, 1913.
18. See Ellen Key, *The Renaissance of Motherhood* (New York, 1914). See also the contemporary texts of Charles Leland, *The Alternate Sex* (New York, 1904); Emmet Densmore, *Sex Equality: A Solution of the Woman Problem* (New York, 1907); and C. Gasquoine Hartley, *The Truth About Woman* (New York, 1914), for some idea of the discussion on the new woman at the time.
19. See Edna Kenton, quoted in *Anti-Suffrage Essays, op. cit.*, p. 143.
20. See R. Riegel, "Women's Clothes and Women's Rights," *op. cit.*
21. *The Revolution*, July 22, 1869.

XXIV. A VERY AMERICAN TALE

1. Quoted in the Introduction by Irving Howe to the Modern Library edition of *The Bostonians*.
2. *The Bostonians*, pp. 27, 183–184.
3. Charlotte Stewart, "The American Girl in Fiction," *The Woman's World for 1889* (London, 1889), pp. 100–103.
4. Ellen Glasgow, *The Sheltered Life* (New York, 1932), p. 293.
5. Henry Adams, *op. cit.*, pp. 446–447.

XXV. THE HEIRS OF ANNE HUTCHINSON

E. Dakin has written a penetrating biography, *Mrs. Eddy* (New York, 1929). Also interesting are the writings of her rejected follower, Augusta Stetson, *Sermons and Other Writings* (New York, 1924). On Charlotte Gilman, the best source is Charlotte Gilman in her *The Living of Charlotte Perkins Gilman* (New York, 1935). Particularly excellent are her *Woman and Economics* (Boston, 1898) and *The Home: Its Work and Influence* (New York, 1910).
1. A. Stetson, *op. cit.*, p. 60.
2. *The Living of Charlotte Perkins Gilman, op. cit.*, pp. 5, 40, 70.
3. *The Home, op. cit.*, pp. 46, 51.

XXVI. THE ENGLISH EXAMPLE

An accessible and large collection of work on English feminism can be found in the library of the Fawcett Society in London. The standard sources are summed up in O. McGregor's bibliography, "The Social Position of Women in England, 1850–1914," *British Journal of Sociology*, March, 1955. Seminal for understanding the militant movement are E. Sylvia Pankhurst, *The Suffragette* (Boston, 1911) and *The Suffragette Movement* (London, 1931); also Teresa Billington-Grieg, *The Militant Suffrage Movement* (London, 1912), for her description of why she rebelled from the militants.

For the moderate suffragists' point of view, Millicent Fawcett's *Women's Suffrage* (London, 1912) and *The Women's Victory—And After* (London, 1920) and Rachel Strachey's *The Cause: A Short History of the Women's Movement in Great Britain* (London, 1928) are important. There is also an urbane account of suffragism in England by Roger Fulford, *Votes for Women* (London, 1957), and a good period piece on England before the First World War in George Dangerfield, *The Strange Death of Liberal England* (New York, 1935). I am also indebted to an unpublished paper by Andrew Bird, "Militancy and the Suffrage Movement in Great Britain."

1. Rebecca West, "These American Women," *Harper's Magazine,* November, 1925.
2. R. Fulford, *op. cit.,* p. 91.
3. *Proceedings of N.W.S.A.,* 1884, p. 97.
4. R. Fulford, *op. cit.,* p. 80.
5. Elizabeth Blackwell to Henry Blackwell, November 29 (?), *LC.*
6. R. Fulford, *op. cit.,* p. 75.
7. Jane Addams, "The Larger Aspects of the Woman's Movement," *Annals of the American Academy,* November, 1914.
8. Speech by the Hon. Stanley E. Bowdle to the Pennsylvania Association Opposed to Woman Suffrage (undated), N.A.W.S.A. papers, *LC.*
9. Interviews with Mrs. Blatch and Mrs. Pankhurst on militancy in *Pearson's Magazine,* February, 1910.
10. Mary Winsor, "The Militant Suffrage Movement," *Annals of the American Academy,* November, 1914.
11. *Ibid.*
12. *New York Times,* July 9, 1917.
13. Carrie Catt to Harriet Upton, April 19, 1915, *LC.*
14. Julia Howe to Mrs. Doggett, December 1, 1871, *RWA.*
15. Anna Shaw on the Congressional Union, July 27, 1916, N.A.W.S.A. papers, *LC.*
16. See Catherine Cleverdon's excellent book on *The Woman Suffrage Movement in Canada* (University of Toronto, 1950).

XXVII. THE CONTINUING DIVISION

The most useful sources were C. Catt and N. Shuler, *op. cit.;* E. Flexner, *op. cit.;* and the *History of Woman Suffrage* (vols. 3 to 6, New York, 1886–1922). A. Kraditor has an excellent chapter on the Southern question, L. Merk is useful on the situation in Massachusetts, and I am further indebted to David Morgan, who is working on the relationship between Congress and the suffrage movement.

1. Lucy Stone to Margaret Campbell, March 17 and April 7, 1888, *LC.*
2. Lucy Stone to Henry Blackwell, May 1, 1887, *LC.*

3. *Proceedings of N.A.W.S.A.,* 1893, p. 79. See also Clavia Goodman, *Bitter Harvest: Laura Clay's Suffrage Work* (Lexington, Ky., 1946).

4. Carrie Catt to Alice Blackwell, August 4, 1900, *LC.*

5. Susan Anthony to William Garrison II, July 14, 1898, *HL* (copy of a letter in the Sophia Smith Collection).

6. *Proceedings of N.A.W.S.A.,* 1894, pp. 23, 99.

7. *Ibid.,* 1903, quoted in Myrdal, *op. cit.,* II, p. 506.

8. Ella Chamberlain, quoted by A. Elizabeth Taylor, "The Woman Suffrage Movement in Florida," *Florida Historical Quarterly,* No. 36, 1957.

9. *Proceedings of N.A.W.S.A.,* 1896, p. 76.

10. Elizabeth Saxon in *Proceedings of N.A.W.S.A.,* 1884, p. 94.

11. Anti-suffrage literature, in the files of N.A.W.S.A., *LC.*

12. Susan Anthony to Jessie Anthony, April 3, 1902, *HL.*

13. Walter White to Mary Terrell, March 4, 1919, quoted by A. Kraditor, *op. cit.,* p. 203.

14. Letter of Elizabeth Stanton to the First International Woman Suffrage Convention, 1902, Anthony papers, 1902 scrapbook, *LC.*

15. Alice Miller, *Are Women People?* (New York, 1915), p. 45.

16. Mary Dennett to Mrs. Medill McCormick, December 30, 1913, N.A.W.S.A. papers, *LC.* For the story of the Women's Political Union, see Harriot Blatch and Alma Lutz, *Challenging Years* (New York, 1940).

17. Susan Anthony to Thomas Bowman, September 7, 1894, and to Mary Keith, March 20, 1896, *HL.*

18. Inez Irwin, *The Story of the Woman's Party* (New York, 1921), p. 17. This account is very much on the side of the militants, and should be corrected by the account of N.A.W.S.A. at its centennial celebration, *Victory—How Women Won It* (New York, 1940). Equally, the files of the militant newspaper, *The Suffragist,* 1914–1920, should be balanced by a reading of the files of the *Woman's Journal* and *Woman Citizen.*

XXVIII. UNIONS FOR WOMEN

Generally useful are the relevant chapters in E. Flexner, *op. cit.; Women's Work in America, op. cit.; America Through Women's Eyes, op. cit.;* E. Groves, *op. cit.;* Dale Kramer, *The Wild Jackasses* (New York, 1956); and Florence Kelley, *Some Ethical Gains Through Legislation* (New York, 1910).

1. See E. Flexner, *op. cit.,* pp. 199–200, and *Women's Work in America, op. cit.,* p. 299.

2. *Autobiography of Mother Jones* (Chicago, 1925), pp. 203–204, 238.

3. MS of the autobiography of Mary Kenney (O'Sullivan), p. 54, *RWA.*

4. Pamphlet of Leonora O'Reilly, 1913, *RWA.*

5. See Mary Dreier, *Margaret Dreier Robins* (New York, 1950).

6. Ella Reeve Bloor, *We Are Many* (New York, 1940), pp. 92–93, 116.
7. Elizabeth Gurley Flynn, *I Speak My Own Piece* (New York, 1955), p. 35.
8. See R. Drinnon's excellent biography of Emma Goldman, *Rebel in Paradise* (University of Chicago, 1961), pp. 60, 143.

XXIX. THE PROGRESSIVE ANSWER

Out of the voluminous literature on the Progressive movement, I have relied chiefly on Richard Hofstadter's seminal work.

1. Julia Howe, "The Relation of the Woman Suffrage Movement to Other Reforms," *Transactions of the National Council of Women of the United States,* Washington, D.C., February 22–25, 1891, p. 242.
2. Clifford Howard, "Why Man Needs Woman's Ballot," *Bulletin of the University of Texas,* June 1, 1915.
3. Jane Addams, "The Larger Aspects of the Woman's Movement," *op. cit.*
4. Professor John Graham Brooks, quoted in *Eminent Opinions on Woman Suffrage* (N.A.W.S.A., New York, undated).
5. Address by Miss Emily Bissell of Delaware, *op. cit.*
6. Mary Wood, "Civic Activities of Women's Clubs," *Annals of the American Academy,* November, 1914. See also Mrs. J. C. Croly, *The History of the Woman's Club Movement in America* (New York, 1898).
7. Grover Cleveland in the *Ladies' Home Journal,* May and October, 1905, answered by the *Bulletin of the General Federation of Women's Clubs,* June and November, 1905.
8. See Mark Sullivan, *Our Times* (Vol. 2 of 6, New York, 1927), p. 522.
9. Margaret Robinson, "Woman Suffrage a Menace to Social Reform," *Cambridge Chronicle,* October 16, 1915.
10. *Bulletin No. 15 of the Illinois Association Opposed to the Extension of Suffrage to Women.*
11. Annie Bock, "Women Suffrage," 63 Cong., 1 Sess., S.D. 160.
12. *Proceedings of N.A.W.S.A.,* 1905, p. 90.
13. James Bryce, *op. cit.,* p. 611.
14. Jack London, *John Barleycorn* (New York, 1913), pp. 335–336.
15. F. P. Dunne, *The Best of Mr. Dooley, op. cit.,* p. 212.
16. H. Pringle, *Theodore Roosevelt: A Biography* (New York, 1931), p. 470.
17. J. Bishop, *Theodore Roosevelt and His Time* (2 vols., London, 1920), II, p. 127.
18. Theodore Roosevelt to F. M. Qvam, May 6, 1910, Catt papers, *NYPL.*
19. "Reasons Why The Non-partisan Policy of the N.A.W.S.A. Is Practical" and "Objections To The Policy Of The Congressional Union," N.A.W.-S.A. papers, *LC.*
20. Louis Seibold in the New York *World,* November 25, 1916.
21. *Ibid.*

22. Woodrow Wilson to Carrie Catt, May 8, 1917, Catt papers, *NYPL.*
23. See H. H. Gardener to T. W. Brahany, July 25, 1917, Catt papers, *NYPL.* See also Margaret Clark to Carrie Catt, October 11, 1918, Catt papers, *LC;* Maud Park, *Front Door Lobby* (Boston, 1960); and Doris Stevens, *Jailed for Freedom* (New York, 1920).
24. See William McAdoo, *Crowded Years* (Boston, 1931), pp. 496–498, and Arthur Link, *Wilson: The New Freedom* (Princeton University, 1956), p. 257.
25. Quoted in G. Mowry, *The Era of Theodore Roosevelt, 1900–1912* (London, 1958), p. 33.
26. "The Suffrage Single Plank," 1915, Catt papers, *NYPL.*
27. See Helen Sumner, *op. cit.,* pp. 214–260.
28. Quoted in the N.A.W.S.A. papers, *LC.*
29. Herbert Croly, "The Vote As a Symbol," *Nation,* October 9, 1915.
30. *Proceedings of the Victory Convention, N.A.W.S.A., (1869–1920), and First National Congress, League of Women Voters,* Chicago, February 12–18, 1920, pp. 35, 81–87.

XXX. CHANGING PATTERNS

Invaluable in writing this chapter were R. Smuts, *Women and Work, op. cit.;* the Lynds' path-breaking *Middletown* (New York, 1929) and *Middletown in Transition* (New York, 1937); Sophinisba Breckinridge's *Women in the Twentieth Century* (New York, 1933); *American Women, Report of the President's Commission on the Status of Women, 1963* (Washington, D.C., 1964); and a conversation with Paul Taylor, who is working on the political role of women after 1920.

1. P. Lazarsfeld, B. Berelson, and H. Gaudet, *The People's Choice* (Columbia University, 1948), p. 141.
2. See Frank Kent, *The Great Game of Politics* (New York, 1923) and *Political Behaviour* (New York, 1928).
3. Alice Blackwell to Carrie Catt, September 4, 1929, Blackwell papers, *LC.*
4. See Mathilde and Mathias Vaerting, *The Dominant Sex* (New York, 1923).
5. F. P. Dunne, *The Best of Mr. Dooley, op. cit.,* p. 212.
6. See the excellent article by Philip Hastings, "Hows and Howevers of the Woman Voter," *New York Times,* June 12, 1960.
7. R. and H. Lynd, *Middletown in Transition, op. cit.,* pp. 178–179.
8. Margaret Hagood, *Mothers of the South* (University of North Carolina, 1939).
9. See J. Dunn, *Massacres of the Mountains* (London, 1886), pp. 220–221.
10. Frances Gage, quoted in Elizabeth Stanton's speech on Reconstruction, *op. cit.*

11. E. Lincoln Frazier, quoted in L. Bennett, Jr., "The Negro Woman," *Ebony*, September, 1963.
12. Edwin Muir, "Woman—Free For What?," *Our Changing Morality*, (Freda Kirchwey, ed., New York, 1924), pp. 81–82.

XXXI. THE NEW VICTORIANS

Simone de Beauvoir's *The Second Sex* (New York, 1953) has probably influenced more women in the direction of independence than any other modern work. I have also found important Viola Klein, *The Feminine Character* (New York, 1949), and Betty Freidan, *The Feminine Mystique* (New York, 1963), which has some striking insights despite the use of propagandist and journalistic exaggerations. Also valuable are David Potter's *People of Plenty* (University of Chicago, 1954) and *American Women and the American Character* (Stetson University, Fla., 1962) and Alice Rossi, "Equality Between the Sexes: An Immodest Proposal," *Daedalus*, Spring, 1964.

1. Quoted in A. Schlesinger, Sr., *Learning How to Behave, op. cit.,* p. 16.
2. Mary Ross, "The New Status of Women in America," *Woman's Coming of Age, op. cit.*
3. H. Keyserling, *America Set Free* (London, 1930), p. 309.
4. I have relied for my statistics on Charles Kiser's excellent collection of *Research in Family Planning* (Princeton University, 1962).
5. See Agnes Rogers, *Vassar Women* (Poughkeepsie, New York, 1940).
6. Anthony Ludovici, *Man: An Indictment* (London, 1927).
7. F. Lundberg and M. Farnham, *Modern Woman: The Lost Sex* (New York, 1947). This book is a model of the distortion of social history by self-styled Freudians. Nearly every one of its historical judgements is wrong. I am not qualified to speak of its psychological judgements.
8. *Godey's Lady's Book*, February, 1839.
9. See A. Rossi, *op. cit.*
10. *Ladies' Home Journal*, September, 1890.
11. P. Blanchard and C. Manasses, *New Girls for Old* (New York, 1930), p. 175.
12. Brigid Brophy, "Women Are Prisoners of Their Sex," *Saturday Evening Post*, November 2, 1963.

INDEX

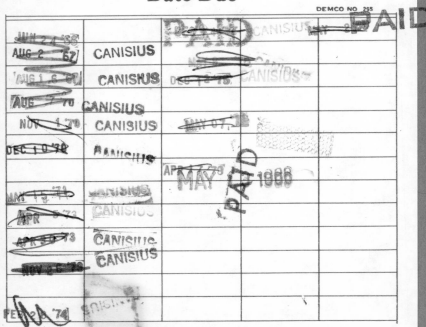